Library of
Davidson College

Studies in
Labor Markets

 A Conference Report
Universities—National Bureau
Committee for Economic Research

Number 31

National Bureau of Economic Research

Studies in Labor Markets

Edited by **Sherwin Rosen**

The University of Chicago Press

Chicago and London

SHERWIN ROSEN is professor of economics at the University of Chicago and a senior research fellow of the National Bureau of Economic Research.

The University of Chicago Press, Chicago 60637
The University of Chicago Press, Ltd., London

© 1981 by The National Bureau of Economic Research
All rights reserved. Published 1981
Printed in the United States of America
88 87 86 85 84 83 82 81   5 4 3 2 1

Library of Congress Cataloging in Publication Data
Main entry under title:

Studies in labor markets.

(A Conference report / Universities–National Bureau Committee for Economic Research ; no. 31)
Includes bibliographical references and index.
1. Labor economics—Congresses. 2. Labor and laboring classes—United States—1970–   —Congresses. I. Rosen, Sherwin. II. Series: Conference report (Universities–National Bureau Committee for Economic Research ; no. 31)
HD4813.S78   331   81-7488
ISBN 0-226-72628-2   AACR2

National Bureau of Economic Research

Officers

Eli Shapiro, *Chairman*
Franklin A. Lindsay, *Vice Chairman*
Martin Feldstein, *President*

Charles E. McLure, Jr., *Vice President*
Charles A. Walworth, *Treasurer*
Sam Parker, *Director of Finance and Administration*

Directors at Large

Moses Abramovitz
George T. Conklin, Jr.
Morton Ehrlich
Solomon Fabricant
Martin Feldstein
Edward L. Ginzton
David L. Grove
Walter W. Heller

Franklin A. Lindsay
Roy E. Moor
Geoffrey H. Moore
Michael H. Moskow
James J. O'Leary
Peter G. Peterson
Robert V. Roosa
Richard N. Rosett

Bert Seidman
Eli Shapiro
Stephen Stamas
Lazare Teper
Donald S. Wasserman
Marina v.N. Whitman

Directors by University Appointment

Charles H. Berry, *Princeton*
Otto Eckstein, *Harvard*
Walter D. Fisher, *Northwestern*
J. C. LaForce, *California, Los Angeles*
Paul McCracken, *Michigan*
Daniel McFadden, *Massachusetts Institute of Technology*
Almarin Phillips, *Pennsylvania*

James L. Pierce, *California, Berkeley*
Lloyd G. Reynolds, *Yale*
Nathan Rosenberg, *Stanford*
James Simler, *Minnesota*
William S. Vickrey, *Columbia*
Dudley Wallace, *Duke*
Burton A. Weisbrod, *Wisconsin*
Arnold Zellner, *Chicago*

Directors by Appointment of Other Organizations

Carl F. Christ, *American Economic Association*
Robert C. Holland, *Committee for Economic Development*
Stephan F. Kaliski, *Canadian Economics Association*
Albert G. Matamoros, *National Association of Business Economists*
Douglass C. North, *Economic History Association*

Rudolph A. Oswald, *American Federation of Labor and Congress of Industrial Organizations*
Joel Popkin, *American Statistical Association*
G. Edward Schuh, *American Agricultural Economics Association*
James C. Van Horne, *American Finance Association*
Charles A. Walworth, *American Institute of Certified Public Accountants*

Directors Emeriti

Arthur F. Burns
Emilio G. Collado
Frank Fetter
Thomas D. Flynn

Gottfried Haberler
Albert J. Hettinger, Jr.
George B. Roberts
Murray Shields

Boris Shishkin
Willard L. Thorp
Theodore O. Yntema

Since this volume is a record of conference proceedings, it has been exempted from the rules governing critical review of manuscripts by the Board of Directors of the National Bureau (resolution adopted 6 July 1948, as revised 21 November 1949 and 20 April 1968).

Universities–National Bureau Committee for Economic Research

This committee is a cooperative venture of universities and the National Bureau. Its guiding objective is the encouragement of economic research on problems susceptible of objective treatment and of sufficiently broad scope to merit attention by institutions serving a scientific and public interest.

Participating Universities and Their Representatives

Brown, Jerome L. Stein
California (Berkeley), Daniel McFadden
California (Los Angeles), J. C. La Force
California (San Diego), Robert E. Engle
Carnegie-Mellon, Edward C. Prescott
Chicago, Lester G. Telser
Columbia, Robert Mundell
Cornell, S. C. Tsiang
Duke, T. Dudley Wallace
Harvard, John V. Lintner
Illinois, Robert Resek
Indiana, Franz Gehrels
Iowa State, Dudley G. Luckett
Johns Hopkins, Carl F. Christ
Maryland, Barbara Bergman
Massachusetts Institute of Technology, Richard S. Eckaus
McGill, Alex G. Vicas
Michigan, Harold T. Shapiro
Michigan State, Victor Smith
Minnesota, James M. Henderson
New School for Social Research, Thomas Vietorisz
New York, M. Ishaq Nadiri
New York State (Buffalo), Daniel Hamberg
North Carolina, Henry A. Latané
Northwestern, Robert Eisner
Ohio State, Donald O. Parsons
Pennsylvania, Jere R. Behrman
Pittsburgh, S. H. Chou
Princeton, Edwin S. Mills
Purdue, Patric H. Hendershott
Queen's, Martin F. J. Prachowny
Rochester, Walter Y. Oi
Stanford, Moses Abramovitz
Texas, Samuel L. Myers, Jr.
Toronto, Richard Bird
Vanderbilt, Anthony M. Tang
Virginia, Richard T. Selden
Washington (Saint Louis), Hyman Minsky
Washington (Seattle), Richard W. Parks
Wisconsin, Leonard W. Weiss
Yale, Richard Ruggles

National Bureau of Economic Research Representative

Robert E. Lipsey

Members at Large

Irma Adelman
Bela A. Balassa
Carl E. Beigie
Daniel Creamer
Frank de Leeuw
Walter S. Salant
George J. Stigler

The officers of the Universities–National Bureau Committee are: Edwin S. Mills, chairman; Leonard W. Weiss, vice-chairman; and Christine Mortensen, secretary. The members of the Executive Committee are: Irma Adelman, Richard Bird, Robert Eisner, Robert E. Lipsey, Dudley G. Luckett, Edwin S. Mills, and Leonard W. Weiss.

Contents

	Prefatory Note	ix
	Introduction Sherwin Rosen	1
1.	**Labor Mobility and Wages** Jacob Mincer and Boyan Jovanovic	21
2.	**Wage Growth and Job Turnover: An Empirical Analysis** Ann P. Bartel and George J. Borjas *Comment:* Gilbert Ghez	65
3.	**Heterogeneity and State Dependence** James J. Heckman	91
4.	**Anticipated Unemployment, Temporary Layoffs, and Compensating Wage Differentials** John M. Abowd and Orley Ashenfelter	141
5.	**Structural and Reduced Form Approaches to Analyzing Unemployment Durations** Nicholas M. Kiefer and George R. Neumann	171
6.	**Layoffs and Unemployment Insurance** Frank Brechling *Comment*: Daniel S. Hamermesh	187
7.	**Employment in Construction and Distribution Industries: The Impact of The New Jobs Tax Credit** John Bishop	209

8.	**Black Economic Progress after 1964: Who Has Gained and Why?** Richard B. Freeman	247
9.	**Risk Shifting, Statistical Discrimination, and the Stability of Earnings** Herschel I. Grossman and Warren T. Trepeta *Comment*: Dennis W. Carlton	295
10.	**Signaling, Screening, and Information** Michael Spence	319
11.	**Learning by Observing and the Distribution of Wages** Stephen Ross, Paul Taubman, and Michael Wachter *Comment*: John G. Riley *Comment*: Charles Wilson	359
	List of Contributors	387
	Author Index	391
	Subject Index	394

Prefatory Note

This volume contains the papers presented at the Conference on Low Income Labor Markets held at the University of Chicago's Center for Continuing Education 9 and 10 June 1978, sponsored by the Universities–National Bureau Committee for Economic Research. Funds for the conference were provided by the National Science Foundation; we are indebted for its support. We also thank Sherwin Rosen, who served as chairman of the conference and editor of this volume.

Executive Committee, June 1978
Edwin S. Mills, Chairman
Irma Adelman
Richard Bird
Robert Eisner
Dudley G. Luckett
Leonard W. Weiss
Robert E. Lipsey, NBER Representative

Introduction

Sherwin Rosen

When the Universities–National Bureau Committee for Economic Research requested me to investigate the possibility of a conference on the theme "Low-Income Labor Markets," I undertook the task with some trepidation. My own belief is that simple class distinctions never show up in the data and that modern research in labor economics has proven that more general and wide-ranging investigations ultimately bear better fruit than narrow and perhaps parochial ones. In a word, why censor the data? If the theories are any good, they should be able to account for at least middle-income markets as well! My investigations into the possibility of a conference and discussions with friends and the Committee resulted in a conference of somewhat wider scope and a slightly altered title. Its substantive content is, however, related to several issues that were closely connected to discussions of "low-income labor markets" in those days. The papers and comments presented here are concerned with four major themes: (1) labor mobility, job turnover, and life cycle dynamics; (2) analysis of unemployment compensation and employment policy; (3) labor market discrimination; and (4) labor market information and investment. I hope the reader will agree with me that the decision was a good one. In fact, the papers that follow present an excellent sampling of the best of modern research in labor economics, combining some of the most sophisticated theory, econometric methods, and high-quality data on a host of empirically relevant problems.

In what follows I present a detailed reader's guide to each of the papers and, befitting an enterprise of this sort, offer some suggestions on where the work might be pushed or extended in the future.

Labor Mobility, Turnover, and Life Cycle Dynamics

The paper by Jacob Mincer and Boyan Jovanovic is a fine substantive contribution in its own right, but also serves as an excellent introduction to the modern study of labor mobility, whose main analytical difficulty lies in its relation to the theory of stochastic processes. Clearly, viewing the mobility problem as a probabilistic process, as in part 2 of the paper, especially with the time series or panel data now becoming available, is at the frontier of the subject and, if I may make a prediction, will be a major innovative development in labor econometrics in the years to come. The paper is also interesting for its simple empirical results that are basically obtained by standard methods applied to averages over the underlying microprocess, results which the subsequent paper by Ann Bartel and George Borjas extend, using similar ensemble average methods. James Heckman's paper then links up very nicely with many of the econometric issues raised.

In the economics of ordinary exchange it is the gains from trade that are fundamental and not the personal identities of the traders. Thus, for example, the amount of bread a consumer buys and the price paid are objects of analysis, whereas whether or not the bread was purchased from store A, B, C, or Z is of no consequence. Until very recently most modern empirical research in labor economics has followed this line. Why, therefore, should mobility be an important subject for study? I believe there are two reasons. First, to follow the analogy above a bit further, it would be interesting to know that if seller C offered the good at a lower price than the rest, the probability of a buyer's going to outlet C increased. Otherwise the law of one price and the efficiency of the market institution would be impaired. So it is in labor markets as well. Labor mobility is the primary means for getting labor resources to their highest-valued uses. The separation decisions examined by Borjas and Bartel and the labor supply decisions examined by Heckman can be thought of in this way. Second, there is empirical evidence that a great deal of job mobility throughout the life cycle, i.e., unstable work histories, is associated with low earnings and poverty. It is important to understand the dynamics leading up to such outcomes of life cycle behavior. Mincer and Jovanovic analyze the the problem in the context of the theory of general and firm-specific human capital: wage dispersion induces mobility as individuals attempt to take advantage of unusual circumstances; firm-specific human capital investments give rise to rents that tend to reduce mobility. Somewhere a balance is struck.

The particular problem addressed by Mincer and Jovanovic is how to use panel data on mobility and wages to ascertain the proportions by which human capital investments are general or firm specific, i.e., are tied to labor market experience or current job tenure. Specific human capital creates a wedge between actual wages paid or received and opportunity wages, the differences representing returns on specific investments. Larger specific investments increase the wedge and therefore reduce mobility. Consequently the probability of separation should diminish with tenure if specific investment increases with tenure. However, in a group of measurably similar people a whole distribution of job tenure will be observed, indicating either considerable unobserved differences in specific investments, or heterogeneity. Thus, it is possible to observe a declining relation between separation probabilities and tenure that has no causal significance, since those with greater propensities to move will always exhibit greater separation rates and lower tenure than those with the opposite propensities. The difficulty for analysis therefore is to purge the data of this mechanical effect arising from heterogeneous populations.

Mincer and Jovanovic control for this effect by introducing measures of previous mobility. While specific job tenure remains an important determinant of mobility, supporting the specific human capital argument, its influence is much smaller if these controls are introduced. A similar argument, with similar empirical results, is also applied to the observed positive relationship between wages and specific job tenure. Drawing on these results and other work, the authors tentatively conclude that general human capital accounts for about one-half of the total, that specific investments account for about one-fourth, and that the remainder is due to interfirm mobility as arbitrage activity. This is an extremely important question to which this paper is the first, to my knowledge, to propose a workable and plausible answer. Clearly, an even better answer should be a major goal on the research agenda.

Bartel and Borjas present an empirical analysis of the relationship between wage growth and job mobility, using the theory of human capital as the central concept for organizing the data. Two effects of job mobility are examined: (1) the effect on differential life cycle wage growth between jobs of "origin and destination"; (2) the influence on life cycle wage growth in any given job. The data used come from panel surveys of older and young men in the 1969–73 period.

A number of interesting results are obtained. First, the effects of mobility on wage growth are different for young men and for older men. Generally, greater gains were associated with mobility among young men, reflecting the differential role of turnover between these two groups: the search-investment aspect of turnover in discovering a life career and a conformable job has greatest value for youth. The results of the analysis, at least for quits, are broadly consistent with this notion of investment. On the other hand, turnover among adult workers tends either to have a greater element of surprise (e.g., an unanticipated plant closing) or to be representative of workers who for one reason or another tend to turn over at much higher than average rates. While the latter selectivity effect is not precisely modeled by Bartel and Borjas, some simple tests that utilize the panel feature of the data strongly suggest that it is not the most important source of variation. In addition, the effects of turnover on wage growth vary with the cause of turnover, (permanent) layoffs tending to reduce subsequent wage growth and quits tending to increase it, or at least not to decrease it as much as layoffs. This presents a theoretical puzzle that remains to be resolved in future research; economic theory suggests that there should be no difference in response, since job separations should occur if and only if productivity on the current job is less than productivity on an alternative job. Therefore, who initiates the turnover decision should be irrelevant to the outcome. It may be, however, that nonpecuniary factors (working conditions) intervene in this process and somehow cause the asymmetry, or that jobs subject to permanent layoff probabilities are inherently riskier than others, calling for a compensatory differential wage that would tend to reduce subsequent wage growth. Both of these possibilities as well as others remain to be explored.

Second, the authors examine wage growth within a given job spell, predicting that greater expected tenure should result in greater investment and therefore greater wage growth. The method used is conceptually very interesting: it is found that those with longer spells exhibit greater life cycle wage growth, as the theory predicts. However, as Gilbert Ghez notes in his comment, the theory predicts some interactions that are not tested; and, in addition, use of completed spells as a measure of expected employment duration is subject to substantial error of measurement. One might add on this latter point that the measurement error tends to bias their result toward zero and against accepting the economic hypothesis. Also, the statistical method should be extended to cases where the current spell of employment has not ended. The fact that such individuals are not utilized in the comparisons undoubtedly also biases the estimated effects toward zero since it tends to censor longer-tenure people from the sample.

Finally, the panel or time series aspect of the data is used to help resolve some of the difficulties of distinguishing between general and job-specific experience in cross-section data. The empirical results apparently show that specific training is an important component of life cycle wage determination, since those individuals who have greater specific firm experience have greater lifetime wage growth. The methods used try to net out individual fixed effects on earnings levels, but heterogeneity in turnover propensities is not completely handled by these methods. Again, much work remains to be done in this important area.

James Heckman begins to develop a dynamic model of labor force participation behavior of married women that can be used to explain panel data. The work is related to, but also considerably extends, his earlier work on selection and heterogeneity in cross-section data. The statistical models are complicated, but are necessary to account for the dynamic behavior observed in the data, and while the emphasis here is on the decision of whether or not to participate in the market, it is clear that these methods will prove useful for other related problems, such as unemployment behavior.

The paper begins with an extremely clear exposition of the statistical issues by analogy with a class of statistical models known as "urn schemes." What is especially intriguing is how the problem is put in the context of some very elementary and easily understood stochastic processes, which are required to complete the description of dynamic behavior in panel data. These models have several distinct components. They include (1) a pure random effect, where the decision to participate in any given period is independent of the decision in other periods; (2) the effect of heterogeneous populations, whereby unobserved differences in tastes and opportunities imply permanent differences in participation decisions among individuals; (3) the possibile effect of "state dependence," whereby the decision to participate in any given period alters the probability of participating in future periods; and (4) a serially correlated random effect whereby the unobserved error is not independent from period to period, but rather displays some temporary persistence, a "half-life" of greater than a single period, but not a permanent effect.

The effects of permanent differences or heterogeneity are well understood from previous work. The decision to participate depends on whether the market wage exceeds the reservation wage, and both market wages and reservation wages depend on observable factors such as schooling and number of children and on unobservable factors such as ability and health status that are known to market participants but not to the econometric analyst, and therefore are best treated in the statistical analysis by various distributional assumptions. Panel data allow for a generalization of these urn schemes to the effect of state dependence, a phenomenon which has clear theoretical foundations, but which cannot be analyzed in cross-section data. The fundamental reason for expecting previous participation decisions to influence future decisions lies in the theory of investment in human capital. The decision to participate today implies some capital accumulation which affects the decision to participate tomorrow. Costs of making decisions or fixed costs of participating might have similar effects as well. These issues are of obvious importance to a host of phenomena in labor economics as well as to labor force participation.

Treating the problem as an investment decision suggests a theoretical formulation in terms of a dynamic programming model of decisions over the life cycle. Although that formal apparatus is not developed in his paper, Heckman adopts a relatively simple empirical specification that is a natural first approximation. The empirical work itself is a careful investigation of various aspects of the model, of course using panel data. Heckman finds that previous labor market decisions are determinants of current participation decisions for older women but not for younger women, a finding that is consistent with and explained by the theory of human investment. Younger women, who anticipate childbirth, have lower incentives to invest in labor market skills than women who anticipate a longer future participation and hence higher return on investment. A considerable amount of heterogeneity among both older and younger women is found, and neglect of these interpersonal differences leads to marked overestimates of labor market turnover and to biased estimates of the effects of exogenous variables on the probability of participation. Finally, Heckman discovers that the unobservables determining participation follow a first-order Markov process, and, although the serial correlation is quite high, any initial differences among people tend to vanish with the passage of time, at least if the period considered is long enough. In earlier work on this problem, a fixed effect specification has been used to model unobservable differences among people, which literally imposes a "serial correlation" of unity. Writing the disturbance as a Markov process relaxes that assumption, and it is found that a pure fixed effect model is not entirely appropriate.

Unemployment Compensation and Employment Policy

In their imaginative and innovative paper, John Abowd and Orley Ashenfelter examine the effect of anticipated temporary unemployment on wage rates, a subject dear to the hearts of all labor economists, representing as it does modern variations on a theme by Adam Smith. Even apart from the obvious intellectual interest of this problem, it has much practical interest, in that it concerns the extent to which the labor market itself provides a form of unemployment insurance or compensation in addition to that provided through the public sector. The considerable empirical work underlying this paper is among the first serious substantive studies and unquestionably the most sophisticated investigations of Smith's ancient point.

The theoretical model used to organize the data parallels Smith's theory very closely, albeit in a neoclassical language and notation. Beginning with the theory of labor supply based on the demand for leisure, the authors first define unemployment as a situation in which a worker desires to work more hours than the employer desires to employ at the going wage. For whatever reason, an hours constraint is binding for an unemployed worker. This calls for a wage-compensating variation for an hours-constrained job in order for it to achieve equal utility with an unconstrained job and hence be consistent with supply of workers. This wage-compensating variation is the value of rationed hours with imputations for the value of leisure. Next, the hours constraint is considered to be a random variable, binding with probability rather than with certainty.

In this case, a wage-compensating variation is required not merely for the actuarial adjustment of probability of occurrence, as in the first case, but also for the fear and uncertainty of temporary unemployment on the part of risk-averse workers. To these two effects, both identified by Smith, Abowd and Ashenfelter add an offset factor arising from eligibility for government-sponsored unemployment insurance.

In this model a labor market contract specifies a fixed probability of layoff, with a given expected duration and variance. If the offered attributes differ among firms or industries, labor market clearing through supply equalization requires compensatory wage differentials depending on workers' preferences for leisure and for risk bearing.

As is true of many of the papers in this volume, the model is implemented empirically using panel data, with the theoretical counterparts of contract terms estimated by computer-intensive methods from employment histories of workers in the sample in 1967–75. To avoid employment instability having to do with search and career development activities, which are beyond the scope of the paper, the sample is confined to stably employed individuals with lengthy records of labor force experience and job tenure. First, the unemployment probabilities and expected durations unemployed are estimated, conditional upon previous unemployment history, personal variables, and industry-specific effects. Layoff incidence, duration unemployed, and duration variance by industry that arise from these estimates are of substantial interest in their own right, indicating considerable risk in the construction industry and durable manufacturing and much less in government and professional service. These estimates are used to construct contract unemployment attributes suggested by the theoretical formulation.

The results provide strong confirmation of the utility-maximizing hypothesis: workers demand a significant amount of wage compensation for risk bearing and constrained employment opportunities, with the former accounting for the bulk of the differential. While these differentials vary by industry and year, depending on the actual characteristics of the contract, they average as large as seven percent in some of the estimates and fourteen percent in some industries. The differential is also found to fall as eligibility for public unemployment insurance increases, though the estimated replacement effect is rather too large for the model. Two other structural parameters are identified by the model. The compensated labor supply elasticity (for prime-age white males) is found to be in the neighborhood of that estimated from other studies, or approximately .10. The coefficient of relative risk aversion is found to be very large.

This interesting study clearly deserves replication and extension to new data. The model also needs to be extended to the decisions of firms, beginning, as the authors suggest, with the implicit contracts literature.

Additional evidence should also be available from the sorting patterns of workers with different preferences among firms offering different risk and constraint characteristics. If sorting by personal characteristics and preferences is the rule rather than the exception in this kind of world, some difficult conceptual and econometric issues arise in precisely ascertaining and measuring the extent of unemployment risk attributable to firms and therefore in need of compensation. One could even imagine a dual set of compensating variations on the other side of the market, if continuity, reliability, and turnover probabilities are of importance to firms as contributions to specific human capital or for other considerations. Clearly this work opens new territory on an important subject.

In their paper on job search, Nicholas Kiefer and George Neumann contrast and compare two econometric methods for inferring behavioral response patterns to the stimulus of varying official unemployment compensation parameters, such as the benefit rate, or of other policies, such as a wage subsidy to the unemployed. The methods are discussed in the context of data on unemployed persons who had permanently lost their jobs owing to plant closings. The standard method of analyzing such data, and a natural first approach, is to observe the outcomes of the job search process. Then completed duration unemployed is statistically related to personal variables such as schooling and previous job experience and also to unemployment compensation parameters such as benefit rate and benefit duration. Similarly, the wage on the new job might be related to the same set of variables. Kiefer and Neumann call this a reduced form approach and argue convincingly that, here as in many other areas of applied economics, a structural approach may be more useful than, or at least a useful supplement to, the reduced form model.

A structural model of unemployment duration and subsequent wage gain or loss is constructed on the basis of the sampling theory of search now familiar in the literature. The decision to accept a job is based on comparing the wages actually encountered in the search process with a reservation wage calculated on the basis of the perceived offer-wage distribution and the costs of search. The structural model consists of an offer-wage distribution and a nonstochastic reservation-wage function. These are inherently related to each other from the theory of search, but are separately identified because some measurable factors affect the costs of search and shift the reservation wage, independently of the given offer-wage distribution. Such separation would be problematic at the macro level where it might be supposed that anything shifting the reservation wage of everyone would, through the forces of supply and demand, ultimately be reflected in the offer-wage distribution. However, the independence assumption seems to be a tolerable approximation at the micro level of the data or for differences among people operating in the same general market. In this setup, the actual data on the reemployment wage and unemployment duration distributions are considered to be the outcomes of the stochastic process modeled by the theory of search. Indeed, the likelihood function in the structural method is the probability of observing the sample joint distribution. The reduced form approach may be most easily thought of as the expected unemployment duration and subsequent wage, conditional on personal characteristics and program parameters, whereas the structural estimates attempt to reveal the stochastic process itself.

There are two advantages of the structural approach, although the reduced form estimates are clearly complementary to it. First, it allows one to ask more questions concerning interventions into the stochastic process. For example, in the paper, Kiefer and Neumann ask what a personal wage subsidy would do to unemployment duration and subsequent wages. This simply cannot be answered from reduced form estimates, but can be answered from the structural estimates if the subsidy is viewed as a shifter of the offer-wage distribution. Second, the reduced form approach is most useful in comparing the whole histories of experience of those in the sample. If at some time in the sampling period there remain individuals who have not found jobs, data on them cannot be utilized in the reduced form estimation, and this censorship of the sample may lead to biased estimates if not handled appropriately. The structural approach utilizes the information on those who have not found employment and makes an imputation for them based on some distributional assumptions.

Kiefer and Neumann's basic results are that for those individuals who were permanently laid off their previous jobs, unemployment insurance parameters have little effect on unemployment duration and subsequent wage. The same conclusions emerge from both reduced form and structural estimates. The wage subsidy is found to be far more successful in increasing subsequent wages. Another interesting empirical result is that the true variance of the wage-offer distribution is very small relative to interpersonal differences in permanent earnings capacity due to corresponding differences in ability, health status, and so on. This suggests to me that the search theory in its pure form cannot in any case explain a great deal of the unemployment behavior of this group of workers. This estimate of variance, whatever its interpretation, is of course something that could not have been known in advance and without a structural model. In fact, it is one of the few actual estimates of such parameters to be found in the literature. Finally, I do not believe, and I am sure the authors would concur, that these results are informative about the effects of unemployment compensation for those who are not on permanent layoff status, which according to some estimates is a very large fraction of the unemployed. It is ironic that the present system appears to have greater influence on transitory behavior and temporary unemployment than on the disaster of a permanent loss of job due to adverse shifts in demand for labor for particular uses.

By way of contrast, the paper by Frank Brechling is devoted to an empirical analysis of the effects of official unemployment compensation on aspects of employment and labor turnover using pooled state cross-section and time series data. While most empirical research on the effects of unemployment compensation has been conducted at the micro level of worker behavior, Brechling's work is best read as one of the few studies that have attempted to ascertain the firms' responses to changes in various program parameters. The emphasis here is on the role of experience rating in decisions concerning layoffs, rehires, unemployment durations, and hours of work.

Recent research on unemployment insurance, including some by Brechling himself, has keyed on two fundamental parameters of the unemployment insurance (UI) system: the tax treatment of benefits and the degree of experience rating. The fact that UI benefits are exempt from personal income taxation has the effect of subsidizing temporary periods of full-time leisure instead of uniformly shorter work schedules or work weeks. Shorter workdays tend to be an inferior alternative to complete absence from work because the income earned while working is subject to tax and UI benefits are not. This feature of the insurance system increases the demand for temporary layoffs on the part of workers. Insofar as layoffs are temporary, the firm need not greatly fear that it will suffer large subsequent hiring and training expenses either. On the other side of the coin, imperfect experience-rating schemes, which are characteristic of our system, tend actually to increase the "supply" of jobs subject to temporary layoffs. Imperfect experience rating is another way of saying that there are actuarial imbalances built into the system. These largely come from limitations on the maximum tax rate that tend to subsidize cyclical and seasonal firms and to tax the firms in more stable industries. This alters relative costs and, through corresponding variations in relative product prices, tends artifically to encourage demand in cyclically sensitive sectors as well as the adoption of a more volatile employment policy by any given firm. Brechling adds an additional twist, suggesting that imperfect experience rating directly affects duration unemployed by encouraging firms to use greater inventory stockpiling to meet transitory changes in demand.

The empirical work uses time series data on layoff and unemployment durations, combined with state averages for various industry classifications. Variation in program parameters arises from changes over time and differences among the states in tax and benefit levels. As noted in the comment by Daniel Hamermesh, some of the time series variation in these parameters cannot be entirely exogenous, since changes in state balances due to experience in previous years often call for corresponding overall changes in taxes within a given state. Therefore the results must rest upon the pooled nature of the data; interstate differences in program parameters must constitute the essential source of independent variation. Published benefit levels at this level of aggregation are available in less detail than various features of the tax system, and Brechling accordingly concentrates on the latter, achieving the most careful and detailed specific empirical specification of the experience-rating system currently available. Since the actual payroll tax system is subject to several nonlinearities, at least five parameters are necessary in order fully to characterize it. Of all these parameters, the tax rate applying to firms with negative balances, i.e., the tax rate which is most responsible for the lack of experience rating in the system, is found to have the largest effect. Increases in this tax reduce not only layoffs and rehires, but also unemployment duration and hours of work of the remaining employed, as the theory would suggest.

John Bishop represents one of the first attempts to assess the effects of employment tax credits on the demand for workers in the construction, trucking, and trade sectors of the economy. It is a familiar proposition to students of macroeconomics schooled in the IS-LM tradition that governmental tax and expenditure policy may produce stimulus or contraction tending to offset the opposite tendencies in the private economy. Up to recent years it was commonly felt that direct employment through public works was not sufficiently sensitive in timing to be countercyclical. In addition, it was also held that tax policies had widespread effects on general business expansion or contraction. Changes in federal income tax rates or in corporate or business tax schedules, including depreciation provisions, thus became the main focus of fiscal policy. While policies directly affecting employment had been advocated in the thirties and unemployment and related indicators have always been the major signals of recessions and booms, it is only in recent years that policies directly affecting employment have been seriously considered. Thus the modern equivalent of public works, perhaps, is public employment subsidies through state governments; and the fiscal counterpart to stimulating investment through investment tax credits is direct employment tax credits. Such a policy was tried in 1977–78 under the Federal Unemployment Tax Act. Since the credits were limited in amounts, it is likely that their major impact would be on smaller firms located in the industries that Bishop studies.

The basic methodology followed by Bishop is to estimate the equivalent of labor demand functions for each industry from monthly time series data, including relevant factor prices, a rental price for capital that allows for the effect of investment tax credits and the like, and direct shift variables accounting for the influence of employment tax credits. An interesting aspect of the employment tax credit put into operation in 1977 was that it applied only to incremental employment over and above existing levels of employment in the firm. This nonlinear subsidy properly reduces the fiscal burden while at the same time giving appropriate marginal incentives to increase employment. However, it also gives incentives to reduce hours of work, so that the total effect on overall labor input employed could be less than the direct employment effect. Bishop therefore appropriately investigates both employment and hours responses. Measuring the tax credit variable by proportion of firms who were aware of the tax credit, and allowing for a lagged effect, Bishop reports a fairly substantial effect of the credit on total employment by March of 1978, perhaps as much as one-half million additional employed. While this increment is a small fraction of total employment in these industries, it is a much higher fraction of unemployment originating in these industries. Bishop also reports the anticipated negative effect on hours, so the combined effect is roughly half as large as that on employment alone.

It would be interesting to check these results against direct evidence of effects on employment, by examining tax returns to see the extent to which credits were actually taken by firms. There are broader issues raised by these kinds of policies as well that need further analysis, the primary one of course being the cost-benefit calculus that would support them from the point of view of economic efficiency. There are also questions, as Bishop notes, of their effects on employment stability if maintained as a permanent fixture on the economic scene, as well as questions of tax incidence and shifting and effects on labor supply.

Labor Market Discrimination

Using a variety of sources, and in a veritable onslaught of data and figures, Richard Freeman presents an extensive empirical analysis of the economic status of blacks relative to whites in the decades of the sixties and seventies. The best data available on family and personal incomes come from various survey sources, and Freeman combines them in an imaginative way. He makes a convincing case that relative labor market discrimination against blacks has declined markedly in these two decades. He goes on to argue that the decline in discrimination has been so great that other factors determining economic status, such as family background, are by now the most important causes of black-white income differentials among young workers, to the extent of swamping any residual "pure" discrimination that might remain for these workers. That is, the really large gains made by blacks has been predominantly among those who came from families with higher socioeconomic status. These status differentials are a relatively new phenomenon among black workers. If these findings represent permanent structural shifts, the results imply further barriers to racial income equality until the dynamics of the intergenerational transfer mechanism and the influence of home environment on economic success become fully worked out. Finally, Freeman uses some time series comparisons to argue the controversial position that the progress of blacks was in large measure caused by government antibias activity, and in particular the Civil Rights Act of 1964.

Two main sources of data are used to establish the improvement of black economic status. The first is various census surveys and the Current Population Survey (CPS) in alternative years. These show an advance in the ratio of black-white incomes that accelerates in the 1960s and continues through the mid-seventies. It is not impeded, as many had feared, by cyclical variations in aggregate employment conditions. These comparisons also show relative gains among blacks for young workers, relatively skilled workers, and women. Part of the improvement in black incomes is shown also to be due to a relative improvement in the extent to which black workers are found on higher paying jobs (i.e., a relative occupational shift) as well as to an increase in salaries relative to white workers, at least for a selected group of jobs.

The second source of data used is the panels from the National Longitudinal Survey, which imply convergence of blacks and whites in educational attainment of youth. Here the change in the role of family background is manifest as well. For older men in this sample, family background variables play a much smaller role in determining educational attainment for blacks than whites, while for younger men its role is approximately equal for both groups. Furthermore, regional differentials (particularly Southern and rural) that were a major explanatory factor for older black men have about equal effects and explanatory power for both white and black young men. These changes in social mobility patterns are summarized by Freeman in the form of standardized comparisons, which tend to show that family background differences are a much more important cause of black-white schooling differences among young men than among old men, presumably because of the decline in the discriminatory effects of rural residences and region. These same data are also used to show that family background has become a much more important factor in determining earnings differentials among young men than among older men as well: by 1969 schooling and occupational status differences were by far the major source of earnings differences among young workers, with residual measured discrimination having a very small impact, though a somewhat larger one for older men.

The most controversial part of Freeman's paper is the attribution of the erosion of wage discrimination to the Civil Rights Act of 1964 and the Equal Employment Opportunities Commission of 1965. A time series regression of relative wage and salary earnings of nonwhites to whites over the 1948–75 period is the main empirical support for this argument.

Independent variables are trend and cycle variables, relative employment and relative participation variables (to capture various aspects of supply and demand), and relative schooling, relative employment, and relative participation rates, all of which serve as control variables for various aspects of demand and supply. The crucial variable then is one that measures cumulated expenditures by the equal employment opportunity agency per nonwhite worker. The equal opportunity variable tends to have a significant coefficient, but it is basically a post-1964 trend variable. Freeman marshals a lot of evidence and makes a strong case that the Civil Rights Act was instrumental in improving economic status of nonwhites. Nevertheless, the case is still not entirely airtight. While it is clear that there was a change in behavior in the 1960s, there is still a problem of ascertaining cause and effect. We know, for example, that the passage of a law is not a fortuitous event and usually reflects the temper of the times. For example, some have maintained that many legislative acts of this sort are passed after the restrictions they impose are already a fait accompli. Were there enough forces in motion prior to 1964 so that, had the act not been passed, relative economic status of nonwhites would have been markedly inferior? Thus, for example, the status of nonwhite women had achieved parity long before 1964, and there were marked differences in status of males across regions. On the other side, it is true that equal opportunity employment agencies have revolutionized employment and personnel practices of large corporations at the present time; yet there still remains a question regarding the extent of their effects in the mid-sixties. In other words, there is a simultaneous equations problem of a most unusual and difficult sort here that remains to be completely analyzed. Whatever the answers might ultimately be, it is clear from this study that black economic progress has been concentrated among younger workers, has increased the value of family background, and has not benefited experienced black workers very much. Why these patterns should have emerged, whatever the effect of the Civil Rights Act, also remains a researchable subject of importance.

Herschel Grossman and Warren Trepeta present a theoretical model that attempts to account for racial differences in earnings stability over time, using a sophisticated variant of the theory of discrimination. Their model is based on the most modern research on unemployment, to which Grossman has been a major contributor, wherein risk-averse workers shift cyclical earnings risk to owners of firms, who are less risk averse or who can diversify through superior portfolio management. The nature of this type of labor contract is to equate earnings and marginal product over an extended time horizon, but not necessarily at every moment in time. Instead, the worker is paid less than marginal product when the state of demand is high, representing the equivalent of an insurance premium, to be paid back as an indemnity in the form of a wage in excess of marginal product when the state of demand is low. In this way the worker's income is stabilized, and there are gains from trade arising from differential risk aversion of employer and employee.

The difficulty of implementing an earnings stabilization scheme of this sort is that one or another party has an incentive to cheat on the arrangement, depending on the state that is realized. For example, when demand for labor is increasing elsewhere in the economy, a worker who is presently paid less than marginal product at some firm has incentives to renege on his "insurance contract" by jumping to a firm that is paying high current wages in the "spot" market. Similarly, firms have incentives to lower wages in low states of demand in the presence of a pool of available alternative unemployed workers, though Grossman and Trepeta assume that the future value of the firm's reputation is sufficient to keep it honest. A worker who does not cheat is called reliable. They assume that different types of workers have different tastes for reliability, which is tantamount to assuming rising supply price of workers cheating on insurance contract terms. The analytical achievement of this paper is to ascertain the general equilibrium insurance contract in the presence of this moral hazard problem. Workers tend to be highly unreliable if there is too great a divergence between the insured wage and opportunity wages, since the returns on leaving the firm rise in that case. Therefore, full insurance is not an equilibrium outcome in this world. Instead, the market equilibrium balances the demand for insurance by risk-averse workers against the supply of it in terms of actuarial imbalances which differential worker reliability might imply. It follows immediately that less insurance, i.e., greater earnings instability, must result when workers are less reliable, because the costs of providing insurance rise and less is purchased (assuming here some regularity conditions on income effects of price changes on the demand for insurance, as is usually necessary in problems of this sort).

A model of statistical discrimination is then appended to this structure whereby employers have different beliefs about reliability of different identifiable groups in the population. Grossman and Trepeta demonstrate that these beliefs can become a self-fulfilling prophecy even if untrue in certain circumstances of the model, which is capable of multiple equilibria. However, as pointed out toward the end of the paper and more forcefully by Dennis Carlton in his comment, multiple equilibria, supporting thoroughgoing statistical discrimination, are possible only in cases where employers are not completely informed of the influence of their own wage policy on the reliability of their own specific work force. Such information would eventually erode statistical discrimination not supported by real differences among groups, though the differences might persist for some time, depending on the speed of learning.

I would add two further points. While it is true that those who discriminate must pay the price in the form of higher wage bills and consequently lower profits, there is no inherent reason why discrimination should vanish so long as the number of potential discriminators is large, because discrimination, by hypothesis, is a "good" for such people and is another argument of their utility function. Second, although Grossman and Trepeta do not particularly develop the point, their model appears to be useful in explaining differences among groups due to objective factors of taste or opportunity differences among groups. These points remain to be developed. For example, discrimination in the market for specific human capital accumulation would tend to make blacks appear less reliable than whites. Young workers might have different attitudes toward risk than older workers, if for no other reasons than that the two groups have different family responsibilities and structure. These and other related points remain to be developed.

Labor Market Information and Investment

In his paper "Signaling, Screening, and Information," Michael Spence provides a survey and some very suggestive ideas for extending the basic model of signaling that he has been instrumental in developing. The basic idea is that when personal productivity is not directly observed but is known to be correlated with observable but endogenous variables such as schooling, individuals have incentives to invest in signals as indicators of personal productivity. This is true whether or not these investments increase actual productivity, so long as they are correlated with perceived productivity. Of course, if the signals are sustainable, perceived and actual productivity must match up in the final equilibrium, for otherwise the wage-signal relationship established in the market would unravel owing to profits or losses by firms. A signaling equilibrium is viable if those who are truly more able in the productivity sense are also more able in the investment sense of being able to purchase the signal on more favorable terms than others. Since the signal is relatively cheaper for more capable individuals, they purchase more of it and earn higher pay supported by their higher inherent market productivity. Indeed, that is the only way they can reveal their productivity to the market.

Spence begins by contrasting the signaling, human capital, and job-rationing models from the point of view of the relationship between earnings and schooling. He shows in a very simple way what is becoming increasingly well understood, that it is very difficult to distinguish among these various hypotheses at a very general level, since each model basically has the same behavioral implications. There are of course important normative differences among them, but it is clearly never possible to assess divergences between social and private productivity on the basis of earnings data alone. This identification problem is particularly well displayed in John Riley's comment, which illustrates the differences in the models with the standard Wicksellian optimal-stopping apparatus. The only difference is shown to lie in a few tangency conditions, and these are not directly revealed by data alone. Spence presents an interesting formulation of the rationing model, whereby productivity resides in the job to which a person is assigned rather than in the person himself, but he does not pursue it very far. This is an old idea in labor economics that has not received as much attention as it probably should and that perhaps could be developed much further than Spence does here.

In the simplest signaling models, it is assumed that unobserved productivity or ability is perfectly correlated with the costs of investing in the signal. Here, Spence relaxes the perfect correlation assumption and allows the signal to be noisy. On the average, persons with greater ability in the market can also purchase the signal on more favorable terms, but at the same time there exist individuals who are very able and who also find it relatively expensive to purchase the signal. This corresponds to the same kinds of analysis as are found in the human capital literature, where, for example, capital market imperfections make it difficult for some people to borrow and finance investment in schooling. Consistent with the identification problem noted above, the behavioral consequences and welfare distortions introduced thereby are not dissimilar to those that come from the human capital model. Spence next uses this model to show the difficulty of identifying the schooling-income productivity effect even when measures of ability are available. The chief difficulty appears to be that even if the ability indicator actually used were orthogonal to schooling, it cannot clean out the effect of signaling on schooling because the schooling effect on earnings always contains both productivity and signaling effects. Indeed, from his discussion it appears as if only the sum of the schooling-human capital and schooling-signal effects is identified and not each one separately. While this result depends on the particular example used by Spence, it brings us back to the original point: how does one choose between nonidentified models when important normative issues are at stake?

Spence also shows that his model leads to no definite predictions concerning the schooling-earnings relationship among the self-employed versus a screened sector, so that tests based on these presumed differences, even if it could be assumed that the self-employed do not signal, which is doubtful (think of why doctors so prominently display their credentials), would not necessarily be conclusive. Finally, Spence analyzes the effects of contingent contracts as a solution to the signaling-asymmetrical information problem, as well as some effects of licensing. A contingent contract is shown to solve the signaling problem in the sense of offering an alternative arrangement that removes the overinvestment inefficiency of signaling. However, in his interesting comment, Charles Wilson demonstrates that there may well be an adverse selection problem with contingent contracts when there are capital market imperfections that make it difficult for workers to borrow on terms as favorable as those available to firms.

One feature of the signaling model that appears to be artificial for many labor economists is the extreme assumption of asymmetrical knowledge, i.e., that workers know exactly who they are but firms have no information other than the signal. It is clear, however, that a great deal of job turnover and search activity engaged in by workers, if not school experiences themselves, is for the sake of acquisition of information about their own skills, tastes, and opportunities. In their paper, Ross, Taubman, and Wachter (RTW) begin to analyze how sequential job assignments might convey information about personal productivities of workers. While the scheme they consider would tend to collapse in the case of extreme asymmetric information, owing to the possibility of contingent contracts, it becomes more interesting in the case where information is equally poor on both sides of the market. Thus, in distinction from the extreme signaling model where schooling has no effect on productivity, the process envisioned by RTW actually yields a productive service to society in slotting people into the correct job.

As RTW set up the problem, a person of type i on job type j produces an output a_{ij}. At the time of initial hire neither the firm nor the workers have information on what types the workers are, but there is prior information on the probabilities of each type in a given group of workers. Hence the optimum strategy is to assign everyone to the one job with highest expected value. After the job assignments are made and output is revealed, information becomes available on the quality of the match for each person, which then yields conditional information on the worker's type. Given that information, new assignments are made, output is revealed again, and more information is yielded about the worker. With competitive labor markets, the wage paid at each step of the process must be the conditional mean productivity (conditional on the information revealed in previous steps). The main conclusion that RTW draw from this is that the wage of each person must tend to increase over the life cycle. This obviously must be true if the sorting process is productive and actually yields information that increases total output by better matching of different types of workers to different kinds of jobs. Although RTW contrast their conclusion with the conventional one that, for example, comes from an on-the-job training model, it strikes me as rash to overstress the conceptual differences: in both cases the process can be described as one of capital accumulation, in the training case the actual learning of skills and in the sorting case the learning about latent skills and comparative advantage.

There are a host of implications yet to be obtained from this way of looking at the problem, which in a formal sense is a variety of optimal-stopping, dynamic-programming problem. Wilson's comments show that the optimum assignment policy depends on the length of the remaining horizon and also on the dispersion of productivities. The latter is closely related to the amount of information obtained from a given assignment. In fact, it seems that if the horizon were long enough, it is not necessarily optimal to assign workers to the job that maximizes expected current product. There might be another job that actually yields more information—lower current expected product, but larger lifetime product through the more efficacious matches it allows later on. Evidently workers would be willing to pay for these kinds of changes if the matching information resides in them. Clearly there is a lot of useful economics yet to be done on this problem.

Note

Though all papers were assigned formal discussants at the conference, only selected comments appear in the published volume. This reflects the intensity of preferences of the discussants themselves, and no editorial judgment is implied or intended.

1 Labor Mobility and Wages

Jacob Mincer and Boyan Jovanovic

In this essay we explore the implications of human capital and search behavior for both the interpersonal and life cycle structure of interfirm labor mobility. The economic hypothesis which motivates the analysis is that individual differences in firm-specific complementarities and related skill acquisitions produce differences in mobility behavior and in the relation between job tenure, wages, and mobility. Both "job duration dependence" and "heterogeneity bias" are implied by this theory. Exploration of longitudinal data sets—National Longitudinal Surveys (NLS) and Michigan Income Dynamics (MID)—which contain mobility, job, and wage histories of men in the 1966–76 decade yield the following findings, among others:

1. The initially steep and later decelerating declines of labor mobility with working age are in large part due to the similar but more steeply declining relation between mobility and length of job tenure.

2. Given tenure levels, the probability of moving is predicted positively by the frequency of prior moves and negatively by education. The inclusion of prior moves in the regression reduces the estimated tenure slope because it helps to remove the "heterogeneity bias" in that slope.

3. The popular "mover-stayer model" is rejected by the existence of tenure effects on mobility.

Jacob Mincer is Professor of Economics, Columbia University, and Research Associate, National Bureau of Economic Research.

Boyan Jovanovic is staff economist at Bell Laboratories.

We are grateful to the National Science Foundation and the Sloan Foundation for support of this work.

The research reported here is part of the NBER's program in Labor Economics. Any opinions expressed are those of the authors and not those of the National Bureau of Economic Research.

4. Differences in mobility during the first decade of working life do not predict long-run differences in earnings. However, persistent movers at later stages of working life have lower wage levels and flatter life cycle wage growth.

5. The analysis calls for a reformulation of earnings (wage) functions. Inclusion of tenure terms in the function permits separate estimates of returns to general and specific human capital after correction for heterogeneity bias. A rough estimate is that fifty percent of lifetime wage growth is due to general (transferable) experience and twenty-five percent to firm-specific experience and interfirm mobility.

Sections 1.1–1.8 contain an exposition and empirical analysis which ranges over somewhat wider subject matter than Sections 1.9–1.11 which focus on the stochastic structure of mobility processes.

1.1 Introduction: Renewed Interest in Labor Mobility

Labor mobility is one of the central topics of labor economics and a long-standing subject of empirical research. Earlier studies reflected primarily a concern with the allocative efficiency of the labor market. They analyzed attitudes, job change decisions, and the direction of observed labor mobility in attempts to ascertain whether information, motivation, and behavior of workers were consistent with the postulates of economic theory.

In a comprehensive survey of this literature, Parnes (1970) concluded that the evidence on the operation of market forces was mixed, both among different studies and even within them. Although research in the 1960s was more sophisticated and utilized larger data sets than prior work, it did not provide any change in perspective.

Reviewing the more recent literature, Parsons (1978) finds promise in the emergence of theories of human capital and of search theories as tools for the analysis of labor mobility, labor turnover, and unemployment. However, applied work in search theory has, thus far, only partially touched on problems of labor mobility and of unemployment: its emphasis has been largely on conditions terminating job search, rather than on circumstances which generate it.

The reformulation of labor mobility as a human capital investment decision has been fruitfully applied to migration (Sjastaad 1962, and other work reviewed by Greenwood 1975). The connection between investments specific to the firm (and to larger units) and the incidence of industrial and occupational labor turnover has been elucidated in studies by Becker (1975), Oi (1961), and Parsons (1972).

The novel approaches suggested by human capital and by search theories are producing a renewed interest in the formerly stagnant field of labor mobility. A further source of interest has come from stochastic models of labor mobility. The first of these, the "mover-stayer" model, appeared two decades ago (Blumen, Kagan, McCarthy 1955) and they have recently reappeared in more sophisticated form (Heckman 1977, 1978; Jovanovic 1978b; for a review, see Singer and Spilerman 1976).

The purpose of this essay is to explore the implications of human capital and search behavior for both the interpersonal and life cycle structure of interfirm labor mobility. The apparent ambiguity in the relation between labor mobility and wages which characterizes much of the literature surveyed by Parnes is implicit and reconcilable in human capital analysis; as a response to perceived gains in wages, mobility promotes individual wage growth, but to the extent that on-the-job investments contain elements of specificity, mobility is a deterrent to wage growth. The study of differences in mobility behavior requires information over time; of special importance, in our approach, is information on time spent in the firm (tenure) and on the life cycle changes in job attachments. The availability of longitudinal microdata (especially NLS and MID panels) enables us to study these phenomena.

The economic hypothesis which motivates the analysis is that individual differences in firm-specific human capital behavior lead, via wage effects, to heterogeneity in mobility behavior, and to "tenure effects" on attachment to the firm. Implications for life cycle mobility are then derived in the absence or presence of "aging" (changes in mobility with age, at given tenure levels). Both "tenure dependence" and "heterogeneity bias" are implied by the theory. We explore data sets which contain mobility histories to ascertain the existence of these phenomena and to correct for the predictable biases. Next we investigate corresponding features of the wage structure. Labor mobility and tenure effects are introduced and tested in a reformulated earnings function in which specific and general human capital accumulation can be distinguished.

Sections 1.9–1.11 present a rigorous formulation of the structure of mobility viewed as a stochastic process.

1.2 Tenure, Working Age, and Mobility: Some Definitions and Facts

We define labor mobility as change of employer, whether or not unemployment intervenes. We exclude exits from and entries into the labor force. This exclusion is a minor one for the male labor force which we study.[1] Consequently, job separation is synonymous with job change in our data. Except for one illustration of observed differences (see table 1.2), we do not distinguish here between separations initiated by (or reported as) quit and layoff. Geographic, industrial, and occupational mobility are components of job mobility which are included in our concept but not singled out for separate treatment.[2]

Two probabilistic relations, or time profiles, are basic in our discussion and measurement of labor mobility. (1) The "tenure turnover profile" $S(T)$ is the relation between the probability of separating from a job in period t and the time spent in that job prior to t (current tenure T). In the language of renewal theory, $S(T)$ is the "hazard function." At the individual level this is a profile of "propensity to move" conditional on tenure. Such a profile is not observable. In large homogeneous groups, that is, groups consisting of individuals with the same propensity $S(T)$, we can observe estimates of the probabilities in each period in the form of relative frequencies or separation rates conditional on tenure. (2) The relation between an individual's propensity to move and working age, regardless of his current tenure, is his "experience turnover profile" $S(X)$. Again, this is observable as a relation between experience and separation rates.

The most firmly established fact about labor mobility of all kinds is that it declines with age. It declines much more sharply with length of tenure. The declines in both $S(X)$ and $S(T)$ are strongest initially and decelerate subsequently. Several tenure and age profiles of separation rates are shown in tables 1.1–1.3.

Table 1.1 shows the decline with age in the proportion of job changers (number of job changers divided by number employed) in 1961. The decline is similar when measured in terms of number of job changes rather than job changers, since a similar fraction (35%–40%) of job movers in each age group changed jobs more than once during the year (BLS 1963, table A).

Table 1.2 shows cross-classifications of separations, quits, and layoffs by experience and tenure in the period 1971–73 in the two NLS samples of men (young men, ages 19–29, and older men, ages 50–64, in 1971). The tenure profiles within working age (experience) classes are steeply declining and decelerating (convex). Mobility does not decline with working age at given tenure levels *within* each of the cohort age ranges. The decline *between* the young and old cohort is pronounced, but it shows mainly in quits.

The separation equations in table 1.3, derived from NLS panel data, summarize the conclusion that *within* the two age panels declines of mobility with working age (experience), shown by $S(X)$ in tables 1.1 and 1.2, are due to the effect of tenure which is revealed in the regression $S(X,T)$: For young men, experience effects (coefficients of X, X^2) vanish when tenure (T, T^2) is included. No experience effects are observed for older men with or without the tenure variables.[3] However, estimates of

Table 1.1   Job Changers as Percent of Employed Men, U.S., 1961

	\multicolumn{6}{c}{Age}					
	18–19	20–24	25–34	35–44	45–54	55–64
Percent	23.5	24.4	14.9	10.2	7.1	4.0

Source: BLS 1963.

Table 1.2   Mobility by Experience and Tenure, Pooled, 1967–73
(Percent moving in a two-year period)

Experience (years)	All	0–1	1–3	3–5	5–7	7–9	9–11	11–15	15–19	19+	n
					A. Separations						
0–4	.47	.73	.58	.28	.07	.12	.04				2,246
5–9	.38	.77	.60	.38	.08	.07	.06				1,197
25–29	.11	.46	.16	.22	.10	.19	.04	.03	.06	.04	441
30–34	.11	.40	.20	.15	.10	.16	.12	.04	.06	.06	1,499
35–39	.12	.51	.19	.19	.11	.08	.08	.06	.04	.04	1,998
40–44	.12	.43	.20	.10	.10	.11	.13	.05	.05	.06	1,542
					B. Quits						
0–4	.32	.48	.41	.20	.06	.08	.04				
5–9	.25	.48	.42	.26	.06	.05	.07				
25–29	.06	.19		.22	.10	.11	.04	0	.01	0	
30–34	.07	.20	.12	.09	.08	.09	.11	.03	.03	.02	
35–39	.05	.18	.10	.10	.06	.05	.06	.03	.02	.01	
40–44	.05	.13	.09	.03	.07	.06	.07	.03	.04	.02	
					C. Layoffs						
0–4	.14	.26	.17	.08	.01	.05					
5–9	.12	.28	.18	.11	.03	.02					
25–29	.05	.27	.16	0	0	.08	0	.02	.03	.01	
30–34	.05	.21	.08	.06	.02	.07	.01	.01	.03	.05	
35–40	.07	.33	.09	.10	.05	.04	.02	.03	.02	.03	
40–44	.07	.30	.12	.06	.03	.05	.05	.03	.01	.03	

$S(X)$ and $S(X,T)$ in Michigan Income Dynamics data which cover the complete age spectrum (table 5, panel C, lines 1 and 2) show that net aging effects remain even after the inclusion of tenure, although they are reduced in size and significance. In all data sets the explanatory power resides mainly in the tenure variables; mobility is convex both in tenure and in experience; and the tenure profile is much steeper than the experience profile.

1.3 Wage and Mobility Structures: Some Theory

We now turn to broad theoretical considerations with which we may analyze the facts of labor mobility. Some skills acquired in a particular firm are not transferable to other firms. The acquisition of such "specific" components of human capital by workers and the consequent wage pattern suffice to produce the tenure effects in the attachment to the firm which we observed in tables 1.2 and 1.3. At the same time, individual differences in amounts of specific capital investment imply a heterogene-

Table 1.3   **Separate Equations (1967–73)**

Young Men, Pooled

$S(X) = .486 - .034X + .002X^2 \quad R^2 = .02$
$(5.2)(3.6)$

$S(X,T) = .692 + .006X - .0000X^2 - .172T + .009T^2 \quad R^2 = .29$
$(1.0)(0)(19.7)(16.3)$

Older Men, Pooled

$S(X) = .015 + .0028X - .000X^2 \quad R^2 = .003$
$(.4)(.5)$

$S(X,T) = .208 + .0035X - .0000X^2 - .024T + .0005T^2 \quad R^2 = .10$
$(.3)(.2)(6.4)(4.1)$

Source: NLS Tapes.

ity in mobility, or in attachment to the firm (length of tenure), as well as in the strength of tenure effects, that is, in slopes of the tenure-separation probability relation.

The effects of acquiring job-specific capital on mobility may be described as follows: successful job matches eventually result in wage levels W which exceed expected alternative wages W_g. The higher the wage W the less incentive to quit, given W_g and the usual fluctuations in demand. Separations are high during the initial "probation" period and then drop to low levels. It is reasonable to assume that a successful match is only a starting point for a continuing employment relation which often involves investments of workers and firms in worker skills, and these are partially nontransferable.[4] Employer investments involve hiring, screening, and training costs which are recouped by a wage policy such that both quits and layoffs are deterred, that is, $W_g < W <$ VMP, where VMP is the worker's value of marginal product in the firm.

Define $W = W_g + W_s$, where W_g is the worker return on his general (transferable) human capital and W_s is the difference between the (higher) wage received in the firm and the opportunity wage elsewhere (also W_g). Similarly, W_e is the employer's return on the costs of investing in workers, the difference between the worker's productivity (VMP) and the wage paid to him (W). Workers are deterred from quitting, and employers from dismissing workers, because of these returns. Total separations are affected by $\Delta = (\text{VMP} - W_g) = W_s + W_e$, that is, by both components of returns to specific capital. In this paper we do not focus on the distinction between quit and layoff or consider the question whether employers and workers engage in joint or in separate optimizing behavior (but see Mortensen 1978). Plausibly, W_s and W_e are expected to be positively related: a good match and opportunity for joint investments are recognized by both employee and employer.

The distribution of returns to specific capital (Δ) creates individual (and group) differences in tenure-turnover profiles. Tenure profiles are horizontal only when $\Delta = 0$, in which case tenure has no effect on mobility or on wages. With $\Delta > 0$, tenure profiles of specific capital do not emerge instantaneously as the worker joins the firm. Specific capital is accumulated over time, given a successful match, and the returns grow over time. Both the rate of growth of these returns and their ultimate level affect mobility: the "tenure effect" is positively correlated with both. The convexity of the tenure-mobility profiles, and concavity of the tenure-wage profiles, are due to the eventual completion of specific capital accumulation in the firm.[5]

Thus the economics of specific human capital formation predict the coexistence of heterogeneity and of "tenure dependence" in accounting for mobility. The two aspects of behavior are related and are not to be viewed as mutually exclusive hypotheses: persons who favor large volumes of specific capital investment exhibit relatively little mobility (except for an initial period of repeated search and occasional later moves) and strong tenure effects.[6] Low levels of specific investment behavior, whether intentional or due to inefficiency in job matching, imply high (persistent) mobility levels independent of tenure (zero or small tenure effects). If rates of decline of experience profiles of mobility reflect primarily the slopes of tenure profiles, as appears to be the case, the flat and high profiles of "movers" and the downward-sloping profiles of "stayers" imply a progressive divergence over the life cycle in observed mobility behavior of a heterogeneous population.

The growing divergence of mobility rates over the working age parallels the repeatedly observed divergence of individual life cycle wage profiles (see Mincer 1974). The human capital model can interpret both divergences as lifetime outcomes of unchanging individual differences in abilities and opportunities. This view cautions against literal impressions that older cohorts are more heterogeneous than younger ones, or against the notion that the experience of longer tenure creates a "reinforcement effect," that is, a desire to invest in specific capital. This is not to say, however, that such views are not valid. Habit formation and unexpected events do modify lifetime histories, but they need not be invoked in an initial analysis.

The major implication of specific capital heterogeneity for the structure of mobility is the existence of differential tenure effects. Levels of $S(T)$ are higher and slopes flatter for individuals and groups who acquire little specificity in their human capital, while steeper slopes and eventually lower levels characterize tenure functions of large specific capital investors. Empirical observations should reveal steep downward slopes in tenure-turnover profiles uncorrected for "heterogeneity bias," as well as "true" negative slopes after correction for bias.

A related set of predictions applies to the wage structure: a major one is the existence of tenure effects on wages which are additional to the effects of general human capital accumulation. This suggests a reformulation of the earnings function to include a tenure term. The experience and tenure coefficients should provide a decomposition of worker returns to general (transferable) and specific (nontransferable) human capital investments. As in the case of mobility, it is also necessary to attempt correction for the danger of upward biases in tenure effects which is posed by the existence of heterogeneity.

Other implications of the theory relate to the effects of age (experience) on mobility and wages $S(X)$ and $W(X)$. An interesting conclusion is that mobility declines and wages grow with age even if there are no "aging" effects, that is, even if mobility depended only on levels of tenure and not directly on age (given tenure). Similarly, wages grow (on average) over the life cycle even if no general (experience) capital is accumulated. Also $W(X)$ should be concave if $W(T)$ is concave, and $S(X)$ convex because $S(T)$ is. Indeed, without specific capital phenomena, the convex shape of the age patterns of mobility $S(X)$ would be difficult to understand.

1.4 Tenure Effects on Mobility in Homogeneous and in Heterogeneous Groups

A simple heuristic model makes the notions intuitively clear:[7] The propensity to move at the individual level, or the separation rate in a homogeneous group, is a function:

(1) $$s = f(T, X)$$

where s is the probability of separation in period t, T is length of current employment in the firm up to time t, and X is total work experience (working age). The slope of the age (experience) profile is:

(2) $$\frac{ds}{dX} = \left(\frac{\partial s}{\partial T} \cdot \frac{dT}{dX} \right) + \frac{\partial s}{\partial X}$$

Here $\partial s/\partial T$ is the slope of the tenure profile, dT/dX is the growth of tenure with working age, and $\partial s/\partial X$ is the true age effect, if any. Note that $0 < dT/dX < 1$. Tenure would grow by the same amount as age only in the case of perfect immobility: it increases initially with age since it is necessarily short at early stages of experience. At later stages dT/dX approaches zero as T approaches the fixed value $[(1/s) - 1]$ in the case of no tenure dependence, that is, when $\partial s/\partial T = 0$. In the case of job specificity or tenure dependence, i.e., when $\partial s/\partial T < 0$, dT/dX remains positive at later ages as well.[8] A regression of T on X, not shown here, reveals a positive slope and slight concavity.

Decomposition (2) yields the following conclusions about the observed decline of mobility with age:

1. Even if there were no "age effects" ($\partial s/\partial X = 0$), mobility would decline with age, because of job specificities, that is, because mobility declines with tenure ($\partial s/\partial T < 0$). No decline would be observed if mobility were independent of tenure (see part 2, theorem 2).

2. Again abstracting from age effects, since $dT/dX < 1$, the slope of the experience profile is less than that of the tenure profile.

3. Convexity in the tenure profile would be reinforced or simply reflected in the age profile if dT/dX decreases over time, or is constant. Moreover, this could happen even if there is an age effect and even if the age effect were concave.

4. Decline of mobility with age is faster the stronger the decline of mobility with tenure, apart from the pure age effect.

Up to this point the analysis applies to a homogeneous group, defined by the identical $S(X,T)$ function for each of its members. Components of life cycle mobility can be observed directly in such groups by estimation of equation (1). Generally, it is not possible to define homogeneous groups empirically, so that estimation of (1) cannot be carried out directly. If in fact individual propensities to move are not reduced by tenure, yet differ among workers, the observed group tenure profile $S(T)$ will have a downward slope, and it is likely to be convex as well, because persons with high propensities to move are more likely to separate at early levels of tenure while those with low propensities are more likely to stay on a long time. The decline in the tenure profile consequently reflects the degree of heterogeneity when measured by the variance in propensities to move, while convexity would reflect a decline in that variance, as only stayers remained in the long-tenure classes.[9]

Let us now define a heterogeneous population in consonance with specific capital heterogeneity as a collection of homogeneous subgroups among which mobility rates differ at given levels of tenure, while tenure curves $S(T)$ decline in some or most of the subgroups. By the preceding argument, any degree of specific capital heterogeneity will lend a downward bias (steeper than average slope) to the observed group tenure curve. We should note that heterogeneity biases can exist without any true tenure effects, for reasons not involving specificity. But, if the tenure effect $(\partial s/\partial T)_i$ is zero in each subgroup i, the observed population experience profile $S(X)$ will be horizontal, since its slope is an average of slopes in the subgroups. Conversely, if $(\partial s/\partial T)_i < 0$ in each or some subgroups, the observed experience profile must slope down. Thus, in the absence of age effects, the age profile of mobility $S(X)$ provides a clear test of the presence or absence of tenure effects in the group, regardless of the group's degree of heterogeneity.

As an example, the popular "mover-stayer" model (see Blumen, Kogen, and McCarthy 1955; Singer and Spilerman 1976), which assumes heterogeneity and neglects tenure effects, must be rejected by the decline in the age-mobility profile, insofar as the latter is not exclusively due to pure age effects [$\partial s/\partial X < 0$ in (1)].

Although the decline in life cycle mobility reflects the existence and strength of tenure effects, it yields no information on the extent of heterogeneity in the population. Assessment of heterogeneity is important, however, both in its own right and as a basis for recognition and correction of bias in the estimated tenure effects.

1.5 Empirical Mobility Functions

An open-ended empirical procedure for estimating tenure effects in the presence of heterogeneity is to enter a number of variables which are likely to capture heterogeneous behavior in a regression of tenure on mobility. The tenure slope estimate in the multiple regression is reduced compared with its value when it is the only right-hand variable. The reduction measures the extent of heterogeneity bias due to these variables. This procedure was applied to the NLS data and the results are shown in table 1.4. In addition to experience, the heterogeneity factors in the regressions were education, health, hours of work, family status variables, industry, and union membership. In terms of controbution to the adjusted coefficient of determination R^2, the last two factors were the most pronounced. The reduction in slope was about 20–30 percent for the young men, and larger (relative to the flatter slope) for the older men. This procedure is clearly incomplete for our purposes here, although of interest in the substantive studies of particular factors.

A scheme that is more general, in the sense that it does not require an enumeration of heterogeneity factors, derives from another definition of

Table 1.4   Gross and Net Tenure-Separations Slope, NLS, 1967–71

	Young Men				Older Men			
	1967–69		1969–71		1967–69		1969–61	
	Slope[d]	R^2	Slope	R^2	Slope	R^2	Slope	R^2
Gross Coefficient[a]	−.1420	.182	−.1100	.151	−.028	.12	−.027	.12
Net Coefficient[b]	−.0845	.200	−.0847	.165	−.016	.17	−.006	.20
Heterogeneity Factors[c]		.131		.110		.07		.11

[a]Linear coefficient in the regression of separation of tenure.
[b]Partial coefficient of tenure (linear term) in the multiple regression.
[c]Regression variables other than tenure.
[d]Tenure coefficients always highly significant (t > 4).

a heterogeneous population: At a given level of tenure, members of a homogeneous group have equal probabilities of moving during the next period regardless of their past mobility, while in a heterogeneous group probabilities differ even at fixed current tenure. Since frequency of past mobility is an indicator of personal probability ("propensity to move"), which differs among workers, its (partial) correlation with mobility in the next period, given tenure, reveals the existence, and estimates the degree, of heterogeneity. And to the extent that the prior mobility variable captures and therefore standardizes for differential mobility levels, its inclusion corrects the bias in the estimated tenure slope.

Information on prior mobility was available in the NLS data for young men as the number of interfirm moves (NM) between 1966 and 1971. For the older men in NLS such information was not available, but we constructed a variable (PM) on the number of (survey to survey) periods between 1965 and 1973 during which at least one move took place.[10]

Table 1.5 presents, in successive steps, regressions for young men (panel A) in which separations (job changes) in the period 1971–73 are predicted by years of work experience (X, X^2) up to 1971; tenure (T, T^2) in 1971; and mobility prior to the current job (NM). The prior mobility variable was also interacted with experience (XNM). The same regressions (except that PM replaces NM) predict job change rates of NLS older men in 1973–75 (panel B), and of all MID men in 1975–76 (panel C).

Briefly, the findings are: Inclusion of tenure (row 2) shows it to be the variable which is responsible for the gross age decline in separations among young NLS men (row 1, panel A). Looking at rows 1 and 2 of panel B, we find that the older NLS men show neither gross nor net age (experience) effects. While net age effects are absent within the limited age ranges in the NLS data (young $\leq$ 29, old $\geq$ 50), they are reduced (going from row 1 to row 2 in panel C) but remain significant in the MID regressions which cover the whole age spectrum. The absence of gross age effects (row 1, panel B) in the older cohort reflects very small tenure effects (slopes) at this stage. This is consistent with a strong convexity of tenure (and age) profiles over the long run. The comparable tenure slopes are much steeper for the young because they are dominated in regressions by early tenure levels. Indeed, in a subsample of older men whose tenure does not exceed eight years (not shown here), the tenure slopes are quite as steep as those of young men. Thus, the differences between the young and the old need not be interpreted as a change in the mobility structure.

The inclusion of prior mobility variables shows the existence of heterogeneity in mobility behavior; the variable is a strong predictor of mobility in the next period given experience and tenure at the beginning of the period. Persons who moved more frequently prior to the current job are

Table 1.5 Mobility Functions $s = f(X, T, NM, Ed)$

A. Job Change Rates of Young Men in NLS, 1971–73 ($n = 1{,}595$, $\bar{s} = .375$)

Constant	X	X^2	T	T^2	NM	$X \cdot NM$	Ed	R^2
.506	−.0424 (3.98)	.0020 (2.44)						.023
.612	−.0064 (.61)	.0002 (.24)	−.1071 (10.41)	.0057 (5.73)				.124
.547	−.0034 (.32)	.0001 (.17)	−.0963 (9.02)	.0051 (5.08)	.0060 (3.65)			.131
.547	−.0171 (1.63)	.0003 (.36)	−.0822 (7.38)	.0048 (4.72)		.0035 (5.56)		.141
.850	−.0253 (2.37)	.0004 (.48)	−.0797 (7.17)	.0047 (4.64)		.0032 (5.04)	−.0211 (3.89)	.149
Sample means	5.05	40.72	2.82	15.75	5.17	17.28	12.54	

Table 1.5 (continued)

Constant	X	X^2	T	T^2	PM	$X \cdot$ PM	Ed	R^2
\multicolumn{9}{c}{B. Job Change Rates of Older Men in NLs, 1973–75 ($n = 1{,}282$, $\bar{s} = .091$)}								
.1645	−.0063 (.16)	.0001 (.22)						.0008
.5060	−.0165 (.44)	.0002 (.5)	−.0172 (7.67)	.0003 (5.78)				.065
.5553	−.0282 (.57)	.0004 (.85)	−.0045 (1.57)	.00009 (1.49)	.0921 (6.82)			.098
.5680	−.0275 (.76)	.0004 (.79)	−.0049 (1.72)	.0001 (1.64)		.0024 (6.77)		.098
.7551	−.0344 (.93)	.0005 (.93)	−.0052 (1.82)	.0001 (1.75)	(.79)	.0024 (6.62)	−.0026 (.79)	.098
Sample mean	38.09	1464.78	16.42	415.26	.5226	19.89	11.67	

Table 1.5 (continued)

Constant	X	X^2	T	T^2	$X \cdot SM$	SM	Ed	R^2
C. Job Change Rates of All Ages, MID, 1975–76 ($\bar{s} = .116$, $n = 1{,}562$)								
.2285	−.0099 (4.08)	.0001 (2.61)						.027
.2402	−.0054 (2.11)	.00009 (1.66)	−.0149 (4.35)	.0004 (3.09)				.043
.2014	−.0063 (2.46)	.0001 (1.95)	−.0097 (2.71)	.0002 (1.91)		.2300 (5.01)		.058
.2329	−.0078 (2.92)	.0001 (2.16)	−.0107 (2.91)	.0003 (2.25)	.0112 (3.09)			.049
.3484	−.0062 (2.42)	.00008 (1.43)	−.0099 (2.82)	.0002 (2.05)		.2175 (4.74)	−.0105 (3.46)	.066
Sample mean	18.71	516.37	7.26	113.38	1.27	.095	12.64	

Note: X = years of work experience; T = years of tenure on the current job; Ed = years of schooling; NM = number of interfirm moves in the period 1966–71 of young men in NLS. Adjusted to length of period if experience started after 1966; PM = number of 2-year periods between 1965 and 1973 during which a job change occurred among older men in NLS; SM = number of annual periods between 1968 and 1975 during which a job change occurred among men in MID. Adjusted work experience started after 1968; w = logarithm of hourly wage; $\bar{w}$ = mean of w; $\bar{s}$ = mean rate of job change (over a 2-year period in NLS, annual in MID); n = sample size; R^2 = adjusted coefficient of determination; t = statistics in parentheses.

more likely to leave the job earlier than others. Prior mobility appears to be a stronger predictor at older than at younger ages. When converted into an elasticity, prior mobility is also several times larger in the older group. Evidently, repeated mobility at an advanced age represents persistent mobility, suggesting little stake in job tenure or lack of opportunity, while repeated mobility at young ages does not have the same connotation. We tried to test the proposition that prior mobility at older ages is a better index of heterogeneity *within* each of the panels: the experience–prior mobility interaction variable, shown in row 4 of each panel, with positive and significant. Incidentally, the existence of this interaction implies that age (experience) profiles of mobility are not only higher but also flatter for movers (PM large) than for stayers (PM small), as we theorized in section 1.3.

The introduction of the prior mobility variable was designed to separate "movers" from "stayers." If effective, such "standardization" should reduce the tenure slope in the regression. Tenure slopes are indeed reduced in row 3 and below in all three data panels. The reduction is small among the young and large among the old, as would be expected since PM is a stronger indicator of persistent mobility at older ages. The average reduction in the linear tenure term at mid-experience levels (MID) is about one-third. That is, heterogeneity biases the steepness of tenure-turnover profile upward by about fifty percent, on average. The education variable shown in the last rows of table 1.5 appears to predict some reductions in mobility at given levels of initial mobility, but has no additional predictive power among the old.

1.6 Net Age Effects on Mobility

Although they do not appear in the NLS regression of table 1.5, age effects (coefficients of experience $\partial s/\partial X$) on mobility are present in the MID regressions in panel C and were seen in the decline of mobility rates at fixed levels of tenure when the older cohort was compared with the younger (table 1.2). The economics of this downward shift in tenure curves may be found in the more traditional aspects of labor mobility: job change is a response to higher wage levels beckoning elsewhere as well as a search for specific investment opportunties.

For a given wage gain, the supply response would diminish with working age (at given levels of tenure), since the payoff period declines. Such effects, however, would not become pronounced until late in the working life, especially in view of positive and not negligible discounting. Emphasis on the effect of finite life (working age) on expected returns cannot produce a convex experience-turnover profile, nor can it rationalize the fact that the observed net age declines ($\partial s/\partial X$) occur relatively early in the working life (see rows 3 to 5, panel C). However, the gain from mobility may decline early in the life cycle not because of the declining payoff period but because of rising costs: in particular, costs of geographic mobility rise with family size and the presence of school-age children.

Age effects are, indeed, more important in migration than in local job mobility. The decline in migration with age is steeper than the decline in local job mobility: one-third of young compared to less than ten percent of older job changers migrate. But the greater costs of migration include also costs due to locational specificities which exist in addition to job specificity, so stronger "pure aging" is not the only reason for a sharper age decline in migration than in local job mobility: Tenure effects which reflect both job and location specificities are, indeed, sharper migrants.

Another set of age factors, unrelated to location, may operate in the early years of work experience: the range of quality of jobs and of the job match cannot be ascertained by mere search, and some knowledge must be acquired by actual experimentation. Also, job training and opportunities for investment in general human capital may present themselves sequentially in different firms. Beyond the first decade of working life, we may expect that human capital investors who eventually find a reasonably compatible work place develop a strong attachment to the job.

1.7 Tenure and Mobility Effects in the Wage Function

Specific capital investments imply tenure effects on wages which cause the tenure effects in mobility. Wage heterogeneity due to differential specificities similarly produces some of the heterogeneity in mobility. Consequently, we should observe tenure effects in addition to general work experience effects in wage functions. Moreover, these effects may be exaggerated in empirical estimates in view of interpersonal diversity in specific investment behavior.

Information on job mobility can and should be built into the standard earnings function. The inclusion of the tenure variable should capture returns to specific (nontransferable) capital accumulation, permitting the experience term to measure returns to general (transferable) capital accumulation. Information on prior mobility should also be used in correcting for heterogeneity bias. The explanatory power of the enriched wage function ought to be enhanced.

The coefficients of experience (X) in the standard wage function, which includes only education in addition to the experience terms, reflect a gross effect dw/dX which is a mixture of returns to general and specific capital:

(2a) $$\frac{dw}{dX} = \left(\frac{\partial w}{\partial t} \cdot \frac{dT}{dX} \right) + \frac{\partial w}{\partial X}$$

The standard wage function has an upward-sloping and concave experience profile (the concavity is more pronounced when $w = \log$ wage) in cross-sections and in longitudinal data.[11] Its slope has been derived in human capital theory and in econometric studies. In view of (2a), it is incorrect to interpret the coefficients of experience dw/dX as measures of returns to general human capital stocks. Such returns are measured by $\partial w/\partial X$, that is, by coefficients of experience when tenure is included in the wage function. Clearly dw/dX overstates $\partial w/\partial X$ if specific capital is of any importance. The experience coefficients in the earnings function which omits tenure is an upward-biased measure of returns to general human capital accumulated on the job.

It is interesting to note, according to (2a), that even if no general capital were accumulated in the work career, wages would still rise over the life cycle, and, as a group average, the wage profile would tend to be concave so long as the tenure wage profile is concave and dT/dX does not increase over the life cycle.

Wage functions with tenure variables $w(X,T)$ can be estimated in homogeneous groups without bias (homogeneity defined as the same tenure wage profile), but no such groups can be defined a priori: in the presence of heterogeneity, the tenure coefficient is likely to be exaggerated, as in the case of mobility, and corrections need to be devised. More precisely, the bias arises because greater specificity produces larger discrepancies between the marginal product in the firm and the opportunity wage $\Delta = \text{VMP} - W_g = W_s + W_e$, where W_s is the specific return to the worker, and W_e to the employer, and Δ as well as W_s differ among workers and firms. Δ affects the length of tenure. It is plausible for W_s and W_e to be positively correlated, because a fruitful match has to be recognized as such by both parties. Therefore W_s is a good index of Δ, and the tenure-wage coefficient which attempts to measure W_s is likely to be correlated with expected tenure (see discussion of theorem 3 below). Heterogeneity in W_s is thus likely to produce an upward bias in the estimates of tenure effects of wages, that is, of returns to specific worker investments. An additional source of bias could result from a positive correlation between general and specific investments; here steeper tenure-wage curves would start at higher levels. To the extent that general returns to capital (W_g) are not fully measured (standardized) by regression variables, the bias will arise.

Of course, positive tenure coefficients need not reflect wage growth in the firm. Higher wage levels (not growing with tenure) for the same labor in some firms also create incentives to stay there longer. Although transitional, this relation is likely to be widespread in a dynamic economy as an equilibrating phenomenon. Such supply adjustments to shifting demands are most likely to involve younger people whose mobility is less costly especially in terms of specific capital losses. Note that in this case prior mobility is not a good index of wage heterogeneity. Similar and more long-lasting effects can be created by above-equilibrium union wages and nepotism.

Can information on prior mobility be used in the wage function as an index of relevant heterogeneity, that is, of individual differences in W_s and consequently in the wage-tenure coefficient? The answer is less clear in the wage equation than in the mobility equation. Positive serial correlation in mobility makes the link between length of tenure and mobility almost definitional whatever the source of heterogeneity in mobility. The problem for the wage equation is that bias in the tenure coefficient is only in part due to heterogeneity in specific capital, and the latter is responsible for only a part of the heterogeneity in mobility. Thus prior mobility may be a weak instrument for elimination of heterogeneity bias. Its role in wage formation is nevertheless of interest to our study.

Table 1.6 presents wage functions of the younger and older NLS men, and of all men in MID. The independent variables are the same as in the mobility functions in table 1.5; the dependent variable is the logarithmic wage.[12] Row 1 is the "standard" wage function where the independent variables are education and experience. In the next row the tenure terms are added. In the third row we add the prior mobility variable, and in the last row we observe its interaction with experience.

In the young men's panel (A), the introduction of tenure reduces the experience coefficients. At this stage (on average, five years of experience), wages grow 6.6 percent per year of experience (row 1); 4.3 percent as returns to general postschool human capital accumulation (row 2); and the remaining 2.3 percent owing to specific capital accumulation. The tenure coefficients are large and significant. Prior mobility is not related to current wages and does not affect the tenure coefficients. The coefficient of the interaction variable (XNM) is positive but quite small, and its introduction raises the tenure coefficient slightly. Apparently differences in early mobility of young men are not indicative of future differences in specific capital investments, nor do they capture differences in wage levels which are positively related to the length of current tenure.

In the wage function for NLS older men (panel B), the experience profile is a plateau, but tenure slopes are positive (and concave) though much flatter than for young men.[13] Still, the observed tenure effect is biased upward. Introduction of prior mobility cuts the linear term in half and reduces its significance. We may conclude that repeated mobility at an advanced stage of the life cycle is an indicator of persistent turnover, denoting little investment in specific capital. The mobility variable has a negative effect, showing that frequent movers have lower wages than stayers, given education, experience, and current tenure. This is in contrast to the young whose past mobility did not imply a downward selection. We may conclude that intensive early mobility—about a half of

Table 1.6   Wage Functions

Constant	Ed	X	X^2	T	T^2	NM	$X \cdot$ NM	R^2
A. Wage Functions of Young Men, NLS, 1971 ($\bar{w}_{71} = 1.28$, $n = 1{,}442$)									
−.0311	.0847 (17.93)	.0658 (7.36)	−.0022 (3.23)					.194
.0021	.0079 (16.50)	.0433 (4.70)	−.0011 (1.52)	.0702 (7.27)	−.0052 (5.24)			.229
.0026	.0779 (16.47)	.0432 (4.69)	−.0011 (1.53)	.0702 (6.99)	−.0052 (5.17)	−.00003 (.03)		.229
−.0343	.0790 (16.64)	.0401 (4.29)	−.0010 (1.46)	.0780 (7.49)	−.0055 (5.49)		.0011 (1.98)	.231
Sample mean	12.52	4.97	39.94	2.78	15.06	5.29	17.48	

Table 1.6 (continued)

B. Wage Functions of Older Men, NLS, 1973 ($\bar{w}_{73} = 1.59$, $n = 982$)

Constant	Ed	X	X^2	T	T^2	PM	$X \cdot PM$	R^2
.6733	.0696 (10.37)	.0113 (.14)	−.0002 (.22)					.175
.5359	.0683 (10.19)	.0130 (.17)	−.0002 (.24)	.0136 (2.99)	−.0002 (1.58)			.199
.6105	.0666 (9.88)	.0157 (.2)	−.0003 (.3)	.0067 (1.09)	−.00006 (.4)	−.0482 (1.8)		.202
.5996	.0668 (9.90)	.0146 (.2)	−.0003 (.28)	.0080 (1.32)	−.00009 (.57)		−.0011 (1.52)	.201
Sample mean	11.58	38.05	1462.28	15.23	367.19	.573	21.83	

Table 1.6 (continued)

Constant	Ed	X	X^2	T	T^2	SM	$X \cdot SM$	R^2
C. Wage Functions of All Ages, MID, 1975–76 ($\bar{w}_{75}=1.69$, $n=1{,}560$)									
.2437	.0741 (17.45)	.0467 (14.07)	−.0007 (9.56)					.263
.2351	.0732 (17.57)	.0372 (10.70)	−.0006 (8.08)	.0305 (6.59)	−.0007 (4.25)			.295
.2791	.0722 (17.33)	.0378 (10.91)	−.0006 (8.32)	.0264 (5.44)	−.0006 (3.49)	−.1842 (2.94)		.298
.2541	.0725 (17.43)	.0404 (11.15)	−.0007 (8.55)	.0249 (5.01)	−.0006 (3.39)		−.0150 (3.04)	.299
Sample mean	12.63	18.72	516.96	7.27	113.53	.094	1.26	

Note: Regression variables same as in table 1.5.

the first decade in our NLS data—is not necessarily an inverse index of longer-run tendencies to acquire specific capital or an index of inability to acquire a good job match. It may even be a positive index of efficiency in making wage gains by moving across firms or of greater intensity of search for an optional career.

Taken together the findings in both NLS panels (A and B) show that tenure effects on wages are significant, reflecting the firm-specific component of wage progress on the job. This component accounts for about one-third of wage growth per year in the early part of working life. At young ages, past mobility does not clearly distinguish tendencies toward firm-specific human capital behavior. It does so, however, at older ages. At that stage lesser specific investments also result in lower wages, apparently as a result of slower growth over the past decades.[14]

The wage function in the MID panel (C), which covers all working ages, indicates that an average (and in mid-career) the firm-specific component accounts for 20–25 percent of wage growth per year (difference between the X-coefficients in rows 1 and 2). Prior mobility is negatively related to wages. The interaction term is also negative suggesting that men who continue to be frequent movers in the third decade of their working lives have both lower wages and flatter experience profiles of wages. The inclusion of prior mobility variables reduces the tenure slope by close to 20 percent. Thus, heterogeneity biases the tenure-wage slope coefficient upward by about 25 percent, half as much as it biased the tenure-mobility slope (panel C of table 1.5).

1.8 Tenure, Experience, and Mobility: Additional Remarks

We used the generalized term "specific human capital behavior" to cover both the informational aspect of job matching and the theory of specific human capital investment. The former is a necessary condition for the latter, and both are required for completeness.

There is another and popular view that the reality of tenure effects on mobility and on wages is largely institutional. The effects we analyzed are seen as "seniority rights" which include job security, pension rights, vacations, and seniority-based pay and promotion advantages. But the distinction is superficial. The "rights" themselves may well derive from human capital specificities in the presence or absence of formal, especially union, regulations. Indeed, recent research shows that tenure turnover profiles decline and tenure wage profiles grow as much and more (!) in the nonunion as in the union sector.[15]

In the past, experience coefficients dw/dX were sometimes crudely interpreted as returns to on-the-job general investments. In the wage function which includes tenure, the experience coefficients $\partial w/\partial X$ effectively segregate returns to general human capital investments, but they contain both returns to on-the-job general investment and across-jobs wage gains due to mobility (but not to tenure). These across-jobs wage changes are positive in purposive quits especially in migration, but are often negative when job change results from layoff, "exogenous" quit, and job dissatisfaction (Bartel and Borjas, chapter 2, below).

Over the life cycle, the effects of mobility on wages become increasingly less favorable at least as measured by money wages. Quits, migration, and occupational upgrading predominate in mobility of the young, but they become relatively unimportant at older ages. Since the frequency of job change declines over the life cycle for reasons already spelled out, the mobility component of wage growth declines over the life cycle as a result of declines both in the size and in the frequency of wage gains across firms. This is another aspect of the well-known concavity of the experience profile of wages.

Some models elevate the across-firm wage change to a single explanation of the typical concave life cycle wage profile: the worker is envisaged as moving up a fixed offer-wage distribution over his lifetime. Successful on-the-job search results in across-jobs wage growth. With a fixed offer-wage distribution, turnover declines with labor market experience. Thus older workers have a higher wage and a smaller probability of future separation.[16]

Although they produce concavity in the wage profiles, such models are quite inadequate as major explanations of magnitudes of wage growth over the life cycle (dw/dX). In a calculation based on the Coleman-Rossi data, Bartel (1975) shows that no more than 25 percent of personal wage growth can be attributed to across-firms wage changes during the first fifteen years of work experience, when mobility is most pronounced. The models, therefore, neglect the bulk of the phenomenon they are trying to explain. Moreover, concavity in the wage profile does not require job mobility, in human capital theory, or in fact: Borjas (1976) found the typically pronounced concavity in wage profiles of NLS workers who spent all of their working life in a single firm.

Although crude, our estimates of tenure and experience wage effects suggest that about 25 percent of life cycle wage growth, which abstracts from economy-wide changes, is due to specific capital investment. Taken together, the estimates provide a complete though very rough decomposition of lifetime wage growth: about 25 percent of it is due to interfirm mobility; another 20–25 percent to firm-specific experience; and over 50 percent to general (transferable) experience.

Perhaps the best way to summarize the life cycle relation between mobility and wages is to recognize that initial (first decade ?) job search has two major purposes: to gain experience, wages, and skills by moving across firms; and to find, sooner or later, a suitable job in which one can settle and grow for a long time. The life cycle decline in mobility is, in part, evidence of successful initial mobility, an interpretation which is corroborated by corresponding life cycle growth in wages.

In both older and younger age groups, stayers and successful searchers grow faster than unsuccessful searchers or "noninvesting" movers. However, a comparison of movers and stayers puts successful searchers in the category of movers among the young, but in the category of stayers (they moved when younger) among the old. As a result, comparisons of stayers and movers show that young movers do as well as or better than stayers, but ultimate stayers show superior wage growth and higher wage levels in the later decades.

We note, in conclusion, that "tenure and heterogeneity effects" are not restricted to job mobility. Whenever specific capital matters, comparable dualities between returns ("wages") and turnover may be expected. Some evidence on this generalization is available in analyses of location decisions (Da Vanzo 1976), and of marital instability (Becker, Landes, Michael 1977).

In the second part of our paper we shall treat labor mobility and wage growth over the life cycle as related stochastic processes. We first focus on the evolution of these processes for a given worker, interpreting our formulation within the context of existing theories of turnover and of wage growth and listing some of the implications of these theories. Next we take up the question of unmeasured heterogeneity in the population, and the problem of sample selection over time, known as the "mover-stayer" problem. A simple result is proved (theorem 3) which relates the behavior of a heterogeneous group to the behavior of the individual members of that group. In interpreting the result, we pay particular attention to the on-the-job-training hypothesis. Lastly, we describe a method to estimate various parametrizations of the separation and wage equations.

1.9 Evolution of Stochastic Processes

Definitions:

z = parameter indexing a particular worker

X = the worker's labor market experience

t = the worker's job tenure

X_0 = market experience at which the worker started on his current job, so that, at each moment in time, $X_0 + t = X$

Let

$F(t|X_0, z) \equiv$ probability that for a worker of type z, job tenure does not exceed t on a job which started at X_0

Let $f(t|X_0, z) = \partial F/\partial t$ be the associated density, and let $\hat{s}(t, X_0, x)$ be the "hazard function" of this distribution, defined by $\hat{s} = f/(1-F)$. Then $\hat{s}$ is the conditional density of job separation at tenure t, given that a tenure level t has been attained. The definitions of $\hat{s}$ and f imply that F may be written as

$$(3) \qquad F(t|X_0, z) = 1 - \exp\left[-\int_0^t \hat{s}(y, X_0, z)\, dy\right]$$

There may be a positive probability that a job episode never terminates, in which case

$$\lim_{t\to\infty} F(t|X_0, z) < 1, \text{ i.e., } \int_0^\infty \hat{s}(y, X_0, z)\, dy < \infty$$

It should be noted that F determines $\hat{s}$ uniquely and vice versa. Since $f \geq 0$, $\hat{s} \geq 0$ so that F is nondecreasing.

One purpose of this section is to draw some parallels between wage rates and separation probabilities. Let $\hat{w}(t, X_0, z)$ be the mathematical expectation of the wage that worker z, with experience $X_0 + t$, and tenure t, will receive. It may be noted that both $\hat{w}$ and $\hat{s}$ are mathematical expectations conditional upon t, X_0, and z.

Hereafter it is assumed that when a particular job episode terminates, it is immediately followed by a new job episode. That is, there are assumed to be no unemployment spells or spells of market nonparticipation. Given this assumption, consider now the special case in which $\partial \hat{s}/\partial X_0 = \partial F/\partial X_0 = 0$. Then each job episode is identically distributed. If, in addition, the job episodes are also assumed to be independently as well as identically distributed, then turnover becomes a pure renewal process (see Feller 1966, chapter 11). In what follows, we study processes that are more general than the renewal process.

Let $a(X, z)$ be the probability density that worker z will experience a job separation at the point in time at which his market experience is equal to X. (For the special case where turnover is a renewal process, $a(X, z)$ is known as the renewal density.) Also let $h(t|X, z)$ be the probability density that a worker with market experience x will have current job tenure equal to t. Note that for this statement to be true, the worker must have experienced a job separation at exactly $X = t$ level of market experience, and no subsequent separations. Therefore,

$$(4) \qquad h(t|X, z) = \begin{cases} 1 - F(X|0, z) & \text{if } t = X \\ a(X-t, z)\,[1 - F(t|X-t, z)] \\ \quad \text{if } 0 \leq t < X \end{cases}$$

Then

(5) $$a(X, z) = \hat{s}(X, 0, z)[1 - F(X|0, z)] + \int_0^X \hat{s}(t, X-t, z) h(t|X, z) dt$$

$$= \hat{s}(X, 0, z)[1 - F(X|0, z)] + \int_0^X \hat{s}(t, X-t, z) a(X-t, z) \times [1 - F(t|X-t, z)] dt$$

Define $y(X, z)$ as the mathematical expectation of worker z's wage conditioned only on his market experience. Then

(6) $$y(X, z) = \hat{w}(X, 0, z)[1 - F(X|0, z)] + \int_0^X \hat{w}(t, X-t, z) \times a(X-t, z)[1 - F(t|X-t, z)] dt$$

Now define two new functions

$$s(t, X, z) = \hat{s}(t, X-t, z) \rightarrow s_X = \hat{s}_{X_0}$$
$$\text{and } s_t = \hat{s}_t - \hat{s}_{X_0}$$

and

$$w(t, X, z) = \hat{w}(t, X-t, z) \rightarrow w_X = \hat{w}_{X_0}$$
$$\text{and } w_t = \hat{w}_t - \hat{w}_{X_0}$$

(where subscripts denote partial derivatives).

Making the substitution into (5) and (6).

(7) $$a(X, z) = s(X, X, z)[1 - F(X|0, z)] + \int_0^X s(t, X, z) \times a(X-t, z)[1 - F(t|X-t, z)] dt$$

and

(8) $$y(X, z) = w(X, X, z)[1 - F(X|0, z)] + \int_0^X w(t, X, z) \times a(X-t, z)[1 - F(t|X-t, z)] dt$$

There are several reasons for choosing this approach. First, the deterministic earnings function approach (see, for example, Mincer 1974) is a special case of the above formulation. In the earnings function approach, turnover is not considered explicitly, so that job tenure is not included in the regressions. Such regression equations are here interpreted as expectations conditional on X and on the measured component of z, and the expressions that characterize such conditional expectations are provided in equations 8 and 11. A set of sufficient conditions under which the conditional expectation of the wage is a monotonically increasing function of experience is provided below.

Second, the job-matching theory of turnover as developed in Jovanovic (1978b) is fully consistent with the above formulation when the latter is restricted to $s_X = w_X = 0$ for all (X, t, z), so that the turnover process is predicted by the theory to be one of pure renewal. The key assumptions in generating such a result are a constant rate of discount and an infinite horizon, and an assumption about the job search process that makes the latter "pure experience search," in the terminology of Nelson (1970). The model implies $w_t > 0$ for all t, and $s_t < 0$ for large enough t and perhaps for all t.

Two other search models that explicitly look at the implications for life cycle mobility are those of Burdett (1973) and of Jovanovic (1978a). Both models involve the worker's moving up a fixed wage-offer distribution over his lifetime, with search of the "pure search" kind (Nelson's terminology again). Both models imply that in the absence of on-the-job training, $s_X < 0$ and $w_X > 0$, while $s_t = w_t = 0$ for given X. When firm-specific human capital investment is introduced (Jovanovic 1978a), the latter prediction changes to $s_t < 0$ and $w_t > 0$ for all workers except the very old, for whom $s_t > 0$ and $w_t < 0$ as they allow their human capital to depreciate toward the end of their lifetime.

General on-the-job training raises wages, implying $w_X > 0$ given a monotonic increase in general training over time. Since general training raises the worker's productivity in many firms, it is not expected to affect turnover, and therefore $s_X = 0$ is consistent with $w_X > 0$ and with the presence of general training. A somewhat different argument asserts that the presence of general training is the cause of turnover at younger ages, because it may be optimal for the training to be acquired in several different firms and such turnover is planned in advance. To the extent that such turnover is significant (and little evidence is available to support its significance), it may produce nonmonotonic effects on $s(t, X, z)$ for young workers as t and X increase.

Next, define

(9) $$H(t, X, z) \equiv \int_0^t h(\tau | X, z) \, d\tau \geq 0$$

so that $H(0, X, z) = 0$ and $H(X, X, z) = F(X|0, z)$. Then, integrating by parts in (7) and (8), one obtains

(10) $$a(X, z) = s(X, X, z) - \int_0^X s_t(t, X, z) H(t, X, z) \, dt$$

and

(11) $$y(X, z) = w(X, X, z) - \int_0^X w_t(t, X, z) H(t, X, z) \, dt$$

Equations 10 and 11 should be compared for their identical structure.

The following results follow directly from equations 10 and 11, and are presented in theorem 1:

Theorem 1: Let $s_t < 0$ and $w_t > 0$ for all values of the arguments. Then

$$a(0, z) = s(0, 0, z) \text{ and } y(0, z) = w(0, 0, z)$$
$$a_X(0, z) = s_X(0, 0, z) + s_t(0, 0, z)$$
$$y_X(0, z) = w_X(0, 0, z) + w_t(0, 0, z)$$
$$a(X, z) > s(X, X, z)$$
$$y(X, z) < w(X, X, z) \text{ for any } X > 0$$

Proof: The assertions follow from the observation that

$$H(t, X, z) > 0 \text{ for any } t > 0 \text{ and from } H(0, 0, z) = 0$$

Next, consider the special case in which $s_X = 0$, as would be true if turnover was a pure renewal process. We then have the following theorem:

Theorem 2: Let $s(t, X, z)$ be independent of X. Then if $s_t < 0$ for all (X, t, z) then $a_X < 0$ for all (X, z).

Proof: Differentiating with respect to X in equation 10 and applying the assumption that $s_X = 0$ yields

$$a_X(X, z) = s_t(X, X, z)[1 - F(X|0, z)] - \int_0^X s_t(t, X, z) H_X(t, X, z) \, dt$$

and since, by assumption, $s_t < 0$, it is sufficient to prove that $H_X < 0$ for all (t, X, z). But since s does not depend on X, neither does F. Therefore, $H_X(t, X, z) = \int_0^t a_X(X - y, z)[1 - F(y|X - y, z)] \, dy$. Therefore, $H_X(t, X, z) < 0$ if $a_X(X - y, z) < 0$ for all $y \in (0, X)$. But then, $a_X(X, z) < 0$ for all X if there exists an $\varepsilon > 0$, no matter how small, such that $a_X(X, z) < 0$ for $X \in (0, \varepsilon)$. But such an ε must exist if $a_X(X, z)$ is continuous at zero, because by theorem 1, $a_X(0, z) = s_t(0, 0, z) + s_X(0, 0, z) < 0$. (The last inequality follows by the assumptions of the theorem.) This completes the proof of the theorem.

Intuitively, one expects that theorem 2 should extend to the case where $s_t < 0$ *and* $s_X < 0$, that is, to the case where the separation propensity declines with both tenure and market experience, and that the decline in the separation propensity considered as a function of market experience alone $[a(X, z)]$ should, if anything, be reinforced. While this conjecture may be true, an attempt at proving it along the lines of the proof of theorem 2 fails, because H_X cannot be signed.

Theorem 2 asserts that the renewal density declines monotonically if the interevent waiting time distribution possesses a monotonically decreasing hazard rate. Note that a parallel result for monotonically increasing hazard rate distribution does not hold. That is, $s_t > 0$ everywhere does not imply that $a_X > 0$ for all X, and an attempt at a proof along the lines of the proof of theorem 2 is quickly seen to fail (a counterexample is given in Brown 1940).

It should be noted that $y(X, z)$ is the wage experience profile for a homogeneous group of type z. By differentiating in equation 8, conditions may be derived under which the wage experience profile will be increasing and concave ($y_X > 0$, $y_{XX} < 0$) for each homogeneous group. These conditions involve restrictions on both $w(t, X, z)$ and $s(t, X, z)$. For example, one set of *sufficient* conditions for a monotonically increasing wage experience profile ($y_X > 0$) is: $s_X = 0$, $s_t < 0$, $w_t > 0$, $w_X > 0$ and $w_{tX} > 0$, as may be verified by direct differentiation in (8) (and by applying the result of theorem 2 which states that $s_t < 0$ and $s_X = 0$ jointly imply $a_X < 0$ everywhere). Assuming that $s_X = 0$ is theoretically consistent with assuming that $w_X > 0$, that is, the accumulation of purely general on-the-job training raises the worker's productivity in all firms by an equal amount, and it raises his wage (hence $w_X > 0$), but it is not expected to have any effect on his separation propensity (hence $s_X = 0$). Sufficient conditions for concavity of the wage experience profile may also be derived but turn out to be much more complicated.

Let $T(X, z)$ be the mathematical expectation of current tenure. The latter is distributed according to (4), and, therefore,

$$(12) \quad T(X, z) = X[1 - F(X|0, z)] + \int_0^X th(t|X, z)dt$$
$$= X - \int_0^X H(t, X, z)dt$$

The second equality follows after integration by parts. Since $H > 0$, $T(X, z)$ cannot exceed X. Differentiating with respect to X,

$$(13) \quad T_X(X, z) = 1 - F(X|0, z) - \int_0^X H_X(t, X, z)dt$$

so that $T_X(0, z) = 1$. If turnover is a pure renewal process, with $s_t < 0$ everywhere, then, from theorem 2, $H_X > 0$, and $T_X > 0$ for all X. In other words, the average current job tenure will always be increasing for a cohort of workers as their market experience increases under these assumptions.

Let $t_1, t_2, \ldots$ be the sequence of completed job durations. Then the distribution function for the length of the nth job episode is $F(t_n | \sum_{j=1}^{n-1} t_j, z)$. The t_i are therefore neither independent nor identically distributed random variables so long as the aging effect (s_X) is not zero. If there is no aging effect, then each job episode has the same distribution, and if, in addition, one assumes that the job episode durations are independently distributed, then turnover is a pure renewal process. Let $n(X, z)$ be the number of job changes (the number of completed episodes or the number of "prior moves") on the experience interval $(0, X)$. Then

$$(14) \qquad E\, n(X, z) = \int_0^X a(t, z)\, dt$$

To see this, note that $a(X, z)\,\Delta X + 0\,[(\Delta X)^2]$ is the probability that exactly one job change will occur in the interval $(X, X+\Delta X)$. The expression in equation 14 is the sum of these probabilities over such disjoint intervals as Δt tends to zero. Dividing both sides of (14) through by X, taking the limit as X tends to infinity, and applying L'Hôpital's rule, one obtains

$$\lim_{X\to\infty} a(X, z) = \lim_{X\to\infty} \frac{E\,n(X, z)}{X}$$

Of course, $(\partial/\partial X)\,[E\,n(X, z)] = a(X, z)$, and $(\partial^2/\partial X^2)\,[E\,n(X, z)] = a_X(X, z)$. Therefore, a monotonically decreasing experience profile of turnover implies concavity of the expected number of moves treated as a function of experience.

1.9.1 Example: A Pure Renewal Process

Let F be the mixed exponential distribution:

$$F(t|X, z) = 1 - \tfrac{1}{2}\,[e^{-zt} + e^{-(z+b)t}]$$

so that no aging effects exist. Then

$$f(t|X, z) = \tfrac{1}{2}\,[ze^{-zt} + (z+b)e^{-(z+b)t}]$$

and

$$s(t, X, z) = z + \frac{b}{1+e^{bt}}$$

$$s_t(t, X, z) = -\frac{b^2 e^{bt}}{(1+e^{bt})^2}$$

The slope of the separation function is in this case independent of z. If $b = 0$, then $s_t = 0$, and so b is a parameter denoting the extent of duration dependence. Then let

$$\hat{T}(X, z) = \tfrac{1}{2}\left(\frac{1}{z} + \frac{1}{z+b}\right) < \frac{1}{z}$$

Labor Mobility and Wages

The renewal equation (5) has for this case explicitly been solved by Bartholomew (1972) to yield

$$a(X, z) = [\hat{T}(X, z)]^{-1} + (z + \tfrac{b}{2} - [\hat{T}(X, z)]^{-1})e^{-(z+\frac{b}{2})X}$$

$$= \frac{2(z+b)z}{2z+b} - \frac{b^2}{2(2z+b)}e^{-(z+\frac{b}{2})X}$$

so that

$$a_X(X, z) = -\frac{b^2}{4}e^{-(z+\frac{b}{2})X}$$

If there is no duration dependence with tenure ($b = 0$), then separations also do not decline when considered as a function of age. Notice also that

$$a_{Xz}(X, z) = -X\, a_X(X, z) > 0$$

so that although the $s(t, X, z)$ curves are parallel in z, that is, ($s_{tz} = 0$), the age curves are not—they diverge. The relationship between the tenure and age curves is depicted in figure 1.1.

The divergence of age profiles therefore can be explained not only by divergences in levels of specific human capital (as argued in part 1) but also as a purely statistical phenomenon.

In this case, convexity of $s(t, X, z)$ implies convexity of $a(X, z)$ in X. As b (the duration-dependence parameter) tends to zero, both $a(z, z)$ and $s(t, X, z)$ tend to a constant, z.

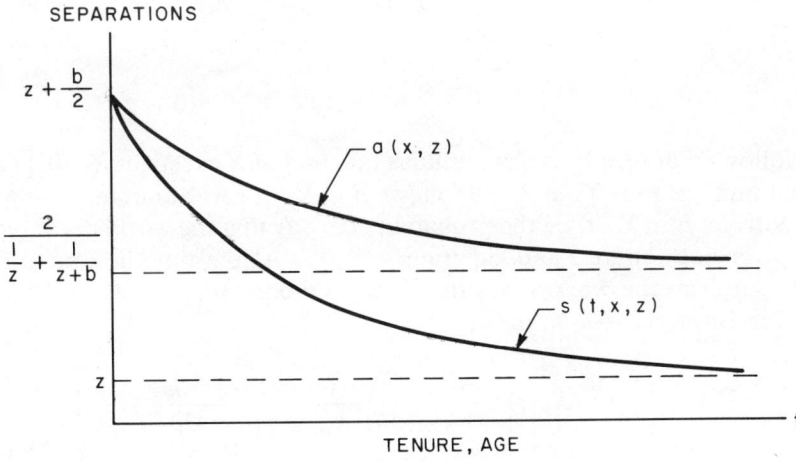

Figure 1.1 Separations by age and by tenure.

1.10 Group Relationships

The individual-specific parameter z is by assumption unobservable. It is an "incidental parameter." The population distribution of z is assumed to be $p(z)$ with mean μ and variance σ. The nondegeneracy of this distribution gives rise to the dynamic version of the sample selection problem studied below.

Upon entering the labor market, a worker is assumed to be a random drawing from the distribution $p(z)$. On the other hand, a worker who is starting out on a job *other* than his first, at a market experience level $X>0$, is *not* representative of the entire population in the sense that he cannot be considered a random drawing from the distribution $p(z)$.

Although $p(z)$ is interpreted to be an unmeasured personal characteristic, it is likely to be correlated with measured personal characteristics such as years of schooling, race, sex, and so on. The unmeaured variability in separation propensities decreases as the number of personal characteristics held constant increases, which is another way of saying that part of the variance of z is "explained" by the variance of a set of personal characteristics. (Note that this is quite different from the statement that the variance of the conditional distribution is never greater than the variance of the marginal distribution. The latter statement is false.)

The objective now is to characterize the distribution of z conditional upon X and t. Let $p(z|X)$ be the distribution of z which applies to workers who are just *starting* a new job at experience level X. Applying Bayes's theorem,

$$(15) \quad p(z|X) = \begin{cases} \dfrac{a(X,z)\,p(z)}{\int a(X,z)\,p(z)dz} & X>0 \\[2mm] p(z) & X=0 \end{cases}$$

It follows that $p(z|X)$ is a continuous function of X except at $X=0$. [The continuity of $p(z|X)$ at $X>0$ follows if $a(X,z)$ is continuous.]

Now let $\hat{p}(z|X_0, t)$ be the probability density that the worker is of type z, given job tenure t and experience X_0+t. At the time he joined his current firm, the worker was drawn from the population $p(z|X_0)$. Applying Bayes's theorem again,

$$(16) \quad \hat{p}(z|X_0, t) = \frac{[1-F(t|X_0,z)]p(z|X_0)}{\int [1-F(t|X_0,z)]\,p(z|X_0)dz}$$

Equation 16 follows because $1-F(t|X_0,z)$ is just the probability that the worker of type z will attain tenure t in a job which he started at experience level X_0.

Writing $\hat{s}(t|X_0, z)$ instead of $\hat{s}(t, X_0, z)$ (thereby emphasizing the nature of the conditioning), let

(17) $\qquad \hat{s}(t, X_0) \equiv \int \hat{s}(t|X_0, z)\, \hat{p}(z|X_0, t)\, dz$

be the probability that the worker will experience a separation at tenure t given X_0 and t. We then have

Theorem 3

$$\hat{s}_t(t, X_0) = \int \hat{s}_t(t|X_0, z)\, \hat{p}(z|X_0, t)dz - \sigma^2(\hat{s}|X_0, t)$$

(18) and

$$\hat{w}_t(t, X_0) = \int \hat{w}_t(t|X_0, z)\hat{p}(z|X_0, t)dz$$
$$- \text{Cov}(\hat{s}, \hat{w}|X_0, t)$$

where $\hat{w}(X_0, t)$ is the mathematical expectation of the wage given X_0 and t, where $\sigma^2(\hat{s}|X_0, t)$ is the variance of $\hat{s}(t|X_0, z)$ in the population $\hat{p}(z|X_0, t)$, and where $\text{Cov}(\hat{s}, \hat{w}|X_0, t)$ is the covariance of $\hat{s}(t|X_0, z)$ and $\hat{w}(t|X_0, z)$ in the population $\hat{p}(z|X_0, t)$. Before proving this theorem, we elaborate on the meaning of its assertions. When t is increased by one unit while X_0 is held constant, tenure and experience both increase by one unit. Therefore, s_t is the sum of the tenure effect and of the pure age effect, and similarly for w_t. In words, the first assertion of the theorem may be expressed as: The slope of the average separation rate is equal to the average of the individual slopes, minus the variance of the separation rates in the *current* population $\hat{p}(z|X_0, t)$. This result is an extension of an earlier result of Barlow, Marshall, and Proschan (1963). Their result states that mixtures of decreasing hazard rate distributions also possess decreasing hazard rates.

Suppose that there are no true age or tenure effects on separations, so that $\hat{s}_t(t|X_0, z) = 0$ everywhere. Then, $\hat{s}_t(t, X_0) = -\sigma^2(\hat{s}|X_0, t)$, so that the group separation rate declines although the individual separation rates are constant. Furthermore, $\hat{s}(t, X_0)$ would in this special case be convex in t (which would be consistent with the evidence presented in table 1.2), if $\sigma^2(\hat{s}|X_0, t)$ declines monotonically with t. For a wide class of distributions $p(z|X_0)$, one would expect such a monotonic decline because the selection out of the sample as t increases is such that "movers" are (on average) selected out leaving behind only "stayers," so that the sample of those left behind becomes increasingly more homogeneous. But σ^2 need not decline monotonically, as is demonstrated by the following example. Assume that at any X_0, $p(z|X_0)$ is such that z takes on only two values, say 1 and 0, and that the $z = 1$ workers have a higher separation propensity than do the $z = 0$ workers. Assume that the initial ($t = 0$) sample is such that nine-tenths of the workers are $z = 1$ types and that the remaining one-tenth are $z = 0$ types. Then the initial variance of z is $(1 - .9).9 = .09$.

As tenure increases, the population proportions shift toward the stayers, and the variance of z increases steadily up to .25, at which point the population proportions are equal. Thereafter, the variance declines monotonically to zero.[17] Of course, a monotonic decline would occur even in this example if the initial proportions happened to be equal, or were weighted in favor of stayers.

According to the first part of equation 18, the change in the group separation rate is always an overstatement (in the negative direction) of the average of the individual changes. However, the same is not true of the group wage change, because the covariance term in the second part of equation 18 may be either positive or negative. The relevant question is whether a "mover" [for whom $\hat{s}(t, X_0) - \hat{s}(t|X_0, z)$ is negative] would expect to receive higher or lower wages than a "stayer" at a certain tenure level *given that it was optimal for both to remain in the firm up to that time*. A theory which predicts that a worker will separate from a job on which wages paid to him were low relative to his prior expectations implies nothing about this question.

The implications of human capital theory for the sign and magnitude of $\text{Cov}(\hat{w}, \hat{s}|X_0, t)$ are ambiguous. In part 1 we emphasized the role of firm-specific human capital in generating a wedge between the worker's productivity in his current firm and his productivity elsewhere. Consider the polar case in which the ratio of general to firm-specific training is fixed and constant across workers, but in which workers differ in the total amount of training that they undertake. Suppose that z is an index inversely related to the worker's propensity to invest in on-the-job training. Under these assumptions, a higher propensity to invest also implies a higher investment in specific training, so that $\hat{s}_z(t|X_0, z) > 0$. Assume that z is not correlated with unmeasured ability components. Then, since investment in training involves foregone earnings early on in return for higher earnings later, this implies that $w_z(t|X_0, z) > 0$ for young workers (for whom X_0 and t are small), and $w_z(t|X_0, z) < 0$ for older workers. Therefore, $\text{Cov}(\hat{w}, \hat{s}|X_0, t)$ is *positive* for the young and *negative* for the old workers.

Suppose instead, however, that the total amount of training across individuals (with given X_0 and t and other observable characteristics) is constant while only the ratio of general to specific training varies positively with z. Now, high-z workers have higher separation propensities because their training is general in nature rather than firm specific. In view of the well-known argument (see Becker 1975) that general training is financed by the workers, such workers earn lower wages initially, and higher wages later on, than do "stayers" whose training is more firm specific in nature. (Again, this conclusion depends on the assumption that the preference for the type of training is not related to unmeasured ability differences.) The implication now is that $\text{Cov}(\hat{s}, \hat{w}|X_0, t)$ is *negative* for the young, and *positive* for the old workers.

Neither polar case is expected to obtain in practice. Both the total amount and the composition of the training may be expected to vary systematically with z. But which dominates? The wage function estimates reported in table 1.6 strongly suggest that the dominant variation is in the total amount of training. This inference is made by comparing the second row with the fourth row in panel A, and the second row with the third in panel B. The variables PM and NIM are indexes of past mobility and are correlated with $\hat{s}(t|X_0, z)$. By definition, z is the unmeasured component of heterogeneity, and the inclusion of PM and NIM therefore has the effect of reducing the *absolute value* of $\text{Cov}(\hat{w}, \hat{s}|X_0, t)$. In both panels, there appears to be an effect of this reduction. The wage growth, measured as the sum of the coefficients on X and T, *increases* for the young men when NIM is included, and *decreases* for the older men when PM is included in the regression, and these changes are consistent with the first polar case, but not the second, as is clear from equation 18.

Proof: Substituting for $\hat{p}$ into (17),

(19) $$\hat{s}(t, X_0) = \frac{\int f(t|X_0, z)\, p(z|X_0)dz}{\int [1 - F(t|X_0, z)]\, p(z|X_0)dz}$$

Differentiating with respect to t in equation 16,

$$\hat{p}_t(z|X_0, t) = \frac{-f(t|X_0, z)\, p(z|X_0)}{\int (1-F)\, pdz}$$

(20) $$+ \frac{[1 - F(t|X_0, z)]p(z|X_0) \int f(t|X_0, z)\, p(z|X_0)dz}{[\int (1-F)\, pdz]^2}$$

$$= [-\hat{s}(t|X_0, z) + \hat{s}(t, X_0)]\, \hat{p}(z|X_0, t)$$

Multiplying both sides by $\hat{s}(t|X_0, z)$ and integrating both sides over z,

(21) $$\int \hat{s}(t|X_0, z)\, \hat{p}_t(z|X_0, t) = \hat{s}(t, X_0)^2 - \int \hat{s}(t|X_0, z)^2\, \hat{p}dz$$

$$= [E(\hat{s})]^2 - E(\hat{s}^2) = -\sigma^2(\hat{s}|X_0, t)$$

and differentiating with respect to t in equation (17) and using equation 21, one obtains the first assertion of the theorem which has therefore been proved. Next,

$$\hat{w}(X_0, t) = \int \hat{w}(t|X_0, z)\, \hat{p}(z|X_0, t)dz$$

and differentiating with respect to t,

$$\hat{w}_t(X_0, t) = \int \hat{w}_t\, \hat{p}dz + \int \hat{w}\hat{p}_t\, dz$$

$$= \int \hat{w}_t\, \hat{p}dz + \int \hat{w}(t|X_0, z)\, [\hat{s}(t, X_0)$$

$$- \hat{s}(t|X_0, z)]\, \hat{p}(z|X_0, t)dz$$

where the second equality follows in view of equation 20, and this completes the proof of the theorem.

1.11 An Estimation Procedure

The following estimation procedure exploits the property of $p(z|X)$ (defined in equation 15) of having two different functional forms, implying, in turn, two different functional forms for $\hat{s}(t, X_0)$ in (17). We demonstrate below how identification of the parameters may be secured by subdividing the sample of all workers into two subsamples: one for which $X_0 = 0$ (workers on their first job ever), and the other for which $X_0 > 0$. In fact, in the following illustration for an *additive* fixed effect parametrization of $s(t, X, z)$, the parameters are overidentified, which suggests that identification may be secured for more complex functional forms which we hope to consider in future work. The following additive fixed effect formulation is perhaps inadequate in capturing the individual differences, but it is adequate as an illustration of the estimation method. Let

$$(22) \qquad s(t, X, z) = z + S(t, X)$$

where, without loss of generality $S(0, 0) = 0$. One possible way to proceed is to take first differences in equation 22 and eliminate z, thereby also eliminating the selection bias. There are two problems with this approach. First, using differences in separation probabilities as the dependent variable leads to coefficients that are not significant. Secondly, there is then no possibility of estimating σ^2, the variance of z. We have therefore chosen a different procedure, which is based on deriving two separate relationships associated with equation 22.

Let $z(t, X)$ be the conditional expectation of z, and $s(t, X)$ the conditional expectation of the separation rate, given t and X. Then, taking conditional expectations in equation 22,

$$(23) \qquad s(t, X) = z(t, X) + S(t, X)$$

where

$$z(t, X) = \int z \hat{p}(z|X - t, t) dz$$

Then since

$$F(t|X - t, z) = 1 - \exp\left[-zt - \int_0^t S(y, X - t + y) \, dy\right]$$

application of (16) and (15) leads to

$$(24) \qquad z(t, X) = \frac{\int z e^{-zt} a(X - t, z) p(z) dz}{\int e^{-zt} a(X - t, z) p(z) dz} \quad \text{for } X > t$$

$$z(X, X) = \frac{\int z e^{-zX} p(z) dz}{\int e^{-zX} p(z) dz} \text{ for } X = t$$

(Workers with $X = t$ are on their first job.) Assume now that $p(z)$ is the normal distribution. Then a straightforward calculation yields

$$z(X, X) = \mu - \sigma^2 X$$

where μ and σ^2 are the mean and variance of z.

So that (for workers on their first job)

(25) $$s(X, X) = \mu + S(X, X) - \sigma^2 X$$

The discontinuity of the $\hat{p}$ distribution at $X = 0$ carries over to $z(t, X)$. It is seen from (24) that

$$z(0, 0) = \mu$$

while taking the limit in (24) and observing (7),

$$\lim_{X \to 0} z(0, X) = \mu + \frac{\sigma^2}{\mu}$$

To obtain a closed form approximation to $z(t, X)$ for $X > t$, a first-order Taylor's expansion is performed in equation 24 around the point $(t = 0, X = \varepsilon)$ where $\varepsilon > 0$. Then

$$z(0, \varepsilon) = \frac{\int z a(\varepsilon, z) p(z) dz}{\int a(\varepsilon, z) p(z) dz}$$

$$z_t(0, \varepsilon) = -\frac{[\int z^2 a(\varepsilon, z) p(z) dz + \int z a_X(\varepsilon, z) p(z) dz]}{\int a(\varepsilon, z) p(z) dz}$$

$$+ \frac{[\int z a(\varepsilon, z) p(z) dz + \int a_X(\varepsilon, z) p(z) dz] \int z a(\varepsilon, z) p(z) dz}{[\int a(\varepsilon, z) p(z) dz]^2}$$

and

$$z_X(0, \varepsilon) = \frac{\int z a_X(\varepsilon, z) p(z) dz}{\int a(\varepsilon, z) p(z) dz} - \frac{\int a_X(\varepsilon, z) p(z) dz}{\int a(\varepsilon, z) p(z) dz} z(0, \varepsilon)$$

For any $X > t$, and any $\varepsilon > 0$ no matter how small,

(26) $$z(t, X) = z(0, \varepsilon) + z_t(0, \varepsilon) t + z_X(0, \varepsilon)(X - \varepsilon)$$

$$+ \text{ higher order terms}$$

$$= \lim_{\varepsilon \to 0} z(0, \varepsilon) + [\lim_{\varepsilon \to 0} z_t(0, \varepsilon)] t$$

$$+ [\lim_{\varepsilon \to 0} z_X(0, \varepsilon)] X$$

$$+ \text{ higher order terms}$$

Evaluating the limits, and using theorem 1,

$$\lim_{\varepsilon \to 0} z(0, \varepsilon) = \frac{\int z\, a(0, z)\, p(z)dz}{\int a(0, z)\, p(z)ds}$$

$$= \frac{\int z\, s(0, 0, z)\, p(z)ds}{\int s(0, 0, z)\, p(z)dz}$$

$$= \frac{\int z^2 p(z)dz}{\int z\, p(z)dz} = \mu + \frac{\sigma^2}{\mu}$$

$$\lim_{\varepsilon \to 0} z_t(0, \varepsilon) =$$

$$-\frac{[\int z^2 s(0, 0, z)\, p(z)dz + \int z[s_X(0, 0, z) + s_t(0, 0, z)]\, p(z)dz]}{\int s(0, 0, z)\, p(z)dz}$$

$$+ \frac{\int z\, s(0, 0, z)\, p(z)dz + \int [s_X(0, 0, z) + s_t(0, 0, z)]\, p(z)dz}{[\int s(0, 0, z)\, p(z)dz]^2}$$

$$= -\mu^{-1}[\int z^3\, pdz + \mu(\alpha + \gamma)] + \mu^{-2}(\int z^2\, pdz + \alpha + \gamma)$$

where $\alpha \equiv S_X(0, 0)$ and $\gamma \equiv S_t(0, 0)$.

If $p(z)$ is a symmetric distribution so that the third order moment about the mean is equal to zero, then one obtains $\int z^3 pdz = \mu^3 + 3\sigma^2\mu$, and therefore

$$\lim_{\varepsilon \to 0} z_t(0, \varepsilon) = (\mu^{-2} - 1)(\alpha + \gamma) + 1 - 3\sigma^2 - \mu^2 + \frac{\sigma^2}{\mu}$$

Also,

$$\lim_{\varepsilon \to 0} z_X(0, \varepsilon) = -\frac{\sigma^2}{\mu^2}(\alpha + \gamma)$$

Taking an expansion in (23),

$$s(t, X) = \alpha X + \gamma t + z(t, X) + \text{higher order terms}$$

But making the substitution into (26),

$$z(t, X) = \mu + \frac{\sigma^2}{\mu} + [(\mu^{-2} + 1)(\alpha - \gamma) + 1 - 3\sigma^2 - \mu^2 + \frac{\sigma^2}{\mu^2}]t$$

$$- \frac{\sigma^2}{\mu^2}(\alpha + \gamma)X + \text{higher order terms}$$

Therefore for $t < X$,

(27) $$s(t, X) = \mu + \frac{\sigma^2}{\mu} + [(\mu^{-2}-1)\alpha + \mu^{-2}\gamma + 1 - 3\sigma^2 - \mu^2 + \frac{\sigma^2}{\mu_2}]t + [\alpha - \frac{\sigma^2}{\mu^2}(\alpha+\gamma)]X$$

$$+ \text{higher order terms}$$

Also, expanding in (25)

(28) $$s(X, X) = \mu + (\alpha + \gamma - \sigma^2)X + \text{higher order terms}.$$

Equations 27 and 28 are the two basic relationships estimated.

The separation propensity is of course unobservable. All that is observed is whether or not an individual has changed jobs within a particular period. Let $y=1$ if the worker has changed jobs within the period $(X, X+\Delta X)$, and zero otherwise.

$$\text{Prob } (y=1) = 1 - \exp\{-\int_0^{\Delta X} s(t+y, X+y, z)dy\}$$

$$= s(t, X, z) \Delta X + 0 [(\Delta X)^2]$$

Similarly

$$\text{Prob } (y=0) = 1 - s(t, X, z) \Delta X + 0 [(\Delta X)^2]$$

Therefore y_X has a mean equal to $s(t, X, z) \Delta X + 0 [(\Delta X)^2]$

Ignoring the $0[(\Delta X)^2]$

$$y_X = [z + S(t, X)] \Delta X + u$$

where u is a disturbance with zero mean. In the data, ΔX was equal to two years. The regressions for the separation equations are reported in the first two columns of table 1.7. (Separate regressions were also run for quits and for layoffs, and they are reported in the table, although they do not have an interpretation within the mathematical structure presented above.) The three linear coefficients and the two constant terms provide five restrictions on the four parameters so that the parameters are overidentified. However, the relative magnitude of the two constant terms is reversed from that implied by the theory, leading to an estimate of σ^2 which is negative, which may mean that the additive fixed effect formulation is inadequate. In future work, we intend to experiment with different functional forms for the separation and wage equations, focusing on the question of the best way to model the individual differences, and to organize the data so that the time interval ΔX is shortened, one year rather than two.

Table 1.7 NLS Young Men's Sample, 1967–73

	Separations		Quits		Permanent Layoffs	
	$X=T$	$X>T$	$X=T$	$X>T$	$X=T$	$X>T$
Constant	.78	.64	.5583	.4439	.103	.1999
X	−.1805	.0137	−.1112	.0051	−.0692	.0086
	(23.22)	(1.13)	(14.55)	(.4)	(12.51)	(.844)
X^2	.0098	−.0012	.0057	−.0005	.0042	−.0006
	(15.38)	(1.27)	(9.02)	(.524)	(9.09)	(.862)
T		−.1819		−.0996		−.0822
		(10.03)		(5.28)		(5.38)
T^2		.0069		.0032		.0037
		(3.02)		(1.34)		(1.92)
XT		.0037		.0016		.0021
		(1.65)		(.696)		(.924)
R^2	.305	.246	.167	.106		.148
n	1,877	1,985	1,877	1,984	1,877	1,984

Notes

1. The subject of women's labor mobility is reserved for separate study.
2. For analysis of geographic mobility see Bartel (1978) and Mincer (1978).
3. This is in contrast to the BLS data of Table 1.1 and may be peculiar to the NLS sample.
4. In his work, Jovanovic (1978b) has shown that job-matching processes produce downward sloping tenure-separation functions and upward sloping tenure-wage functions. Investments of employers and workers in their mutual association are a corollary. We use the language of specific capital to cover the combined phenomena.
5. We may note that even if returns to specific capital accumulation, and in particular W_s, did not decelerate with tenure, but grew in a linear fashion, the resulting growth of the reservation wage in job search would nevertheless lead to decelerating declines in the probability of quit, given a declining upper tail of the wage-offer distribution.
6. We must be careful, however, not to assert the converse: by itself, inertia does not bring about specific investments.
7. The deterministic treatment is for expository convenience only. See part 2 for a more formal and more specialized analysis of the stochastic process.
8. Perhaps a simple way of illustrating the conclusion that dT/dX is larger with than without tenure dependence is to consider a case in which we go from none to some tenure dependence. Let the mean tenure in the group be T_{av} and the overall turnover rate s. Then, after a passage of a year, the $(1-s)$ stayers have increased tenure by one year, while the s movers, without tenure dependence, have lost on average T_{av} years of tenure. The net change dT/dX is therefore $(1-s)-sT$, which approaches zero since T approaches $[(1/s)-1]$. Now, let s remain the same, but the process become tenure-dependent. In this case, the average tenure lost by movers is $T_{mav} < T_{av}$ since proportionately more of them are drawn from low-tenure classes. Consequently the net gain in tenure $dT/dX = (1-s)-sT_m > (1-s)-sT$.

9. Cf. theorem 3 in part 2. Such a decline in the variance need not be inconsistent with a widening of differences in mobility rates.

10. For those men whose current tenure started before the initial year of reported prior mobility (1965 for the older men and 1966 for the young men in NLS, and 1968 for MID), no information on PM is available (12% of young men and 62% of the old men in NLS, and about 50% in MID). As a check on the results in table 1.5 which implicitly assigns a value of PM = 0 to those whose tenure is too long, we used dummy variables on the complete samples, and we also replicated the regressions of table 1.5 on the subsamples which contained information on prior mobility. The results were quite similar to those in table 1.5 with one interesting feature: the tenure coefficients for the old men in NLS (with short tenure in the subsample) were as steep as for the young, and the inclusion of PM reduced the slope by a relatively small amount as it did for the young.

11. The longitudinal evidence is less familar. See Borjas and Mincer (1978) reporting Coleman-Rossi data, and Anderson, Balcer, and Diamond (1976) on the Continuous Work History Sample.

12. Dollar wage equations, not shown here, show similar patterns, but weaker predictive power.

13. This is true also in the sample with $T \leq 8$, in contrast to the short-tenure mobility equation (see note 10).

14. Supporting evidence is shown in the Bartel and Borjas paper in this volume, as well as in previous research by Borjas. Borjas (1975) classified the older NLS men into movers and stayers. The latter were defined by the fact that their current job was the longest ever. Education and experience were only slightly different in the two groups. The movers had lower wages (about 25%) and flatter experience profiles.

15. See Freeman (1978), Borjas (1978), and others. The flatter union tenure slopes have been analyzed as effects of union policy. We suggest that they may also reflect lesser heterogeneity in the union compared with the nonunion sector.

16. See Burdett (1973), Sorensen (1975). Jovanovic (1978a) is an adaptation of Burdett, which allows for on-the-job human capital accumulation. It is doubtful, however, that the assumption of a fixed wage-offer distribution can be maintained for workers whose skills are growing and changing over the life cycle.

17. This example was supplied by R. Shakotko.

18. Helpful comments by J. Heckman on an earlier version of this paper have led to considerable improvement of this section.

References

Anderson, R.; Balcer, Y.; and Diamond, D. "A Model of Lifetime Earnings Patterns," in *Decoupling the Social Security Benefit Structure*. Hearings before the Subcommittee on Social Security, House of Representatives, 94th Congress, 2d Session, on H.R. 14430, 1976. Washington, D.C.: U.S. Government Printing Office, 1976.

Barlow, R. E.; Marshall, A. W.; and Proschan, F. "Properties of Distributions with Monotone Hazard Rates." *Annals of Mathematical Statistics*, Vol. 34 (1963): 375–89.

Bartel, A. "Job Mobility and Earnings Growth." NBER Working Paper No. 117, 1975.

———. "The Economics of Migration: An Empirial Analysis with Special Reference to the Role of Job Mobility." NBER Working Paper No. 198, August 1977.

Bartholomew, D. *Stochastic Models for Social Processes.* New York: Wiley, 1972.

Becker, G. S. *Human Capital.* 2d Ed. New York: Columbia University Press, 1975.

Becker, G. S.; Landes, E.; and Michael, R. "An Economic Analysis of Marital Instability." *Journal of Political Economy*, December 1977.

Blumen, I. M.; Kogan, M.; and McCarthy, P. J. *The Industrial Mobility of Labor as a Probability Process.* Ithaca, N.Y.: Cornell University Press, 1955.

BLS. "Job Mobility in 1961." Special Labor Force Report No. 35, 1963.

———. "Job Tenure of Workers 1973." Special Labor Force Report No. 172, 1975.

Borjas, G. "Job mobility and Earnings Growth over the Life Cycle." NBER Working Paper No. 233, February 1978.

———. "Labor Turnover in the Union and the Public Sector." Xerox, 1978.

Borjas, G., and Mincer, J. "The Distribution of Earnings Profiles in Longitudinal Data," in Zvi Griliches, ed., *Income Distribution and Economic Inequality.* N.Y.: John Wiley, 1978.

Brown, A. W. "A Note on the Use of a Pearson Type III Function in Renewal Theory." *Annals of Mathematical Statistics*, pp. 448–53. 1940.

Burdett, K. "On-the-Job Search." Ph.D. Thesis, Northwestern University, 1973.

Da Vanzo, J. "Why Families Move." Rand Report, September 1976.

Feller, E. *Introduction to Probability.* Vol. 2. N.Y.: John Wiley, 1966.

Freeman, R. "Exit-Voice Tradeoff in the Labor Market." Unpublished MS., Harvard University, April 1978.

Greenwood, M. "Research on Internal Migration in the U.S." *Journal of Economic Literature*, June 1975.

Heckman, J. "Statistical Models for Discrete Panel Data." Xerox, 1977.

Heckman, J., and Willis, R. "A Beta Logistic Model for the Analysis of Sequential Labor Force Participation by Married Women." *Journal of Political Economy*, February 1977.

Jovanovic, B. "Labor Turnover Where Jobs Are Pure Search Goods." Unpublished MS., Columbia University, February 1978a.

———. "Job-Matching and the Theory of Turnover." Ph.D. Thesis, University of Chicago, 1978b.

Leighton, L. "Unemployment over the Life-Cycle." Ph.D. Thesis, Columbia University, 1978.

Mincer, J. *Schooling, Experience and Earnings.* N.Y.: Columbia University Press, 1974.

_____. "Family Migration Decisions." *Journal of Political Economy*, October 1978.
Mortensen, D. "Specific Capital and Labor Turnover." *Bell Journal*, Fall 1978.
Nelson, P. "Information and Consumer Behavior." *Journal of Political Economy*, 1970.
Oi, W. "Labor as a Quasi-Fixed Factor of Production." *Journal of Political Economy*, December 1961.
Parnes, H. S., "Labor Force Participation and Labor Mobility," in *A Review of Industrial Relations Research*, Vol. 1, 1970.
Parsons, D. "Specific Human Capital: Quits and Layoffs." *Journal of Political Economy*, November 1972.
_____. "Models of Labor Turnover," in *Research in Labor Economics*, 1978.
Rosen, S. "Short-Run Employment Variation on Railroads." Ph.D. Thesis, University of Chicago, 1966.
Singer, B., and Spilerman, S. "Some Methodological Issues in the Analysis of Longitudinal Surveys." *Annals of Economic and Social Measurement*, NBER, Fall, 1976.
Sjastaad, L. "Costs and Returns of Human Migration." *Journal of Political Economy*, Part 2, October 1962.
Sorensen, A. "Growth in Occupational Achievement," in *Social Indicator Models*. Russell Sage Foundation, 1975.
Stigler, G. J. "Economics of Information." *Journal of Political Economy*, June 1961.
Tuma, N. B., "Rewards, Resources, and the Rate of Mobility." *American Sociological Review*, April 1976.

2 Wage Growth and Job Turnover: An Empirical Analysis

Ann P. Bartel and George J. Borjas

The question of why an individual's wages grow over and above economy-wide productivity growth is fundamental to the analysis of the earnings distribution. In fact, explanations of the earnings distribution such as human capital investments or random shock models are basically descriptions of the wage growth process for the individual.[1] Despite this importance, and mainly owing to the lack of longitudinal data for a given individual, the empirical analysis of wage growth has lagged behind the empirical analysis of wage levels.[2] This paper is a partial attempt to remedy this asymmetry. We focus on documenting how labor turnover systematically affects the rate of growth in wages both across jobs and within the job. It will be our working hypothesis to interpret wage growth to be the result of human capital investments, both general and specific to the job. We will also interpret wage growth across jobs as being due to changes in the individual's human capital stock resulting from "mobility" investments (e.g., search) and losses of specific training incurred when job separation takes place.

Given this framework, we tackle two important questions in labor economics.[3] The first is a variation of the old question of whether mobility "pays." Note that the cross-section comparison of movers and stayers (or in the migration literature, migrants and nonmigrants) does not necessarily provide an answer to the relevant question: does a person who moved during the time period under investigation do better than he would have done had he stayed? Of course, the fact that the alternative wage is not observed once the individual's decision has been made has

Ann P. Bartel is Associate Professor, Columbia University Graduate School of Business.
George J. Borjas is Associate Professor of Economics, University of California, Santa Barbara.

prevented researchers from answering this question. Recent econometric techniques dealing with selection bias in censored samples (Heckman 1979) provide one method of approaching this problem. In this paper, however, we pursue a somewhat simpler approach that utilizes the longitudinal nature of our data. In particular, we will analyze the on-the-job progress of a *given* individual before and after the move.

A second related question we will analyze is the effect of labor turnover on wage growth *within* the job. It is quite obvious that mobility shifts the earnings profile after each separation occurs. It is less obvious, but equally important, that an individual's intentions to separate from a firm will affect the rate of growth of his earnings in the current job. In particular, we hope to establish that job immobility (i.e., longer tenure) is associated with steeper wage growth than would occur otherwise for a given individual.[4] This finding should prove useful on several grounds. First of all, it establishes that indeed wages grow with tenure for a given individual. Although this may seem like a somewhat trivial empirical result, it should put to rest doubts about the interpretation of the observed positive relationship between wage levels and tenure. In particular, there exists the possibility that this positive correlation is entirely due to population heterogeneity. That is, there exist some unobserved individual characteristics which lead to low wages and high turnover rates for some persons, and to high wages and low turnover rates for other individuals. Then a cross-section correlation of wages and tenure would be positive even if wages did not grow at all in the job.[5]

More importantly, by establishing that wage growth on the job is related to the separation probability, we can obtain some estimates of the importance of specific training in the labor market. In particular, as long as specificity is an important component of human capital investments, the human capital hypothesis predicts a positive correlation between investment costs per year and *completed* job tenure. Since lower probabilities of separation are associated with larger incentives to invest, we should observe steeper earnings profiles in longer jobs. Note that the prediction implies not only that wages grow on the job for a given individual, but that they grow faster the better the match (i.e., the longer the tenure). Therefore, in a sense, the "gains to immobility" are due to the fact that job tenure "matters" over and above the accumulation of labor market exposure.

The purpose of this paper, therefore, is to provide a systematic empirical analysis of the relationship between wage growth and job turnover. We will use two data sets in the study: the National Longitudinal Surveys (NLS) of Young and Mature Men. Section 2.1 provides a systematic examination of the relationship between labor turnover and wage growth across jobs. Section 2.2 analyzes the effects of job immobility on wage growth. In section 2.3 we consider the implications of labor turnover for lifetime wage growth. Section 2.4 briefly describes the effects of personal and labor market characteristics on individual wage growth. Finally, section 2.5 summarizes the results of the study.

2.1 Labor Turnover and the Wage Profile across Jobs

In this section we use the NLS Young and Mature Men samples to analyze the effects of labor turnover on wage growth across jobs. There are several important restrictions in our use of the data. First of all we define labor mobility to occur when an individual changes employers. Thus transfers within the same firm are viewed as part of the returns to staying in the job. Secondly, to simplify the empirical analysis we do not attempt to distinguish between local movers and individuals who change jobs and migrate simultaneously. In other words, we ignore the role of geographic mobility and its interaction effects with job turnover on wage growth.[6] Third, our sample is composed of individuals who either did not change jobs at all in the period under investigation or did not leave the labor force after the separation took place. Thus individuals who were either retired or in school at the beginning of the period or whose job separation was followed by either retirement or by a return to school are deleted from our sample.[7] For both data sets we concentrate on the interval between 1967 and 1973, and partition this long period into three two-year intervals, 1967–69, 1969–71, and 1971–73. We then pool the information in each of these intervals across the individuals in our sample, in effect tripling the number of observations.[8] The labor turnover variable is defined to equal unity if the employer at the end of the two-year period is not the same as the employer at the beginning of the two-year interval. Section 2.1.1 reports the results of comparing the two-year price-deflated wage growth of individuals who separated from their jobs during the period with the relevant wage increases reported by stayers. In section 2.1.2 we return to the question addressed earlier of whether mobility "pays" for a given individual.

2.1.1 Comparing Movers and Stayers

Table 2.1 contains coefficients on dummy variables that indicate the individual's mobility status over a two-year interval. These coefficients are taken from regressions using absolute or percentage wage growth over the two-year period as the dependent variable and holding constant a set of standardizing variables listed in the note to the table (an exact description of these variables is given in the appendix). It is important to note that these standardizing variables are measured as of the beginning of the two-year period.

The coefficients of the separation dummies may be broadly interpreted as estimates of the "gains" associated with mobility. Table 2.1 shows that among the young men a quit is associated with an increase in earnings but for the older men a quit has either a negative or zero effect on wage growth. Thus, for example, young men who quit receive a wage increase of 11 cents an hour more than those who stayed, while for older men the wage increase is approximately minus 3 cents an hour.[9] On the other hand, in both samples, being laid off from a job leads to lower wage growth than staying, although in the young men's sample the difference is not very significant. For the older men, however, layoffs reduce wage

Table 2.1 The Effects of Turnover on Wage Growth across Jobs Comparing Movers and Stayers (Dependent variable = ΔW or $\Delta \ln W$)

	Absolute Growth			Percentage Growth		
	(1)	(2)	(3)	(4)	(5)	(6)
A. NLS Young Men ($n=3{,}665$)						
QUIT	.1139			.0184		
	(2.02)			(1.31)		
LAYOFF	−.0264	−.0397	−.0485	−.0253	−.0299	−.0322
	(−.35)	(−.53)	(−.64)	(−1.35)	(−1.60)	(−1.72)
JOBREL		.1800			.0382	
		(3.07)			(2.62)	
PERS		−.3545	−.3605		−.1269	−.1284
		(−3.14)	(−3.19)		(−4.53)	(−4.59)
PUSH			.0540			.0055
			(.72)			(.30)
PULL			.2984			.0688
			(4.09)			(3.81)
B. NLS Mature Men ($n=4{,}745$)						
QUIT	−.0259			−.0488		
	(−.29)			(−2.05)		
LAYOFF	−.1888	−.1907	−.1927	−.0972	−.0979	−.0982
	(−2.08)	(−2.10)	(−2.13)	(−4.00)	(−4.03)	(−4.04)
JOBREL		.1342			.0047	
		(1.31)			(.17)	
PERS		−.4641	−.4651		−.1951	−.1953
		(−2.81)	(−2.82)		(−4.42)	(−4.43)
PUSH			−.0973			−.0283
			(−.79)			(−.85)
PULL			.5999			.0711
			(3.46)			(1.53)

Note: Other variables held constant are EDUC, EXPER, JOB, ARMY, UNION, HLTH, MAR, WLFP, WW, WKSUN, SIZE, UN, D67, D69; t-statistics in parentheses.

growth over the two-year period by about 19 cents per hour. An interesting result is obtained by making a direct comparison of quits versus layoffs. In the case of young men, a quit is worth about 14 cents more than a layoff; while for the older men, a quit is worth 16.3 cents more than a layoff. Thus although who gains and loses relative to stayers varies over the life cycle, the gains to quitting as opposed to being laid off remain relatively constant with age.

Of course, it is not surprising that quitters do better than individuals who were laid off at all ages. What is puzzling is that quitters do not do better than stayers systematically over the life cycle. Further analysis of this result can be conducted with the information provided in the NLS on the *reasons* for the quit. Thus we decompose the variable QUIT (1 if change was voluntary, 0 otherwise) into two kinds of voluntary changes: job related or for personal reasons.[10] The reader should, of course, note that these reasons are reported *after* the separation took place, and hence there may be some element of rationalization on the worker's part which may contaminate the results we report. The coefficients of JOBREL (job-related quits) and PERS (personal quits) are shown in columns 2 and 5 of table 2.1. The results are quite striking. In both samples we now find that individuals who quit for personal reasons had significantly smaller wage growth than stayers, while men who had a job-related quit experienced higher wage growth than stayers. This latter effect is significant for the young men's sample, but less significant in the older men's NLS. The results, therefore, imply a very significant differential in the gains from quitting according to the type of quit. Moreover, it is also of interest to note that layoffs and quits for personal reasons have similar qualitative effects on wage growth. This might be due to the fact that both these types of separations have a large exogenous and unexpected component, so that these individuals would have had less search while on the job than individuals whose quit was premeditated.

A further decomposition of the variable QUIT may be examined in columns 3 and 6 where job-related quits have been segmented into quits due to dissatisfaction with the current job (PUSH) and quits occurring because the individual found a better job (PULL).[11] One may argue that it is irrelevant whether the change was due to a pull or a push since basically the voluntary separation occurred because the individual's opportunities were better in the new job. That is, it is irrelevant whether the quit was due to the fact that the present job was bad or to the fact that the new job was better. Either way, the new job improved the individual's situation *relative* to the old job. Although essentially correct, this line of argument ignores an empirical peculiarity of the data: most of the individuals who said they were pushed from the current job gave reasons relating to the nonwage aspects of the job. Thus there is no obvious reason to expect any kind of wage increase for this group. Indeed, table

2.1 shows that the effect of quits on wage growth differs significantly depending on whether the quit was a pull or a push. A pull always leads to significantly higher wage growth than that experienced by stayers, while a push does not seem to affect wage growth at all. In general, the results in table 2.1 suggest that the nature of a quit is a very important determinant of the gains to mobility. Moreover, the results obtained with the detailed decomposition of QUIT provide one explanation of the fact that the QUIT coefficient varies over the life cycle. In particular, a quit is more likely to be due to finding a better job at younger ages, while at older ages the quit is mainly due to dissatisfaction with the current job. These results, however, are not entirely consistent with the matching view of labor turnover since the matching process—and therefore quits due to dissatisfaction with the present employer—is more likely to take place early in the life cycle. The fact that our data show the opposite is somewhat puzzling.

Finally, one way of measuring the magnitude of the wage increase due to PULL is to calculate the present value of this increase assuming both that the individual works full time until his retirement and that the wage increase due to the quit is general in the sense that it remains with him throughout his working life.[12] From column 3 the observed wage increase is worth $2,940 for the young men and $570 for the older men. Obviously the longer payoff period for young men clearly increases the return on mobility investment.

2.1.2 Wage Growth prior to, during, and after the Move

In the previous section we conducted an analysis calculating the "gains" associated with mobility by comparing movers and stayers. As was pointed out earlier, this procedure could create problems if population heterogeneity is an important phenomenon in the labor market. The existence of heterogeneity raises two distinct types of problems. First, the separation dummies that compare movers and stayers can be proxying unobserved individual characteristics indicating both the propensity for turnover and the individual's ability to "grow" on the job. Since individuals with high propensities for turnover find it harder to "hold onto a job," population heterogeneity would create a negative correlation between wage growth and the separation probabilities. Moreover, if one reason that stayers stay in the job is their better progress (or prospects for progress), clearly this would give a further downward bias to the "gains" to mobility.

Thus unless we resort to somewhat more complicated statistical procedures, ordinary least-squares comparisons of movers and stayers will yield hopelessly biased estimates of the returns to moving. A correct answer to the question of whether the individual gained by moving can be obtained only by a comparison of the individual's new wage progress to that which he would have obtained had he stayed at the previous job. Clearly the relevant alternative wage is unavailable once the individual's separation decision is taken. A simple approximation, however, exists if we utilize fully the longitudinal nature of our data. For example, suppose we have a sample of individuals who either did not change jobs between 1967 and 1973 or changed only between 1969 and 1971. Thus the basic difference between the two groups of men lies in their 1969–71 separation propensities. Suppose that we estimate wage growth equations similar to those given in columns 3 and 6 of table 2.1 for each of the subperiods 1967–69, 1969–71, and 1971–73 as a function of the 1969–71 separation probabilities. The coefficients on these dummies can then be studied to show how the mover's wages were growing *before* he changed jobs, *during* the period in which he changed jobs, and *after* the job change took place. If we are willing to assume that the effect of the 1969–71 mobility dummy on 1967–69 wage growth is indicative of how movers were doing in the job prior to separation, we can then determine conclusively whether a mover gained from moving by analyzing the behavior of the separation dummies over the six-year period. In particular, the individual improved his situation by moving if the mobility coefficient is more positive after the move than before the move. Thus by looking at *changes* in the mobility coefficient we are, in effect, controlling for population heterogeneity, since these unobserved individual characteristics are assumed to be constant over time.

The results of estimating these equations are presented in table 2.2. Panels A and B give the results for young and older men using the sample of men who either moved during 1969–71 only or did not move at all during the six-year period. To show how these results should be interpreted, let us consider in detail the effect of being "pushed" from the 1969 job on the wage profile of young men. We find that prior to the separation, individuals who were "pushed" from the job had significantly lower wage growth than individuals who stayed in that job subsequently. Two factors explain this result. Clearly, the movers were not progressing well on the job and eventually quit because of this. Secondly, if the job was a mismatch, as it eventually turned out to be, and if this information was known to both firm and workers, the incentives for investment in the job were weak, leading to smaller wage growth (see section 2.2, below). During the 1969–71 period, when the move actually occurred, we find that these *same* individuals had larger wage growth than stayers. Again, assuming that the difference between movers and stayers in the 1967–69 period is the correct comparison between the mover's old job and the stayers' job, clearly the positive coefficient of PUSH on 1969–71 wage growth provides very strong evidence that the movers improved their situation significantly through job mobility. Moreover, we find that these gains were not temporary since the comparison of movers to stayers in the 1971–73 period (after the move took place) yields the finding that there is

Table 2.2 The Effects of 1969–71 Mobility on Wage Growth (Dependent variable = ΔW or $\Delta \ln W$)

	Absolute Growth			Percentage Growth		
	67–69	69–71	71–73	67–69	69–71	71–73
	A. NLS Young Men ($n = 392$)					
LAYOFF	.0885 (.57)	−.0391 (−.23)	.0579 (.47)	.0785 (1.24)	.0201 (.39)	.0575 (1.14)
PERS	−.1250 (−.59)	−.3029 (−1.34)	.2169 (.80)	−.0320 (−.37)	−.1223 (−1.75)	.1347 (1.95)
PUSH	−.2455 (−1.66)	.3083 (1.94)	−.0440 (−.23)	−.0693 (−1.15)	.1105 (2.26)	.0153 (.32)
PULL	−.1027 (−.57)	.6174 (3.23)	.3287 (1.44)	.0384 (.53)	.1784 (3.02)	.0599 (1.03)
	B. NLS Mature Men ($n = 1{,}016$)					
LAYOFF	.2111 (.99)	−.5501 (−2.80)	.1534 (.69)	.0802 (1.75)	−.1818 (−3.45)	.0579 (.95)
PERS	−.2156 (−.44)	−1.1024 (−2.46)	−.1143 (−.23)	−.0301 (−.29)	−.3780 (−3.13)	.0062 (.04)
PUSH	.1202 (.32)	−.0932 (−.27)	−.2345 (−.59)	.0129 (.16)	−.0437 (−.47)	−.0098 (−.09)
PULL	.1083 (.22)	−.6126 (−1.37)	−.7372 (−1.45)	.0407 (.39)	−.0656 (−.54)	−.1102 (−.79)
	C. NLS Young Men ($n = 1{,}032$)					
LAYOFF	.0922 (1.90)	.1157 (1.40)	−.5305 (−.43)	.0515 (1.47)	.0163 (.60)	−.0069 (−.22)
PERS	−.1040 (−.80)	−.1187 (−.92)	.0417 (.22)	−.0223 (−.41)	−.0465 (−1.09)	.0521 (1.07)
PUSH	−.1801 (−1.91)	.1637 (1.75)	−.0467 (−.34)	−.0363 (−.91)	.0535 (1.74)	−.0028 (−.08)
PULL	−.0033 (−.03)	.2202 (2.01)	−.0197 (−.12)	.0477 (1.02)	.0587 (1.62)	−.0144 (−.35)
	D. NLS Mature Men ($n = 1{,}379$)					
LAYOFF	.1552 (.89)	−.1687 (−1.00)	−.1519 (−.82)	.0183 (.47)	−.0455 (−1.03)	−.0518 (−1.08)
PERS	−.2006 (−.55)	−.3616 (−1.03)	.4840 (1.24)	−.0096 (−.12)	−.1559 (−1.68)	.1579 (1.56)
PUSH	.0220 (.08)	−.0223 (−.08)	−.1771 (−.58)	−.0340 (−.53)	.0327 (.45)	−.0248 (−.31)
PULL	−.0096 (−.03)	−.1769 (−.44)	.1511 (.34)	.0294 (.32)	−.0016 (.00)	−.0453 (−.39)

Note: The variables (excluding JOB) held constant in table 2.1 are held constant here; t-statistics in parentheses.

no difference in the wage progress of the two groups. Therefore, we can safely conclude that individuals who moved used job mobility as a tool to achieve a better wage package.

The reader can easily verify that almost (qualitatively) identical results are obtained for the other types of voluntary separations in the NLS young men's sample. For the mature men, this exercise yields somewhat mixed results. The reason is probably due to the fact that the separation dummies have very low means. For example, the frequencies of PUSH, PULL and PERS are .0098, .0059, and .0059, respectively.

It may be argued that these findings are seriously biased by the existence of selectivity bias since our sample consists of individuals who either did not change jobs at all or who moved in only the 1969–71 period, so that the move was, in a sense, successful. In fact, the use of an unrestricted sample, where we include all individuals and relate their wage growth in all three periods to their 1969–71 separation behavior, barely affects our results as can be seen in panels C and D of table 2.2. If anything, we obtain somewhat more reasonable results for the mature men.

2.2 Labor Turnover and Wage Growth within the Job

In the previous section we have shown that labor turnover affects the wage profile *across* jobs. In this section we demonstrate how labor turnover also affects the earnings profile *within* the job. In section 2.2.1 we present a simple framework for analyzing the relationship between labor turnover and on-the-job wage growth, and in section 2.2.2 we document empirically that labor turnover systematically affects the slope of the earnings profile within the job.

2.2.1 A Framework for Analyzing On-the-Job Wage Growth

One way in which on-the-job wage growth can be studied is to interpret it as the result of human capital investment. If no mobility occurs during the period $t-1$ to t, then the absolute change in the individual's earnings capacity during that period can be written as:

(1) $$\Delta E_t = E_t - E_{t-1} = r_n C_{t-1}$$

where E_t is earnings capacity at experience year t; C_t denotes dollar investment costs in t, and r_n is the rate of return to postschool investments on the current (nth) job. Note that C_t is composed of all investment costs borne by the individual. That is, it is composed of general investments as well as the share of specific training costs paid by the individual.

The change in earnings capacity given by equation (1) is unobserved. However, if all investment costs are foregone earnings, observed earnings, Y_t, are defined by $Y_t = E_t - C_t$. Thus equation (1) can be rewritten as:

(2) $$\Delta Y_t = r_n C_{t-1} - (C_t - C_{t-1}) = r_n C_{t-1} + \beta_n$$

where $\beta_n = -(C_t - C_{t-1})$. Since, by assumption, no job change has occurred, observed wage growth on the job is composed of the returns to on-the-job training plus the change in investment costs from period to period. If the investment profile is assumed to be continuous and linearly declining (within the job), the change in investment costs is given by the constant rate of decline in investment in the current job, β_n. Thus observed wage growth incorporates the saving in investment costs as job tenure increases.

To convert equation (2) into observables, we hypothesize that investment costs are a negative function both of previous experience and of current job experience.[13] That is, more investment is undertaken the younger the individual was when he started the job and the shorter the tenure on the job. Of course, both these implications must be qualified by the fact that at low levels of tenure there is a considerable amount of learning taking place as both the individual and the firm consider whether the job match is worthwhile. Moreover, at younger ages, as the individual learns about the labor market, "job shopping" might lead to an initial increase in investment. Thus it is possible that human capital investments may be zero or rise initially both with age and with job tenure. We assume that these matching periods are reasonably short so that our linear approximations do not greatly distort reality. In particular, if π_n measures experience prior to the current job and e_n measures current job tenure, a simple relation determining investment costs would be:[14]

(3) $$C_t = C_{0n} - \sigma_n \pi_n - \beta_n e_n$$

Note that C_{0n} measures the level of investment that would take place initially if the current job were the first job in the life cycle. Substituting (3) into (2) yields:

(4) $$\Delta Y_t = (r_n C_{0n} + \beta_n + r_n \beta_n) - r_n \sigma_n \pi_n - r_n \beta_n e_n$$

Thus a simple regression of wage growth on previous and current experience gives coefficients that are proportional to the effect of aging both prior to the job and within the job.

We can introduce the relationship between labor turnover and on-the-job wage growth by noting that C_{0n} will vary systematically with the probability of separation. That is, since a part of dollar investment costs is specific to the current job, there will be a positive correlation between the level of the investment profile (measured by C_{0n}) and expected completed job duration. In other words, the individual and the firm will invest more in longer jobs because they can both collect the returns to specific training over a longer period of time. Simultaneously, those individuals who have invested more on the job will have an incentive to stay longer.[15]

Denoting by t_n^* the expected completed tenure in the job as of the beginning of the job, this implies:

(5) $$C_{0n} = \alpha_n + \rho_n t_n^*$$

If longitudinal data are used, information on t_n^* is generally available as long as actual events closely parallel expectations. If we make the simplifying assumption that *actual completed* tenure equals t_n^* as a first-order approximation, and if we observe a sample of individuals changing jobs at some point during the survey, then it is possible to estimate the parameter ρ_n (times a constant). In particular, rewrite t_n^* as:

(6) $$t_n^* = e_n + R_n$$

where e_n is current job tenure and R_n is time remaining in the current job. Using equations 4–6 we can derive:

(7) $$\Delta Y_t = (r_n \alpha_n + \beta_n + r_n \beta_n) - r_n \sigma_n \pi_n + r_n(\rho_n - \beta_n) e_n + r_n \rho_n R_n$$

The human capital hypothesis would predict that the coefficient on R_n is positive, i.e., wage growth is steeper in longer jobs. It is important to note that this relationship cannot be measured by observing the coefficient on current tenure, e_n. As equation 7 shows, the coefficient on e_n is ambiguous because longer observed tenure (as of the time of the survey) implies both that the individual is older (the aging effect β_n) and that more will be invested, since for given R_n the job will be longer (the investment effect ρ_n). The key to demonstrating that labor turnover and on-the-job wage growth are related is the availability of longitudinal data which enable us to observe an individual's *completed* tenure.[16]

It is important to note, however, that an alternative interpretaton can be given to the observation of a positive coefficient on R_n. One could simply argue that in jobs where an individual is progressing, i.e., where his wages are growing faster than they would elsewhere (perhaps because of better opportunities for investment), the individual will have an incentive to stay. Again, we would observe a positive correlation between on-the-job wage growth and *completed* job tenure. Actually, either interpretation highlights the importance of specific human capital in explaining labor turnover.

2.2.2 Empirical Results on Wage Growth within the Job

Table 2.3 presents the results of estimating equation 7 on both NLS samples. In both cases, we selected a group of individuals who had stayed on the job between 1967 and 1969 but who had changed jobs at any time during 1969 and 1973. Thus we have a sample of individuals for whom time remaining on the job is observed.[17] The equations in table 2.3 relate

Table 2.3 Effects of "Time Remaining on the Job" on 1967–69 Wage Growth

	(1) Absolute Growth $Y_{69} - Y_{67}$	(2) Percentage Growth $\ln Y_{69} - \ln Y_{67}$
A. NLS Young Men ($n = 156$)		
PREV	−.0120 (−.56)	−.0109 (−1.53)
JOB	−.0500 (−1.47)	−.0225 (−2.00)
REMTEN	.0837 (.87)	.0238 (.76)
B. Mature Men ($n = 747$)		
PREV	−.0144 (−2.13)	−.0045 (−1.62)
JOB	−.0195 (−2.90)	−.0062 (−2.25)
REMTEN	.0245 (1.26)	.0013 (.16)

Note: The variables held constant in table 2.1 (except D67 and D69) are also held constant here.
The sample is restricted to individuals who stayed on the job between 1967 and 1969 but left that job between 1969 and 1973.

wage growth in 1967–69 to previous experience (PREV), current job tenure (JOB), time remaining on the job measured as of 1967 (REMTEN), and a set of standardizing variables listed in the note to table 2.1. As before, the wage growth equations are estimated in two alternative ways: in column 1, the absolute change in wages over the 1967–69 period is the dependent variable, while in column 2, the percentage change in wages is analyzed.

Although the results are not statistically very strong, the coefficient of time remaining on the job, REMTEN, has the right sign and seems to be more significant for the older men sample.[18] For example, an extra year of job tenure in the older men sample increases the hourly wage rate by about 2.5 cents more over the 2-year time period under investigation. An interesting exercise that can be carried out is to ask how much does the positive correlation between completed tenure and wage growth contribute to total wage gains on the job? This calculation can be done roughly in the following way. First of all, in terms of yearly earnings (i.e., 2,000 hours supplied to the labor market), we obtain the increase in annual earnings of expecting to stay *one* additional year on the job by multiplying .0125 by 2,000;[19] this amount is $25.70. The individuals in our sample, in fact, stayed 20 years on the job (15 years prior to the survey and 5 after the survey). Therefore, from an ex ante point of view, staying an additional 20 years on the job is equivalent to an increase in annual earnings of $514. The present value of this increase in annual earnings over the completed job span (20 years of tenure) is $4,446. Thus there is substantial wage growth on the job over and above that obtained if there were no positive correlation between wage growth and completed job tenure. In the case of young men, even though the coefficient of REMTEN is 8.4 cents, the completed tenure is significantly smaller, only 6.6 years (2.9 years before the survey, 3.7 years after the survey). Thus the present value of the wage gains due to the correlation between completed job tenure and wage growth is $2,700.[20] Of course, we recognize that the insignificance of REMTEN in our equations indicates the need for further research on this question.

2.3 Labor Turnover and Lifetime Wage Growth

Parts 2.1 and 2.2 have shown the role that labor turnover plays in determining wage growth both across jobs and within the job. We have observed that individuals who change jobs voluntarily experience wage gains while individuals who stay on the job appear to experience steeper wage growth within the job. Thus one cannot predict a priori whether turnover leads to smaller or larger lifetime wage growth. In this section we suggest how this question can be answered.

It might seem appropriate to estimate an earnings function of the form:

(8) $$Y_t = \alpha_0 + \alpha_1 t + \alpha_2 t^2 + \alpha_3 e + \alpha_4 e^2$$

where t is total labor force experience and e denotes current job tenure. This type of earnings function is essentially based on the argument that on-the-job training is composed both of general and specific training. The coefficients of t capture the earnings growth of the individual over the life cycle, while the coefficients of e measure any growth which is specific to the current job *over and above* the growth which would have occurred due to general labor force experience. Thus, in principle, the estimation of (8) would provide some insight into the importance of job-specific skills in determining the observed wage structure. Unfortunately, a problem with this interpretation arises when (8) is applied to a cross-section of individuals. In particular, consider an extreme case in which there is no specific training, and thus α_3 and α_4 are truly zero. If individuals self-select themselves into different types of jobs because they differ in their propensities to separate—in other words, there is population heterogeneity—it may be that individuals who match into a "good" job receive high wages and therefore show low propensities to separate and individuals with "bad" matches receive low wages and are therefore observed to have high propensities to separate.[21] In this case, in the cross-section, α_3 may turn out to be positive *artificially*! Thus the cross-section estimates of (8) may not be very meaningful in analyzing the relationship between turnover and lifetime wage growth.

Using longitudinal data, however, we can provide a solution to this problem. In particular, consider the equation:

(9) $\quad\quad\quad Y_t - Y_0 = \gamma_1 t + \gamma_2 t^2 + \gamma_3 e + \gamma_4 e^2$

where Y_0 gives earnings in the first year of the life cycle. Thus by looking at wage growth we net out any individual differences that are unobserved but affect the individual's earnings throughout the working life. The coefficients γ_i ($i = 1, \ldots, 4$) can be interpreted as the effects of experience and job tenure on total life cycle wage progress. In particular, consider the extreme case in which there is no specific training. Clearly the coefficients γ_1 and γ_2 simply capture scale effects and are expected to be positive and negative respectively. If there is only general training, there is no obvious reason why length of current job tenure should provide any additional information on total life cycle wage growth. In fact, if mobility "pays" (that is, if there are nonnegative gains associated with changing jobs), longer tenure implies a smaller propensity for separation. If there is serial correlation in this propensity over the individual's life cycle, this implies less turnover in the individual's previous experience $t - e$. But under the assumption that mobility pays, the net effect of current tenure should then be negative! On the other hand, if wage progress over the life cycle is a function not only of total experience but of current job tenure, we would expect γ_3 and γ_4 to be positive and negative respectively in equation 9. If this is the case, however, the results can be interpreted as an indication of the fact that specific training is an important component of wage determination.[22] In other words, job tenure matters over and above the passage of labor market exposure.

Unfortunately, the two data sets we use in this paper do not contain any information on initial earnings in the life cycle. Moreover, in the young men's NLS the individuals are much too young and both labor market experience and job tenure too short to get any robust estimates of the parameters. However, in the older men's NLS we do have a measure of labor market progress made by the individual over the life cycle, since we are given the Duncan scale for the initial and current occupations. One distinct advantage of using the Duncan scale is that the measure of "earnings" is of a more permanent nature.[23] Table 2.4 presents the lifetime earnings growth regression estimated for the older men's NLS. The linear job tenure coefficient is positive and significant, indicating that holding total labor force experience constant, longer job tenure is associated with higher levels of total life cycle wage growth. Therefore, the results unambiguously show that while mobility that takes place early in

Table 2.4 Effects of Job Tenure on Lifetime Wage Growth, NLS Mature Men (Dependent Variable = $Y_t - Y_0$)

Variable	Coefficient	t
Constant	−24.1973	
EDUC	.4470	(2.13)
EXPER	1.8399	(2.04)
EXPER^2	−.0284	(−2.23)
JOB	.4860	(3.29)
JOB^2	−.0077	(−1.78)
R^2	.028	

the life cycle may pay, individuals who have finally settled in a firm experience larger lifetime wage growth than individuals who are still changing jobs.

2.4 Effects of Other Variables

In the previous sections we have documented that turnover is an important determinant of wage growth. In this section we explore in more detail the other determinants of wage growth for both the young men's and the mature men's NLS samples. The basic results are presented in table 2.5 where wage growth regressions are estimated separately for stayers, quitters, and layoffs in both age samples. In order to conserve space we present only the results using arithmetic wage growth.

The effects of the other variables are interesting. For example, education has a strong positive effect on the wage growth of young men. Moreover, within the young men's sample, education affects the wage growth of men who separated from the job much more strongly than that of stayers. In the older men sample, however, education has a significant effect only for those who quit. Therefore the results seem to suggest that education helps to increase the gains from mobility for young men and the gains from quitting at older ages.

The coefficients of experience are quite interesting in the young men's sample. In particular, as predicted in section 2.2, experience has a negative effect on the wage growth of stayers. Note, however, that experience is *positive* (though very weak) for both quitters and layoffs, indicating that the accumulation of labor market experience may be helpful in creating the gains from mobility. A similar pattern is found for older men: experience has a negative effect on the wage growth of stayers, a positive effect on the wage growth of quitters and a zero effect on the wage growth of people who were laid off.

Other variables of some interest include a union coefficient which seems to have a zero or negative effect on the wage growth of stayers. Marital status and the labor force participation status of the wife have significantly positive and negative effects respectively on the wage growth of the young men stayers. These effects can be interpreted by arguing that marriage increases the labor market investment incentives of males (perhaps due to the household division of labor), while if the wife works these incentives are diminished.

Finally, one of the most significant variables in the regression is the size of the local labor market. This variable has a strong positive effect on the wage growth of stayers. Surprisingly, it has a negative effect on the wage growth of older men who were laid off from their jobs.

Table 2.5 Effects of Other Variables on Wage Growth (Dependent variable = ΔY_i)

	Stayers		Quitters		Layoffs	
	Coeff.	t	Coeff.	t	Coeff.	t
		A. Young Men				
D67	.0020	(.03)	.0927	(.54)	.2099	(1.12)
D69	−.0467	(−.40)	−.0331	(−.08)	−.0806	(−.23)
EDUC	.0250	(2.69)	.0710	(2.35)	.0796	(2.71)
EXPER	−.0094	(−1.40)	.0123	(.53)	.0103	(.49)
JOB	−.0068	(−.94)	−.0488	(−1.40)	.0209	(.59)
ARMY	−.0018	(−1.27)	−.0028	(−.57)	−.0005	(−.11)
UNION	−.0713	(−1.80)	−.1051	(−.66)	−.0766	(−.55)
HLTH	−.0684	(−1.02)	−.2184	(−1.08)	−.0959	(−.53)
MAR	.0934	(1.90)	−.0883	(−.53)	−.2598	(−1.61)
WLFP	−.1032	(−1.83)	.0855	(.44)	.5517	(2.51)
WINC	.0014	(1.06)	.0033	(.75)	−.0057	(−.98)
WKSUN	−.0023	(−.51)	−.0027	(−.26)	.0054	(.96)
SIZE	.0057	(3.09)	.0140	(2.12)	.0020	(.31)
UN	−.0086	(−.75)	.0010	(.03)	.0381	(1.01)
R^2	.029		.021		.049	
n	2145		1046		474	
		B. Mature Men				
D67	.0531	(.97)	1.124	(2.24)	.7686	(3.68)
D69	−.0078	(−.14)	.6508	(1.28)	.5883	(2.86)
EDUC	.0033	(.41)	.1082	(1.71)	−.0061	(−.19)
EXPER	−.0081	(−1.68)	.0731	(1.83)	.0105	(.54)
JOB	.0011	(.60)	−.0266	(−1.36)	−.0019	(−.25)
UNION	−.0146	(−.35)	.0773	(.17)	.5189	(3.49)
HLTH	−.0210	(−.43)	.2883	(.81)	.1391	(.78)
MAR	.0022	(.03)	.2708	(.46)	−.5184	(−2.14)
WLFP	.0116	(.28)	.5285	(1.36)	.0370	(.23)
WW	.0046	(.93)	−.1899	(−1.01)	−.0005	(−.29)
WKSUN	−.0064	(−1.29)	.0027	(.14)	−.0037	(−.87)
SIZE	.0025	(1.48)	.0032	(.23)	−.0177	(−2.61)
UN	−.0011	(−.10)	.0224	(.21)	.0234	(.57)
R^2	.004		.060		.130	
n	4213		252		280	

2.5 Summary

In this paper we have presented a systematic empirical analysis of wage growth in the National Longitudinal Surveys of Young and Mature Men. We have demonstrated that labor turnover is a significant factor in understanding wage growth since it affects both wage growth *across* jobs and wage growth *within* the job. Some specific findings are summarized below.

1. Although the gains to quitting appear to be positive for young men and zero or negative for older men, this was clarified by distinguishing among three types of quits: quits due to finding a better job, quits due to being dissatisfied with the current job, and quits due to personal reasons. It was then shown that in both age groups, individuals who quit because they said they found a better job experienced significant wage gains. At older ages a quit is mainly due to dissatisfaction with the current job and these types of quits do not in general significantly increase earnings. The change in the nature of a quit over the life cycle is the reason for the age differences in the impacts of quits on wages.

2. We extended our analysis of the wage gains from mobility by comparing not only movers and stayers but individuals to themselves in the sense that we analyzed the individual's wage profile before, during, and after the move to determine whether it had been significantly affected by mobility. It was shown that at least for the young men, this type of exercise led to the conclusion that a mover significantly gained from his actions.

3. Labor turnover and wage growth within the job are related through a weak positive correlation between wage growth and *completed* job tenure. Individuals who expected to remain on the job an additional year experienced steeper wage growth in the current period, ceteris paribus.

4. Since labor turnover was found to have offsetting effects on wage growth, i.e., to lead to wage gains across jobs but flatter growth in shorter jobs, its effect on lifetime wage growth could not be predicted. Our empirical analysis showed, however, that, even when total labor force experience is held constant, there exists a strong positive correlation between length of current tenure and total life-cycle wage growth. Thus, while early mobility may pay, individuals who are still changing jobs later in life experience lower overall wage growth.

In summary, this paper has tried to show that labor turnover affects not only the growth of wages across jobs but also the rate at which wages grow on the job. It is therefore an important factor that must be taken into account in any study of the earnings distribution.

Appendix

List of Variables

QUIT	= 1 if individual changed jobs voluntarily
LAYOFF	= 1 if the individual changed jobs involuntarily
JOBREL	= 1 if individual quit for job-related reasons (see note 10)
PERS	= 1 if individual quit for personal reasons (see note 10)
PUSH	= 1 if individual quit because of dissatisfaction with current job (see note 11)
PULL	= 1 if individual quit because he found better job (see note 11)
EDUC	= years of education
EXPER	= potential experience since date of completion of schooling
JOB	= years of job tenure
ARMY	= years in the military (Young Men only)
UNION	= 1 if individual was a member of a union
HLTH	= 1 if individual's health limits kind or amount of work
MAR	= 1 if individual married with spouse present
WLFP	= 1 if individual's wife was employed
WW	= wife's wage rate (Older Men)
WINC	= wife's earnings (Young Men)
WKSUN	= weeks unemployed during the two-year interval
SIZE	= size of labor force in 1960 of area in which individual lives
UN	= unemployment rate in area in which individual lives
D67	= 1 if observation refers to 1967–69
D69	= 1 if observation refers to 1969–71

Notes

1. See Mincer (1970) and Sahota (1978) for surveys of alternative explanations of the determinants of the earnings distribution.
2. Some exceptions are found in the papers by Lazear (1976) and Wise (1975).
3. In previous work (Bartel and Borjas 1977) we have analyzed the problem of *why* people move. Here we concentrate on establishing the consequences of labor turnover for the individual's wage-experience profile.
4. Jovanovic (1979) provides a model that predicts wage growth on the job based on the matching process between the individual and the firm.
5. An extensive discussion of the role and effects of heterogeneity in the labor market is given in Heckman, chapter 3, below. Further analysis of the problem, with labor turnover used as the focus, is provided by Jovanovic and Mincer, chapter 1, above.
6. See Bartel (1979) for a detailed analysis of the relationship between job turnover and migration.

7. These sample selection rules are far more serious than they appear to be. In particular, in the extreme age groups sampled in the NLS, a significant portion of turnover may be due to either retirement or school enrollment changes.

8. There are two important qualifications to be noted here. First, in the young men's NLS, many individuals were enrolled in school in the early years of the survey. Since we concentrate on the labor market behavior of men permanently attached to the labor force, we do not have observations for these individuals in the early years, so that pooling cross-section and time series less than triples the number of observations. Secondly, the efficiency of ordinary least squares can be improved upon by utilizing one of the many methods now available for pooling cross-section and time series. We do not pursue this refinement in this paper.

9. Recall that these numbers refer to the gains made over the two-year period. To obtain annual effects of labor mobility, simply divide the coefficients by two.

10. A job-related quit is one that occurred because the individual (a) was dissatisfied with wages, hours, working conditions, and/or location of his job; (b) disliked his fellow employees; or (c) found a better job. A personal quit is one that occurred because of (a) health problems or (b) family reasons. For young men, 85 percent of the quits were job related while for the older men 73 percent were job related.

11. PUSH is defined as a quit that occurred because the individual (a) was dissatisfied with wages, hours, working conditions or location of his job; or (b) disliked his fellow employees. PULL is a quit where the individual reports that he found a better job. Among the young men, 50 percent of job-related quits were "pulls," while for the older men only 35 percent of these quits were "pulls."

12. The calculation uses the formula:

$$PV - 2,000 \cdot (\Delta W) \int_0^{T-1969} e^{-rt} \, dt$$

where ΔW is the absolute wage increase, 2,000 is the number of hours worked each year, and T is the year of retirement. For young men, $T - 1969$ is 43 years while for older men it is 10 years. We assume r equals 10 percent.

13. These implications follow easily from life cycle optimization models developed by Ben-Porath (1967), Becker (1975) and Heckman (1976).

14. The implications of this investment function for the wage level equation are derived in Borjas (1975, 1981).

15. If firm and individual investments are positively correlated, then clearly the firm too has a smaller incentive to lay off the worker, further lowering the probability of separation.

16. Although the derivations in this section are in terms of absolute wage growth, similar equations can be derived for percentage wage growth. In particular, the analysis would then be conducted in terms of time-equivalent investment ratios. These ratios, in turn, would then be expected to decline both over the life cycle and within the job. Moreover, if higher levels of investment can take place only by spending a larger portion of work time investing, one would expect a positive correlation between these investment ratios and completed job tenure. Thus the analysis may carry over to percentage wage growth.

17. These sample restrictions, of course, raise the possibility of sample selection bias; see Heckman (1979) for a thorough discussion of this problem.

18. There are two possible reasons for the insignificance of REMTEN in the young men's NLS. First, these men are in the very early years of their jobs when investment may not be taking place. Second, the usable sample is very small because during 1967–69 approximately half of the individuals were enrolled in school and are deleted from the sample; among the remaining 50 percent, the job separation rate is very high thus resulting in further deletions. It is interesting to note that by enlarging the young men's sample to include individuals who did not leave the job by 1973 and assigning an arbitrary value of 10 for REMTEN for these individuals, the REMTEN coefficient becomes positive and significant.

19. We use .0125 rather than .025 because the wage growth equations refer to two-year intervals.

20. Note that the coefficient of REMTEN is never significant in column 2 when we deal with percentage wage growth. In principle, the correlation between investment and completed tenure need hold only in terms of dollar investment costs and not in terms of time-equivalent investment ratios since it is not clear a priori how initial earnings capacities are correlated with completed job tenure.

21. The problem of heterogeneity versus state dependence is discussed in detail in Heckman (chapter 3, below) and Jovanovic and Mincer (chapter 1, above).

22. Of course, the results could also be consistent with the hypothesis that wages grow on the job because of a successful "match" between employer and employee. In other words, an individual's mobility ultimately led to his finding a firm in which he was able to "move up the ladder."

23. The Duncan index is described in Reiss (1961). It is very highly correlated with earnings in the occupation.

Comment   Gilbert R. Ghez

The paper by Ann Bartel and George Borjas is an interesting investigation of the relationship between wage growth and turnover. It seeks to shed light on this relationship using the theory of human capital. The authors succeed in showing some important empirical regularities characterizing job mobility. It is precisely the soundness of many of their findings which prompts me to take a more careful look at their methods.

I begin with four general comments on the model, followed by a number of shorter comments on empirical implementation.

1. My first observation is that the wage path of movers is surely a function of their whole history of job turnover. Repeat job losers presumably will fair worse than nonrepeaters not only because each successive job loss pushes them into worse options but also because a repeater may come to acquire a poor reputation. Employers tend to screen applicants on the basis not only of education but also on their work history. This feature is not recognized in the Bartel-Borjas paper, or for that matter in the voluminous literature on screening that has emerged in recent years. Even for job quitters, a series of former quits may be regarded adversely by prospective employers in that they may believe that this applicant's probability of quitting soon is higher than that of other comparable workers. This would reduce the market options of the repeat quitter. Repeat quits may of course also have a beneficial effect: in so far as search effort is more intense around the time of quitting, a repeat quitter may well have acquired more information about labor market options than other workers and thereby may be able to secure a more rewarding job.

Gilbert R. Ghez is Associate Professor of Management and Economics, Roosevelt University, Walter E. Heller College of Business Administration.

The direction of net impact of repeat quits on wage growth is thus an empirical question.

Because of these lagged effects, the error terms in the Bartel-Borjas empirical investigation are temporarily correlated. Repeat job changes over a given span of time are a more likely occurrence for young men than for mature ones. (Although to be sure the total number of job changes is a nondecreasing function of age.) The neglected lags are therefore more damaging to the regressions in the sample of young men. This may help explain why the effects of current layoffs are less significant there: current layoffs are a less perfect measure of total recent layoffs for young men than for older men. The neglected lags may also help explain why in both samples the effect of quits due to dissatisfaction with the current job (PUSH) does not have a statistically significant effect.

It would be most welcome if in future empirical work more attention was paid to this problem. There would be several ways to proceed. A natural and simple way would be to run regressions of wage growth on current separation, given that the individual had the same employer for, say, the previous five years and compare it to the wage growth of current movers who also changed jobs in the previous five years, as well as to the wage growth of those who did not change jobs over the five-year span. Presumably job separations in the very distant past carry no weight currently. A more complex procedure would allow for differential weights to past separations depending on exactly how far in the past they occurred.

2. My second comment pertains to modeling the effect of expected completed tenure on current investment costs. Bartel and Borjas assume in equation 5 that expected tenure t^* affects investment costs C independently of years of experience. However, a moment of reflection should convince the reader that optimizing theory predicts that a lengthening of expected tenure should have a larger effect on investments the closer the worker is to that expected date, for then the returns from longer tenure are discounted less heavily. Take for instance the Ben Porath neutral model of investment planning, modified to account for tenure on the current job until t^* and for tenure in a subsequent job from t^* to t^{**} (we could introduce more jobs without altering the gist of the argument). The discounted value of returns $b(t)$ from a unit of investment undertaken at time t is:

$$(1) \qquad b(t) = \int_t^{t^*} a^* \, e^{-(i+\delta)(s-t)} ds + \int_{t^*}^{t^{**}} a^{**} \, e^{-(i+\delta)(s-t)} ds$$

where a^* is the return per period from a unit of human capital when the worker works in the firm where the training is undertaken, a^{**} is the return per period in the subsequent job from a unit of human capital acquired in the current job, i is the opportunity cost of funds, and δ is the constant rate of depreciation. If we assume that a^* and a^{**} are constant within each job spell, then $b(t)$ can be written more compactly as:

$$b(t) = \frac{a^*}{i+\delta}[1-e^{-(i+\delta)(t^*-t)}] + \frac{a^{**}}{i+\delta}[e^{-(i+\delta)(t^*-t)} - e^{-(i+\delta)(t^{**}-t)}]$$

$$= \frac{a^*}{i+\delta} - \frac{(a^*-a^{**})}{i+\delta}e^{-(i+\delta)(t^*-t)} - \frac{a^{**}}{i+\delta}e^{-(i+\delta)(t^{**}-t)}$$

Presumably $a^{**} < a^*$ if the current investment contains a specific component. So long as the worker is still investing, he equates marginal cost of investing to its marginal benefit. Total investment cost per period in the current job, denoted by C, is then simply (assuming that the production function of human capital does not shift over time):

$$C(t) = C[b(t)] \text{ with } \frac{dC}{db} > 0$$

The effect on marginal benefits of a change in expected completed tenure on this job, holding constant the total expected work length, is:

(2) $$\frac{\partial b(t)}{\partial t^*} = (a^* - a^{**})e^{-(i+\delta)(t^*-t)} > 0$$

This effect is larger the closer t is to t^*, as long as $i+\delta > 0$:

(3) $$\frac{\partial^2 b(t)}{\partial t^* \partial t} = (a^* - a^{**})(i+\delta)e^{-(i+\delta)(t^*-t)} > 0$$

Hence[1]:

$$\frac{\partial^2 C(t)}{\partial t^* \partial t} > 0$$

when $i+\delta > 0$ and $a^* > a^{**}$.

To avoid excessive notation here, assume that the current job is the first job. The empirical function used by Bartel-Borjas is:

$$C_t = \alpha + \rho t^* - \beta t$$

(I use t where they use e in their notation, since my discussion is centered on the first job in order to get at the main point). This linear function allows t^* to affect levels of investments but not slopes. A more appropriate specification which conserves much simplicity for the purpose of estimation is:[2]

(4) $$C_t = \alpha' + \rho'(t^* - t) + \rho''(t^* - t)^2 + \gamma'(t^{**} - t) + \gamma''(t^{**} - t)^2$$

where the prediction is that $\rho' > 0$, $\rho'' < 0$, $\gamma' > 0$, $\gamma'' < 0$. Viewed in this framework, Bartel-Borjas are implicitly assuming that $\rho'' = 0$ and $\gamma'' = 0$. It is useful to point out that if t^{**} is the same for all individuals in the sample, this equation can be implemented with data on expected completed tenure and experience (past and current experience). The earnings growth equation would be:

$$\Delta Y_t = rC_{t-1} - (C_t - C_{t-1})$$

(5)
$$\Delta Y_t = r[\alpha' + \rho'(t^* - t - 1) + \rho''(t^* - t - 1)^2]$$
$$+ \gamma'(t^{**} - t) + \gamma''(t^{**} - t)^2 - (\rho' + \gamma')$$
$$+ (\rho'' + \gamma'') + 2\rho''(t^* - t) + 2\gamma''(t^{**} - t)$$

That is, the wage growth equation is a quadratic function of t and t^*:

(6) $$\Delta Y_t = k_0 + k_1 t + k_2 t^2 + k_3 t^* + k_4 (t^*)^2 + k_5 t t^*$$

where the coefficients are:

$$k_0 = r\alpha' - (1+r)(\rho' + \gamma') + (1+r)(\rho'' + \gamma'')$$
$$+ [r\gamma' - 2(1+r)\gamma''] t^{**} + r\gamma''(t^{**})^2$$
$$k_1 = -r(\rho' + \gamma') + 2(1+r)(\rho'' + \gamma'') - 2r\gamma'' t^{**}$$
$$k_2 = r(\rho'' + \gamma'') < 0$$
$$k_3 = r\rho' - 2(1+r)\rho'' > 0$$
$$k_4 = r\rho'' < 0$$
$$k_5 = -2r\rho'' > 0$$

3. This brings me to another comment. The assumption made by Bartel-Borjas that actual completed tenure is a good estimate of expected completed tenure is a dubious one. The assumption of perfect cohort expectations was introduced in my NBER study on life cycle consumption (Ghez and Becker 1975, chapter 2) and is embedded in all studies using rational expectations, but the assumption of perfect predictions is a poor choice at the level of the individual. Moreover although the assumption of rational expectations makes sense in the context of variables that are moving with some regularity, I think it is improper to use it in the context of turnover where chance events bulk large and where it is difficult to extract information from the past.

At the least, I would suggest breaking up the sample by variables that strongly influence completed tenure: characteristics of workers such as their level of education, and characteristics of firms (perhaps an industry classification). Then make the assumption that for any individual his completed tenure is equal to the average tenure of the group plus a random term. In this way, by constructing a synthetic group, estimates of completed tenure effects are less likely to be biased.

In a more complete framework, expected completed separation from the current job is likely to vary over time for the worker. In this case, the change in income would partly reflect these changed expectations: a revised prospect that separation will occur sooner than had been anticipated earlier will reduce the incentive to invest currently. In practice I grant that it is difficult to come up with empirical counterparts to these expectation variables.

4. An equally fundamental problem with the Bartel-Borjas model is the assumption that job separations are exogenous. Rather than using ordinary least squares, they would have done better to construct and estimate a turnover equation also. Many of the standardizing variables used by Bartel-Borjas in their wage growth equations are also good controls for turnover. Such a turnover equation would depend also on anticipated returns from job mobility. The point is not simply that a simultaneous equation format would have been more appropriate, but also that predicted turnover could have been used as a more correct expected tenure variable. It might then also have been possible to estimate separately the contribution of anticipated turnover and that of turnover shocks (less fully anticipated separations) on wage growth.

I will make a few more brief comments. Their brevity is conditioned by the desire to conserve on space.

5. The 1967–73 period is composed of two distinct periods: 1967–69 is a period of full employment; 1970–73 is characterized by considerably more unemployment, recession in 1970–71, followed by a mild recovery in 1972–73. Bartel-Borjas analyze the effects of 1969–71 separations on 1967–69 wage growth. To the extent that the downturn in 1970 was unanticipated, it would make sense to compare the effect of 1969–71 separations on 1967–69 wage growth with the effect of 1971–73 separations on 1969–71 wage growth.

6. Presumably much turnover occurs immediately or soon after leaving school. The Bartel-Borjas sample contains only continuous labor force participants: those young men (aged 15–25 in 1967) in school full time who take summer jobs are excluded from the sample, whereas those in school holding continuous part-time jobs are included. Since people are likely to change jobs abruptly upon completion of school, it might be appropriate to include at least a dummy variable indicating whether or not the respondent is in school. This in itself does not solve the sample selection problem, but does provide some standardization.

7. Some additional standardization would have been appropriate. In particular the length of the workweek is an obvious candidate.

8. Another standardizing variable which might have been included is whether job mobility was accompanied by geographic mobility. These effects are important, as shown in previous work by Bartel. Why not include at least a dummy for geographic mobility on the slope coefficients of quits and layoffs?

9. Bartel-Borjas control for unemployment. I presume this reflects unemployment prior to job separation. Why not also control for unemployment at the place of destination?

10. Bartel-Borjas find that the size of the local labor market has a stronger effect on the wage growth of young quitters than on that of young stayers. This finding makes sense in the context of search theory, and could have been emphasized.

The virtual absence of effects of the size of local labor markets on the wage growth of mature quitters is puzzling. Perhaps if the regressions were standardized by geographic mobility, a stronger positive effect would be borne out.

11. Clearly a more appropriate measure of rewards from work would include nonpecuniary benefits on the one hand and fringe benefits in the form of paid vacations, health insurance plans, pensions, and bonuses on the other hand. It is remarkable that Bartel-Borjas get so much mileage from their less inclusive wage variable. Eventually, of course, human capital models with more comprehensive measures of rewards from work will have to be tested, when data sets suitable for that purpose become available.

Notes

1. These results generalize to the case of nonneutral investments using the methods developed in my unpublished paper "A Note on the Earnings Function When Human Capital Is Biased toward Earnings" (1973).

2. The Mincer-Polachek (1974) equation is different: it makes investment ratios decline with years of experience within work spells, but holds constant the anticipated duration of work in the current (and future) job.

References

Bartel, A. P. "The Migration Decision: What Role Does Job Mobility Play?" *American Economic Review*, December 1979.

Bartel, A. P., and Borjas, G. J. "Middle-Age Job Mobility: Its Determinants and Consequences," in S. Wolfbein, ed., *Men in the Pre-Retirement Years*. Philadelphia: Temple University, 1977.

Becker, G. S. *Human Capital*. 2nd Ed. N.Y.; Columbia University Press, 1975.

Ben-Porath, Y. "The Production of Human Capital and the Life Cycle of Earnings." *Journal of Political Economy*, August 1967.

Borjas, G. J. "Job Investment, Labor Mobility, and Earnings." Ph.D. Thesis, Columbia University, 1975.

———. "Job Mobility and Earnings over the Life Cycle." *Industrial and Labor Relations Review*, April 1981.

Ghez, G. R., and Becker, G. S. *The Allocation of Time and Goods over the Life Cycle*. N.Y.: Columbia University Press, 1975.

Heckman, J. J. "Life-Cycle Model of Earnings, Learning and Consumption." *Journal of Political Economy*, August 1976.

———. "Sample Selection Bias as a Specification Error." *Econometrica*, January 1979.

Jovanovic, B. "Job Matching and the Theory of Labor Turnover." *Journal of Political Economy*, December 1979.

Lazear, E. "Age, Experience and Wage Growth." *American Economic Review*, September 1976.

Mincer, J. "The Distribution of Labor Earnings." *Journal of Economic Literature*, October 1970.

Mincer, J., and Polachek, S. "Family Investments in Human Capital: Earnings of Women." *Journal of Political Economy*, March-April 1974.

Reiss, A. J., et al. *Occupations and Social Status*. N.Y.: Free Press, 1961.

Rosen, S. "Learning and Experience in the Labor Market." *Journal of Human Resources*, Summer 1972.

Sahota, G. "Theories of Personal Income Distribution: A Survey." *Journal of Economic Literature*, March 1978.

Wise, D. "Academic Achievement and Job Performance." *American Economic Review*, June 1975.

3 Heterogeneity and State Dependence

James J. Heckman

In a variety of contexts, such as in the study of the incidence of accidents (Bates and Neyman 1951), labor force participation (Heckman and Willis 1977) and unemployment (Layton 1978), it is often noted that individuals who have experienced an event in the past are more likely to experience the event in the future than are individuals who have not experienced the event. The conditional probability that an individual will experience the event in the future is a function of past experience. There are two explanations for this empirical regularity.

One explanation is that as a consequence of experiencing an event, preferences, prices, or constraints relevant to future choices (or outcomes) are altered. In this case past experience has a genuine behavioral effect in the sense that an otherwise identical individual who did not experience the event would behave differently in the future than an individual who experienced the event. Structural relationships of this sort give rise to true state dependence as defined in this paper.

A second explanation is that individuals may differ in certain unmeasured variables that influence their probability of experiencing the event

James J. Heckman is Professor of Economics, University of Chicago, and Research Associate, National Bureau of Economic Research.

This research is supported by NSF Grant SOC 77-27136, Grant 10-P-90748/9-01 from the Social Security Administration, and a fellowship from the J. S. Guggenheim Memorial Foundation. Comments by Tom MaCurdy and R. A. Pollak have been especially valuable in preparing this draft of the paper. I have also benefited from comments by Gary Chamberlain, Chris Flinn, Zvi Griliches, Jan Hoem, Samuel Kotz, Marc Nerlove, Guilherme Sedlacek, and Donald Waldman. The first draft of this paper circulated in July 1977, and was presented at the Harvard-MIT Workshop on Econometrics and Jacob Mincer's Columbia University Workshop on Labor Economics (October 1977). Ralph Shnelvar performed the calculations. I am solely responsible for any errors.

but that are not influenced by the experience of the event. If these variables are correlated over time, and are not properly controlled, previous experience may appear to be a determinant of future experience solely because it is a proxy for such temporally persistent unobservables. Improper treatment of unmeasured variables gives rise to a conditional relationship between future and past experience that is termed spurious state dependence.

The problem of distinguishing between structural and spurious dependence is of considerable substantive interest. To demonstrate this point, it is instructive to consider recent work in the theory of unemployment. Phelps (1972) has argued that short-term economic policies that alleviate unemployment tend to lower aggregate unemployment rates in the long run by preventing the loss of work-enchancing market experience. His argument rests on the assumption that current unemployment has a real and lasting effect on the probability of future unemployment. Cripps and Tarling (1974) maintain the opposite view in their analysis of the incidence and duration of unemployment. They assume that individuals differ in their propensity to experience unemployment and in their unemployment duration times and that differences cannot be fully accounted for by measured variables. They further assume that the actual experience of having been unemployed or the duration of past unemployment does not affect future incidence or duration. Hence in their model short-term economic policies have no effect on long-term unemployment. The model developed in this paper is sufficiently flexible to accommodate both views of unemployment and can be used to test the two competing theories.

As another example, recent work on the dynamics of female labor supply assumes that entry into and exit from the labor force can be described by a Bernoulli probability model (Heckman and Willis 1977). This view of the dynamics of female labor supply ignores considerable evidence that work experience raises wage rates and hence that such experience may raise the probability that a woman works in the future, even if initial entry into the work force is determined by a random process. The general model outlined in this paper extends the econometric model of Heckman and Willis by permitting (1) unobserved variables that determine labor force choices to be freely correlated, in contrast with the rigid permanent-transitory error scheme for the unobservables assumed in their model; (2) observed explanatory variables to change over time (in their model these variables are assumed to be time invariant); and (3) previous work experience to determine current participation decisions. Empirical work reported below reveals that these three extensions are important in correctly assessing the determinants of female labor supply and in developing models that can be used in policy simulation analysis.

The problem of distinguishing between the two explanations for the empirical regularity has a long history. The first systematic discussion of this problem is presented in the context of the analysis of accident proneness. The seminal work on this topic is by Feller (1943) and Bates and Neyman (1951). Bates and Neyman demonstrate that panel data on individual event histories are required in order to discriminate between the two explanations. Papers preceding the Bates and Neyman work unsuccessfully attempted to use cross-section distributions of accident counts to distinguish between true and spurious state dependence. (See Feller 1943; Heckman and Borjas 1980.)

The problem of distinguishing between spurious and true state dependence is very similar to the familiar econometric problem of estimating a distributed lag model in the presence of serial correlation in the errors (Griliches 1967, Malinvaud 1970, Nerlove 1978). It is also closely related to previous work on the mover-stayer model that appears in the literature on discrete stochastic processes (Goodman 1961, Singer and Spilerman 1976).

This paper presents a new approach to this problem. A dynamic model of discrete choice is developed and applied to analyze the employment decisions of married women. The dynamic model of discrete choice presented here extends previous work on atemporal models of discrete choice by McFadden (1973a) and Domencich and McFadden (1975) to an explicitly dynamic setting. Markov models, renewal models, and "latent Markov" models emerge as a special case of the general model considered here. The framework presented here extends previous work on the mover-stayer problem (Singer and Spilerman 1976) by broadening the definition of heterogeneity beyond the "mixing distribution" or "components of variance" models employed in virtually all current work on the analysis of discrete dynamic data.

The major empirical finding reported in this paper is that past employment experience is an important determinant of current employment decisions for women past the childbearing years, even after accounting for heterogeneity of a very general type. This relationship can be interpreted as arising *in part* from the impact of both general and specific human capital investment on current labor market choices, but it is consistent with other explanations as well. Empirical evidence on the importance of heterogeneity is presented. Estimates of structural state dependence based on procedures that improperly control heterogeneity dramatically overstate the impact of past employment on current choices.

The estimates for younger married women, most of whom are in their childbearing years, suggest a weak effect of past participation on current choices, but empirical evidence on the importance of heterogeneity is still strong.

This paper also presents evidence that the unobserved variables that determine employment follow a stationary first-order Markov process. Initial differences in unmeasured variables tend to be eliminated with the passage of time. This homogenizing effect is offset in part by the impact of prior work experience that tends to accentuate initial differences in the propensity to work.

The empirical evidence on heterogeneity reported in this paper calls into question the implicit assumption maintained in previous work that addresses the problem of heterogeneity (Singer and Spilerman 1976; Heckman and Willis 1977). That work assumes that unmeasured variables follow a components of variance scheme; an individual has a "permanent" component to which a serially uncorrelated "transitory" component is added. The work reported here suggests that the heterogeneity process for married women cannot be modeled so simply. Unmeasured components are better described by the first-order Markov process. Omitted variables determining choices are increasingly less correlated as the time span between choices widens. Misspecification of the heterogeneity process gives rise to an erroneous estimate of the impact of the true effect of past employment on current employment probabilities.

This paper is in four parts. Part 3.1 provides an intuitive motivation to the problems and models considered in this paper. Part 3.2 presents the model used here, and discusses econometric issues that arise in implementing it. Part 3.3 presents estimates of the model and some qualifications. Part 3.4 presents an interpretation of the estimates. The paper concludes with a brief summary. An appendix presents a decomposition of estimated structural state dependence effects into wage and nonwage components.

3.1. Heterogeneity and State Dependence: An Intuitive Introduction

In order to motivate the analysis in this paper, it is helpful to consider four simple urn models that provide a useful framework within which to introduce intuitive notions about heterogeneity and state dependence. In the first scheme there are I individuals who possess urns with the same content of red and black balls. On T independent trials individual i draws a ball and then puts it back in his urn. If a red ball is drawn at trial t, person i experiences the event. If a black ball is drawn, person i does not experience the event. This model corresponds to a simple Bernoulli model and captures the essential idea underlying the choice process in McFadden's (1973a) work on discrete choice. From data generated by this urn scheme, one would not observe the empirical regularity described in the introduction. Irrespective of their event histories, all people have the same probability of experiencing the event.

A second urn scheme generates data that would give rise to the empirical regularity solely due to heterogeneity. In this model individuals possess distinct urns which differ in their composition of red and black balls. As in the first model sampling is done with replacement. However, unlike the first model, information concerning an individual's past experience of the event provides information useful in locating the position of the individual in the population distribution of urn compositions.

The person's past record can be used to estimate the person-specific urn composition. The conditional probability that individual i experiences the event at time t is a function of his past experience of the event. The contents of each urn are unaffected by actual outcomes and in fact are constant. There is no true state dependence.

The third urn scheme generates data characterized by true state dependence. In this model individuals start out with identical urns. On each trial, the contents of the urn change *as a consequence of the outcome of the trial*. For example, if a person draws a red ball, and experiences the event, additional new red balls are added to his urn. If he draws a black ball, no new black balls are added to his urn. Subsequent outcomes are affected by previous outcomes because the choice set for subsequent trials is altered as a consequence of experiencing the event. This model is a generalized Polya urn scheme.[1]

A variant of the third urn scheme can be constructed that corresponds to a renewal model (Karlin and Taylor 1975). In this scheme new red balls are added to an individual's urn on successive drawings of red balls until a black ball is drawn, and then all of the red balls added to the most recent continuous run of drawings of red balls are removed from the urn. The composition of the urn is then the same as it was before the first red ball in the run was drawn. A model corresponding to fixed costs of labor force entry is a variant of the renewal scheme in which new red balls are added to an individual's urn only on the first draw of the red ball in any run of red draws.

The crucial feature that distinguishes the third scheme from the second is that the contents of the urn (the choice set) are altered as a consequence of previous experience. The key point is not that the choice set changes across trials but that it changes in a way that depends on previous outcomes of the choice process. To clarify this point, it is useful to consider a fourth urn scheme that corresponds to models with more general types of heterogeneity to be introduced more formally below.

In this model individuals start out with identical urns, exactly as in the first urn scheme. After each trial, but independent of the outcome of the trial, the contents of each person's urn are changed by discarding a randomly selected portion of balls and replacing the discarded balls with a randomly selected group of balls from a larger urn (say, with a very large number of balls of both colors). Assuming that the individual urns are not completely replenished on each trial, information about the outcomes of previous trials is useful in forecasting the outcomes of future trials, although the information from a previous trial declines with its remoteness in time. As in the second and third urn models, previous outcomes give information about the contents of each urn. Unlike the second model, the fourth model is a scheme in which the information depreciates since the contents of the urn are changed in a random fashion. Unlike in the third model, the contents of the urn do not change as a consequence of any outcome of the choice process. This is the urn model analogue of Coleman's (1964) latent Markov model.

The general model presented below is sufficiently flexible that it can be specialized to generate data on the time series of individual choices that are consistent with samples drawn from each of the four urn schemes just described as well as more general schemes including combinations of the four. The principle advantage of the proposed model over previous models is that it accommodates very general sorts of heterogeneity and structural state dependence as special cases and permits the introduction of explanatory exogenous variables. The generality of the framework proposed here permits the analyst to combine models and test among competing specifications within a unified framework.

In the literature on female labor force participation, models of extreme homogeneity (corresponding to urn model one) and extreme heterogeneity (corresponding to urn model two with urns either all red or all black) are presented in a paper by Ben Porath (1973) which is a comment on Mincer's model (1962) of female labor supply. Ben Porath notes that cross-section data on female participation are consistent with either extreme model. Heckman and Willis (1977) pursue this point somewhat further and estimate a model of heterogeneity in female labor force participation probabilities that is the probit analogue of urn model two. They assume no state dependence. There is no previous work on female labor supply that estimates models corresponding to urn schemes three and four.

Urn model three is of special interest. It is consistent with human capital theory, and other models that stress the impact of prior work experience on current work choices. Human capital investment acquired through on the job training may generate structural state dependence. Fixed costs incurred by labor force entrants may also generate structural state dependence as a renewal process. So may spell-specific human capital. This urn model is also consistent with psychological choice models in which, as a consequence of receiving a stimulus of work, women's preferences are altered so that labor force activity is reinforced (Atkinson, Bower, and Crothers 1965).

Panel data can be used to discriminate among these models. For example, an implication of the second urn model is that the probability that a woman participates does not change with her labor force experience. An implication of the third model in the general case is that participation probabilities change with work experience. One method for discriminating between these two models utilizes individual labor force histories of sufficient length to estimate the probability of participation in different subintervals of the life cycle. If the estimated probabilities for a given woman do not differ at different stages of the life cycle, there is no evidence of structural state dependence.[2]

A more general test among the first three urn models utilizes labor force history data of sufficient length for *each woman* in a sample to estimate a regression of current participation status on previous participation status (measured by dummy variables indicating whether or not a woman worked at previous stages in her life cycle). If previous labor force experience has no effect on the current probability of participation, the first and third urn models would describe the data. If past experience predicts current participation status, but not perfectly, the third model describes the data.

Considerable care must be taken in utilizing panel data to discriminate among the models. The second test must be performed on data drawn from the work history of one person. One could utilize data on the histories of a sample of people by permitting each person to have his own fixed effect or intercept in the regression just described. If one were to pool data on individuals to estimate the regression on the entire sample, and not allow each person to have his own intercept, one would risk the danger that individual differences in participation probabilities, which would be relegated to a disturbance term in a pooled regression across people that does not permit individual intercepts, will be correlated with past participation status. If some individuals have a higher probability of participation than others, and if these differences are relegated to the disturbance term of the regression of current participation status on past participation status, regression analysis would produce a spurious positive relationship between current and previous experience that would appear to demonstrate the presence of structural state dependence that did not, in fact, exist, since people with higher participation probabilities are more likely to be in the labor force in the current period as well as in the past.

This point can be stated somewhat more precisely. Let $d(i, t)$ be a dummy variable that assumes the value of one if woman i works in period t and is zero otherwise. Define $\varepsilon(i, t)$ as a disturbance with the following structure:

$$\varepsilon(i, t) = \phi(i) + U(i, t) , t = 1, \ldots , T$$
$$i = 1, \ldots , I$$

where $\phi(i)$ is an individual-specific effect and $U(i, t)$ is a mean zero random variable of innovations uncorrelated with other innovations $U(i, t')$, $t \neq t'$.[3] There are I individuals in the sample followed for T time periods.

For each individual, write the regression

(1) $$d(i, t) = \phi(i) + \delta \sum_{t' < t} d(i, t') + U(i, t), \quad t+1, \ldots, T$$

where $d(i, 0)$ is a fixed nonstochastic initial condition.[4] Note that $\phi(i)$ is the intercept in the regression. More general models allowing for depreciation in the effect of past participation on current participation could be written out, but for present purposes nothing is gained by increasing the level of generality of the model. If this regression were fit on data for a single individual, a statistically significant value for δ would indicate that the third urn scheme is more appropriate than the second, i.e., that there is evidence for true state dependence at the individual level. If δ were estimated to be zero, the second urn model would fit the data better.[5]

If regression 1 is computed across people and time, and no allowance is made for individual differences in intercepts, the regression model for the pooled sample could be written as

(2) $$d(i, t) = \bar{\phi}(i) + \delta \sum_{t' < t} d(i, t') + U(i, t) + \phi(i) - \bar{\phi}(i)$$

$$i = 1, \ldots, I$$
$$t = 1, \ldots, T$$

where $\bar{\phi}(i)$ is the average intercept in the population. The composite disturbance in the regression is $U(i, t) + \phi(i) - \bar{\phi}(i)$. Because of equation 1, the term $\sum_{t' < t} d(i, t')$ would be correlated with the composite disturbance. Regression estimates of δ would be upward biased because past work experience is positively correlated with the composite disturbance. This bias could be avoided by permitting each individual to have his own intercept.[6]

Note further that if there is some variable, such as the number of children, that belongs in equation 1, the effect of children estimated from equation 2 will be biased. If children depress participation, and $\delta > 0$, the estimated effect of children on the probability of participation will be upward biased. This follows from a standard simultaneous equation bias argument if current numbers of children are negatively correlated with previous participation, and cumulated previous experience is positively correlated with the error term. Thus, uncorrected heterogeneity not only leads to an overstatement of the state dependence effect but also leads to an understatement of the negative effect of children on participation.[7]

The empirical analysis in this paper could be based on more general versions of equations 1 and 2.[8] However, estimation in the generalized linear probability model gives rise to well-known econometric difficulties; the errors are heteroscedestic, and estimated values of probabilities may not lie inside the unit interval.[9] Moreover, the interpretation of the statistical model as an economic model is unclear.

Instead, the model used here is a dynamic extension of cross-section models of discrete choice developed by the author in other work. (Heckman 1981a b). The essential features of this model are described in the next section.

3.2 A Dynamic Model of Labor Supply

This section presents a dynamic model of discrete choice that can be used to analyze unemployment, labor force participation, and other dynamic events. For specificity we focus on a dynamic model of female employment. The model presented here is based on Heckman (1978b, 1981a b).

Women are assumed to make employment decisions in successive equispaced intervals of time. Each woman has two options in each period in her life cycle: to work or not to work.[10] Let $v(1, i, t)$ be the expected lifetime utility that arises if woman i works in period t. This utility is a function of all relevant decision variables including her expectations about demographic events, such as the birth of children and divorce, and state variables such as her stocks of human capital. "$v(1, i, t)$" is the highest level of lifetime utility that the woman can attain *given* that she works today. "$v(0, i, t)$" is the highest level of lifetime utility that the woman can attain *given* that she does not work today. Implicit in both value functions is the notion that subsequent employment decisions are optimally chosen *given* the current choice, and given any new information, unknown to the agent at t, that becomes known in future periods when future employment decisions are being made.

Employment occurs at age t for woman i if $v(1, i, t) > v(0, i, t)$, i.e., if the expected lifetime utility of employment at age t exceeds the expected lifetime utility that arises from nonemployment. This view of employment is consistent with a wide variety of economic models. In particular, as is demonstrated below, under special assumptions it is consistent with McFadden's (1973b) random utility model applied in an intertemporal context or models of lifetime decision making under perfect certainty developed by Ryder, Stafford, and Stephan (1976) and others. The model is also consistent with fixed costs of entry into and exit from the work force.

For the present analysis, the difference in utilities $V(i, t) = v(1, i, t) - v(0, i, t)$ is the relevant quantity. If $V(i, t)$ is positive, a woman works at time t; otherwise she does not.

The difference in utilities $V(i, t)$ may be decomposed into two components. One component $\bar{V}(i, t)$ is a function of variables that can be observed by the economist, while the other component $\varepsilon(i, t)$ is a function of variables that cannot be observed by the economist. The difference in utilities may thus be written as

$$V(i, t) = \bar{V}(i, t) + \varepsilon(i, t)$$

We record whether or not woman i works at time t by introducing a dummy variable $d(i, t)$ that assumes the value of one when a woman works and is zero otherwise. Thus, $d(i, t) = 1$ if $V(i, t) > 0$, while $d(i, t) = 0$ if $V(i, t) \leq 0$.

To make the model empirically tractable we assume that the difference in utilities $V(i, t)$ can be approximated by

$$(3) \quad V(i, t) = Z(i, t)\beta + \sum_{t' < t} \delta(t, t') \, d(i, t') + \sum_j \lambda(t, t-j) \prod_{\ell=1}^{j} d(i, t-\ell) + \varepsilon(i, t)$$

where $i = 1, \ldots, I$ and $t = 1, \ldots, T$. $E(\varepsilon(i, t)) = 0$, $E(\varepsilon(i, t)\varepsilon(i, t')) = \sigma_{t, t'}$. $E(\varepsilon(i, t)\varepsilon(i', t')) = 0$, $i \neq i'$.

For the moment, we assume that the initial conditions of the process $d(i, 0), \ldots, d(i, -k), \ldots$, are fixed, nonstochastic constants.

"$Z(i, t)$" is a vector of exogenous variables that determine choices in period t. β is a suitably dimensioned vector of coefficients. Included among the components of $Z(i, t)$ are variables such as education, income of the husband, number of children, and the like, as well as expectations about future values of these variables.

The effects of prior work experience on choice in period t are captured by the second and third terms on the right hand side of equation 3. The second term indicates the effect of all prior work experience on choice in period t. The third term indicates the effect on choice in period t of work experience in the most recent continuous spell of work for those who have worked in period $t - 1$. The coefficients associated with these terms are written to allow for depreciation of the effects of previous work experience and to capture the idea that the effect of previous work experience depends on conditions prevailing in the period in which experience occurs as well as on conditions in period t.

Alternative specifications of δ and λ generate different models. For example, setting $\delta(t, t') = \delta$ and $\lambda(t, t-j) = 0$ generates a stochastic process for which the entire work history is relevant for determining choices in period t. Such a model is consistent with (but not necessarily limited to) models of general human capital. Setting $\delta(t, t') = \delta(t - t')$ for $t - t' \leq K$, $\delta(t, t') = 0$ otherwise, generates a Kth-order Markov process. A first-order Markov process is consistent with a model of fixed costs of labor force entry. Once an individual is working she need not pay further fixed costs to continue working. Setting $\delta(t, t') = 0$ for all t', and letting $\lambda(t, t-j)$ be free, generates a renewal process which describes spell-specific human capital accumulation. (See Jovanovic 1978.) For a more complete discussion of alternative specifications of this model see Heckman (1981a).

Heterogeneity arises in this model from $\varepsilon(i, t)$, an unmeasured disturbance due to essential uncertainty (as perceived by the consumer) as well as to factors unknown to the observing economist but known to the consumer. The assumption that disturbances across individuals are uncorrelated is an implication of the random sampling scheme used to generate the data analyzed below.[11]

It is plausible that $\sigma_{tt'} \neq 0$ for $t \neq t'$, i.e., that unmeasured variables like ability are correlated over time for a consumer. Even if the only source of randomness in the model arose from variables that operate on the consumer at a point in time, and are themselves uncorrelated over time, the disturbances are serially correlated. This is so because the difference in utilities in periods t and t' depend on some of the same set of unmeasured expected future variables that determine remaining *lifetime* utility. The empirical work presented below suggests that the unobservables obey a first-order stationary autoregression (i.e., first-order Markov process).

The model of equation 3 can be used to characterize all of the urn models previously considered. The first urn scheme, in which all women face identical urns, and successive drawings are independent, is given by a specialization of equation 3 in which $Z(i, t) = 1$, $\sigma = \lambda = 0$, and $\varepsilon(i, t)$ is distributed independently of all other disturbances. Under these assumptions the probability that $V(i, t)$ is positive is the same for all women at all times, and is independent of any past events.

McFadden's (1976) random utility model corresponds to a special case of equation 3 in which $Z(i, t)$ is not restricted, $\delta = \lambda = 0$, and $\varepsilon(i, t)$ is a mean zero random variable which is distributed independently of other disturbances.

An urn scheme in which a woman's work status is perfectly correlated over time is a special case of equation 3 in which $Z(i, t) = 1$, $\delta = \lambda = 0$, and $\varepsilon(i, t)$ is perfectly correlated over time.[12]

The second urn scheme in which each woman in a population makes independent drawings from her own (distinctive) urn is a special case of equation 3 in which $Z(i, t) = Z(i)$ (regressors are constant over time for a given person but may vary among people), $\delta = \lambda = 0$, and $\varepsilon(i, t)$ has a components of variance structure, i.e., $\varepsilon(i, t) = \phi(i) + U(i, t)$, where $\phi(i)$ and $U(i, t)$ are realizations of mean zero random variables, $\phi(i)$ is a person effect that does not change over the life cycle, and $U(i, t)$ is an independently identically distributed random variable with zero mean. In this model, the term $Z(i)\beta + \phi(i)$ corresponds to the idiosyncratic person-specific loading of balls in the second urn scheme. For each woman, successive draws are independent, but women differ in the composition of red and black balls in their urns. In essential detail this model is that of Heckman and Willis (1977).

The third urn scheme, in which all women start life alike but receive a red ball each time they work, corresponds to a special case of equation 3 in which $Z(i, t) = 1$, $\delta(t, t') = \delta > 0$, $\lambda = 0$, and $\varepsilon(i, t)$ is an independently identically distributed random variable with zero mean.[13] Setting $\delta(t, t') = 0$, but letting λ be nonzero, generates a renewal process version of the third urn scheme.

The fourth urn scheme corresponds to a special case of equation 3 in which $Z(i, t) = 1$, $\delta = \lambda = 0$, and $\varepsilon(i, t)$ is a mean zero random variable following a first-order Markov process, i.e., $\varepsilon(i, t) = \rho \varepsilon(i, t-1) + U(i, t)$, where $U(i, t)$ is independently identically distributed with mean zero.

The general model that is estimated below contains all of these schemes as a special case of a more general model in which the exogenous variables $Z(i, t)$ are permitted to change over time, δ and λ are permitted to be nonzero, and $\varepsilon(i, t)$ is permitted to have a very general serial correlation pattern.

3.2.1 The Econometric Specification

The model of equation 3 is estimated by the method of maximum likelihood. The disturbance terms are assumed to be jointly normally distributed so that the statistical model is a "multivariate probit model with structural shift." A formal analysis of this model is presented elsewhere (Heckman, 1978a, 1981a b).[14] In estimating the model, special care is taken to avoid bias that arises from the correlation of $\varepsilon(i, t)$ with previous work experience $d(i, t')$, $t > t'$. Such bias would arise in estimating the coefficients of the model if values of $\varepsilon(i, t)$ are serially correlated, which is the plausible case. In the presence of serial correlation, the work experience variables are correlated with the disturbance term for period t since prior work experience is determined by prior values of the disturbances, and prior disturbances are correlated with the disturbance in period t.

The statistical model used here avoids large-sample bias in estimating the structural coefficients by correcting the distribution of $\varepsilon(i, t)$ for the effect of previous work experience using the model of equation 3 to form the correct conditional distribution. The distribution of $\varepsilon(i, t)$ conditional on previous work experience may be written as

$$(4) \qquad g[\varepsilon(i, t) \mid d(i, t-1), d(i, t-2), \ldots]$$

For details on constructing this distribution see Heckman (1978a, 1981a) or appendix B. The probability that $d(i, t)$ is unity (i.e., that woman i works in period t) is the probability that $V(i, t)$ is positive. This probability is computed with respect to the appropriate *conditional* distribution of $\varepsilon(i, t)$. Defining $P(i, t)$ as the probability of participation in period t by woman i conditional on previous work experience,

$$P(i, t) = \Pr[V(i, t) > 0 \mid d(i, t-1), d(i, t-2), \ldots]$$
$$= \Pr[\varepsilon(i, t) > -Z(i, t)\beta - \sum_{t' < t} \delta(t, t') d(i, t') - \sum_j \lambda(t, t-j) \prod_{\ell=1}^{j} d(i, t-\ell)]$$

$$= \int_K^\infty g(\varepsilon(i, t) \mid d(i, t-1), \ldots) d\varepsilon(i, t)$$

where
$$K = [-Z(i, t)\beta - \sum_{t'<t} \delta(t, t') d(i, t')$$
$$- \sum_j \lambda(t, t-j) \prod_{\ell=1}^j d(i, t-\ell)].$$

Conditioning the distribution of $\varepsilon(i, t)$ on previous experience using the model of equation 3 to construct the correct conditional distribution avoids large-sample bias in the estimated coefficients.

The same likelihood function for random variables $d(i, t)$, where $t = 1, \ldots, T$, and $i = 1, \ldots, I$, is

$$\pounds = \prod_{i=1}^I \prod_{t=1}^T [P(i, t)]^{d(i, t)} [1 - P(i, t)]^{1 - d(i, t)}$$

This function is maximized with respect to the parameters of the model. The properties of the maximum likelihood estimators are discussed in Heckman (1978a). Under standard conditions, they possess desirable large-sample properties.

The information that woman i works in period t reveals that $V(i, t) > 0$. The inequality is not reversed if both sides are divided by the standard deviation of the unobservables $\sigma_{tt}^{1/2}$. This implies that from sample information about a sequence of work patterns it is possible to estimate the coefficients β, $\delta(t, t')$, and $\lambda(t, t-j)$ in equation 3 only up to a factor of proportionality. However, if there are regressors in equation 3, and β is invariant across periods, it is possible to estimate the ratios $\sigma_{tt}/\sigma_{t't'}$ among variances (Heckman, 1981a). Normalizing σ_{11} to unity, it is possible to estimate $\sigma_{22}, \ldots, \sigma_{TT}$.

If the latent variables $\varepsilon(i, t)$ are covariance stationary (Koopmans 1974), $\sigma_{tt'} = \sigma_{t+k}\sigma_{t'+k}$ for all t, t', and k. Since it is possible to estimate $\sigma_{tt}/\sigma_{t't'}$, it is possible to test for stationarity in the disturbances of equation 3. This test is performed below.

To facilitate computations, it is assumed that the disturbances in equation 3 can be one-factor analyzed. This means that it is possible to represent the correlation matrix in the following fashion. Define the correlation coefficient between disturbance $\varepsilon(i, t)$ and disturbance $\varepsilon(i, t')$ as $r_{tt'}$. If the disturbances can be one-factor analyzed

$$r_{tt'} = \alpha_t \alpha_{t'} \text{ for } t \neq t', t' \text{ and } t = 1, \ldots, T$$

Since the number T of panel observations per person is three in the empirical analysis of this paper, this restriction is not serious.[15]

Because of computational considerations the number of panel observations per person is small. Thus it is impossible to estimate all of the models of structural state dependence that could be generated by equation 3. Instead, in the empirical work reported below attention is confined to a model with $\delta(t, t') = \delta$ and $\lambda(t, t-j) = 0$. This specification assumes that prior work experience has the same impact on labor force decisions in period t independent of the time period in which it occurred. In fact, this rigid specification is relaxed to a certain degree in the empirical work.

Two types of prior work experience are considered: presample experience and within-sample experience. It is likely that presample experience exerts a weaker measured effect on current participation decisions than more recent experience because of depreciation and also because the data on presample experience, which are based on a retrospective question, are likely to be measured with error.

Moreover, the data source utilized in the empirical analysis is not sufficiently rich to correctly adjust conditional distribution 4 using the model of equation 3. As demonstrated in appendix B and Heckman (1981b), appropriate conditioning requires, in general, the entire life cycle history of individuals including presample values of exogenous variables. Elsewhere (Heckman 1981b) exact and approximate solutions to this problem of correctly initializing the process are proposed. One estimator, which is shown to work well especially for testing the null hypothesis of no structural state dependence, predicts presample experience by a set of regressors and utilizes the predicted value as another element of $Z(i, t)$. This estimator is utilized to generate the empirical estimates reported in this paper. Within-sample work experience is treated in the manner described in the preceding paragraphs. Thus, conditional distribution 4 is constructed using actual within-sample realizations of prior work experience, and predicted values of presample work experience.

3.3 Empirical Results

This section presents evidence from an empirical analysis of the dynamics of married female labor supply. Empirical results are presented for two groups of white women: women of age 30–44 in 1968 and women of age 45–59 in 1968. Both groups of women were continuously married to the same spouse in seven years of panel data drawn from the probability sample of the Michigan Panel Survey of Income Dynamics.[16] For the sake of brevity, we focus on the results for older women and the contrasts in the empirical findings between the two age groups. Our discussion focuses on the central empirical issue of distinguishing heterogeneity and structural state dependence.

The major finding reported here is that for older women there is some evidence of structural state dependence in individual probabilities. For younger women, there is much less evidence of structural state dependence. The results reported here question the validity of the simple "permanent-transistory" or "convolution" scheme commonly used to characterize heterogeneity in much applied work in social science. A first-order Markov process for the disturbances describes the data better. Tests for nonstationarity in the unobservables reject that hypothesis.

A mostly conventional set of variables is used to explain employment. These are (1) the woman's education; (2) family income excluding the wife's earnings; (3) number of children younger than six; (4) number of children at home; (5) presample work experience; (6) within-sample work experience; (7) unemployment rate in the county in which the woman resides; (8) the wage of unskilled labor in the county—a measure of the availability of substitutes for the woman's time in the home; and (9) the national unemployment rate for prime-age males—a measure of aggregate labor market tightness. Mean values for each of these variables in both samples are presented in table 3.A.2 in appendix C. A woman is defined to be a market participant if she worked for money any time in the sample year. This definition departs from the standard census definition in two respects. First, participation is defined as work, and excludes unemployment. The second way in which the definition used here departs from the standard one is that the time unit of definition of the event is the year and not the usual census week. For both reasons, our results are not directly comparable with previous cross-section empirical work by Cain (1966) and Mincer (1962). Our definitions are comparable with those of Heckman and Willis (1977).

A noteworthy feature of the data is that roughly 80 percent of the women in the sample of older women either work all of the time or do not work at all. (See table 3.1A) The corresponding figure for younger women is 75 percent. (See table 3.1B) Both samples are roughly evenly divided between full-time workers and full-time nonworkers. There is little evidence of frequent turnover in these data, nor is there much evidence of turnover in the full seven years of data.[17]

We first present results for the older group of women. Then results for the younger women are briefly discussed.

Coefficient estimates of equation 3 for women aged 45–59 for the most general model estimated in this paper are presented in column 1 of table 3.2. A positive value for a coefficient means that an increase in the associated variable increases the probability that a woman works, while a negative value for a coefficient means that an increase in the associated variable decreases the probability. Inspection of the coefficients arrayed in column 1 reveals that more children and a higher family income (excluding wife's earnings) depress the probability of female employment.

Higher rates of unemployment (both local and national) tend to depress the probability of female participation.[18] This finding suggests that the net impact of labor market unemployment is to discourage female

Table 3.1 Runs Patterns in the Data (1 corresponds to work in the year, 0 corresponds to no work)

Runs Pattern (1968, 1969, 1970)			No. of Observations	Runs Pattern (1971, 1972, 1973)			No. of Observations
A. Women Aged 45–59 in 1968							
0	0	0	87	0	0	0	96
0	0	1	5	0	0	1	5
0	1	0	5	0	1	0	4
1	0	0	4	1	0	0	8
1	1	0	8	1	1	0	5
0	1	1	10	0	1	1	2
1	0	1	1	1	0	1	2
1	1	1	78	1	1	1	76
B. Women Aged 30–44 in 1968							
0	0	0	126	0	0	0	133
0	0	1	16	0	0	1	13
0	1	0	4	0	1	0	5
1	0	0	12	1	0	0	16
1	1	0	24	1	1	0	8
0	1	1	20	0	1	1	19
1	0	1	5	1	0	1	8
1	1	1	125	1	1	1	130

employment. The estimated effect of the wage of unskilled labor in the county on participation is statistically insignificant.

The estimated values of the ratios of the second and third-period variances in the disturbances to the first-period disturbance variance (i.e., σ_{22} and σ_{33} respectively) are close to one. Utilizing conventional test criteria, one cannot reject the hypothesis that both of these estimated coefficients equal one. Thus the variance in the unobservables is the same in each period. When the model is recomputed constraining σ_{22} and σ_{33} to unity (see the results reported in column 2), the decrease in log likelihood for the model is trivial (.82), and well below the variation that would arise solely from chance fluctuations. The remaining coefficients in the model are unaffected by the imposition of this restriction, lending further support to the assumption of constant variances.

Coefficients α_1, α_2 and α_3 are normalized factor-loading coefficients which, when multiplied, yield estimates of the correlation coefficients among the unobservable variables $\varepsilon(i, t)$. Utilizing the estimates reported in column 1 of table 3.2, the estimated correlation between disturbances in year 1 and year 2 is $(.922) \times (.992) = .915$ while the estimated correlation between disturbances in year 2 and year 3 is $(.992) \times (.926) = .918$. The estimated two-year correlation is $(.922) \times (.926) = .854$. Note that the product of the estimated one-year correlation coefficients (.840) is very close to the estimated two-year correlation

Table 3.2 Estimates of the Model for Women Aged 45–59 in 1968 (asymptotic normal test statistics in parentheses; these statistics are obtained from the estimated information matrix)

Variable	(1)	(2)	(3)	(4)	(5)
Intercept	−2.498(4.1)	−2.576(4.6)	−1.653(2.5)	−2.325(5.1)	−2.367(6.4)
No. of Children aged less than 6	−.803(2.8)	−.816(2.7)	−.840(2.3)	−.741(2.6)	−.742(2.6)
County unemployment rate (%)	−.039(1.4)	−.035(1.5)	−.027(1.0)	−.030(1.4)	−.030(1.5)
County wage rate ($/hr.)	.106(.96)	.104(.91)	.104(.91)	.100(.93)	.099(.93)
Total no. of children	−.141(3.2)	−.146(4.3)	−.117(2.2)	−.127(3.5)	−.124(4.9)
Wife's education (yrs.)	.157(5.0)	.162(6.5)	.105(2.8)	.145(5.3)	.152(7.3)
Family income excluding wife's earnings	−.36 × 10^{-4}(4.1)	−.363 × 10^{-4}(4.8)	−.267 × 10^{-4}(2.7)	−.32 × 10^{-4}(4.3)	−.312 × 10^{-4}(5.2)
National unemployment rate	−.098(.5)	−.106(.51)	−.254(1.4)	−.035(.34)	−.003(.38)
Current experience (δ)	.136(.97)	.143(.95)	.273(1.5)	—	—
Predicated presample experience	.069(4.0)	.072(5.8)	.059(3.4)	.062(4.3)	.062(6.2)
α_1	.922(33)	.921(3.)	—	.922(35)	.920(35)
α_2	.922(124)	.991(116)	—	.996(164)	.997(196)
α_3	.926(19)	.919(14)	—	.948(41)	.949(42)
σ_{22}	.935(4.8)	1	1	.895(4.4)	1
σ_{33}	1.114(4.5)	1	1	1.079(4.7)	1
ρ	—	—	.873(14.0)	—	—
η	—	—	—	—	—
ln likelihood	−236.92	−237.74	−240.32	−238.401	−239.81

Table 3.2 (continued)

Variable	(6)	(7)	(8)	(9)	(10)
Intercept	−2.011(3.4)	−1.5(0)	−2.37(5.5)	.227(.4)	−3.53(4.6)
No. of children aged less than 6	−.793(2.1)	−.69(1.2)	−.70(2.0)	−.814(2.1)	−1.42(2.3)
County unemployment rate (%)	−.027(1.2)	.046(11)	−.03(1.6)	−.018(.57)	−.059(1.3)
County wage rate ($/hr.)	.139(1.5)	.105(.68)	.13(1.4)	.004(.02)	.27(1.1)
Total no. of children	−.116(2.2)	−.160(6.1)	−.161(4.9)	−.090(2.4)	−.203(3.9)
Wife's education (yrs.)	.095(2.5)	.105(3.3)	.077(3)	.104(3.7)	.196(4.8)
Family income excluding wife's earnings	−.207×10⁻⁴(2.3)	−.385×10⁻⁴(20)	−.2×10⁻⁴(2.6)	−.32×10⁻⁴(3.6)	−.65×10⁻⁴(5.1)
National unemployment rate	−.021(.26)	−.71(0)	.02(.3)	−1.30(6)	1.03(.14)
Current experience (δ)	—	—	—	1.46(12.2)	—
Predicted presample experience	.062(3.5)	.095(11.0)	.091(7.0)	.045(3.4)	.101(5.4)
α_1	—	—	—	—	—
α_2	—	—	—	—	—
α_3	—	—	—	—	—
σ_{22}	1	1	1	1	1
σ_{33}	1	1	1	1	1
ρ	.942(50)	—	—	—	—
η	—	.941(4.1)	.92(4.5)	—	—
ln likelihood	−243.11	−242.37	−244.7	−263.65	−367.3

(See following page for source notes)

coefficient, a result that strongly suggests that the disturbances obey a first-order stationary Markov process, i.e., that

$$\varepsilon(i, t) = \rho\varepsilon(i, t-1) + U(i, t) \quad i = 1, \ldots, I$$

$$t = t, \ldots, T$$

where $U(i, t)$ is independently identically distributed across people and time.

Column 3 of table 3.2 reports estimates of a model that constrains the disturbances to follow a first-order Markov scheme. The Markov model is a special case of the general model in which $\alpha_1 = \alpha_3$, and $\alpha_2 = 1$. The empirical results appear to support the hypothesis of a Markov error process. Comparing the value of the likelihood function presented in column 2 with the value presented in column 3, one cannot reject the null hypothesis that the Markov model describes the distribution of disturbances. Twice the difference in log likelihood (5.25) is to be compared with a value of the χ^2 statistic with two degrees of freedom, 5.99, for a five percent significance level.[19] Most of the estimated coefficients presented in column 3 are essentially the same as the corresponding coefficients presented in the two preceding columns of the table so the Markov restriction appears to be innocuous. However, the coefficient on presample work experience drops slightly while the coefficient on recent experience almost doubles, and almost becomes statistically significant using conventional test statistics.

For reasons already presented, the measured effect of previous work experience on current employment is broken into two components: (a) the effect of work experience acquired prior to the first year of the sample (1968), and (b) the effect of more recent experience measured in the sample. The coefficient of recent experience is roughly twice the size of the coefficient on presample experience. Both coefficients are positive, as expected, but only the coefficient on predicted presample experience is statistically significant using conventional asymptotic "t" test statistics.

Table 3.2 Source Notes
Source: First three years of the Michigan Panel Survey of Income Dynamics, 1968, 1969, 1970.
Note: Increase in variables with positive coefficients increase the probability of employment, while increases in variables with negative coefficients decrease the probability of employment.
Presample experience is predicted from all of the other regressors in $Z(i,t)$, a set of dummy variables for education, city size variables, regional variables and family background variables (mother's and father's education). Note that utilizing predicted experience in place of actual experience in the probit model assumes that the errors from prediction are approximately normally distributed. Even if this is not a correct assumption, this procedure permits a valid statistical test of the important null hypothesis that past labor force experience has no effect on current experience. The standard errors of the estimated coefficients must be interpreted as *conditional* on the predicted values of presample experience variables.

Testing the null hypothesis that work experience does not affect the probability of employment is a central issue in this paper. It is important to proceed cautiously before any final conclusions are reached on this matter.

Testing this hypothesis raises a technical issue that cannot be evaded. There are a variety of asymptotically equivalent test statistics available to test the same hypothesis (Rao 1973). These alternative test statistics lead to the same inference in large samples but may lead to conflicting inferences in small samples. In the model considered in this paper, there is no theoretical basis for preferring one statistic over another. A recent Monte Carlo study of a nonlinear model somewhat similar (in its degree of nonlinearity) to the one estimated in this paper that compares the asymptotic "t" statistics of the sort presented in table 3.2 with the likelihood ratio statistics obtained from likelihood functions evaluated at restricted and unrestricted values concludes with the advice, "use the likelihood ratio test when the hypothesis is an important aspect of the study" (Gallant 1975).

Following this advice, the statistical models displayed in columns 1, 2, and 3 are reestimated deleting the recent work experience variable from each model. The empirical results from this procedure are reported in columns 4, 5, and 6 which correspond, respectively, to the models associated with the estimates reported in columns 1, 2, and 3.

At a ten percent significance level, one would reject the hypothesis that within-sample work experience does not affect the probability of employment in each of the models. Maintaining the assumption of stationarity in the unobserved variables (see columns 5 and 6) leads to rejection of the hypothesis at five percent significance levels. From these tests we provisionally conclude that recent work experience determines the probability of employment. However, it must be acknowledged that with these data, if the stationarity assumption is not maintained this inference is not strong.

We tentatively conclude that the most appropriate model is one with both recent and presample work experience as determinants of employment and with the disturbances in the equations generated by a stationary first-order Markov process. In order to place these empirical results in perspective, it is useful to compare the model just selected with a recent model presented by Heckman and Willis (1977). Their model is a special case of the general model of equation 3 in which (a) the impact of past participation on the current probability of participation is ignored; (b) the disturbances obey a "permanent-transistory" model so that

$$\varepsilon(i, t) = \phi(i) + U(i, t)$$

where $U(i, t)$ is independently identically distributed, and $\phi(i)$ is a person effect that is not assumed to change over the course of the sample;[20] and

(c) no variation is permitted in the regressors $Z(i, t)$ for an individual during the same period, although differences among individuals are permitted.[21]

Empirical estimates of their model are presented in column 7, table 3.2. Strictly speaking, the model displayed there is "too generous" to Heckman and Willis because it includes predicted presample experience in the model, deleting the effect of *recent* experience on participation. The only innovation in notation is the symbol "η" defined as the ratio of the variance in $\phi(i)$ to the variance in $\varepsilon(i, t)$. This parameter is important in the Heckman-Willis analysis because as they show in their appendix, a value of η in excess of ½ implies that the distribution of participation probabilities among a group of women with identical observed characteristics is U-shaped with most of the mass of the distribution concentrated near zero or one (i.e., most women work nearly all of the time or not at all). Since η is estimated to be .94, the implied distribution of probabilities is strongly U-shaped.

A direct comparison between the new model with estimated coefficients reported in column 3 and the Heckman-Willis model is not possible using conventional testing criteria since neither model nests the other as a special case. However, as previously noted, examination of the empirical results for the general models of columns 1 or 4 suggests that the correlation pattern for the unobservables favors the first-order Markov structure and not the "permanent-transistory" structure which imposes the restriction of equicorrelation among disturbances ($\alpha_1 = \alpha_2 = \alpha_3$). Moreover, as previously noted, there is evidence that recent work experience determines employment.

One way to compare the two models is to examine their predictive power on fresh data. Table 3.3 displays the results of such a comparison. In column 1, the actual numbers in each pattern of labor force activity are recorded. In the remaining columns, the numbers predicted from the model described at the top of the column are recorded. In particular, the predicted numbers from the new model are recorded in column 2 while predicted numbers from the Heckman-Willis model are recorded in column 3. The bottom row of the table records the χ^2 goodness of fit test. A lower value of the χ^2 statistic implies a better fit for a model.

A major difference in predictive power between the two models comes in the interior cells of the table that register labor market turnover. The model developed in this paper is more accurate in predicting labor force turnover than is the Heckman-Willis model, especially for the turnover pattern of women who work most of the time.

Given that Heckman and Willis ignore the impact of past participation on current participation, and hence relegate this effect to the disturbance term in their model, it is plausible that their disturbance terms exhibit a greater degree of intertemporal correlation than is present in the model

Table 3.3 Comparisons of Models Using Runs Data—Women Aged 45–59 in 1968 (Data for 1971, 1972, 1973, Three years following the sample data used to estimate the model)

Runs Pattern[a]	(1) Actual Number	(2) Number Predicted from the New Model (Column 3, Table 3.2)	(3) Number Predicted from Heckman-Willis Model (Column 7, Table 3.2)	(4) Probit Model That Ignores Heterogeneity (Column 9, Table 3.2)	(5) Probit Model That Ignores Heterogeneity and Recent Sample State Dependence (Column 10, Table 3.2)
0, 0, 0	96	94.2	139.5	145.3	36.1
0, 0, 1	5	17.6	4.1	38.5	20.5
0, 1, 0	4	1.8	4.1	1.9	20.2
1, 0, 0	8	2.6	4.1	.35	20.6
1, 1, 0	5	1.4	3.6	.02	21.2
1, 0, 1	2	2.4	3.6	1.38	21.1
0, 1, 1	2	16.4	3.6	8.51	21.7
1, 1, 1	76	61.5	34.9	2.05	36.6
χ^2[b]	...	48.5	66.3	4,419	221.8

[a] "0" corresponds to not working, "1" corresponds to working. Thus "1, 1, 0" corresponds to a woman who worked the first two years of the sample and did not work in the final year.
[b] This is the standard chi-square statistic for goodness of fit. The higher the value of the statistic, the worse the fit.

estimated in this paper. Moreover, their analysis overstates the amount of heterogeneity in probabilities at a point in time, and ignores the life cycle evolution of the distribution of employment probabilities that arises from the impact of past employment on current employment. Their estimate of heterogeneity, and the U shape in the distribution of employment probabilities, overstate the extent of heterogeneity, especially at the youngest ages, and overstate the degree of intertemporal correlation in error terms, and the persistence over time in the correlation of unobservables. The evolutionary view of the participation process offered in this paper is considerably more dynamic than the view offered by Heckman and Willis.

It is of some interest to estimate the Heckman-Willis model relaxing their assumption that the regressors do not change over the sample period while retaining their other assumptions. Estimates of this model are presented in column 8 of table 3.2.

This model is a special case of the model estimated in column 2 in which the α_j are restricted to equality and current experience is deleted from the model. The model under consideration thus imposes three restrictions on the parameters ($\alpha_1 = \alpha_2 = \alpha_3$, and $\delta = 0$). Twice the difference in log likelihood between the two models is 14 which is to be compared with a χ^2 statistic of 7.8 with three degrees of freedom using a five percent significance level. Accordingly, one would reject the null hypothesis that the model with estimates reported in column 8 explains the data better than the model of column 2.[22]

These tests suggest that the principal defect in the Heckman and Willis scheme is not the assumption that the regressors are fixed over the sample period. The real problem comes in the permanent-transitory error structure for unobservables, and the neglect of "true" state dependence.

In order to illustrate the importance of treating heterogeneity correctly in estimating dynamic models, we consider models that are estimated ignoring heterogeneity. The model presented in column 9 of table 3.2 is the model of column 1 in which no heterogeneity is permitted ($\alpha_1 = \alpha_2 = \alpha_3 = 0$) so that the unobservables in different periods are assumed to be uncorrelated. A likelihood ratio test clearly rejects the hypothesis of no heterogeneity. The effect of recent market experience on employment is dramatically overstated in a model that neglects heterogeneity. Compare the estimated effect of recent market experience on current employment status that is recorded in column 9 (1.46) with the estimated effect reported in column 1 (.136). Ignoring heterogeneity in estimating this effect would lead to an overstatement of the impact of past work experience on current employment by a factor of ten! Too much credit would be attributed to past experience as a determinant of employment if intertemporal correlation in the unobservables is ignored. Moreover, a comparison of estimated effects of national unemployment on employment suggests that the model that ignores heterogeneity dramatically overstates the impact of this variable on employment. The effect of children on employment is *understated* in a model that ignores heterogeneity.

Another way to gauge the importance of heterogeneity in the unobservable variables is to consider how well a model that utilizes past work experience as a regressor but ignores unmeasured heterogeneity predicts sample runs patterns. It is plausible to conjecture that "lagged employment" might serve as a good "proxy" for the effect of heterogeneity. To explore this conjecture, consider the numbers displayed in column 4 of table 3.3.

As is familiar from a reading of the literature on the "mover-stayer" problem, a model that ignores unmeasured heterogeneity underpredicts the number of individuals who either work all of the time or do not work at all. A dynamic model estimated without controlling for heterogeneity will overstate the estimated frequency of turnover in the labor force. In table 3.3 the overstatement is dramatic. The overall "goodness of fit" statistic is decidedly inferior to the goodness of fit statistics for the preceding models. A simple lagged work status "proxy" for heterogeneity does not adequately substitute for a more careful treatment of heterogeneity.

Next, consider a model that ignores both heterogeneity and the effect of *recent* employment on current employment. Estimates of such a model are presented in column 10 of table 3.2. A likelihood ratio test strongly rejects this specification of the general model. The simulations reported in column 5 of table 3.3 suggest that introducing "lagged employment status" into the model as a substitute for a more careful treatment of heterogeneity is an imperfect procedure and is worse than using no proxy at all. Moreover, a model that does not allow for heterogeneity or state dependence dramatically overestimates the extent of labor market turnover.

The two models just discussed have one feature in common: they can be estimated from a single cross section of data.[23] Accordingly, comparisons between the performance of models that ignore heterogeneity, and models that account for heterogeneity, reveal the potential value of panel data for estimating models that can accurately forecast labor market dynamics. Labor supply functions fit on cross-section data overstate the true extent of turnover in the labor force. Ad hoc "proxies" for heterogeneity generate models that yield misleading forecasts of the true microdynamics of the labor market.

We now turn to the empirical results for younger women. Table 3.4 is identical in format to table 3.2. No estimates are given for the models of columns 1, 4, and 5 of the table. The reason for this is that estimated values of α_2 strongly tend to unity leading to numerical instability in

Table 3.4 Estimates of the Model for Women Aged 30–44 in 1968 (asymptotic normal statistics in parentheses)

	(1)	(2)	(3)	(4)	(5)
Intercept	—	.257(.66)	−.15(.27)	—	—
Number of children younger than 6	—	.293(2.7)	−.31(3.1)	—	—
County unemployment rate (%)	—	$-1.21 \times 10^{-3}(.06)$	$-1.03 \times 10^{-3}(.05)$	—	—
County wage rate ($/hr)	—	−.074(.8)	−.080(.71)	—	—
Number of children	—	$9.1 \times 10^{-3}(.2)$	−.0125(.3)	—	—
Wife's education (yrs)	—	.0324(1.9)	.056(1.9)	—	—
Family income excluding wife's earnings	—	$-1.62 \times 10^{-5}(2.1)$	$-1.50 \times 10^{-5}(2.3)$	—	—
National unemployment rate	—	−.378(3)	−.139(1.1)	—	—
Current experience	—	.366(3.7)	.116(1.0)	—	—
Predicted presample experience	—	.057(2.1)	.0324(1.0)	—	—
α_1	—	.93(23)	—	—	—
α_2	—	.9998(6×10^3)	—	—	—
α_3	—	.926(17.8)	—	—	—
σ_{22}	—	1	—	—	—
σ_{33}	—	1	—	—	—
ρ	—	—	.844(16)	—	—
η	—	—	—	—	—
ln likelihood	—	−479.5	−481.1	—	—

Table 3.4 (continued)

	(6)	(7)	(8)	(9)	(10)
Intercept	$-.387(.7)$	$-.91(0)$	$-.397(.77)$	$1.4(2.9)$	$.0379(.08)$
Number of children younger than 6	$-.277(3.0)$	$-.28(2.1)$	$-.270(3.2)$	$-.34(3.3)$	$-.37(3.9)$
County unemployment rate (%)	$-3.5 \times 10^{-3}(.19)$	$-4.4 \times 10^{-3}(.15)$	$-9.58 \times 10^{-4}(.05)$	$.0107(.45)$	$-4.51 \times 10^{-3}(.2)$
County wage rate ($/hr)	$-7.89 \times 10^{-2}(.76)$	$-.21(1.9)$	$-.089(.84)$	$-.265(2.4)$	$-.336(3.3)$
Number of children	$-8.32 \times 10^{-3}(.19)$	$.01(6.1)$	$-9.077 \times 10^{-3}(.22)$	$3.8 \times 10^{-3}(.12)$	$2.2 \times 10^{-3}(.07)$
Wife's education (yrs)	$.055(1.8)$	$.08(3.0)$	$.052(1.8)$	$.065(2.8)$	$.075(3.6)$
Family income excluding wife's earnings	$-1.21 \times 10^{-5}(2.0)$	$-2.3 \times 10^{-5}(2.4)$	$-1.159 \times 10^{-5}(2.0)$	$-2.3 \times 10^{-5}(3.6)$	$-2.76 \times 10^{-5}(4.)$
National unemployment rate	$-.048(.74)$	$-.041(.69)$	$-.045(.7)$	$-1.06(7.2)$	$5.8 \times 10^{-3}(.05)$
Current experience	—	—	—	$1.14(14)$	—
Predicted presample experience	$.042(1.2)$	$.052(1.7)$	$.044(1.4)$	$.02(.69)$	$.038(1.7)$
α_1	—	—	—	—	—
α_2	—	—	—	—	—
α_3	—	—	—	—	—
σ_{22}	—	—	—	—	—
σ_{33}	—	—	—	—	—
ρ	$.886(39)$	$.86$	—	—	—
η	—	—	$.846$	—	—
ln likelihood	-482.05	-489.8	-491.92	-520.4	-652.5

(See following page for source notes)

evaluating the sample likelihood function. At $\alpha_2 = 1$, the likelihood function assumes a limiting functional form that is mathematically different from the model with $\alpha_2 \neq 1$. Because of the instability, the estimates recorded in column 2 of table 3.4 are somewhat suspect.

Since the estimated values of α_1 and α_3 are virtually identical, and since the estimated value of α_2 tends to unity, the data appear to be consistent with a first-order Markov scheme for the unobservables. This result is in accord with the analysis for older women. When the first-order Markov scheme is imposed (see column 3 of table 3.4) the decrease in log likelihood is negligible and well within sampling variation. Moreover, since the computational procedure is much more stable when the first-order Markov restriction for unobservables is imposed, the estimates (and test statistics) reported in column 3 are to be preferred to the estimates reported in column 2.

The major difference in the results for younger women as compared with the results for older women comes in the importance of recent experience for current employment decisions. The "t" statistic on recent experience is 1.0, and would lead to acceptance of the null hypothesis that recent experience is not a determinant of current employment. Anticipating a potential conflict between the statistical inference based on this statistic and the likelihood ratio test, along the lines previously discussed, the model is reestimated deleting current experience (results are reported in column 6). The change in log likelihood is trivial. This suggests that recent work experience does not determine current employment. These tests lead to adoption of the model with estimates reported in column 6 of table 3.4 as the appropriate model for younger married women, i.e., a model without any effect of recent experience on current participation decisions.

Columns 7 through 10 of table 3.4 record estimates of models directly comparable to the models with the corresponding headings in table 3.2. Estimates of the Heckman-Willis analogue are reported in column 7.

Table 3.4 Source Notes
Note: Increases in variables with positive coefficients increase the probability of employment, while increases in variables with negative coefficients decrease the probability of employment.
Presample experience is predicted from all of the other regressors in $Z(i, t)$, a set of dummy variables for education, city size variables, regional variables, and family background variables (mother's and father's education). Note that utilizing predicted experience in place of actual experience in the probit model assumes that the errors from prediction are approximately normally distributed. Even if this is not a correct assumption, this procedure permits a valid statistical test of the important null hypothesis that past labor force experience has no effect on current experience. The standard errors of the estimated coefficients must be interpreted as *conditional* on the predicted values of presample experience variables.

Estimates of the model that retains the permanent-transitory structure, and ignores the impact of recent participation on current choices, but permits the regressors to change over the sample period, are reported in column 8. That model is clearly rejected by the data.

Columns 9 and 10 of table 3.4 report estimates of models that ignore heterogeneity. As in the case of older women, neglect of heterogeneity leads to a systematic overstatement of the effect of recent experience on employment choices. (See the estimate reported in column 9 and compare with the estimates reported in columns 2 and 3.) Assuming that the model of column 6 is the correct model, the misspecified model of column 9 dramatically overstates (in absolute value) the negative effect of aggregate unemployment on employment, leads to an overstatement of the effect of income on employment (again, in absolute value), and overstates the effect of education on employment. Similar remarks apply to the empirical results reported in column 10. Tests of the predictive power of the alternative models are similar to the tests reported for older women and so are not discussed here. (They are available on request from the author.)

The main conclusions of the empirical analysis are as follows. (1) For older women, there is evidence that recent labor market experience is a determinant of current employment decisions. There is no such evidence for younger women. (2) There is considerable evidence that the unobservables determining employment choices follow a first-order Markov process. The estimated correlation coefficients for both age groups are comfortably close. (3) Dynamic models that neglect heterogeneity overestimate labor market turnover. "Proxy methods" for solving the problems raised by heterogeneity such as ad hoc introduction of lagged work experience variables lead to dynamic models that yield exceedingly poor forecast equations for labor force turnover. Models that neglect recent market experience and heterogeneity actually perform better in forecasting turnover on fresh data, but these forecasts are still poor, and considerably overestimate the amount of turnover in the labor market. (4) Models that neglect heterogeneity lead to biased estimates of the effect of all variables on labor force participation probabilities in models that include past employment as a determinant of current employment.

Since the unobservables that determine employment probabilities follow a first-order Markov process, standard procedures for introducing heterogeneity into dynamic models do not work, and may lead to erroneous estimates of structural parameters, especially in models that explicitly allow for state dependence. A simple "components of variance" scheme gives misleading estimates of structural parameters and generates forecasts of work force turnover that are quite erroneous. While the assumption of the "convolution property" or "components of variance" scheme is mathematically convenient, its application in empirical work may result in a misleading characterization of population heterogeneity. Given that heterogeneity arises, in part, from omitted variables that plausibly change over time, it is reasonable to expect that there is decay in the correlation between unobservable variables that determine choices the more distant in time the choices are.

3.3.1 Qualifications and Suggested Extensions of the Empirical Analysis

As is always the case in empirical work, there is considerable room for improvement in the data and in the approach taken to analyze the data. In this paper six improvements seem especially warranted.

First, the rigid separation of presample from within-sample work experience is a crude way to allow for depreciation in the effect of past work experience on current labor supply. A more appropriate procedure would use the general models of equation 3 and Heckman (1981a) on longer panels of data to estimate less ad hoc depreciation schemes.

Second, the procedure used to "solve" the initial conditions problem in this paper is exact only for the construction of test statistics for the null hypothesis of no structural state dependence, although Monte Carlo work presented elsewhere (Heckman 1981b) suggests that the procedure performs reasonably well in generating estimates. The exact solution proposed in Heckman (1981b) remains to be empirically implemented.

Third, more explicit economic models should be estimated. The procedures proposed here are useful exploratory tools but are no substitute for an explicit dynamic economic model.

Fourth, a normality assumption has been employed in the empirical work although it is not essential to the approach. The one-factor model is an especially flexible format within which to relax this assumption. It would be of great interest to examine the sensitivity of the estimates and the accuracy of model forecasts under alternative distributional assumptions. Especially interesting would be an examination of distributions that allow for more general forms of nonstationarity in the unobservables than are permitted in the multivariate normal.

Fifth, the entire empirical analysis has been conducted in discrete time yet employment decisions are more suitably modeled in continuous time. The empirical treatment of the time unit is largely a consequence of the availability of the data. Approximating a continuous time model by a discrete time model results in a well-known time aggregation bias (see Bergstrom 1976). For one continuous time model of heterogeneity and state dependence, see Heckman and Borjas (1980).

Sixth, unemployment has been treated as a form of "leisure" or nonmarket time. A more general approach consistent with much recent work treats measured unemployment as a separate decision variable. While estimation of the more general model is more costly it is also more informative. Estimates of such a model would enable analysts to determine whether being unemployed is, in fact, a separate activity distinct from being out of the labor force. For one approach, see Flinn and Heckman (1981).

3.4 What Does Structural State Dependence Mean?

Granting the validity of the preceding evidence in support of structural state dependence in the employment decisions of older women, it remains to interpret it. This section presents a brief menu of behavioral models that generate structural state dependence. Before these models are presented, however, it is useful to restate the key statistical assumption used to secure this evidence.

In the discussion surrounding equation 3, a distinction is made between the effects of unmeasured variables—the $\varepsilon(i, t)$—and prior work experience—lagged $d(i, t)$—on choices made in period t. The crucial assumption not subject to test in this paper is that the unmeasured variables cause but are not caused by prior choices. "Cause" is used in the sense of Sims (1977) suitably modified for a discrete data model. That is, the conditional distribution of $\varepsilon(i, t)$ given all lagged values of $\varepsilon(i, t)$ and all lagged values of $d(i, t)$ is the same as the conditional distribution of $\varepsilon(i, t)$ given all lagged values of $\varepsilon(i, t)$.

Structural state dependence is defined to exist if the conditional distribution of $d(i, t)$ given all past values of $\varepsilon(i, t)$ and lagged $d(i, t)$ is a nontrivial function of the latter set of variables. Structural dependence is tested in this paper by a discrete data analogue of time series causality tests. Correctly conditioning the distribution of current $\varepsilon(i, t)$ "controls" for the effect of past $\varepsilon(i, t)$ on current $d(i, t)$.

The validity of the estimates of and tests for structural state dependence presented here depends on the validity of this untested assumption. If, in fact, the unmeasured variables are caused by lagged $d(i, t)$, the statistical procedures discussed in section 3.2 and implemented in section 3.3 are inappropriate. Evidence of serial correlation derived from these procedures may, in fact, be evidence of structural state dependence. Evidence for or against structural state dependence derived from the procedures presented in this paper will necessarily be inconclusive.

In any empirical application of our procedures, the maintained hypothesis will be controversial. In our analysis of the employment decisions of women this is the case. Following the analysis of Ryder, Stafford, and Stephan (1976), women may devote more time to human capital investment in periods in which they work than in other periods if the cost of investing is lower on the job than off. Since investment time is not observed, and is not an exact function of employment status, controlling for prior work experience as we have done only imperfectly accounts for human capital investment. Estimated heterogeneity will arise from human capital investment. The unobservables are "caused" by past employment.[24] However, there is also structural state dependence as we have defined it in this paper.

Granting the validity of the maintained assumption, at least as a first approximation, it is of some interest to consider how well-defined economic models can generate structural state dependence. Apart from the model just discussed, three further examples are presented: a model of stimulus-response conditioning of the sort developed by mathematical psychologists, a model of decision making under uncertainty, and a model of decision making under perfect foresight.

In the stimulus-response model developed by behavioral psychologists (e.g., Bush and Mosteller 1955; Restle and Greeno 1970; Johnson and Kotz 1977), the individual who makes a given "correct" response is rewarded, so that he is more likely to make the response in the future. Decision making is myopic. This model closely resembles the generalized Polya process discussed above. Models that resemble the stimulus-response model have been proposed by dual labor market economists who assume that individuals who are randomly allocated to one market are rewarded for staying in the market and are conditioned by institutions in that market so that their preferences are altered. The more time one has spent in a particular type of market, the more likely one is to stay in it (Cain 1976).

The model of myopic sequential decision making just discussed is unlikely to prove attractive to many economists. Nonmyopic sequential models of decision making under imperfect information also generate structural state dependence. Such models have been extensively developed in the literature on dynamic programing (e.g., Dreyfus 1965, pp. 213–15; Astrom 1970). An example is a model in which an agent at time t maximizes expected utility over the remaining horizon, given all the information at his disposal and given his constraints as of time t. Transition to a state may be uncertain. As a consqeuence of being in a state, costs may be incurred or information may be acquired that alters the information set or opportunity set or both relevant for future decisions. In such cases the outcome of the process affects subsequent decision making, and structural state dependence is generated.

The disturbance in this model consists of unmeasured variables known to the agent but unknown to the observing economist as well as unanticipated random components unknown to both the agent and the observing economist.

Structural state dependence can also be generated as *one representation* of a model of decision making under perfect certainty. In such a model there are no surprises. Given the initial conditions of the process, the full outcome of the process is perfectly predictable from information available to the agent (but not necessarily available to the observing economist).

To illustrate this point in the most elementary way, consider the following three-period model of consumer decision making under perfect certainty with indivisibility in purchase quantities: a consumer's strictly concave utility function is specified as

$$U[a(1)d(1), a(2)d(2), a(3)d(3)]$$

where the $a(i)$ are the fixed amounts that can be consumed in each period. The consumer purchases amount $a(i)$ if $d(i) = 1$, otherwise $a(i) = 0$. Resources M are fixed so that

$$\Sigma a(i)d(i) \leq M$$

The agent has full information and selects the $d(i)$ optimally. Optimal solutions are denoted by $d^*(i)$.

An alternative characterization of the problem is the following sequential interpretation. Given $d^*(1)$, maximize utility with respect to remaining choices. Thus

$$\underset{d(2),d(3)}{\text{Max}} U[a(1)d^*(1), a(2)d(2), a(3)d(3)]$$

$$\text{subject to} \sum_{i=2}^{3} a(i)d(i) \leq M - a(1)d^*(1)$$

The demand functions (really the demand inequalities) for $d(2)$ and $d(3)$ may be written in terms of $d^*(1)$ and available resources $M - a(1)d^*(1)$. This characterization is a discrete choice analogue of the Hotelling (1935), Samuelson (1960), Pollak (1969) treatment of ordinary consumer choice and demonstrates that the demand function for a good can be expressed as a function of quantities consumed of some goods, the prices of the remaining goods, and income. (Pollak's term, "conditional demand function," is felicitous.)[25]

The choice of which characterization of the decision problem to use is a matter of convenience. When the analyst knows current disposable resources $M - a(1)d^*(1)$ and past choices $d^*(1)$ but not $a(1)$ or M, the second form of the problem is econometrically more convenient. The conditional demand function gives rise to structural state dependence in the sense that past choices influence current decisions. The essential point in this example is that past choices serve as a legitimate proxy for missing M and $a(1)$ variables known to the consumer but unknown to the observing econometrician. The conditional demand function is a legitimate structural equation.[26]

Both a model of decision making under uncertainty and a model of decision making under perfect foresight may be brought into sequential form so that past outcomes of the choice process *may* determine future outcomes. In principle one can distinguish between a certainty model and an uncertainty model if one has access to all the relevant information at the agent's disposal. In a model of decision making under perfect certainty, if all past prices are known and entered as explanatory variables for current choices, past outcomes of the choice process contribute no new information relevant to determining current choices. In a model of decision making under uncertainty, past outcomes would contribute information on current choices not available from past prices since uncertainty necessarily makes the prediction of past outcomes from past prices inexact, and the unanticipated components of past outcomes alter the budget set and cause a revision of initial plans.[27] In practice it is difficult to distinguish between the two models given limitations of data. The observing economist usually has less information at his disposal than the agent being analyzed has at his disposal when he makes his decisions.

The key point to extract from these examples is that structural state dependence as defined in this paper may be generated from a variety of models. It is not necessary to assume myopic decision making to generate structural dependence. Nor does empirical evidence in support of structural state dependence prove that agents make their decisions myopically. The divergence in estimated state dependence effects for the two age groups of women *may* be reconciled, in part, by an appeal to human capital theory. Under this interpretation previous work experience may be viewed as a proxy for investment in market human capital. The higher the stock of market-oriented human capital, the more likely is the event that a woman works (ceteris paribus). It is likely that the investment content of recent work experience is lower for women in their child-rearing years, when there are many competing demands for their time, than it is for older women past the child-rearing period who are reentering the work force in earnest. However, the empirical evidence on structural state dependence presented here is consistent with a variety of interpretations, and without further structure imposed we cannot be precise about which source of state dependence explains our empirical results.

Appendix A presents a first attempt at a decomposition of estimated structural state dependence effects into wage and nonwage components. It is estimated that forty-nine percent of an estimated structural state dependence effect arises from the effect of work experience on raising wage rates and the subsequent effect of higher wage rates on employment. A full fifty-one percent of estimated structural state dependence arises from other sources.

2.5 Summary

This paper presents a statistical model of discrete dynamic choice and applies the model to address the problem of distinguishing heterogeneity from structural state dependence. The concept of heterogeneity is generalized, and the concept of structural state dependence is given an economic interpretation. The methodology developed here is applied to analyze the dynamics of female labor supply. Evidence of structural state dependence is found for older women. There is little evidence that recent work experience determines the labor supply of younger women once heterogeneity is properly controlled. Heterogeneity arising from unobservables is found in the data for both groups of women. However, the traditional permanent-transitory model of heterogeneity is found to be inappropriate; for women, a first-order Markov model is a better description of the error process. Ad hoc shortcut procedures for controlling for heterogeneity are shown to produce erroneous estimates and forecasts.

Appendix A

A Procedure for Identifying Separate Components of the Effect of Previous Work Experience on Current Participation, and Some Preliminary Empirical Results

In the text, a procedure for estimating the impact of work experience on employment is proposed and implemented. As noted in the text, evidence for the existence of structural state dependence is consistent with several different hypotheses. One hypothesis is that work experience raises wage rates and that wage rates in turn influence employment. A second hypothesis is that fixed costs of entry into and exit out of the work force cause women to bunch their employment spells. A third hypothesis is that household-specific capital is acquired by women who do not participate in the market and that this nonmarket capital causes women who have not worked in the past to be less likely to work in the future. Closely related to this hypothesis is the hypothesis of "reinforcement" of work or nonwork activity of the sort considered by mathematical learning theorists. Other hypotheses have been advanced, and each hypothesis can be further specialized (Heckman 1981a), but for the purposes of the present discussion it will be assumed that these hypotheses are exhaustive explanations of structural state dependence.

In this appendix, a method for isolating these three effects is proposed, and some preliminary empirical evidence with this method is presented. Forty-nine percent of the estimated effect of work experience on employment is estimated to be due to the effect of market experience on wage growth.

The basic idea underlying the methodology is very simple. If measures of wage rates and nonmarket capital are available, it is possible to estimate the effect of work experience on these measures, as well as the direct effect of work experience on employment. If one can determine how nonmarket capital, fixed costs, and wage rates determine employment, one can apportion an estimated structural state dependence effect among these three sources.

The following equation system underlies the analysis in this appendix.

(A1) $$V(i, t) = Z(i, t)\tilde{\beta} + \delta_W W(i, t) + \delta_H H(i, t)$$
$$+ \delta_F F(i, t) + \tilde{\varepsilon}(i, t)$$

and $d(i, t) = 1$ iff $V(i, t) > 0$

$d(i, t) = 0$ otherwise

(A2) $$W(i, t) = Z_W(i, t)\gamma_W + \eta_W \sum_{t > t'} d(i, t') + U_1(i, t)$$

(A3) $$H(i, t) = Z_H(i, t)\gamma_H + \eta_H \sum_{t > t'} d(i, t') + U_2(i, t)$$

(A4) $$F(i, t) = Z_F(i, t)\gamma_F + \eta_F \sum_{t > t'} d(i, t') + U_3(i, t)$$

for $i = 1, \ldots, I$ $t = 1, \ldots, T$

Equation A1 corresponds to equation 3 in the text except that it distinguishes a wage effect on employment $\delta_W W(i, t)$, a nonmarket capital effect on employment $\delta_H H(i, t)$, and a fixed cost effect on employment $\delta_F F(i, t)$. Equations A2–A4 are, respectively, equations explaining wage rates $W(i, t)$, nonmarket capital $H(i, t)$, and fixed costs $F(i, t)$. $Z_W(i, t)$, $Z_H(i, t)$, and $Z_F(i, t)$ are the exogenous explanatory variables in the equations in which they appear. Substituting these equations into equation A1, leads to a specialization of equation 3 in the text

$$V(i, t) = Z(i, t)\beta + \delta \sum_{t > t'} d(i, t') + \varepsilon(i, t)$$

where $\delta = \delta_W \eta_W + \delta_H \eta_H + \delta_F \eta_F$ and $\varepsilon(i, t) = \delta_W U_1(i, t) + \delta_H U_2(i, t) + \delta_F U_3(i, t) + \tilde{\varepsilon}(i, t)$.

If one can estimate $\delta_W \eta_W$, $\delta_H \eta_H$, and $\delta_F \eta_F$, one can allocate the structural state dependence effect δ into wage sources, nonmarket sources, and fixed costs sources.

Equation system A1–A4 is a special case of a dummy endogenous variable model (see Heckman 1978a, especially appendix B). If the disturbances $\tilde{\varepsilon}(i, t)$, $U_1(i, t)$, $U_2(i, t)$, $U_3(i, t)$ are jointly normally distributed with mean zero and variance covariance matrix Σ, the analysis of estimation and identification developed for the dummy endogenous variable model carries over to the model discussed in this appendix. In particular, without using covariance restrictions, and relying solely on classical exclusion restrictions, if one variable appears in $Z_W(i, t)$ that does not appear in $Z(i, t)$, $Z_H(i, t)$, and $Z_F(i, t)$, it is possible to estimate δ_W up to a factor of proportionality given by the standard deviation of $\bar{\varepsilon}(i, t)$.[28] Permuting the subscripts W, H, and F generates necessary conditions for identifiability of normalized values of δ_H and δ_F.

In order to estimate the contribution of each of the three components of structural state dependence to the (normalized) total effect, δ, only two of the three left-hand-side variables that appear in equations A2–A4 need be observed, and the exclusion restrictions must be satisfied for the two equations for which observations on the dependent variable are available. To see why this is so, assume that data are available on $W(i, t)$ and $H(i, t)$ but not on $F(i, t)$. Given exclusion restrictions, this information can be used to estimate γ_W, η_W, γ_H, η_H and hence (normalized) δ_W and δ_H.[29] From the reduced form equation 3 it is possible to estimate (normalized) δ. Thus one can estimate (normalized) $\delta_F \eta_F = \delta - \delta_W \eta_W - \delta_H \eta_H$. If data are available on only one of the three variables and the exclusion restrictions are satisfied for the equation for which the dependent variable is available, one can estimate the fraction of the (normalized) total effect, δ, due to the variable that is observed.

In the analysis of female labor supply, a direct measure of market capital is available: the market wage rate, $W(i, t)$. Direct measures of fixed costs or household capital are not available, although children variables might be used to "proxy" household capital. Accordingly, with the available data, it is possible only to estimate the fraction of structural state dependence due to the effect of work experience on wage rates and the effect of wage rates on employment.

The specific econometric model used to derive the estimates presented in this appendix is based on a *fixed effect*–multiple equation Tobit model developed by the author and T. MaCurdy. That model is a conditional version of the general dummy endogenous variable model, and is described in detail elsewhere (Heckman and MaCurdy 1980, appendix A). In this paper, only the probit wage equation component of that model is used to estimate equation 3 and equation A2.[30] To achieve identification of a wage effect on employment, it is assumed that the local unemployment rate affects labor force participation only through its effect on wage rates—an assumption that could easily be challenged, and which would be counterfactual in a model of labor supply under uncertainty of employment in which local unemployment rates affect expectations of employment. This assumption is maintained here. Then (normalized) δ_W is just identified.

The variables that appear in the wage equation and affect employment are the same as those used by Heckman and MaCurdy (1980), except that in place of their market experience variable (age minus schooling minus six), actual work experience is used. Log wage rates are assumed to depend on (a) local labor market unemployment; (b) work experience; and (c) schooling variables. Labor force participation is assumed to depend (in reduced form) on these three types of variables used in the wage equation, and on (d) variables representing family composition; (e) family income exclusive of the wife's earnings; (f) the wife's age; and (g) variables representing the head's health status. A sample of 672 white women aged 25–65 in 1968 interviewed in the Michigan Panel Survey of Income Dynamics who were continuously married to the same spouse during the sample period 1968–75 was used to generate the estimates.

In order to focus the discussion on the main topic of this appendix, only the key wage and state dependence parameters are presented in 3.A.1.

For the full sample of women of all ages, the estimated normalized total state dependence effect δ is .163—a number that is between the estimates for the two age groups presented in the text. As is apparent from table 3.A.1, only 49 percent of the estimated effect of market experience on employment is due to the effect of market experience on wage growth and the effect of wage rates on market participation. Fifty-one percent of the estimated structural state dependence effect is due to the acquisition of nonmarket capital (including psychological reinforcement effects) and the effect of fixed costs. This estimate, though clearly tentative, suggests that a considerable part of the effect of work experience on employment is due to factors other than the wage-rate-enhancing

Table 3.A.1. Estimates of the Total State Dependence Effect and Its Wage Component (asymptotic normal test statistics derived from the estimated information matrix in parentheses)

(Normalized) Total State Dependence Effect δ	Effect of Experience on $\ln$ Wage Rates η_W	(Normalized) Effect of Wage Rates on Employment $\delta_W{}^*$	Fraction of Total State Dependence Effect Due to the Effect of Experience on Wage Growth**
.163	.032	2.45	.49
(1.9)	(4.9)	(2.9)	(3.6)

*This is obtained by dividing the estimated effect of local unemployment rates on participation by the estimated effect of local unemployment rates on $\ln$ wage rates.
**This is obtained by multiplying η_W and δ_W, and taking the ratio of this product to δ.

Appendix B

The derivation of the likelihood function used in this paper is presented in Heckman (1981a). Here we present the essential features of the derivation and the problem of initial conditions discussed extensively in Heckman (1981b).

Write equation 3 in the text in shorthand notation as

$$V(i, t) = \bar{V}(i, t) + \varepsilon(i, t)$$

for $i = 1, \ldots, I$ and $t = 1, \ldots, T$ where

$$\bar{V}(i, t) = Z(i, t)\beta + \sum_{t > t'} \delta(t, t') \, d(i, t')$$

$$+ \sum_j \lambda(t, t-j) \prod_{\ell=1}^{j} d(i, t-\ell)$$

Let $\varepsilon(i, t)$ be arrayed in a $1 \times T$ vector $\varepsilon(i)$, and array $\bar{V}(i, t)$ in a $1 \times T$ vector $\bar{V}(i)$. The initial conditions of the process are assumed to be fixed nonstochastic constants $d(i, 0), d(i, -1), \ldots$; $V(i, t) > 0$ iff $d(i, t) = 1$; $V(i, t) \leq 0$ otherwise.

The disturbances are assumed to be joint normally distributed

$$\varepsilon(i) \sim N(0, \Sigma)$$

Define diagonal matrix D as the square root of the diagonal elements of Σ. Normalize $\sigma_{11} = 1$. Define the correlation matrix by

$$\tilde{\Sigma} = D^{-1} \Sigma \, D^{-1}$$

and define the normalized $\bar{V}(i)$ by

$$\tilde{\bar{V}}(i) = \bar{V}(i) \, D^{-1}$$

and the normalized $\varepsilon(i)$ vector by

$$\tilde{\varepsilon}(i) = \varepsilon(i) \, D^{-1}$$

Conditional density (equation 4 in the text) is most conveniently defined in recursive fashion. Here we simply start the recursion. The remaining steps are obvious and hence are deleted. Define the joint density of $\tilde{\varepsilon}(i, 2)$ and $\tilde{\varepsilon}(i, 1)$ as

$$f_{21}[\tilde{\varepsilon}(i, 2), \tilde{\varepsilon}(i, 1)]$$

The conditional density of $\tilde{\varepsilon}(i, 2)$ given $d(i, 1)$ is

$$g[\varepsilon(i, 2) \mid d(i, 1)] =$$

$$\left[\frac{\int_{-\bar{V}(i, 1)}^{\infty} f_{21}[\tilde{\varepsilon}(i, 2), \tilde{\varepsilon}(i, 1)] \, d\tilde{\varepsilon}(i, 1)}{\int_{-\bar{V}(i, 1)}^{\infty} f_1[\tilde{\varepsilon}(i, 1)] \, d\tilde{\varepsilon}(i, 1)}\right]^{d(i, 1)} \cdot$$

$$\left[\frac{\int_{-\infty}^{-\bar{V}(i, 1)} f_{21}[\tilde{\varepsilon}(i, 2), \tilde{\varepsilon}(i, 1)] \, d\tilde{\varepsilon}(i, 1)(1 - d(i, 1))}{\int_{-\infty}^{-\bar{V}(i, 1)} f_1[\tilde{\varepsilon}(i, 1)] \, d\tilde{\varepsilon}(i, 1)}\right]^{1 - d(i, 1)}$$

where f_1 is the marginal density of $\tilde{\varepsilon}(i, 1)$. $\tilde{\varepsilon}(i, 2)$ *conditioned* on $d(i, 1)$ is independent of $d(i, 1)$. Thus the probability of $d(i, 2) = 1$ conditional on $d(i, 1)$ is, in the notation of the text,

$$P(i, 2) = \int_{-\bar{V}(i, 2)}^{\infty} g[\varepsilon(i, 2) \mid d(i, 1)] \, d\varepsilon(i, 2)$$

Recall that $\bar{V}(i, 2)$ contains $d(i, 1)$. This creates no simultaneity problem in forming $P(i, 2)$ because $\varepsilon(i, 2)$ is conditionally independent of $d(i, 1)$ by construction.

Define $P(i, 1)$ as

$$P(i, 1) = \int_{-\bar{V}(i, 1)}^{\infty} f_1[\varepsilon(i, 1)] d\varepsilon(i, 1)$$

The joint density of $d(i, 1)$ and $d(i, 2)$ is

$$k[d(i, 1), d(i, 2)] = [P(i, 1)]^{d(i, 1)} [1 - P(i, 1)]^{1 - d(i, 1)}$$
$$\cdot [P(i, 2)]^{d(i, 2)} [1 - P(i, 2)]^{1 - d(i, 2)}$$

The procedure to be used to derive the full distribution of $d(i)$ should now be clear.

A convenient representation of the probability of $d(i)$ that exploits the symmetry of the normal around its mean is the following. Define F as the multivariate cumulative normal integral. The probability that $d(i) = \underline{d(i)}$ given the values of the exogenous variables, the parameters, and the initial conditions is

$$\text{Prob }[d(i) = \underline{d(i)}] = F[\bar{V}(i) * (2\underline{d(i)}) - \iota;$$
$$\tilde{\Sigma}_* (2\underline{d(i)} - \iota)'(2\underline{d(i)} - \iota)]$$

where "*" denotes a Hadamard product (Rao 1973), and ι is a $1 \times T$ vector of ones. Maximizing the sample product of these probabilities with respect to the parameters of the model produces the maximum likelihood estimator. Modifying this expression for nonnormal symmetric and nonsymmetric densities is straightforward.

A crucial assumption in writing down the expression is that presample values of $d(i, 0)$, $d(i, -1)$, . . . are fixed nonstochastic constants. If they are not, correct conditioning for the process requires treating the presample values in the same fashion as the sample values (i.e., conditioning to correct for simultaneity). In life cycle models of the sort considered in the text, this requires the entire history of the process. For a more complete discussion of this problem and for some exact and approximate solutions see Heckman (1981b).

Appendix C Data Summaries

Table 3.A.2 Mean Value of Variables

	1968	1969	1970	1971	1972	1973	1974
			A. Women Aged 45–59				
No. of children aged less than 6	.035	.020	.040	.010	.015	.015	.015
County unemployment rate (%)	4.01	3.61	4.92	5.89	5.85	4.87	5.54
County wage rate ($/hr)	1.90	1.99	2.05	2.09	2.21	2.29	2.48
Total no. of children	2.68	2.68	2.74	2.79	2.86	2.93	2.97
Presample work experience (yr.)[a]	11.22	11.22	11.22	11.22	11.22	11.22	11.22
Wife's education	11.71	11.71	11.71	11.71	11.71	11.71	11.71
Family income excluding wife's earnings ($)	1.26×10^4	1.30×10^4	1.34×10^4	1.39×10^4	1.42×10^4	1.53×10^4	1.56×10^4
Cumulated sample experience[b]	0	.459	.969	1.44	1.91	2.34	2.77
National unemployment rate prime-age males 35–44	1.4	1.4	2.3	2.9	2.5	1.8	2.4
Participation rate	.46	.51	.47	.46	.44	.43	.41
No. of observations	198						

Table 3.A.2 (continued)

	1968	1969	1970	1971	1972	1973	1974
			B. Women Aged 30–44				
No. of children aged less than 6	.392	.325	.280	.250	.204	.135	.123
County unemployment rate (%)	3.83	3.53	4.92	5.81	5.74	4.71	5.40
County wage rate ($/hr)	1.94	2.0	2.05	2.12	2.25	2.30	2.51
Total no. of children	3.20	3.23	3.31	3.37	3.42	3.49	3.54
Presample work experience (yr)[a]	6.51	6.51	6.51	6.51	6.51	6.51	6.51
Wife's education	12.24	12.24	12.24	12.24	12.24	12.24	12.24
Family income excluding wife's earnings ($)	1.28×10^4	1.39×10^4	1.46×10^4	1.59×10^4	1.70×10^4	1.92×10^4	2.08×10^4
Cumulated sample experience[b]	0	.50	1.02	1.52	2.00	2.49	3.00
National unemployment rate prime-age males 35–44	1.4	1.4	2.3	2.9	2.5	1.8	2.4
Participation rate	.5	.52	.50	.49	.49	.51	.54
No. of observations	332						

Source: University of Michigan Panel on Income Dynamics 1968–74.
[a] Defined as the number of years since age 18 that the woman has worked prior to 1968.
[b] Defined as the number of years the woman has worked in the sample years.

Notes

1. For a complete description of the Polya process and its generalizations see Johnson and Kotz (1977, Chapter 4). They note (pp. 180–81) that in the special case in which a person draws a ball and receives the *same number* of the balls of the color drawn whether a black or red ball is drawn, urn model three (in this case a strict Polya model) generates sequences of outcomes identical in probability with the same sequences generated from urn model two provided that the population distribution of the proportion of red and black balls in the urn is *Beta*. In this case, panel data cannot be used to distinguish between the two urn models. In a stationary environment, in which urn contents are not exogenously changed, as long as the number of red balls placed in the urn differs from the number of black balls placed in the urn when a black ball is drawn, it is possible to use panel data to discriminate between the two models. This observation is one of the key insights in the Bates-Neyman paper (1951). A similar nonidentification result appears in the multivariate probit model discussed below. (See note 13).

2. Throughout this section, variables such as children, family income, etc., are ignored solely to simplify the presentation of the main ideas, *not* because they are deemed to be unimportant determinants of participation. Clearly, in actual empirical work it is necessary to control for the effects of such variables on participation probabilities. Note further that the proposed test assumes that model four does not generate the data.

3. Thus this model abstracts from the serial correlation process of the fourth urn scheme.

4. $U(i, t)$ is defined by $U(i, t) = d(i, t) - \phi(i) - \delta \sum_{t>t'} d(i, t')$. The requirement that $U(i, t)$ has a zero mean implies that the probability that $d(i, t) = 1$ conditional on $d(i, t-1), \ldots, d(i, 0)$, and $\phi(i)$ is

$$\Pr[d(i, t) = 1 \mid \phi(i), d(i, t-1), \ldots, d(i, 0)] = \phi(i) + \delta \sum_{t>t'} d(i, t').$$

The conditional probability that $d(i, t) = 0$ is the complement of the preceding probability. Clearly $U(i, t)$ is uncorrelated with $U(i, t')$, $t \neq t'$.

5. The asymptotic test statistics required to perform the test would have to adjust for the heteroscedasticity in the $U(i, t)$. GLS could be used to compute more efficient estimators and test statistics.

6. Readers familiar with the Work of Balestra and Nerlove (1966) will recognize that the model in the text closely resembles the Balestra-Nerlove scheme.

7. Thus, letting β be the effect of children on current participation (assumed to be negative), the probability limits of least squares estimators of β and δ in regression 2 (augmented to include children) are

$$\text{plim} \begin{bmatrix} \hat{\beta} \\ \bar{\delta} \end{bmatrix} = \begin{bmatrix} \beta \\ \delta \end{bmatrix} + \frac{1}{D} \begin{bmatrix} m_{cc} & -m_{ch} \\ -m_{ch} & m_{hh} \end{bmatrix} \begin{bmatrix} 0 \\ m_{h\varepsilon} \end{bmatrix}$$

where D is the probability limit of the regressor matrix, m_{cc} is the population variance in children, m_{ch} is the population covariance between the number of children and the history of participation $h = \sum_{t>t'} d(i, t')$, and m_{hh} is the population variance participation histories. Finally, $m_{h\varepsilon}$ is the covariance between the disturbance $\varepsilon(i, t) = U(i, t) + \phi(i) - \bar{\phi}(i)$ and the participation history h. D is positive. Under the assumptions made in the text, $m_{h\varepsilon} > 0$ and $m_{ch} < 0$. Thus, least squares estimators overstate the true value of δ and overstate the true value of β.

8. For discussion of this generalized linear probability model, see Heckman and MaCurdy (1978).

9. In addition, the small sample properties of the least squares estimator are very undesirable. For example, for $T=2$, least squares estimators of δ in equation 1 are either undefined or nonpositive, even when the true value of δ is positive.

10. Thus we abstract from unemployment. Unemployment is viewed as one form of nonmarket activity, on the same footing as leisure.

11. However, unmeasured business cycle factors and local labor market variables may induce correlation in the errors across individuals.

12. These conditions on equation 3 are sufficient but not necessary. In particular, it is possible for $\delta > 0$.

13. Note the asymmetry. If a woman receives a black ball each time she does not work, the model would have to be augmented to include a time effect. In this case, we obtain a nonidentification result similar to the result mentioned in note 1. For example, consider the following alteration of equation 3. Let

$$V(i, t) = \beta_0 t + \delta \sum_{j=1}^{t} d(i, t-j) + \delta' \sum_{j=1}^{t} [1 - d(i, t-j)] + \varepsilon(i, t)$$

$$= \beta_0 t + (\delta - \delta') \sum_{j=1}^{t} d(i, t-j) + \delta' t + \varepsilon(i, t)$$

$$= (\beta_0 + \delta') t + (\delta - \delta') \sum_{j=1}^{t} d(i, t-j) + \varepsilon(i, t).$$

In this model, if individual i does not experience the event in time period t, she receives a dose of "nonmarket capital" δ'. This model is a special case of equation 3 with t contained among the regressors $Z(i, t)$ (so long as $\beta_0 + \delta' \neq 0$). This underscores the point that the structural state dependence parameters δ in the text are measured only *relative to* nonmarket alternatives.

If $\delta - \delta' = 0$, there is no structural state dependence as defined in the text even though the woman receives a dose of δ when she works and a dose of δ' when she does not. If the doses are of equal strength there is no way to measure the dose, provided $\beta_0 \neq 0$. The nonidentification in this model corresponds to the nonidentification result for the classical Polya urn scheme mentioned in note 1.

14. As discussed in Heckman (1981a), the normality assumption is not critical to this approach. Indeed, the one-factor scheme proposed below can be readily adapted to handle nonnormal disturbances. The advantage of the normality assumption in the general case is that it permits one to control for nonstationarity in the environment. An arbitrary nonstationary distribution would generate an unidentified model. The normal distribution permits the analyst to control for the sorts of nonstationarity in first and second moments usually considered in econometrics.

15. For discussion of one-factor probit model see Heckman (1981a). There it is noted that if $T > 3$, the one-factor assumption imposes nonstationarity onto the error process, except in certain special cases. However, for $T \leq 3$, the one-factor model is consistent with a wide variety of interesting error processes. The principal advantage of the one-factor model is that a multivariate normal integral can be written as one numerical integration of a product of simply computed univariate cumulative normal distributions. This representation greatly facilitates computation.

16. For a complete description of these data, see Morgan, et al. (1974). The restriction to seven years was made to facilitate comparability of samples with other studies, in particular, that of Heckman and MaCurdy (1980).

17. In the complete seven-year sample, fully two-thirds of the women either work all of the time or do not work at all. Again, the numbers of full-time workers and nonworkers are roughly the same.

18. While the coefficient associated with each unemployment variable is not statistically significant at conventional levels, the joint set is statistically significant.

19. The Markov model imposes two restrictions on the α_t coefficients, $\alpha_1 = \alpha_3$, and $\alpha_2 = 1$. Thus two degrees of freedom are lost when this restriction is imposed.

20. This implies that all disturbances have the same correlation with other disturbances ($\alpha_1 = \alpha_2 = \alpha_3$) and the idiosyncratic component is not permitted to decay.

21. Heckman and Willis discuss this model but actually estimate a "beta logistic" approximation to it. The model estimated in the text is the analogue of the Heckman-Willis model estimated in a multivariate probit framework.

22. Note that it is not possible to test the model directly with estimates reported in column 3 against the model with estimates reported in column 8 since neither model nests the other as a special case.

23. Of course, a model in which past participation affects current participation requires retrospective data on participation.

24. To capture this model, a random-coefficient simultaneous equation multivariate probit model is required. Development of such a model is deferred to another occasion.

25. In this example, if the utility function is additive $d^*(1)$ would have no effect on future choices except through its effect on current resources $M - a(1)d^*(1)$. Thus a test of structural state dependence in this model is a test of intertemporal independence in preferences.

26. Another model that generates structural state dependence in an environment of perfect certainty is a model with fixed costs. In some dynamic models of labor supply, training costs are assumed to be incurred by labor force entrants. Once these costs are incurred, they are not incurred again until reentry occurs. Labor force participation decisions taken by labor force participants take account of such costs. In this way structural state dependence is generated.

27. If the uncertainty comes in the form of price uncertainty, ex ante prices are required to perform the test.

28. This condition implicitly assumes that the disturbances $\bar{\varepsilon}(i, t)$ are stationary. If they are not, and variances are normalized relative to first-period disturbances as in the text, the factor of proportionality is the standard deviation of the first-period disturbance.

29. The most direct way to verify this statement is to substitute equations A2–A4 into equation A1. Assuming that the necessary conditions for identifiability are sufficient, from the exogenous variables unique to $Z_W(i, t)$ and $Z_H(i, t)$ one can estimate δ_W and δ_H (up to a common factor of proportionality), since direct estimates of γ_W and γ_H can be achieved from (A2) and (A3). The factor of proportionality is the standard deviation of $\varepsilon(i, t)$.

30. The model that is estimated is

(3) $$V(i, t) = Z(i, t)\beta + \delta \sum_{t > t'} d(i, t') + \varepsilon(i, t) \text{ for}$$

$i = 1, \ldots, I, t = 1, \ldots, T$ and

$d(i, t) = 1$ iff $V(i, t) > 0$

$d(i, t) = 0$ otherwise

(A1) $$W(i, t) = Z_W(i, t)\gamma_W + \eta_W \sum_{t > t'} d(i, t')$$

$$+ U_1(i, t) \text{ for } i = 1, \ldots, I, t = 1, \ldots, T$$

where $\varepsilon(i, t) = \phi_1(i) + V_1(i, t)$ and $U_1(i, t) = \phi_2(i) + V_2(i, t)$. $\phi_1(i)$ and $\phi_2(i)$ are permanent components, and $V_1(i, t)$ and $V_2(i, t)$ are mean zero, jointly normally distributed, temporally independent components with variances σ_{11} and σ_{22}, respectively, and contemporaneous covariance σ_{12}.

The model is estimated treating $\phi_1(i)$ and $\phi_2(i)$ as parameters. Statistical properties of this model are discussed in Heckman and MaCurdy (1980). However, an intuitive justification of the procedure may be of interest, and is given here.

The discussion in the text has already demonstrated that consistent estimates of (normalized) β and σ can be achieved. The procedure for estimating the parameters of equation A1 requires further argument because the wage $W(i, t)$ is observed only for working women (and hence there may be selection bias in estimating equation A1 on a subsample of working women for whom wage data are available) and because $\sum_{t>t'} d(i, t')$ is likely to be correlated with the error term $U_1(i, t)$ because previous wage rates determine previous labor force participation.

The likelihood function conditions the distribution of $V_2(i, t)$ on the fixed effects $\phi_1(i)$, $\phi_2(i)$ and the event $d(i, t) = 1$ (the condition required to be able to observe a wage rate for woman i at time t). The conditional distribution of $V_2(i, t)$ given $\phi_1(i), \phi_2(i)$, and $d(i, t) = 1$ is

(A5) $$g(V_2(i, t)|\phi_1(i), \phi_2(i), d(i, t) = 1) = \frac{\int_{-\infty}^{-[\phi_1(i) + Z(i, t)\beta + \delta \sum_{t>t'} d(i, t')]} f(V_1(i, t), V_2(i, t))dV_1(i, t)}{\int_{-\infty}^{-[\phi_1(i) + Z(i, t)\beta + \delta \sum_{t>t'} d(i, t')]} f_1(V_1(i, t))dV_1(i, t)}$$

where $f[V_1(i, t), V_2(i, t)]$ is the joint distribution of $V_1(i, t)$ and $V_2(i, t)$, and $f_1[V_1(i, t)]$ is the marginal distribution of $V_1(i, t)$. The mean of this conditional distribution is $\lambda(i, t)$.

Given $\lambda(i, t)$, the conditional mean of $W(i, t)$ given $Z_W(i, t), \sum_{t>t'} d(i, t'), \phi_1(i), \phi_2(i)$, and $d(i, t) = 1$, is

$$E[W(i, t)|Z_W(i, t), \sum_{t>t'} d(i, t'), \phi_1(i), \phi_2(i), d(i, t) = 1] = Z_W(i, t)\gamma_W + \eta_W \sum_{t>t'} d(i, t') + \phi_2(i) + \lambda(i, t)$$

The difference between the conditional mean of $W(i, t)$ and $W(i, t)$, $\omega(i, t)$, is uncorrelated with $\sum_{t>t'} d(i, t')$ and $\phi_2(i)$. Thus, given $\lambda(i, t)$ and $\phi_2(i)$, consistent estimates of γ_W and η_W can be achieved by a conventional fixed effect regression of $W(i, t)$ on $Z_W(i, t), \sum_{t>t'} d(i, t')$, and $\lambda(i, t)$. Estimates of the (normalized) parameters of equation 3 can be used to estimate $\lambda(i, t)$. It is thus possible to enter $\lambda(i, t)$ as a regressor in the wage equation, and hence it is possible to secure consistent estimates of the parameters of equation A2 using regression methods.

The likelihood approach used by Heckman and MaCurdy (1980) essentially corrects for selection bias and simultaneous equation bias by adjusting the conditional distribution of $V_2(i, t)$ to account for selectivity and simultaneity. Their estimation procedure is more efficient than the two-step estimator discussed in this note because it incorporates all available prior information. The essential principle underlying the two methods is the same.

An advantage of the fixed effect procedure is that it provides a more satisfactory solution to the problem of "initial conditions" or the problem of endogeneity of presample experience than the procedure used in the text of the paper (see Heckman 1981b).

References

Astrom, K. *Introduction to Stochastic Control Theory.* New York: Academic Press, 1970.

Atkinson, R.; Bower, G.; and Crothers, E. *An Introduction to Mathematical Learning Theory.* New York: Wiley, 1965.

Balestra, P., and Nerlove, M. "Pooling Cross-Section and Time-Series Data in the Estimation of a Dynamic Model." *Econometrica* 34 (July 1966).

Bates, G., and Neyman, J. "Contributions to the Theory of Accident Proneness II: True or False Contagion." *University of California Publications in Statistics* 1 (1951): 215–53.

Ben Porath, Y. "Labor Force Participation Rates and the Supply of Labor." *Journal of Political Economy* 81 (May/June 1973): 697–704.

Bergstrom, A. R. *Statistical Inference in Continuous Time Economic Models.* North Holland, 1976.

Bush, R., and Mosteller, F. *Stochastic Models for Learning.* New York: Wiley, 1955.

Cain, G., *Labor Force Participation of Married Women.* Chicago: University of Chicago Press, 1966.

———. "The Challenge of Segmented Labor Market Theories to Orthodox Theory: A Survey." *Journal of Economic Literature* 14 (December 1976): 1215–57.

Coleman, J. *Models of Change and Response Uncertainty.* Englewood Cliffs, N.J.: Prentice Hall, 1964.

Cripps, T., and Tarling, R. "An Analysis of the Duration of Male Unemployment in Great Britain, 1932-1973." *Economic Journal* 84 (June 1974): 289–316.

Domencich, T., and McFadden, D. *Urban Travel Demand: A Behavioral Analysis.* Amsterdam: North Holland, 1975.

Dreyfus, S. *Dynamic Programming and the Calculus of Variations.* New York: Academic Press, 1965.

Feller, W. "On a General Class of Contagious Distributions." *Annals of Mathematical Statistics* 14 (May 1943): 389–400.

Flinn, C., and Heckman, J. "Models for the Analysis of Labor Force Dynamics," in R. Basmann and G. Rhodes, eds., *Advances in Econometrics.* JAI Press, 1981.

Gallant, A. R. "Testing a Subset of Parameters of Nonlinear Regression Models." *Journal of the American Statistical Association* 70 (December 1975): 927–32.

Goodman, L. "Statistical Methods for the Mover-Stayer Model." *Journal of the American Statistical Association* 56 (1961): 841–68.

Griliches, Z. "Distributed Lags: A Survey." *Econometrica*, vol. 35 (1967).

Heckman, J. "Dummy Endogenous Variables in a Simultaneous Equation System." *Econometrica* 46 (1978a) 931–59.

———. "Simple Statistical Models for Discrete Panel Data Developed and Applied to Test the Hypothesis of True State Dependence against the Hypothesis of Spurious State Dependence." *Annales de l'Insee* (Paris), nos. 30–31 (1978b), pp. 227–70.

———. "Statistical Models for Discrete Panel Data," in C. Manski and D. McFadden, eds., *The Structural Analysis of Discrete Data.* Cambridge: MIT Press, 1981a.

———. "The Incidental Parameters Problem and the Problem of Initial Conditions in Estimating a Discrete Time-Discrete Data Stochastic Process," in C. Manski and D. McFadden, eds., *The Structural Analysis of Discrete Data.* Cambridge: MIT Press, 1981b.

Heckman, J., and Borjas, G. "Does Employment Cause Future Unemployment? Definitions, Questions and Answers from a Continuous Time Model of Heterogeneity and State Dependence." *Economica* (1980): 247–83.

Heckman, J., and MaCurdy, T. "Estimation of a Simultaneous Equation Linear Probability Model." Unpublished Ms., University of Chicago, 1978.

———. "A Dynamic Model of Female Labor Supply." *Review of Economic Studies*, January, 1980.

Heckman, J., and Willis, R. "A Beta Logistic Model for the Analysis of Sequential Labor Force Participation of Married Women." *Journal of Political Economy* 85 (February 1977): 27–58.

Hotelling, H. "Demand Functions with Limited Budgets." *Econometrica* 3 (1935): 66–78.

Johnson, N., and Kotz, S. *Urn Models and Their Application: An Approach to Modern Discrete Probability Theory.* New York: Wiley and Sons, 1977.

Jovanovic, B. "State Dependence in a Continuous Time Stochastic Model of Worker Behavior." Mimeograph, Columbia University, New York, 1978.

Karlin, S., and Taylor, H. *A First Course in Stochastic Processes.* 2d ed. New York: Academic Press, 1975.

Koopmans, L. H. *The Spectral Analysis of Time Series.* New York: Academic Press, 1974.

Layton, L. "Unemployment Over the Work History." Ph.D. dissertation, Department of Economics, Columbia University, New York, 1978.

Lucas, R., and Rapping, L. "Real Wages, Employment and Inflation," in E. Phelps, ed., *Microfoundations of Employment and Inflation Theory.* New York: W. W. Norton, 1970.

McFadden, D. "Conditional Logit Analysis of Qualitative Choice Behavior," in P. Zarembka, ed., *Frontiers in Econometrics.* New York: Academic Press, 1973a.

———. "Analysis of Qualitative Choice Behavior," in Zarembka, ed., *Frontiers in Econometrics*, 1973b.

———. "Quantal Choice Analysis: A Survey." *Annals of Economic and Social Measurement* 5 (December 1976): 363–90.

Malinvaud, E. *Statistical Methods of Econometrics.* 2d ed. Amsterdam: North-Holland, 1970.

Mincer, J. "Labor Force Participation of Married Women," in H. G. Lewis, ed., *Aspects of Labor Economics.* Princeton: Princeton University Press, 1962.

Morgan, J., et al. *Five Thousand American Families: Patterns of Economic Progress.* Vols. 1 and 2. Ann Arbor: ISR Press, 1974.

Nerlove, M. "Econometric Analysis of Longitudinal Data," in *Annales de l'Insee* (Paris), nos. 30–31 (1978).
Phelps, E. *Inflation Policy and Unemployment Theory.* New York: Norton, 1972.
Pollak, R. "Conditional Demand Functions and Consumption Theory." *Quarterly Journal of Economics* 83 (April 1969): 209–27.
Rao, C. R. *Linear Statistical Inference and Its Applications.* 2d ed. New York: Wiley, 1973.
Restle, F., and Greeno, J. *Introduction to Mathematical Psychology.* Reading, Mass.: Addison-Wesley, 1970.
Ryder, H.; Stafford, F.; and Stephan, P. "Labor, Leisure and Training over the Life Cycle." *International Economic Review* 17 (October 1976): 651–74.
Samuelson, P. "Structure of Minimum Equilibrium Systems," in R. Pfouts, ed., *Essays in Economics and Econometrics: A Volume in Honor of Harold Hotelling.* Chapel Hill: University of North Carolina Press, 1960.
Sims, C. "Exogeneity and Causal Ordering in Macroeconomic Models," in C. Sims, ed., *New Methods in Business Cycle Research: Proceedings from a Conference.* Minneapolis: Federal Reserve Bank of Minneapolis, 1977.
Singer, B., and Spilerman, S. "Some Methodological Issues in the Analysis of Longitudinal Surveys." *Annals of Economic and Social Measurement* 5 (December 1976): 447–74.

4 Anticipated Unemployment, Temporary Layoffs, and Compensating Wage Differentials

John M. Abowd and Orley Ashenfelter

This paper models the competitive equilibrium wage rate when employment offers vary according to the amount of anticipated unemployment and unemployment risk. The competitive wage reflects a compensating differential which includes a certainty equivalent compensation proportional to the squared expected unemployment rate and a risk compensation proposal to the coefficient of unemployment variation. The factors of proportionality are half the inverse compensated labor supply elasticity and half the relative risk aversion, respectively. We use panel data to construct a model of anticipated unemployment and unemployment variance which depends on personal employment history and industry-wide and economy-wide factors. Compensating wage differentials ranging from less than one percent to more than fourteen percent are estimated for a two-digit industry classification over the years 1970–75.

4.1 Introduction

The appropriate theoretical framework for the interpretation of measurements of unemployment is once again a matter of controversy. The issues involved are important both because of the overwhelming role

John M. Abowd is Assistant Professor of Economics, University of Chicago Graduate School of Business.
Orley Ashenfelter is Professor of Economics, Princeton University.

We wish to acknowledge helpful comments on previous drafts from Peter Linneman, Robert Lucas, Sherwin Rosen and workshop participants at the University of Chicago, London School of Economics, and Michigan State University. We owe a special thanks to John Pencavel for his discussions throughout the life of the paper. Financial assistance was provided by the Industrial Relations Section, Princeton University. Research assistance was provided by Anthony Abowd and Mark Plant. We are, of course, responsible for any remaining errors.

that measured unemployment plays in the discussion of public policies designed to mitigate it and because of the research strategies implied for understanding the causes and consequences of movements in it. One natural research strategy is to interpret unemployment as the equilibrium outcome of a worker's choices about job search or the intertemporal allocation of nonmarket time.[1] Of course, labor supply theoretic explanations of movements in unemployment are not complete without further specification, but this approach does imply a general strategy for the necessary research. An alternative approach is to treat unemployment as a constraint on individual behavior rather than a result of it.[2] Although this demand theoretic approach is also incomplete without further specification, it also implies a general strategy for further research.

Treating unemployment as a constraint on behavior may appear to have immediate normative implications for public policies regarding unemployment benefits or compensation. It may seem plausible that workers would, as a group, purchase insurance against an unpredictable exogenous constraint on the hours they are able to sell in the market. Whether this insurance is provided privately or governmentally would seem, then, to be a matter of form rather than substance. Predictable variations in the nature and extent of the risks of unemployment are surely extensive, so that a uniform governmental insurance benefit scheme would still leave considerable variation in the incidence of unemployment constraints to be compensated within the labor market. The purpose of this paper is to examine a theoretical model of market wage adjustments to compensate for the uninsured differences in the incidence of unemployment. We examine the empirical significance of these compensations using data from the Panel Study of Income Dynamics for the years 1967 to 1975 (Survey Research Center 1972ab 1973 1974 1975 1976).

Our analysis concerns two different but related issues. First, we extend the emerging empirical and theoretical analyses of the sources of compensating wage differentials to include a systematic treatment of the impact of constraints on hours at work.[3] Our analysis shows clearly how the determination of wage rates in the presence of fully anticipated constraints is systematically related to the determination of labor supply in the absence of such constraints, and demonstrates that these two issues are connected in a way that has not been fully appreciated in the past. The analysis provides a theoretical framework for measuring the impact of risky labor supply constraints on the determination of market wages. At the same time, our model also provides some evidence of how fruitful a research strategy that treats unemployment as a constraint on behavior is likely to be. We find that the labor market compensates anticipated layoffs and unemployment by 2–6 percent per year. The estimated compensations vary from industry to industry but are relatively stable from year to year within industries. Section 4.2 provides a theoretical analysis of equilibrium wage compensations. Section 4.3 disusses the empirical methodology and results.

4.2 A Theoretical Model of Compensating Differentials and Employment Constraints

In this section we consider the determination of wages when workers may choose employment in either of two sectors. In the unconstrained sector the worker may choose the optimum labor supply given the prevailing wage. In the constrained sector the worker accepts a fixed wage and employment conditions contract which sets the average number of work hours and employment variability. In a competitive equilibrium with identical workers, the utility of these two employment situations will be equal. This condition is used to characterize the relationship between the wage in the constrained sector and the conditions of employment. Specifically, we relate the equilibrium wage to the expected extent of unemployment and hours variability.

In the absence of a constraint on the hours a worker may sell in the market, the usual assumptions about preferences between nonmarket time and commodities lead to an optimal offer of labor supply $h^0(w, p, y)$ and optimal commodity demands of $x^0(w, p, y)$ that depend on the wage rate w, commodity prices p, and nonlabor income y. The indirect or maximal utility for this consumer-worker is than $V(w, p, y)$ which also depends on w, p, and y. Consider now a constraint $\bar{h} < h^0(w, p, y)$ which prevents the worker from selling more than $\bar{h}$ hours on the labor market. Faced with a binding constraint, the worker will supply $\bar{h}$ hours of work, demand commodities $x^*(\bar{h}, p, w\bar{h} + y)$, and achieve maximal utility of $V^*(\bar{h}, p, w\bar{h} + y)$. For the same w, p, and y the constraint on hours will, of course, lead to a maximal utility $V^*(\bar{h}, p, w\bar{h} + y)$ which is less than $V(w, p, y)$. The constrained worker would then reach a lower utility level than would be the case in the unconstrained job. The maximum of V^* with respect to $\bar{h}$ is simply $V(w, p, y)$ and is achieved at the point $\bar{h} = h^0$. V^* is graphed in figure 4.1 as a function of $\bar{h}$ for given w, p, and y. We assume V^* is concave in the relevant region although this is necessary only at the point $\bar{h} = h^0(w, p, y)$.

If the worker is faced with a choice of a job in the unconstrained sector versus a job in the constrained sector at the same wage rate, the worker would always prefer employment in the unconstrained sector. Labor market equilibrium will entail the condition

(1) $$V^*(\bar{h}, p, w^*\bar{h} + y) = V(w, p, y)$$

where w is the prevailing wage in the unconstrained sector and w^* is the equilibrium wage rate when the employment contract requires labor

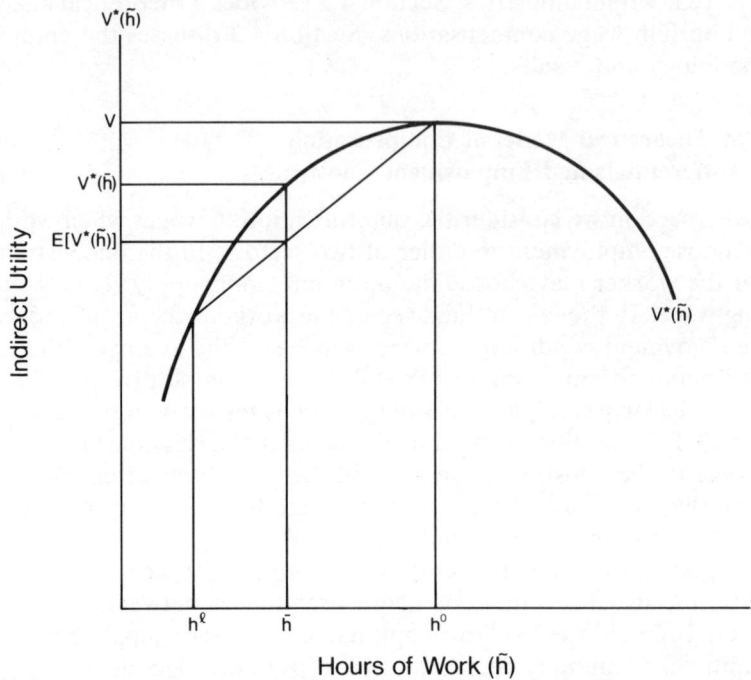

Figure 4.1 Sources of Compensating Differentials Illustrated Using Hours of Work and Constrained Maximal Utility

supply of $\bar{h}$ hours.[4] Equation 1 defines the proportionate compensating wage differential $(w^* - w)/w \approx \ell n(w^*/w)$ implicitly. Figure 4.1 demonstrates this idea for the choice between jobs that entail h^0 and $\bar{h}$ hours at work. The compensating wage differential is simply the increase in the wage rate sufficient to eliminate $V - V^*(\bar{h})$, the utility difference.[5] The consumer worker is indifferent between the wage-hours package w, h^0 and the wage-hours pair w^*, $\bar{h}$. Both allow the attainment of the same utility level.[6] Formally, w^* is the solution of the implicit equation 1 and may be written as

(2) $\qquad w^* = w^*(\bar{h}, w, p, y)$

We will discuss some straightforward approximations to equation 2 below.

The preceding alalysis supposes that the hours of work constraint $\bar{h}$ is known with certainty. In some situations it may be more realistic to assume that $\bar{h}$ is a random drawing from a distribution of possible hours constraints with expected value $\bar{h}$. The worker must choose between a job in the constrained sector which offers the known wage w^{**} and a known distribution of hours of work, versus a job in the unconstrained sector with the known combination w, h^0. Labor market equilibrium will then require that w^{**} compensate for the riskiness of fluctuations in hours worked and for the presence of the mean constraint on hours worked. Figure 4.1 also illustrates this point. We have assumed in the figure that $\bar{h} = h^0$ with probability π, and $\bar{h} = h^\ell$ with probability $1 - \pi$. The probability is chosen such that $E[\bar{h}] \equiv \bar{h} = \pi h^0 + (1 - \pi)h^\ell$. Expected utility is then $E[V^*(\bar{h})] = \pi V^*(h^0) + (1-\pi)V^*(h^\ell)$. The wage difference $w^{**} - w^*$ compensates for the utility difference $E[V^*(\bar{h})] - V^*(\bar{h})$, which is the incremental utility loss associated with the addition of risk to the model with only a mean constraint. As usual, the sign of the compensating differential depends on the worker's attitude toward risk. The case of risk aversion, represented by the concavity of the function $V^*(\bar{h})$ in figure 4.1 implies that additional risk adds to the compensating wage differential $w^{**} - w^*$. This may be seen by noticing that a mean preserving decrease in h^ℓ would lead to greater variance in hours, a greater (absolute) difference in $E[V^*(\bar{h})] - V^*(\bar{h})$, and a greater compensating wage differential. The concavity of the function $V^*(\bar{h})$ is guaranteed in the neighborhood of $\bar{h} = h^0$ so that for small deviations of $\bar{h}$ from h^0, increased risk will generally imply an increased compensating wage differential.

In general, labor market equilibrium will now require that

(3) $$V^{**}(w^{**}, p, y; \theta) = V^*(\bar{h}, p, w^*\bar{h} + y)$$

where $V^{**} = \int V^*(\bar{h}, p, w^{**}\bar{h} + y) f(\bar{h}; \theta) \, d\bar{h}$ is expected utility and θ represents the parameters of the density function for hours of work offered. Equation 3 defines w^{**} implicitly as

(4) $$w^{**} = w^{**}(w^*, p, y; \theta)$$

which is the wage rate which must accompany an employment contract which offers expected constraints and uncertain employment.

The representation of a simplified unemployment insurance (UI) system does not add any major complications. We use the simple specification that the UI system replaces a fixed proportion γ of lost earnings. Labor income is, then, $w^{**}[\bar{h} + \gamma(h^0 - \bar{h})]$. The number of hours actually compensated is $\bar{h} + \gamma(h^0 - \bar{h})$, which we call effective hours.[7] Equilibrium condition 1 is replaced by

(1') $$V^{\gamma*}(\bar{h}, p, w^*[\bar{h} + \gamma(h^0 - \bar{h})] + y) = V(w, p, y)$$

Effective hours, and not actual hours, enter the relevant budget constraint. It should be noted that we used h^0 which depends on w and not w^* as the hours base for calculating lost earnings. The relevant comparison for determining the opportunity cost of the layoff or hours reduction is with the labor supply in the unconstrained sector. The wage w is the only wage at which the worker can optimize hours of work directly. The market operates to make the utility level provided by the insured constrained job equal to the utility level provided by $h^0(w, p, y)$. The utility level provided by $h^0(w^*, p, y)$ is irrelevant since no worker can achieve it. Condition 1' introduces an important new twist into the analysis. Depending on the values of γ and $h^0 - \bar{h}$, it is possible for w^* to be less than w. This occurs whenever the utility payment for the UI benefits exceeds the utility loss from being required to consume too much leisure. The nature of this tradeoff is clear from the approximations below. When the hours offer $\bar{h}$ is a random variable with mean $\bar{h}$ in the insured sector, the equilibrium condition 3 becomes

$$(3') \qquad V^{\gamma**}(w^{**}, p, y; \theta) = V^{\gamma*}(\bar{h}, p, w^*[\bar{h} + \gamma(h^0 - \bar{h})] + y)$$

The compensating wage differentials defined implicitly by (1') and (3') will, of course, depend on γ as well as the wage, price, nonlabor income triple w, p, y, and the θ parameters.[8]

We now address the problem of deriving useful approximations to the compensations expressed in equations 2 and 4. The results reveal that the parameters of the approximations have familiar interpretations which relate to conventional labor supply and risk analysis. We combine the approximations to form an estimating equation for the wage-generating function for a panel of continuously employed (or temporarily laid off) workers.

Let $U(x, 1 - h)$ be a strictly quasiconcave, twice continuously differentiable utility function, and let $px = wh + y$ be the budget constraint. It is convenient[9] to work with the minimum expenditure function $R(w, p, v)$, defined as

$$(5) \qquad R(w, p, v) = \min_{\{x, h\}} px - wh$$

subject to $v = U(x, 1 - h)$ and $0 < h < 1$. In the absence of unemployment insurance the minimum expenditure function for an individual constrained by $h = \bar{h}$ with certainty is given by

$$(6) \qquad R^*(\bar{h}, p, v) - w\bar{h} = \min_{\{x\}} px - w\bar{h}$$

subject to $v = U(x, 1 - \bar{h})$. Equilibrium condition 1 is equivalent to

$$(7) \qquad R^*(\bar{h}, p, v) - w^*\bar{h} = R(w, p, v)$$

Expanding the left-hand side of (7) around the point $\bar{h} = h^c(w, p, v)$, the compensated labor supply function, yields the second order approximation

$$(8) \qquad \frac{w^* - w}{w} \approx \frac{1}{2}\frac{1}{e}\frac{[\bar{h} - h^0(w, p, y)]^2}{\bar{h}h^0(w, p, y)}$$

where e is defined as the compensated labor supply elasticity for the unconstrained individual. The compensating differential is approximately proportional to the squared expected unemployment rate $u \equiv (h^0 - \bar{h})/h^0$. The factor of proportionality is half the inverse compensated labor supply elasticity. The more inelastic the compensated labor supply schedule, the greater the compensating differential will be for anticipated underemployment or anticipated spells of unemployment. The formula is symmetric. It also determines the overtime premium for anticipated overemployment although equation 8 expresses the overtime premium as if it applied to the average rather than the marginal wage rate.

Next consider the introduction of a UI system which pays benefits as γ percent of lost earnings $w^*(h^0 - \bar{h})$. Replacing constrained hours $\bar{h}$ by effective hours in the budget constraint implies that the constrained minimum expenditure function is

(6') $$R^{\gamma*}(\bar{h}, p, v) - w\{\bar{h} + \gamma[h^c(w, p, v) - \bar{h}]\}$$
$$= \min_{\{x\}} px - w\{\bar{h} + \gamma[h^c(w, p, v) - \bar{h}]\}$$

subject to $v + U(x, 1-\bar{h})$.[10] Replacing R^* in equation 7 with $R^{\gamma*}$ and expanding the left-hand side around $\bar{h} = h^c$ yields, to second order,

(8') $$\frac{w^* - w}{w} = \frac{-\gamma(h^0 - \bar{h})}{h^0 + \gamma(h^0 - \bar{h})} + \frac{1}{2}\frac{1}{e}\frac{(h^0 - \bar{h})^2}{h^0[\bar{h} + \gamma(h^0 - \bar{h})]}$$

where $h^0 = h^0(w, p, y)$. The presence of the UI benefits causes the compensating differential to fall in proportion to the expected unemployment rate. The factor of proportionality is exactly the UI system replacement rate. Equation 8' shows explicitly the tradeoff between UI benefits and the labor supply compensation. The function describing the compensating differential is approximately quadratic in the expected unemployment rate. For small expected unemployment rates the compensating differential is negative. As the expected unemployment rate increases, the compensating differential falls to a (negative) minimum and then increases. The unemployment rate corresponding to the minimum compensating differential and the rate corresponding to a zero compensating differential depend on the values of γ and e as well as on the optimal and constrained labor supplies. Because (8') is approximately quadratic in the expected unemployment rate, however, the basic dependence is on the product γe. It is approximately true that the minimum differential occurs at the unemployment rate $u = \gamma e$ and the two zero compensating differentials occur at unemployment rates of zero and γe.[11] These three points determine the quadratic approximation.

If the labor supply constraint $\bar{h}$ is drawn from a distribution with $E[\bar{h}] = \bar{h}$ and $Var[\bar{h}] = \sigma^2$ then, in the absence of UI insurance, equilibrium condition 3 can be expanded in a Taylor series around $\bar{h}$ to yield the approximation

$$(9) \quad \frac{w^{**}-w^*}{w^*} \approx \frac{1}{2} r \frac{\sigma^2}{\bar{h}^2}$$

where r is the relative risk aversion function when $\bar{h}$ is the sole source of randomness in V^*.[12] Equation 9 implies that the incremental compensating differential implied by positive hours variance is approximately proportional to the squared coefficient of variation in hours of work. The factor of proportionality is half the relative risk aversion, r, which must be positive, at least when $\bar{h}$ is near h^0. When a UI system is in effect, equation 9 is modified to be

$$(9') \quad \frac{w^{**}-w^*}{w^*} = \frac{1}{2} r \frac{\sigma^2}{\bar{h}[\bar{h}+\gamma(h^0-\bar{h})]}$$

where h^0 is evaluated at $h^0(w, p, y)$ as in (8') above.

Although we apply the approximations 8 and 9 to individual data using individual unemployment rates, the theory has some implications for the use of aggregate unemployment rates in wage determination equations as well. Two points should be remembered. First, the error in hours of work, $\bar{h}-\tilde{h}$, is not a determinant of the compensating differential. Consequently, the individual's realized unemployment rate is not relevant; only the predictable component $h^0-\bar{h}$ affects the wage. Using the aggregate unemployment rate in the individual's wage determination equation is justified only if this variable is the appropriate expected unemployment rate for the individual. Second, the use of the squared aggregate unemployment rate confounds two effects. The coefficient on the squared expected unemployment rate measures the inverse labor supply elasticity, while the coefficient on the expected squared error (squared coefficient of variation) measures the risk compensation. Unless the aggregate unemployment rate is decomposed into predicted and error components, these effects will be confounded.

The approximations in equations 8' and 9' make clear the relationship between our model and labor supply decisions when layoffs are correctly anticipated. Workers may enter into explicit contracts such as collective bargaining agreements or implicit contracts with particular employers in order to secure employment in the constrained sector. A temporary layoff is one tool which the employer may use to make the expected constraint a realized constraint. If temporary layoffs were the only form of hours reduction that an employer used, then the key parameters θ in the distribution of $\bar{h}$ would be the layoff probability π; the conditional expected completed duration given a layoff δ; and the conditional variance of the layoff duration ϕ^2. The implied compensating wage differential is

$$\frac{w^{**}-w}{w} = -\gamma\frac{\pi\delta}{h^0+(\gamma-1)\pi\delta} + \frac{1}{2}\frac{1}{e}\frac{\pi^2\delta^2}{h^0[h^0+(\gamma-1)\pi\delta]}$$

(10)

$$+\frac{1}{2}r\frac{\pi[(1-\pi)\delta^2+\phi^2]}{(h^0-\pi\delta)[h^0+(\gamma-1)\pi\delta]}$$

Equation 10 forms the basis of our empirical analysis. It shows clearly that the theoretical constructs—expected constrained hours and hours variance—may be replaced with the parameters of the layoff structure associated with the job. The probability of temporary layoff, the conditional mean layoff duration, and conditional duration variance are all observable characteristics of a given job, in principle. Consequently, equation 10 implies that $\ell(w^{**}/w)$ can be specified in terms of employment conditions that are identifiable in many survey data sets. In addition, this formulation does not require a priori determination of which workers are employed in constrained labor supply situations. As the probability of experiencing a layoff approaches zero, the compensating differential also approaches zero. Hence, the layoff probability for every worker can be used as a continuous indicator of the extent to which labor supply constraints are an important aspect of the worker's job.

In this section we have shown that the appropriate compensating differential for employment situations involving anticipated spells of unemployment can be expressed in terms of familiar labor supply parameters. The job-specific variables affecting the size of the differential can be expressed in terms of quantifiable properties of the layoff incidence and layoff duration characteristics of the job. In the next section we calculate empirical analogues of these variables and estimate the compensating wage differentials.

4.3 Empirical Analysis of Compensating Wage Differentials

The wage function in equation 10 holds at the market level under the assumptions of section 4.2. Specifically, given data on individual opportunity wages w, expected unemployment $\pi\delta$, and unemployment variance $\pi[(1-\pi)\delta^2+\phi^2]$, we could estimate the parameters γ, e, and r directly from (10). There are no genuine issues of simultaneous determination as long as unobserved individual heterogeneity is confined to opportunity wages, unemployment incidence, and layoff duration.[13] The common utility function parameters e and r will still determine the market-equilibrium-compensating differential. On the other hand, if individuals vary substantially in either the value of the compensated labor supply elasticity or the relative risk aversion parameter, the market will induce a sort in which firms are matched with employees who supply the appropriate constrained hours and hours variance at minimum cost to the firm. For example, if e varies over the population while r does not, then individuals with the highest e will be sorted into the firms which use temporary layoffs the most—large $\pi\delta$. This combination provides the firm with its demanded employment flexibility at the lowest cost. Individuals with small e, however, are sorted into jobs with small expected unemployment, since these individuals require the largest compensating differentials. If the distribution of e is known, then, in principle, the market sorting of individuals into jobs according to $\pi\delta$ can be inferred directly. In practice, these equilibria are difficult to generate and analyze except in the simplest of cases.[14] We will confine our analysis to the model in which all workers share a common γ, e, and r but may differ systematically and permanently according to w, π, δ, and ϕ^2. That is, we will allow personal heterogeneity in the opportunity wages and job characteristics but not in the utility function. This preserves equation 10 as an operational form of the equilibrium without requiring that all individuals be observationally identical, given observed characteristics.

Panel data permit us to construct measures of the probability of layoff and layoff duration parameters which control for the individual's personal characteristics, past layoff durations, industry-specific past layoff durations, and economy-wide layoff histories. Although this information is probably inferior to the individual's own information, there is no doubt that controlling for personal history differences gives a substantially more accurate measure of the individual's employment situaton than we could get from annual survey averages produced separately for different industries and occupations. As in other empirical analyses of expectational equilibria, our task is to identify the consistent patterns in the employer's behavior and estimate the relationship between these forecastable actions and the market wage. We do observe that there are permanent differences across industries in the extent and duration of layoffs; however, there is also substantial intraindustry variability which reflects firm-specific and individual-specific differences in employment conditions. Our method of constructing π, δ, and ϕ^2 will capture these employer and individual components as well as industry-specific and economy wide differences in the unemployment expectations of the workers.

Formally, let d_{it} be the duration of unemployment for individual i in year t. Let z_{it} be the individual's employment history and personal characteristics up to year t, including d_{it-1}, d_{it-2}, d_{it-3} and economy histories. Consider the two equation systems for the latent variables y_{1it} and y_{2it}:

(11)
$$y_{1it} = z'_{it} \beta_1 + \varepsilon_{1it}$$
$$y_{2it} + z'_{it} \beta_2 + \varepsilon_{2it}$$

where $\varepsilon_{it}(2 \times 1)$ is distributed $N(0, \Sigma)$ independently and identically for all i and t, and β_1 and β_2 are unknown parameter vectors. Define the event

(12) $$\ell_{it} = \begin{cases} 1 \text{ if } i \text{ is laid off in year } t \\ 0 \text{ otherwise} \end{cases}$$

We use equation system 11 along with the following sample selection rules to determine the individual's employment-specific layoff parameters

(13) $$d_{it} = \begin{cases} y_{1it} \text{ if } \ell_{it} = 1 \\ 0 \text{ if } \ell_{it} = 0 \end{cases}$$

and

(14) $$\ell_{it} = \begin{cases} 1 \text{ if } y_{2it} > 0 \\ 0 \text{ otherwise} \end{cases}$$

Following Heckman (1979), the selection rules 13 and 14 imply that

(15) $$\pi_{it} \equiv \Pr\{\ell_{it} = 1\} = \int_{-\frac{z'_{it}\beta_2}{\sqrt{\sigma_{22}}}}^{\infty} f(s)ds$$

(16) $$\pi_{it}\delta_{it} \equiv E[d_{it}|z_{it}] = \pi_{it}(z'_{it}\beta_1 + \frac{\sigma_{12}}{\sqrt{\sigma_{22}}}\gamma_{it})$$

and

(17) $$\phi_{it}^2 = \sigma_{11}[(1 - \frac{\sigma_{12}^2}{\sigma_{11}\sigma_{22}}) + \frac{\sigma_{12}^2}{\sigma_{11}\sigma_{22}}(1 - \frac{z'_{it}\beta_2}{\sqrt{\sigma_{22}}}\lambda_{it} - \lambda_{it}^2)]$$

where $f(s)$ is the standard normal density, $F(s)$ is the cumulative normal distribution function, and

$$\lambda_{it} \equiv f(\frac{z'_{it}\beta_2}{\sqrt{\sigma_{22}}})/F(\frac{z'_{it}\beta_2}{\sqrt{\sigma_{22}}})$$

Equation 15 models π_{it} as a probit function given the history contained in z_{it}. Equation 16 defines the unconditional mean duration as the expectation of the conditional mean durations δ_{it} and zero. Equation 17 defines the conditional variance ϕ_{it}^2. We use these quantities to form the unconditional variance $\pi_{it}[(1 - \pi_{it})\delta_{it}^2 + \phi_{it}^2]$. The statistical model of equations 15–17 provides an empirical counterpart to each of the required theoretical employment condition measures. We turn next to the estimation of the parameters of the layoff duration model and the compensating differentials.

4.3.1 The Data

Estimates are based on waves 1–9 of *The Panel Study of Income Dynamics*, (PSID) corresponding to calendar years 1967–75.[15] Only the 3,318 households in the wave 9 release of the probability sample were eligible for inclusion in the estimation sample. Since we used three years of employment history to calculate the unemployment measures, estimated differentials cover the period from 1970 (wave 4) to 1975 (wave 9). In order to be included in a particular year's estimation sample, an observation was required to come from a household with a white male head who was interviewed in the employed battery in the current year and each of the three previous years. This last requirement means that an individual must have been employed or temporarily laid off at the time of the interview (usually March of the following year) for four consecutive years. The unemployed battery is given to individuals who have experienced a prolonged layoff or who are unemployed and do not anticipate returning to their previous jobs. This selection rule, although primarily dictated by data availability considerations, results in an analysis sample of very stably employed individuals. On average, the sampled individuals have twenty-four years of labor force experience and over nine years of employer tenure. We are not concerned here with extending our conclusions to a population of less stably employed individuals such as youths or females. Rather, we realize that our conclusions apply primarily to individuals who have made relatively long-term employment commitments in industries and occupations which display substantial differences in short-term unemployment and temporary layoff patterns.

About forty percent of the 3,318 cases qualify for inclusion in any one year's estimation sample. Changes in the head of household and failure of the requirement of four consecutive interviews in the employed battery were about equally responsible for deletions. Experienced users of the PSID data will recognize that samples of 1,200–1,300 are common when continuous histories of individuals (as opposed to households) are drawn from the probability sample. Table 4.A.1 presents definitions and annual summary statistics for all variables used in the analysis.

4.3.2 Extimation and Measurement of the Unemployment Variables

The basic unemployment variable used in our analysis is $DSCRP_{it}$, which is defined as the number of hours individual i spent unemployed in year t.[16] Hours unemployed are measured as the product of days spent unemployed, or on strike, times the average hours worked per week when employed regularly. The variable $DUNEM_{it}$ is defined as one when $DSCRP > 0$ and zero otherwise. Table 4.1 presents the results of estimating a probit equation for DUNEM (column 1) and a selection-bias-corrected conditional expectation equation for DSCRP (column 2), given that layoff duration is positive.

The probit equation in column 1 of table 4.1 measures the effect of the individual's employment history on π_{it}. The determinants of π_{it} are the individual's history of layoff durations for the past three years (DSCRPM1–DSCRPM3), the industry-specific average layoff durations for the past three years (MDSCRPM1–MDSCRPM3), and the economy-

Table 4.1 Estimates of the Parameters of the Layoff Probability and Conditional Duration Equations (Standard errors in parentheses)

Variable	DUNEM[a] (Probit) (1)	DSCRP[b] (Lambda) (2)
DSCRPM1	1.813 (.100)	.384
DSCRPM2	.726 (.098)	.277
DSCRPM3	.492 (.083)	.131
MDSCRPM1	−3.848 (.749)	−1.395
MDSCRPM2	−2.031 (.879)	−.376
MDSCRPM3	−.986 (.684)	−.914
YDSCRPM1	.053 (2.537)	3.761
YDSCRPM2	−10.809 (3.737)	−3.284
YDSCRPM3	7.021 (2.205)	3.404
SCHCLASS1	.987 (.066)	−.014
SCHCLASS2	.654 (.063)	−.022
SCHCLASS3	.451 (.065)	.028
EXPERIENCE	−.010 (.007)	−.001
EXPERIENCE^2/100	.006 (.014)	.007
TENURE	−.028 (.008)	−.012
TENURE^2/100	.085 (.027)	.020
LAMBDA	n.a.	.135
Constant	−.871 (.176)	.117

Table 4.1 (continued)

Variable	DUNEM[a] (Probit) (1)	DSCRP[b] (Lambda) (2)
R^2	n.a.	.111
S. E. equation	n.a.	.314
ℓn likelihood	−2185.870	n.a.
χ^2 (16)	9698.044	n.a.

[a]Estimated by maximum likelihood. Equation also includes industry dummy variables.
[b]Estimated by OLS. Equation also includes industry dummy variables. The reported S. E. equation and R^2 have been corrected.

wide average layoff durations for the same period (YDSCRPM1–YDSCRPM3). Permanent interindustry differences are captured by a set of fifteen industry dummy variables. Personal characteristics are measured by schooling dummy variables (relative to college graduates) (SCHCLAS1–SCHCLAS3), total labor force experience (EXPERIENCE, EXPERIENCE^2), and total time spent with the same employer (TENURE, TENURE^2). Although the determinants of π_{it} are not the major concern of this analysis, it is worth noting that personal unemployment history is an important predictor of current unemployment probability, even when industry average durations and economy-wide durations have been held constant. We interpret this effect as measuring employer and individual elements of the employment contract. No attempt is made to separate the employer-specific effect from the individual-specific effect since we remove a person effect from the wage equation used later in the analysis. The effects of common influences on all employers in a given industry are captured by the industry-specific variables. These allow both permanent and serially correlated transitory effects of unemployment history to influence predicted layoff probabilities. It is interesting to note that lagged industry layoff durations decrease the probability of a current layoff, given the industry dummy variables. This indicates that workers (and employers) expect unemployment to undershoot the long-term average after an exceptionally bad year and to overshoot the long-term average after an exceptionally good year. Economy-wide influences are mixed and rather imprecisely estimated. Personal characteristics have reasonable effects. High school dropouts (SCHCLAS1) are the most like to suffer layoffs, followed by high school graduates (SCHCLAS2), college dropouts (SCHCLAS3) and college graduates. Increases in employment tenure substantially reduce layoff probabilities (at a decreasing rate); lifetime labor force experience has a weak negative effect on layoffs (also at a decreasing rate).

Column 2 of table 4.1 shows the selection-bias-corrected estimates of the conditional duration equation. The pattern of effects is similar to the layoff probability equation, but no assessment of statistical significance can be made from the least-squares estimates. The implied interequation correlation coefficient is $\sigma_{12}/\sqrt{\sigma_{11}\sigma_{22}} = .43$. Under the null hypothesis of $\sigma_{12} = 0$, the standard error of the coefficient on LAMBDA is .181. Although the hypothesis that $\sigma_{12} = 0$ cannot be rejected at conventional significance levels, we do not want to ignore a sample correlation of .43; hence, we maintain the selection bias correction when calculating δ_{it} and ϕ_{it}^2.

Table 4.2 provides a comprehensive summary of observed layoff incidence and duration as well as the layoff incidence, expected duration, and duration variance implied by the equations in table 4.1. Table 4.2 reveals the substantial and relatively permanent interindustry differences in the use of temporary layoffs as a means of reducing work hours for long-term employees.[17] The row labeled DUNEM shows the actual annual average layoff frequency for each industry. The row labeled FDUNEM is the predicted layoff probability π_{it}, based on table 4.1. The DSCRP row shows the average layoff duration in thousands of hours.[18] The row EXPDURAT shows the expected layoff duration $\pi_{it}\delta_{it}$, based on table 4.1. The unconditional variance based on table 4.1 is shown in the row VARDURAT. Durable manufacturing industries (30–33) and the construction industry (51) have the highest layoff incidences and expected durations. Nondurable manufacturing (40, 45) also shows substantial use of layoff unemployment. These same industries exhibit higher unemployment risk (measured by VARDURAT) also.[19] Government (92) and professional service industries (86, 87) use layoff unemployment relatively little. Overall, 1975 was the year with the highest predicted unconditional unemployment duration (47 hours) and the highest observed unconditional unemployment duration (64 hours). The year 1971 had the largest overprediction (10 hours) while 1975 had the largest underprediction (-17 hours).

4.3.3 Estimation of the Wage Equation

The empirical counterparts of the variables in equation 10 were defined using the predicted probabilities, durations, and variances estimated in table 4.1 and summarized in table 4.2. We used reported hours (HACT_{it}) plus unemployed hours (DSCRP_{it}) as our measure of desired hours (HOPT_{it}). The empirical counterparts of the expressions in (10) are:

(18) $\quad \text{HEFF}(\gamma) \equiv h^0 + (\gamma - 1)\pi\delta = \text{HOPT}_{it}$
$\quad\quad\quad + (\gamma - 1)\text{EXPDURAT}_{it}$

(19) $\quad \text{CERTEG}(\gamma)_{it} \equiv \dfrac{-\pi\delta}{h^0 + (\gamma - 1)\pi\delta} = \dfrac{-\text{EXPDURAT}_{it}}{\text{HEFF}(\gamma)_{it}}$

Table 4.2 Unemployment, Expected Unemployment, and Compensating Differential Measures for Annual Industry Aggregates

		1970	1971	1972	1973	1974	1975			1970	1971	1792	1973	1974	1975
1.	DSCRP	.0017	.0558	.0235	.0402	.0802	.0595	55.	DSCRP	.0758	.0558	.0517	.0436	.0604	.0456
	EXPDURAT	.0325	.0532	.0327	.0455	.0496	.0567		EXPDURAT	.0364	.0588	.0265	.0407	.0576	.0653
	VARDURAT	.0184	.0309	.0152	.0217	.0240	.0318		VARDURAT	.0211	.0298	.0148	.0205	.0278	.0286
	DUNEM	.0203	.1194	.0458	.0685	.1473	.1429		DUNEM	.3239	.2727	.1312	.1129	.2121	.1667
	FDUNEM	.0910	.1079	.0705	.0906	.1114	.1160		FDUNEM	.1725	.2001	.1171	.1685	.2079	.1967
	Comp. Diff.	2.564	5.205	6.779	7.469	4.888	4.441		Comp. Diff.	2.865	4.233	3.492	3.746	5.372	5.820
	(Std. Error)	(.430)	(.961)	(1.592)	(2.232)	(1.072)	(.815)		(Std. Error)	(.507)	(.783)	(.678)	(.787)	(1.125)	(1.386)
30.	DSCRP	.0095	.0522	.0638	.0278	.0596	.0573	57.	DSCRP	.0050	.0395	.0088	.0025	.0075	.0383
	EXPDURAT	.0332	.0537	.0208	.0442	.0501	.0394		EXPDURAT	.0126	.0219	.0167	.0226	.0190	.0224
	VARDURAT	.0183	.0288	.0121	.0209	.0214	.0198		VARDURAT	.0079	.0124	.0065	.0120	.0112	.0126
	DUNEM	.1207	.1429	.2143	.0943	.2076	.1818		DUNEM	.0862	.1452	.0400	.0208	.0417	.0208
	FDUNEM	.1320	.1539	.0963	.1337	.1475	.1428		FDUNEM	.0661	.0761	.0520	.0700	.0811	.0800
	Comp. Diff.	3.968	4.792	2.087	4.878	4.881	3.859		Comp. Diff.	1.354	1.992	1.818	2.215	1.786	1.908
	(Std. Error)	(.681)	(.846)	(.349)	(1.130)	(1.130)	(.721)		(Std. Error)	(.221)	(.329)	(.510)	(.458)	(.303)	(.318)
31.	DSCRP	.0097	.0375	.0149	.0267	.0117	.0593	61.	DSCRP	.0133	.0159	.0149	.0128	.0242	.0309
	EXPDURAT	.0204	.0355	.0166	.0307	.0349	.0329		EXPDURAT	.0153	.0252	.0113	.0205	.0258	.0318
	VARDURAT	.0117	.0196	.0092	.0142	.0186	.0179		VARDURAT	.0090	.0140	.0066	.0112	.0141	.0158
	DUNEM	.0435	.0769	.0864	.0648	.0865	.1628		DUNEM	.0674	.0315	.0516	.0446	.0828	.0898
	FDUNEM	.0859	.0999	.0624	.0891	.1045	.0965		FDUNEM	.0678	.0802	.0504	.0753	.0874	.0896
	Comp. Diff.	1.860	2.977	1.748	3.454	3.260	4.871		Comp. Diff.	1.672	2.042	.812	2.433	2.026	2.625
	(Std. Error)	(.311)	(.507)	(.308)	(.814)	(.584)	(.915)		(Std. Error)	(.287)	(.343)	(.134)	(.451)	(.344)	(.511)
32.	DSCRP	.2073	.0747	.0360	.0584	.1062	.1292	81.	DSCRP	.0107	.0000	.0057	.0413	.0248	.0637
	EXPDURAT	.0909	.0744	.0669	.0615	.1177	.1118		EXPDURAT	.0180	.0288	.0117	.0231	.0257	.0376
	VARDURAT	.0439	.0317	.0310	.0315	.0538	.0468		VARDURAT	.0103	.0161	.0068	.0129	.0142	.0163
	DUNEM	.4456	.2410	.1714	.3000	.4407	.3529		DUNEM	.0333	.0000	.0286	.1316	.0811	.1471
	FDUNEM	.2851	.2262	.1795	.2511	.3388	.2853		FDUNEM	.0691	.0843	.0493	.0774	.0853	.0870
	Comp. Diff.	8.450	8.101	5.992	7.047	14.011	10.281		Comp. Diff.	1.327	2.075	.964	2.094	2.200	3.337
	(Std. Error)	(1.621)	(1.933)	(1.288)	(1.313)	(2.744)	(2.317)		(Std. Error)	(.218)	(.348)	(.158)	(.348)	(.370)	(.786)

Table 4.2 (continued)

		1970	1971	1972	1973	1974	1975			1970	1971	1972	1973	1974	1975
33.	DSCRP	.0161	.0329	.0097	.0197	.0374	.0782	85.	DSCRP	.0162	.0047	.0177	.0204	.0353	.0319
	EXPDURAT	.0191	.0351	.0166	.0286	.0357	.0354		EXPDURAT	.0167	.0340	.0153	.0230	.0286	.0353
	VARDURAT	.0112	.0179	.0087	.0158	.0177	.0187		VARDURAT	.0095	.0150	.0086	.0128	.0148	.0184
	DUNEM	.0870	.1154	.0571	.0308	.1967	.1667		DUNEM	.0676	.0333	.0769	.0526	.0794	.0625
	FDUNEM	.0852	.1056	.0702	.0990	.1165	.1086		FDUNEM	.0653	.0794	.0519	.0759	.0892	.0895
	Comp. Diff.	1.964	3.134	1.450	2.519	3.120	3.381		Comp. Diff.	1.801	3.854	1.635	1.925	3.887	3.739
	(Std. Error)	(.327)	(.591)	(.268)	(.435)	(.637)	(.616)		(Std. Error)	(.299)	(.872)	(.285)	(.323)	(.689)	(.707)
40.	DSCRP	.0095	.0176	.0034	.0241	.0117	.0310	86.	DSCRP	.0119	.0000	.0025	.0000	.0131	.0190
	EXPDURAT	.0093	.0220	.0055	.0127	.0187	.0225		EXPDURAT	.0120	.0204	.0119	.0145	.0211	.0291
	VARDURAT	.0104	.0143	.0070	.0111	.0138	.0146		VARDURAT	.0072	.0114	.0063	.0084	.0118	.0158
	DUNEM	.0588	.2051	.1290	.1667	.1250	.1026		DUNEM	.0351	.0000	.0208	.0000	.0600	.0328
	FDUNEM	.1121	.1256	.0766	.1151	.1378	.1291		FDUNEM	.0559	.0646	.0408	.0613	.0740	.0752
	Comp. Diff.	1.509	2.438	1.151	1.879	2.269	4.330		Comp. Diff.	1.303	1.817	1.382	1.170	1.907	3.392
	(Std. Error)	(.245)	(.403)	(.187)	(.306)	(.398)	(.804)		(Std. Error)	(.213)	(.302)	(.279)	(.194)	(.318)	(.657)
45.	DSCRP	.0399	.0188	.0049	.0351	.0465	.1261	87.	DSCRP	.0011	.0189	.0006	.0002	.0040	.0216
	EXPDURAT	.0372	.0367	.0258	.0429	.0580	.0562		EXPDURAT	.0104	.0219	.0070	.0155	.0216	.0220
	VARDURAT	.0205	.0196	.0143	.0189	.0234	.0244		VARDURAT	.0074	.0122	.0053	.0095	.0124	.0124
	DUNEM	.2118	.0488	.0241	.1333	.1487	.2647		DUNEM	.0230	.0460	.0116	.0130	.0274	.0811
	FDUNEM	.1326	.1186	.0893	.1296	.1459	.1423		FDUNEM	.0697	.0812	.0503	.0792	.0915	.0870
	Comp. Diff.	3.330	3.607	2.150	4.052	6.019	6.305		Comp. Diff.	1.351	2.049	.944	1.473	2.368	2.248
	(Std. Error)	(.564)	(.626)	(.364)	(1.057)	(1.683)	(1.569)		(Std. Error)	(.227)	(.347)	(.155)	(.241)	(.394)	(.372)
51.	DSCRP	.1226	.0427	.0411	.0574	.1072	.1982	92.	DSCRP	.0176	.0022	.0252	.0176	.0035	.0050
	EXPDURAT	.0604	.0835	.0537	.0725	.0938	.1006		EXPDURAT	.0160	.0197	.0116	.0160	.0203	.0196
	VARDURAT	.0257	.0348	.0255	.0317	.0402	.0450		VARDURAT	.0081	.0109	.0057	.0084	.0113	.0109
	DUNEM	.2761	.1667	.1683	.1682	.2789	.4078		DUNEM	.0652	.0274	.0225	.0538	.0194	.0206
	FDUNEM	.1781	.2095	.1594	.2061	.2360	.2356		FDUNEM	.0502	.0564	.0346	.0529	.0624	.0601
	Comp. Diff.	5.824	9.277	5.721	7.065	10.645	10.673		Comp. Diff.	1.862	1.627	3.797	1.509	5.182	2.057
	(Std. Error)	(1.379)	(2.310)	(1.226)	(1.613)	(2.619)	(2.437)		(Std. Error)	(.377)	(.274)	(.921)	(.266)	(.891)	(.344)

(20) $$\text{CERTSQG}(\gamma)_{it} \equiv \frac{.5\pi^2\delta^2}{h^0[h^0 + (\gamma-1)\pi\delta]}$$

$$\equiv \frac{.5\,(\text{EXPDURAT}_{it})^2}{\text{HOPT}_{it}\,\text{HEFF}(\gamma)_{it}}$$

(21) $$\text{COEFVSQG}(\gamma)_{it} \equiv \frac{.5\pi[(1-\pi)\delta^2 + \phi^2]}{(h^0 - \pi\delta)[h^0 + (\gamma-1)\pi\delta]}$$

$$= \frac{.5\,\text{VARDURAT}_{it}}{(\text{HOPT}_{it} - \text{EXPDURAT}_{it})\text{HEFF}(\gamma)_{it}}$$

From the definitions in equations 18–21 it is clear that there is a nonlinear dependence on γ (the UI replacement rate) in all three of the expressions which enter the equation for $\ell n(w^{**})$. We deal with this problem in two different ways. First, we estimate γ along with e, r, and the determinants of $\ell n(w)$ by nonlinear methods. Second, we compute the sample average UI replacement rates by industry for each year (MCOMPRAT_{it}) and use these replacement rates instead of γ in the formation of the effective hours variable $\text{HEFF}(\gamma)$.[20]

Table 4.3 reports the results of direct estimation of γ, e, and r by nonlinear least squares. Columns 1 and 2 report the use of the reported hourly wage $\ell n(\text{WAGE})$ as the dependent variable and columns 3 and 4 use the calculated hourly wage $\ell n(\text{EARN/HACT})$ as the dependent variable. We use as variables determining the opportunity wage—last year's wage (LAGW)—collective bargaining status (UNION), schooling, labor force experience, tenure, region, and year.[21] Columns 1 and 3 show the results from the specification implied by equation 10. Columns 2 and 4 show the results from the specifications implied by equation 10 but allowing unanticipated unemployment (UNANTIC) expressed as a percentage of desired hours to enter the equation.[22] The first three rows of table 4.3 show the implied estimates of γ, $1/e$, and r. The row labeled $\hat{e}_{\text{MELO}}$ shows the implied estimate of e using Zellner's (1978) method.[23] The row labeled average compensating differential shows the percentage compensating differential gross of the implicit UI purchase payment.

In general, the results of columns 1 and 2 are quite favorable to our model. The implied ninety percent confidence interval estimate of $.093 \pm .085$ for labor supply elasticity is rather imprecise but certainly consistent with previously reported values for white males in both magnitude and precision of estimation.[24] The estimated γ is too large to be a UI replacement rate; however, we will discuss this problem in more detail below. The estimated relative risk aversion of 14.048 (± 3.714) reveals substantial distaste for unemployment risk. This result supports the hypothesis that the difference in risk aversion between employees and employers results in a demand for implicit labor contracts of the type developed here.[25] Overall, the compensating differential is 3.82 percent ($\pm 1.26\%$) which is not an unreasonably large price for employers to pay for the right to set π, δ, and ϕ^2. Of this differential, .60 percent ($\pm .55\%$)

Table 4.3 Nonlinear Least-Squares Estimates of Wage Parameters under Alternative Specifications (Standard errors in parentheses)

Variable Parameter	ℓn (WAGE)[a] (1)	ℓn (WAGE)[a] (2)	ℓn (EARN/HACT)[a] (3)	ℓn (EARN/HACT)[a] (4)
CERTEQG[b] γ	2.486 (.530)	2.485 (.531)	4.035 (.600)	4.312 (.618)
CERTSQG l/e	8.107 (4.572)	8.102 (4.592)	7.283 (5.292)	9.234 (5.624)
COEFVSQG r	14.048 (2.258)	14.044 (2.263)	28.177 (3.073)	29.555 (3.171)
UNANTIC		−.001 (.058)		.241 (.059)
LAGW	.767 (.009)	.767 (.009)	.772 (.009)	.773 (.009)
UNION	.029 (.009)	.030 (.009)	.042 (.009)	.041 (.009)
SCHOOL	.015 (.002)	.015 (.002)	.015 (.002)	.015 (.002)
EXPERIENCE	.006 (.001)	.006 (.001)	.007 (.001)	.007 (.001)
EXPERIENCE^2 /100	−.013 (.003)	−.013 (.003)	−.014 (.003)	−.015 (.003)
TENURE	.003 (.001)	.003 (.001)	.003 (.001)	.004 (.002)
TENURE^2 /100	−.002 (.005)	−.002 (.005)	−.004 (.005)	−.004 (.005)
Average compensating differential (%)[c]	3.820 (.767)	3.820 (.768)	7.000 (.995)	7.460 (1.041)
$\hat{e}_{MELO}$	.093 (.052)	.093 (.053)	.090 (.065)	.079 (.048)
R^2	.693	.693	.699	.700
S. E. equation	.075	.075	.076	.076
Residual d.f.	5551	5550	5551	5550

[a]Regressions include annual regional dummy variables.
[b]This variable is defined as the negative of the theoretical variable so that its coefficient is γ and not $-\gamma$.
[c]Computed at the sample averages of CERTSQG and COEFVSQG, .00074 and .002293, respectively.

is attributable to the certainty equivalent compensation arising from the mean constraint, while 3.22 percent (±.85%) is attributable to risk compensation arising from the variability of unemployment, given the mean constraint. The addition of the unanticipated part of unemployment to the equation (UNANTIC) has no effect on the results.

The rows labeled Comp. Diff. and (Std. Error) in table 4.2 show the industry by year-estimated compensating differentials and associated standard error implied by column 1 of table 4.3. The reported compensating differentials are gross of the implicit payment for UI. The interindustry patterns reveal that automobile workers (32) received compensating differentials varying from 6.00 percent (1972) to 14.01 percent (1974) of hourly wages in exchange for bearing the mean constraints and employment risks discussed above. Construction workers (51) received compensating differentials ranging from 5.72 percent (1972) to 10.67 percent (1975). Workers in the public sector (92), however, received substantially smaller compensations ranging from 1.51 percent (1973) to 5.18 percent (1974). Other interindustry and time series comparisons are obvious from the results reported in table 4.2.

The results in table 4.3, columns 3 and 4, show that the parameter estimates are sensitive to the choice of dependent variable. The general pattern of results remains the same except for two points. First, the estimated effects are larger when calculated wage rates are used. The implied average compensating differential becomes 7.00 percent (±1.64%). Second, the addition of unanticipated unemployment to the equation using calculated wages as the dependent variable (column 4) does produce a substantial effect of .241 (±.097). This suggests that directly measured wage rates (WAGE) are probably more reliable measures of the hourly compensation relevant to implicit or explicit labor contracts than are the ex post calculated wage rates.

Table 4.4 reports estimates based on our second solution to the nonlinear dependence on γ. The compensating differential variables have been calculated using the observed industry average values of UI replacement rates (MCOMPRAT) reported in table 4.A.1. Using these variables we can remove a person-specific effect from each individual's opportunity wage by standard fixed effect methods. The results are presented in columns 1 and 2 for reported wages and columns 3 and 4 for calculated wages. Once again, the results for reported wages are highly supportive of the model. The estimated labor supply elasticity is .224 (±.729), which is more imprecise than the result in table 4.3 but still consistent with the previous estimates. The estimated risk aversion parameter, 8.982 (±1.828), is smaller in the fixed effect model. The estimated UI replacement rate $\hat{\gamma} = 1.206$ (±.681) now includes reasonable values in its ninety percent confidence interval. The average compensating differential is 2.14 percent (±.55%), which is smaller than the values

Table 4.4　Fixed Effect Estimates of the Compensating Differential Parameters
(Standard errors in parentheses)

Variable Parameter	ℓn (WAGE)[a] (1)	ℓn (WAGE)[a] (2)	ℓn (EARN/HACT)[a] (3)	ℓn (EARN/HACT)[a] (4)
CERTEQG[b] γ	1.206	1.082	.718	.184
	(.414)	(.426)	(.413)	(.423)
CERTSQG l/e	1.140	.806	−2.327	−3.758
	(2.258)	(2.272)	(2.250)	(2.257)
COEFVSQG r	8.982	9.041	10.523	10.782
	(1.111)	(1.112)	(1.109)	(1.106)
UNANTIC		.083		.357
		(.066)		(.065)
Average compensating differential (%)[c]	2.144	2.133	2.241	2.194
	(.334)	(.334)	(.333)	(.332)
$\hat{e}_{\text{MELO}}$	.224	.139	[d]	[d]
	(.443)	(.391)		
R^2	.856	.859	.865	.866
S. E. equation	.223	.223	.222	.221
Residual d.f.	3863	3862	3863	3862

[a]Regressions include all variables in table 4.3.
[b]This variable is defined as the negative of the theoretical variable so that its coefficient is γ and not $-\gamma$.
[c]Computed as in footnote c, table 4.3.
[d]Coefficient of CERTSQG has the wrong sign.

in table 4.3. Finally, the addition of UNANTIC has a larger effect in column 2 than the comparable effect in table 4.3, column 2, but the effect is imprecisely estimated—.083 (±.109)—and its presence does not change any of the other effects substantially. As in the nonlinear model, the results are sensitive to the specification of the dependent variable. Columns 3 and 4 show that calculated wages give wrong-signed estimates of e and depend importantly on unanticipated unemployment. This is consistent with the conclusions for calculated wages shown in table 4.3.

Finally, we consider the implied wage payments for UI benefits. According to equation 10 and definition 19, the appropriate price is $\gamma\text{CERTEG}(\gamma)$. This price implies that wages fall by exactly the expected UI benefits in percentage terms. Table 4.5 shows the annual lower and upper 90 percent confidence bounds for the implicit UI price based on table 4.3, column 1, and data for CERTEQG found in table 4.A.1. It also shows the unconditional sample average UI benefits as a percentage of labor earnings. As we noted above, the estimated γ is too large to reflect the UI replacement rate parameter. Nevertheless, the implied wage payments are quite close to the observed unconditional averages con-

Table 4.5 Annual Average UI Benefits Compared with Benefit Expectations Implied by Estimates of γ

	1970	1971	1972	1973	1974	1975	Overall
Lower bound (%)[a]	2.30	3.18	1.97	2.75	3.45	3.62	2.87
Upper bound (%)[a]	4.78	6.62	4.11	5.72	7.17	7.53	5.97
Observed average (%)[b]	1.06	2.47	.72	1.10	1.58	2.38	1.54

[a]Lower and upper bounds of 90% confidence interval computed using $\hat{\gamma} = 2.486$ (table 4.3, column 1) and standard error of $\gamma = .530$. Values of CERTEQG are in table 4.A.1.
[b]Annual average UI benefits expressed as a percentage of total labor earnings (EARN + benefits) for the whole sample (MCOMPRAT·DUNEM).

sidering the fact that the actual UI benefits were not ever used in the analysis leading to the estimates in table 4.3. Furthermore, an estimated γ of about 1 would give values for the implicit price of UI which are fully consistent with the observed percentages. This is, essentially, the value of γ produced by the estimation technique used in table 4.4.[26] It is reasonable to conclude that our high estimates of γ give an approximate consistency with the competitive requirement that the wage in the constrained job should fall by the expected UI benefit level.

4.3.4 Conclusions

The empirical analysis supports our major theoretical points. Estimated compensating differentials range from less than one percent in industries where the workers experience little anticipated unemployment to over fourteen percent in industries which experience substantial anticipated unemployment and unemployment risk. We find the implied estimate of the compensated labor supply elasticity is around .09, which is consistent with the prevailing evidence on this parameter. Our estimate of a relative risk aversion parameter of 14 is high, but, when coupled with the low values of the coefficient of variation for unemployment, the implied risk premium is modest. Finally, we present some evidence that the implicit price of UI implied by our model is somewhat large under one estimation method and approximately equal to the expected UI benefits under the alternative estimation method.

Appendix

Table 4.A.1 contains variable definitions and summary statistics for all variables used in the analysis. All data manipulations and estimation were performed using the *Statistical Analysis System* (1979 version).

Table 4.A.1 Definitions and Means for All Variables Used in the Empirical Analysis (Standard deviations in parentheses)

Variable	Definition
WAGE	Reported wage in current \$/hr for main job
ℓn(WAGE)	Natural logarithm of reported wage
EARN	Reported total labor income in current \$
ℓn(EARN/HACT)	Natural logarithm of EARN/HACT
HACT	Reported average hours per week × reported weeks worked (thousands of hours)
HOPT	HACT plus hours unemployed and hours on strike (thousands of hours)
DSCRP	HOPT-HACT
DUNEM	Equals 1 if DSCRP>0, equals 0 otherwise
FDUNEM	Predicted probability of layoff spell
CONDDURA	Equals DSCRP if DSCRP>0, missing otherwise (Summary statistics are conditional sample means and standard deviations)
EXPDURAT	Predicted unemployment using the formula in the text
VARDURAT	Predicted variance of unemployment using the formula in the text
HBAR	HOPT-EXPDURAT
MCOMPRAT	Industry average unemployment benefits received as a percentage of lost labor earnings
HEFF	HBAR + MCOMPRAT × EXPDURAT (Note: in table 4.3 HEFF is evaluated at the estimate of γ, not at MCOMPRAT)
CERTEQG	$-$EXPDURAT/HEFF (expected percentage unemployment, defined as the negative of the theoretical quantity)
CERTSQG	$.5(\text{EXPDURAT}^2)/(\text{HOPT} \times \text{HEFF})$ (Half of squared expected percentage unemployment. Table entries $\times 10^{-3}$)
COEFVSQG	$.5\ \text{VARDURAT}/(\text{HBAR} \times \text{HEFF})$ (Half of the squared coefficient of variation of unemployment duration. Table entries $\times 10^{-3}$)

	1970	1971	1972	1973	1974	1975	Overall
	5.146	5.456	5.764	6.036	6.478	7.216	5.992
	(2.952)	(3.313)	(3.425)	(3.187)	(3.531)	(3.862)	(3.447)
	1.517	1.571	1.624	1.681	1.750	1.858	1.663
	(.481)	(.488)	(.494)	(.479)	(.484)	(.492)	(.499)
	11501	12121	12917	13662	14403	15155	13243
	(5932)	(6493)	(6980)	(7305)	(7828)	(8293)	(7261)
	8.423	8.477	8.528	8.581	8.657	8.716	8.560
	(.488)	(.488)	(.501)	(.501)	(.501)	(.508)	(.509)
	2.329	2.311	2.319	2.333	2.279	2.259	2.306
	(.610)	(.558)	(.551)	(.558)	(.548)	(.563)	(.567)
	2.369	2.343	2.339	2.360	2.321	2.316	2.342
	(.583)	(.538)	(.537)	(.537)	(.524)	(.525)	(.542)
	0.040	0.032	0.021	0.027	0.042	0.064	0.038
	(.46)	(.136)	(.110)	(.127)	(.157)	(.207)	(.150)
	0.129	0.105	0.074	0.085	0.136	0.153	0.114
	0.111	0.120	0.079	0.108	0.129	0.126	0.112
	(.093)	(.110)	(.096)	(.108)	(.122)	(.124)	(.111)
	0.312	0.309	0.279	0.325	0.307	0.416	0.331
	(.283)	(.303)	(.303)	(.308)	(.317)	(.365)	(.319)
	0.030	0.042	0.024	0.034	0.043	0.047	0.036
	(.048)	(.060)	(.053)	(.069)	(.071)	(.073)	(.063)
	0.016	0.021	0.012	0.017	0.021	0.023	0.018
	(.016)	(.020)	(.020)	(.020)	(.023)	(.024)	(.021)
	2.339	2.302	2.316	2.327	2.277	2.269	2.306
	(.587)	(.541)	(.543)	(.544)	(.530)	(.528)	(.547)
	0.082	0.236	0.097	0.130	0.116	0.156	0.136
	(.087)	(.414)	(.096)	(.211)	(.010)	(.091)	(.211)
	2.342	2.311	2.319	2.330	2.284	2.278	2.312
	(.586)	(.539)	(.542)	(.543)	(.528)	(.528)	(.546)
	.0142	.0197	.0122	.0170	.0214	.0224	.0178
	(.0246)	(.0365)	(.0391)	(.0538)	(.0431)	(.0404)	(.0404)
	.352	.703	.644	.970	.927	.902	.740
	(2.526)	(5.310)	(5.733)	(12.879)	(6.516)	(4.671)	(6.966)
	1.866	2.451	1.759	2.120	2.835	2.779	2.293
	(2.872)	(4.102)	(7.536)	(5.239)	(7.288)	(4.892)	(5.528)

Table 4.A.1 (continued)

Variable	Definition
SCHOOL	Years of school (SCHCLAS1 < 12, SCHCLAS2 = 12, SCHCLAS3 > 12 and/or S < 16, SCHCLAS4 > 16)
EXPERIENCE	Years of actual labor force experience
TENURE	Years employed with the same employer
UNION	Equals 1 if covered by a collective bargaining agreement (1975) or member of a labor union (1970–74)
UNANTIC	(DSCRP–EXPDURAT)/HOPT (Unanticipated unemployment as a proportion of desired hours)
DSCRPM1 DSCRPM2 DSCRPM3	Lagged values of individual DSCRP; 1, 2, 3 years, respectively (Means only shown. Overall standard deviation = .130)
MDSCRPM1 MDSCRPM2 MDSCRPM3	Lagged values of industry average DSCRP; 1, 2, 3 years, respectively
YDSCRPM1 YDSCRPM2 YDSCRPM3	Lagged values of overall average DSCRP; 1, 2, 3 years, respectively
INDUSTRY	Aggregates of the PSID 2-digit industry classification (Sample percentages shown)
1	All industures not classified
30	Metal manufacturing
31	Machinery, including electrical, manufacturing
32	Motor vehicles, other transportation equipment manufacturing
33	Other durable manufacturing
40	Food and tobacco manufacturing
45	Other nondurable manufacturing
51	Construction
55	Transportation
57	Other public utilities
61	Retail, wholesale, other trade
81	Repair services
85	Business, personal, amusement services
86	Professional, noneducational services
87	Educational services
92	Government (nonmedical, noneducational)

n

	1970	1971	1972	1973	1974	1975	Overall
	12.090	12.233	12.228	12.312	12.477	12.711	12.335
	(3.157)	(3.112)	(3.131)	(3.083)	(3.004)	(2.870)	(3.069)
	26.017	25.598	24.696	23.525	22.496	21.534	24.033
	(11.204)	(11.207)	(11.502)	(11.024)	(11.396)	(11.580)	(11.429)
	9.416	10.250	9.569	9.389	8.862	8.473	9.335
	(8.540)	(8.990)	(8.564)	(8.728)	(8.702)	(9.140)	(8.791)
	.356	.330	.325	.299	.297	.286	.317
	.0049	−.0041	−.0017	−.0025	−.0007	.0083	.0007
	(.0591)	(.0616)	(.0513)	(.0535)	(.0652)	(.0879)	(.0642)
	.019	.042	.031	.025	.029	.042	.031
	.026	.019	.041	.036	.030	.028	.029
	.024	.027	.023	.045	.049	.043	.035

Same as above

Same as above

	10.64	10.53	12.68	11.98	10.57	10.97	11.21
	4.17	3.85	3.48	4.35	4.34	3.63	3.97
	6.61	8.17	6.71	8.86	8.52	7.10	7.64
	7.26	6.52	5.80	4.10	4.83	5.61	5.73
	6.61	6.13	5.80	5.33	5.00	4.95	5.66
	2.44	3.06	2.57	3.45	3.28	3.22	2.99
	6.11	6.44	6.88	6.15	6.06	5.61	6.21
	9.63	9.90	8.37	8.78	8.52	8.50	8.97
	5.20	5.18	5.05	5.09	5.41	5.45	5.21
	4.17	4.87	4.14	3.94	3.93	3.96	4.17
	12.80	12.49	12.84	12.88	12.86	13.78	12.93
	2.16	1.81	2.90	3.12	3.03	2.81	2.62
	5.32	4.71	4.31	4.68	5.16	5.28	4.92
	4.10	3.77	3.98	3.36	4.10	5.03	4.05
	6.25	6.83	7.12	6.32	5.98	6.11	6.43
	6.61	5.73	7.37	7.63	8.44	8.00	7.27
	1,391	1,273	1,207	1,219	1,221	1,212	7,523

Notes

1. See Mortensen (1970) and Lucas and Rapping (1969) for examples of unemployment as an optimal labor supply strategy.
2. See Malinvaud (1977) and Ashenfelter (1980) for examples of unemployment viewed as a constraint on labor supply behavior.
3. See especially Rosen (1978 1974). Lewis (1969) provides an early theoretical analysis of the problem of joint worker-employer determination of work hours.
4. Other terms of employment may vary in order to force equality between V^* and V. For example, a lump sum payment could be made to the worker or the fringe benefit package could be altered. We assume that the full adjustment occurs in wage rates.
5. In figure 4.1, V^* depends only on $\bar{h}$ since w, p, and y are being held constant.
6. This condition of equilibrium follows from the same type of argument as Feldstein (1978 1976) uses in analyzing the effects of the unemployment insurance system on temporary layoffs.
7. Later we will use Taylor series approximations around h^0 to provide estimating formulas. Only the linear term $\gamma(h^0 - \bar{h})$ enters these formulas even if the UI system is modeled in a completely general way.
8. The wage w^{**} is an example of an implicit contract equilibrium wage in the spirit of Azariadis (1975) and Baily (1977). Condition 3' ensures that the contract $w^{**}, f(\bar{h}; \theta)$, which leads to unemployment or underemployment is just as desirable as the full employment contract, w, h^0. The firm's production and demand conditions determine which type of contract it will offer.
9. It is easier to derive the relevant approximations using the minimum expenditure function rather than the indirect utility function when there are no risk problems. Of course, we will use the utility function when we consider risk.
10. For the appropriate value of $v = V(w, p, y)$, $h^c(w, p, v) = h^0(w, p, y)$. Hence, the UI system in equation 6' is identical to the system underlying 1'.
11. The reader is reminded that the unemployment rate used here is the expected personal unemployment rate $u = (h^0 - \bar{h})/h^0$ and not the economy-wide unemployment rate.
12. The reader is referred to Abowd and Ashenfelter (1979) for the derivation of this result. The relative risk aversion function used here is a straightforward extension of the concept in Pratt (1964) and Arrow (1970).
13. Duncan and Stafford (1980) consider simultaneous determination of wages and compensating differentials in the context of union wages and working conditions. In this model, personal heterogeneity is assumed to influence the size of the required compensation.
14. Rosen (1974) works an example.
15. See Survey Research Center (1972a) for a description of the methods and sampling frame. See Survey Research Center (1972b 1973 1974 1975 1976) for the relevant questionnaires and variable definitions.
16. All annual hours variables, including DSCRP, are defined in thousands of hours.
17. Sherwin Rosen provided some valuable comments concerning the usefulness of identifying industry patterns when forecasting the hours of work constraint.
18. The average shown is unconditional so that it can be compared with EXPDURAT and VARDURAT. The data for DUNEM and the industry proportions in table 4.A.1 can be used to calculate the conditional average duration.
19. EXPDURAT and VARDURAT are not independent since $\pi\delta$ and $\pi[(1-\pi)\delta^2 + \phi^2]$ will, in general, be correlated when π, δ, and ϕ all depend on z_{it}. The sample correlation coefficient is .91.
20. PSID reports a variable: income from unemployment and workmen's compensation. The sample replacement rates were calculated as industry by year averages of the ratio of

this UI income variable to the implied lost earnings (WAGE*DSCRP) of the head. The average is taken only over nonzero values of DSCRP.

21. The use of last year's wage is intended to remove a person effect from the nonlinear regression. We do not mean to imply any dynamics. As is well known, a fixed person effect cannot be consistently estimated in a nonlinear regression model by the usual deviation from time average method.

22. Ken Wolpin suggested this variation.

23. The method minimizes the posterior expected loss from a Bayesian viewpoint and improves the mean squared estimate error from the sampling theory viewpoint. The method is designed for problems where the parameter of interest is the inverse of the estimated parameter.

24. Ashenfelter and Heckman (1974) estimated the ninety percent confidence interval for the compensated labor supply elasticity at .06 ($\pm$ .05) at their sample means in their table 1. Keeley, et al. (1978a b) estimated the ninety percent confidence interval at .23 ($\pm$ .17) at our sample means using their table 2.

25. See Azariadis (1975) and, especially, Baily (1974) for a discussion of the differential risk aversion hypothesis.

26. We have produced summary measures based exclusively on table 4.3, column 1, since it is, overall, the most reasonable equation. The ninety percent confidence interval for the UI price implied by the estimate in table 4.4, column 1, is 2.14 percent ($\pm$ 1.21%) which includes all the observed values reported in table 4.5. We should also note, however, that Feldstein (1978) reports that reported UI benefits received by CPS respondents understate the aggregate payments by fifty percent. This supports our estimate of γ in table 4.3, column 1, summarized in table 4.5.

References

Abowd, J., and Ashenfelter, O. "Unemployment and Compensating Wage Differentials." Unpublished MS., University of Chicago, CMSBE, Chicago, 1979.

Arrow, K. *Essays in the Theory of Risk Bearing*. Amsterdam: North-Holland, 1970.

Ashenfelter, O. "Unemployment as Disequilibrium in a Model of Aggregate Labor Supply." *Econometrica* 48 (April 1980): 547–64.

Ashenfelter, O., and Heckman, J. "The Estimation of Income and Substitution Effects in a Model of Family Labor Supply." *Econometrica* 42 (January 1974): 73–85.

Azariadis, C. "Implicit Contracts and Underemployment Equilibria." *Journal of Political Economy* 83 (December 1975): 1183–1202.

Baily, M. N. "Wages and Employment under Uncertain Demand." *Review of Economic Studies* 41 (1974): 37–50.

Duncan, G., and Stafford, F. "Do Union Members Receive Compensating Wage Differentials?" *American Economic Review* 70 (June 1980): 355–71.

Feldstein, M. "Temporary Layoffs in the Theory of Unemployment." *Journal of Political Economy* 84 (October 1976): 937–57.

———. The Effects of Unemployment Insurance on Temporary Layoff Unemployment." *American Economic Review* 68 (December 1978): 834–46.
Heckman, J. J. "Sample Selection Bias as a Specification Error." *Econometrica* 47 (January 1979): 153–62.
Keeley, M. C., et al. "The Estimation of Labor Supply Models Using Experimental Data." *American Economic Review* 68 (December 1978a): 873–87.
———. "The Labor Supply Effects and Costs of Alternative Negative Income Tax Programs." *Journal of Human Resources* 13 (Winter 1978b): 3–36.
Lewis, H. G. "Interes del empleador en las horas de Trabajo del empleado" (Employer Interests in Employee Hours of Work). *Cuadernos de Economica* (Chile), 1969.
Lucas, R. E., and Rapping, L. A. "Real Wages, Employment and Inflation." *Journal of Political Economy* 77 (October 1969): 721–54.
Malinvaud, E. *The Theory of Unemployment Reconsidered.* N.Y.: John Wiley, 1977.
Mortensen, D. "Job Search, the Duration of Unemployment and the Phillips Curve." *American Economic Review* 60 (December 1970): 847–62.
Pratt, J. "Risk Aversion in the Small and in the Large." *Econometrica* 32 (January 1964): 122–36.
Rosen, S. Hedonic Prices and Implicit Markets: Product Differentiation in Pure Competition." *Journal of Political Economy* 82 (February 1974): 34–55.
———. "Substitution and Division of Labour." *Economica* 45 (August 1978): 235–50.
Survey Research Center. *A Panel Study of Income Dynamics: Waves I-V Procedures.* Ann Arbor: Institute for Social Research, 1972a.
———. *A Panel Study of Income Dynamics: Waves I-V Tape Codes.* Ann Arbor: Institute for Social Research, 1972b.
———. *A Panel Study of Income Dynamics: Wave VI Procedures and Tape Codes.* Ann Arbor: Institute for Social Research, 1973.
———. *A Panel Study of Income Dynamics: Wave VII Procedures and Tape Codes.* Ann Arbor: Institute for Social Research, 1974.
———. *A Panel Study of Income Dynamics: Wave VIII Procedures and Tape Codes.* Ann Arbor: Institute for Social Research, 1975.
———. *A Panel Study of Income Dynamics: Wave IX Procedures and Tape Codes.* Ann Arbor: Institute for Social Research, 1976.
Zellner, A. "Estimation of Functions of Population Means and Regression Coefficients Including Structural Coefficients: A Minimum Expected Loss (MELO) Approach." *Journal of Econometrics* 8 (October 1978): 127–58.

5   Structural and Reduced Form Approaches to Analyzing Unemployment Durations

Nicholas M. Kiefer and George R. Neumann

5.1 Introduction

Workers with low current earnings comprise two types of individuals: those whose personal characteristics lead to their being permanently in the low-wage state, and those who are, owing to some exogenous event, only transitorily in the low-wage state. This distinction is recognized implicitly in public policies designed to aid such workers. Workers who are viewed as "permanent" low wage earners are provided programs which attempt to alter their personal characteristics—e.g., manpower training programs. For those workers viewed as only transitorily in the low earning state, services provided tend to be short-term income maintenance, e.g., unemployment insurance following losses in jobs and Workmen's Compensation following debilitating work injuries. The distinction between permanent and transitory is not rigid, however, since not all workers recover from a transitory shock such as the loss of a high-wage job. Similarly, some workers with characteristics normally associated with permanent low wage earnings escape to the high-wage sector. The size of the pool of low wage at any time depends then upon the magnitudes of these inflows and outflows. Although economists cannot claim to understand fully how public programs affect all movements between the two states, a clearer picture is emerging on the effects of manpower training programs and the movement out of the low-earnings state.

Our understanding of the effect of public programs on the transition into the low-earnings state is much less precise, however, partially because we have only a limited knowledge of the adjustments individuals

Nicholas M. Kiefer is Associate Professor of Economics, Cornell University.
George R. Neumann is Associate Professor of Economics, University of Chicago Graduate School of Business.

make to such events as job loss. Why is it, for example, that one individual will become reemployed in a short time with only minimal loss of earnings while another individual with a similar earnings history finds a new job only after a considerable period of time and then experiences a substantial decline in earnings? Is this merely an example of "bad luck," or does it indicate a systematic means whereby a transitory event leads some workers into permanent low-wage status? Although much has been written on the job search behavior of individuals, comparatively little empirical evidence exists to shed light on why some individuals succeed and others fail. Moreover, the evidence that does exist is generally of little use for exploring questions about the efficacy of alternative labor market programs. This latter problem arises because customary approaches of analyzing the outcome of the job search process—that is, the wage offer accepted and the length of time required to obtain it—produce, at best, a reduced form relationship which confounds differences in market opportunities with differences in personal characteristics. Consequently, the true effect of a particular program is difficult to determine. For the purposes of policy analysis, an identification of the underlying structural relationship is necessary if one desires to measure the effects of programs designed to affect the job search process.

In this paper we consider the effects of two alternative labor market programs designed to smooth the transition from the unemployed state: a modified version of regular unemployment insurance and a wage subsidy program. In the data used in this study, one of these programs—the modified unemployment insurance—actually operated, and we can therefore consider variations in policy parameters. The alternative wage subsidy program was not available to any individuals, but it has attracted some attention recently as a means of reducing unemployment. While no direct evidence—that is, of the experiences of treatment and control groups—is available, we show that knowledge of the *structural* parameters—but not the *reduced form* parameters—is sufficient to identify the effects of this type of program. In examining the effects of the different programs, we contrast the policy implications that flow from the reduced form estimates and the structural estimates. These differences provide a useful insight into the gains obtainable from a precise model specification.

5.2 Outcomes of the Job Search Process

Analysis of the effects of unemployment has focused on the length of time required to find employment, and the resulting wage obtained; in particular, the analysis has focused on measuring the effects of programs such as unemployment insurance (UI) on the outcome of the job search process. The theory motivating this analysis is given by the well-known papers by Mortensen (1970) and McCall (1970) on search behavior. To state this theory somewhat loosely, empirical studies proceed from the observation that anything which lowers the cost of search increases an individual's reservation wage and thereby leads to both longer durations of unemployment and higher wages upon reemployment.

Empirical efforts to measure the relationship between duration and wage change have taken two directions. The first approach, typified by Classen (1977) and Ehrenberg and Oaxaca (1976), treats the outcomes of the job search process as jointly determined and attempts to estimate a *reduced form* system. The specific model is:

(1a) $\quad D_i = X'_{1i}B + E_{1i}$

(1b) $\quad W_i = X_{2i}B_i + E_{2i}$

where D_i is the number of weeks of unemployment and W_i is reemployment wage. Parameters of the UI system, i.e., the replacement rate, are included in X_1 and X_2, and their coefficients are interpreted as the net effects of the UI system on the job search process.

An alternative approach has been taken in Kiefer and Neumann (1978 1979a b). In this approach the job search process is viewed as a selection problem following Heckman (1979). Individuals accept employment if and only if the market wage offer exceeds their reservation wage. Expected wages are then just a drawing from a truncated distribution, with the point of truncation depending upon the reservation wage, and the expected duration of unemployment is distributed geometrically about the inverse of the per period probability of finding an acceptable job offer.[1] A difficulty encountered in the approach is that reservation wages are not observable; they must be inferred from the observed choices of individuals. This problem, which motivated the use of a reduced form solution in other papers, can be solved in the following manner (see also Kiefer and Neumann 1979b).

Assume that the wage offer distribution facing the ith individual is:

(2) $\quad \ln w^o_{it} + X'_i B + f_i + \varepsilon^o_{it}$
$\quad\quad \varepsilon^o_{it} \sim \text{i.i.d. } N(0, \sigma^2_o) \; \forall t$

where X_i represents all measured characteristics of an individual (age, education, labor market characteristics, etc.), f_i represents all unmeasured characteristics, which are assumed known by the individual and potential employers, and ε^o_{it} is a random error term representing the "pure" amount of wage variability. The characterization in (2) implies that the wage offer distribution is stationary, an assumption which seems reasonable in light of the span of time covered by a typical spell of unemployment, and that observed wages have two sources of variation—systematic, but unmeasured, differences in "ability" f_i, and randomness in the wage offer process, represented by ε_{it}^o.

Facing (2), an optimal strategy is to select a reservation wage with the property that offers which match or exceed this critical value are accepted and those that fall short are rejected. The reservation wage can be shown to be of the form:

(3) $$r_{it} = g[F(w_i^o), m, \theta, t]$$

where $F(w_i^o)$ is the distribution of wage offers, m is the direct cost of search, θ is the discount factor, and t represents the effect of state dependence—that is, reservation wages may systematically vary with the length of time searching. Using results from Kiefer and Neumann (1979a b), a first-order Taylor expansion of (3) can be shown to yield

(3') $$r_{it} = k_i(X'_i B + f_i) + Z_i(t) \cdot \gamma$$

where k_i is defined as

$$k_i = \frac{\int_{r_{it}}^{\infty} F(w_i^o) dw^o}{\int_{r_{it}}^{\infty} F(w_i^o) dw^o + \theta} = \frac{\alpha_i}{\alpha_i + \theta} = k_i(XB, Z\gamma, k_i)$$

Note that there is no stochastic element in (3'); individuals who search optimally in this model choose a strategy—a reservation price—which is not random, although it may vary over time as reflected in the time subscript on Z, i.e., in response to time-dependent factors which directly affect the costs of search.

Individuals accept employment if and only if the wage offer exceeds the reservation wage. Using (2) and (3'), the employment condition is that

(4) $$s_i(t) = (1 - k_i)(X'_i B + f_i) - Z_i(t)\gamma > -\varepsilon_i^o$$

defining $s_i(t) = -[(1 - k_i)(X'_i B + f_i) - Z_i(t)\gamma]/\sigma$. The probability of finding a job in any period α is, for a given individual,

(5) $$\alpha[s_i(t) | f_i] = \Pr(w_i^o > w_i^r | f_i) = 1 - \Phi[s_i(t) | f_i]$$

where Φ is the standard normal distribution function. The statement in (5) is the probability of an individual's finding a job in period t, conditional on his unmeasured ability f_i. Although by definition we do not have measures of f_i, an implication of the optional choice of a reservation wage is that randomness in wage offers should be independent of f_i. Hence the unconditional probability of finding an acceptable job offer is

(6) $$\alpha[s_i(t)] = \int_{-\infty}^{\infty} [1 - \Phi(s_i | f_i)] d\Phi\left(\frac{f_i}{\sigma_F}\right)$$

Using (6) and results from conditional normal theory, the probability of observing a particular outcome—that is, a wage w_i^o, and a length of unemployment D_i—is given by

(7) $$\Pr(w_i^o, D_i) = \int_{-\infty}^{\infty} \left(\{\Pi \; \Phi[s_i(t)|f_i]\} \cdot \frac{1}{\sigma_o} \phi(\varepsilon_i) \cdot [1 - \Phi(s_i|f_i)] \right) d\Phi\left(\frac{f_i}{\sigma_F}\right)$$

as t goes from 1 to $D_i - 1$ and $d\phi(f_i/\sigma_F)$ goes from $-\infty$ to ∞. Subject to identification criteria discussed in Kiefer and Neumann (1979a b), all parameters in equation 7 can be estimated by maximum likelihood methods.[2] In particular one can identify B, γ, σ_o^2 (the pure variation in wage offers), and σ_F^2 (the variation in unmeasured ability).

The issues which arise in estimating the model described above are discussed at length elsewhere (see Kiefer and Neumann 1979b). For the present purposes it is sufficient to note that two structural equations relating unemployment and reemployment earnings are embedded in (7). The expected length of search for a randomly chosen individual is given by:

(8) $$E(D_i) = \sum_{j=1}^{\infty} \int_{-\infty}^{\infty} \left(\prod_{\ell=1}^{j-1} \Phi[s_i(\ell)|f_i] \right) [1 - \Phi(s_i(j)|f_i] \cdot j \; d\Phi\left(\frac{f_i}{\sigma}\right)$$

The expected reemployment wage is somewhat more cumbersome to derive. Conditional on f_i, and conditional on the length of search being D_i, expected reemployment earnings are:

(9) $$E(w_i^o|f_i, D_i) = X_o'B + f_i + \sigma_o\lambda[s(D)|f_i]$$

where

$$\gamma[s(D)|f_i] = \frac{\phi[s_i(D)|f_i]}{1 - \Phi[s_i(D)|f_i]}$$

If the reservation wage were constant, i.e., s did not vary with D, then unconditional expected earnings would be given by

(10) $$E(w_i^o) = \int_{-\infty}^{\infty} E(w_i|f_i, D) d\Phi\left(\frac{f_i}{\sigma}\right)$$
$$= X_i'B + \sigma_o \int_{-\infty}^{\infty} \lambda(s_i|f_i) d\Phi\left(\frac{f_i}{\sigma}\right)$$

When reservation wages vary with search time, the second term on the right-hand side on (10) must be modified to allow for differences in the probability of receiving an acceptable offer in a given period. Define the probability that an acceptable offer is received in period j as:

$$(11) \qquad g_i(j) = \left(\prod_{\ell=1}^{j-1} \Phi[s(\ell) | f_i] \right) \cdot 1 - \Phi[s(j) | f_i]$$

The unconditional expected reemployment wage is then:

$$(12) \qquad E(w_i^o) = \int_{-\infty}^{\infty} \left(\sum_{j=1}^{\infty} E(w_i^o | f_i, D=j) \cdot g_i(j) \right) d\Phi\left(\frac{f_i}{\sigma_o}\right)$$
$$- X_i'B + \sigma_o \cdot \int_{-\infty}^{\infty} \left(\sum_{j=1}^{\infty} \lambda[s_i(j) | f_i] \cdot g_i(j) \right) d\Phi\left(\frac{f_i}{\sigma_o}\right)$$

Equations 8 and 12 can be thought of as the structural analogues to what we have termed the reduced form solutions of (1a) and (2b). In view of the differences between the reduced form and structural approaches it is useful to examine the merits of each. Two issues are of particular importance: interpreting changes in policy variables such as UI benefits, and drawing inferences from incomplete samples (see Johnson and Kotz 1972; Heckman, in press).

The reduced form approach has one particular advantage—it is simple and cheap to estimate. If reservation wages are constant, the estimated coefficients have a potential interpretation as the coefficients of a Taylor expansion of the inverse of (6) for the duration equation [i.e., $E(D) = 1/\alpha(s_i)$], and as

$$B + \sigma_o \int_{-\infty}^{\infty} \frac{\partial \gamma(\cdot)}{\partial(\cdot)} \frac{\partial(\cdot)}{\partial r} \frac{\partial n}{\partial X_i} d\Phi\left(\frac{f_i}{\sigma}\right)$$

for the earnings equation. In this case, if both forms of the job search model were estimated on a complete sample, the only difference that should arise would be due to the inherent nonlinearity of the structural duration equation. If reservation wages vary over time as well as across individuals, then the correspondence between the two approaches is less obvious. Policies which affect the duration of unemployment also affect the distribution of accepted wages since the point of truncation varies with duration.

The use of a reduced form approach also results in problems of interpretation when certain types of policy simulations are attempted. For example, if a wage subsidy of, say, ten percent were given to all individuals in the sample, it would affect both duration and reemployment earnings, although in opposite ways. In the absence of a controlled experiment—where individuals were randomly assigned to the group receiving the subsidy—it is difficult to see how one could simulate this effect using a reduced form model. The problem is one of identification:

the moments of the wage distribution do not enter explicitly into the reduced form approach. If reservation wages are constant, this problem may not be serious because of the potential interpretation of the reduced form coefficients noted above. In the more general case, however, it is not possible to infer the results of such an experiment from the reduced form estimates.

Perhaps the greatest difference between the two approaches arises when information is available only for an incomplete sample. For example, it is frequently the case that a "follow-up" survey is performed after some event has occurred. At the time of the survey some individuals will have completed their job search, but some will not. Those who have not found employment will tend to have low expected market earnings, relative to their reservation wage—hence the long period of unemployment. Since neither of the dependent variables is observed, the observations are usually excluded from the analysis.[3] For well-known reasons this is likely to result in biased estimates. Apart from the question of bias, there is the question of interpreting the results of any simulation exercise since the composition of an incomplete sample is not likely to be invariant under changes in policy. Consider, for example, the effect of a shift in the mean of the wage offer distribution. Search theory implies that the expected wage should increase, and expected duration decrease, for all individuals. In an incomplete sample, the effect of such a policy would be that some individuals who previously had not found employment would become employed and hence would be included in the sample. If these individuals on average had higher durations of unemployment and lower expected earnings, then *observed* average wages would fall and duration increase, even in a carefully controlled experiment.

The importance of this effect will depend upon the location of reservation wages along the distribution of wage offers. If reservation wages are high, relative to the mean of the wage offer distribution, and if the distribution of offers has small variance, even a small shift in the mean may produce a significant change in unemployment patterns.

In noting these differences, we have only pointed out the potential problems which may exist; the severity of these problems—that is, the extent to which they lead to different policy implications—is ultimately an empirical matter. In the following section, we examine the simulated responses of a group of individuals to two plans which affect their unemployment activities.

5.3 Simulating Job Search Behavior: The Effects of A Wage Subsidy Plan

In this section we apply the models discussed above to a sample of unemployed male workers. This particular sample was generated from a survey of trade-displaced workers conducted by the Institute for Research on Human Resources of the Pennsylvania State University. A complete description of the data source is contained in Neumann (1978). Several features make this group particularly appropriate for discussions about low-wage workers. The sample is constructed solely of individuals who were permanently separated from employment—in most cases because the entire plant shut down. Thus we observe only job search behavior and do not have to be concerned with responses to anticipated, temporary layoffs. Moreover, the nature of the shock conforms to the idea of an exogenous shock to which some individuals adjust reasonably well, and others adjust only with great difficulty. Although many of these individuals would not have been considered low-wage workers prior to displacement, the average loss in weekly earnings upon reemployment was over twenty-five percent: consequently, most would be considered low-wage earners afterward. Summary statistics on this sample are contained in table 5.1.

Estimates of the reduced form equations for duration and reemployment earnings are presented in table 5.2, and the structural estimates of reemployment earnings (wage offers) and reservation wages are contained in table 5.3. Although we will not dwell on the precision of the estimates, we do note that the explanatory power of the OLS regression of unemployment duration is exceedingly small; this appears to be a common finding (see, e.g., Ehrenberg and Oaxaca 1976; Classen 1977).

Both approaches indicate an effect of UI benefits on the outcome of the job search process. The reduced form estimates imply that a ten percent increase in the replacement rate—equivalent here to an average increase of $14.9 per week in UI benefits—would lead to an increase in duration of about one-half week ($.0314 \times 14.9$), and an increase in unemployment earnings of 0.60 percent. The effects of increased UI benefits are apparent in column 2, but the numerical values of the increases in duration and reemployment earnings depend upon the position of the reservation

Table 5.1   **Sample Characteristics of Male Workers**

	Mean	Maximum	Minimum
Education (years)	10.2	21.0	0.0
No. of dependents	1.7	9.0	0.0
Percent married	83.5	—	—
Percent union members	70.4	—	—
Local unemployment rate at layoff (%)	5.30	9.00	2.20
Age	47.8	75.0	19.0
Unemployment benefits per week ($1967)	62.7	117.11	0.0
Maximum benefit period (weeks)	41.5	65.6	0.0
Previous weekly earnings ($1967)	149.0	457.0	19.20

Table 5.2 Reduced Form Estimates of Duration and Reemployment Wage Equation

	Duration (1)	Reemployment Earnings (2)
Constant	18.1566 (2.17)	1.839 (3.16)
Education	0.0161 (0.96)	0.0088 (2.41)
Dependents	0.0261 (0.41)	0.0617 (0.14)
Tenure	0.0040 (1.06)	−0.0069 (1.92)
Marital status	0.0001 (0.00)	0.1139 (0.60)
Unemployment rate	2.1164 (1.97)	−0.0461 (1.27)
Age	+0.0441 (1.40)	0.0210 (1.21)
Age^2	−0.0003 (0.27)	−0.0002 (0.06)
Ed·Age	+0.0143 (0.20)	−0.0011 (1.61)
UI benefits	0.0314 (1.71)	0.0004 (1.30)
Maximum duration	0.0214 (1.40)	−0.0001 (0.01)
$\ell n(W_{t-1})$	−0.3118 (1.11)	0.5406 (7.24)
R^2	.1331	.2480
F	1.478	9.012

wage in the wage offer distribution. We calculate these effects in the simulation reported below.

Before examining the simulation results it is useful to consider one feature of the job search process. Both casual empirical evidence and some previous studies (e.g., Neumann 1978) suggest that losses due to unemployment are greatest for the long-term unemployed. Although a higher reservation wage leads to higher expected reemployment and a greater length of unemployment for any individual ex ante, when one observes the outcomes of the job search process ex post, this investment

Table 5.3   Structural Estimates of the Job Search Process

	Earnings Function (1)	Reservation Wage Function (2)
Constant	2.8263 (6.24)	1.9713 (3.47)
Education	0.0361 (1.87)	0.0101 (1.27)
Dependents	—	−0.0068 (0.47)
Tenure	−0.0078 (3.68)	—
Marital status	—	−0.0824 (3.68)
Unemployment rate	0.0197 (1.68)	0.0161 (2.89)
Age	0.0194 (1.86)	−0.0127 (3.46)
Age^2	−0.0001 (0.61)	0.0001 (0.84)
Ed·Age	−0.0008 (1.87)	−0.0003 (1.71)
Unemployment benefits	—	0.0016 (2.43)
Maximum duration	—	0.0004 (0.59)
$\ln W_{t-1}$	0.2574 (4.57)	—
F_i	—	−0.0014 (0.91)
t	—	−0.0023 (2.01)
$\sigma^2_{w^o}$	0.0283 (2.62)	
σ^2_F	0.2493 (12.41)	
$\ln \ell\ell$	−1,794.83	

Note: t-statistics in parentheses.

aspect is swamped by variations in individual characteristics and by random errors in the process. In the present context this phenomenon is likely to be concentrated among the group of workers who had not found employment by the survey date. Since their behavior is of particular interest in any discussion of low-income workers we present simulation results separately for this group.

The simulated effects of changing UI benefits in steps of five percent on duration of unemployment and the percentage change in reemployment earnings are presented in table 5.4. Panels A and B contain the estimates from the reduced form model (equations 1a and 1b) for the total sample and for those workers who remained unemployed for at least sixty-five weeks; panels C and D contain the equivalent estimates for the structural model (equations 8 and 12). The estimates in table 5.4 show two pronounced patterns. Looking across each panel, we see that, for this sample at least, changes in UI benefit levels would have almost negligible effects. Increasing UI benefits by twenty percent—which for this sample is equivalent to raising the average replacement rate by 8.4 percentage points (from 42.1 percent to 50.5 percent)—would raise reemployment earnings by only about .5 percent and increase the duration of unemployment by about one-half week. These are quite modest effects when one considers that the average reemployed worker in this sample had a decline in real weekly earnings of 26.7 percent and spent 39.1 weeks unemployed. It is interesting to note that although estimates of the precise effect of changing UI benefits would differ depending upon whether one used the reduced form or structural model, the conclusions to be drawn from the evidence would not.

Looking down the columns of table 5.4, we observe a somewhat different picture of the differences between the two approaches to modeling the job search process. Comparison of panels A and B would seem to indicate that there is little difference between those who had not become employed within 65 weeks and those who had; panels C and D indicate the contrary. The expected duration of unemployment was estimated to be 34.7 weeks for those who became employed within 65 weeks, and 47.2 weeks for those who had not become employed by 65 weeks. This amounts to about a seven-week difference in expected duration of unemployment between the two groups. In one sense, this difference between the two models can be considered a contrived one, since the structural model takes into account information on the characteristics and, partially, the job search outcomes, of the group of workers who had not found jobs within 65 weeks.[4] But this is precisely the purpose of a structural model, and the differences observed in table 5.4 represent the basis for using such an approach to design policies to smooth labor market transitions. Under the reduced form approach, the similarity of the estimated duration and wage changes would lead one to conclude that

Table 5.4 Structural and Reduced Form Simulations of the Effect of Alternative Levels of UI Benefits

	% Δ in UI Benefits				
	0.0	5.0	10.0	15.0	20.0
	Reduced Form Estimates A. Total Sample				
Duration (weeks)	39.31	39.41	39.51	39.61	39.72
% Δ in earnings	0.0	0.13	0.25	0.38	0.50
	B. Unemployed after 65 weeks				
Duration (weeks)	39.62	39.73	39.83	39.93	40.03
% Δ in earnings	0.0	0.13	.025	0.37	0.49
	Structural Estimates C. Total sample				
Duration (weeks)	43.10	43.41	43.67	43.85	43.91
% Δ in earnings	0.0	0.17	0.29	0.46	0.54
	D. Unemployed after 65 weeks				
Duration (weeks)	47.21	47.36	47.50	47.61	47.71
% Δ in earnings	0.0	0.11	0.18	0.25	0.31

the two groups are essentially the same; hence it must be random influences—luck—which determine whom the labor market assigns to each group. The structural approach, on the other hand, implies that there are real differences between the two groups and thus, at least in principle, allows the possibility of predicting in advance what types of individuals are likely to be most affected by unexpected job loss.

The results of this simulation raise strong doubts about the ability of what is essentially an income maintenance program to have a significant impact on the reemployment experience of displaced workers. Although the sample used is unique, and certainly not representative of all unemployed workers, our results, both the reduced form and structural versions, are not significantly at odds with the findings of others which are based solely on a reduced form approach. While it is difficult to generalize from a sample of one, there is at least the suggestion that returns from more precise modeling of the job search process may be important for policy purposes.

Although predicting which types of individuals will be most adversely affected by job termination is one possible gain to a structural approach, a more important gain is likely to be in terms of the number of difference policy options which can be considered. As an example, we consider the option of a wage subsidy program. The basic idea of a wage subsidy is to shift the distribution of wage offers facing individuals, thereby making employment more likely. In the reduced form approach there is no obvious way to incorporate such effects, except possibly through a controlled experiment. A structural approach allows for a direct interpretation, however, since the shift in the wage offer distribution affects an individual's expected earnings both directly—i.e., through $X_i'B$—and indirectly through its effects on reservation wages.

In table 5.5 we present the results of a simulation exercise with varying amounts of wage subsidy. Because these simulations, as in the case of the UI subsidy, are partial equilibrium in nature, the results are sensitive to the assumed stability of the wage offer distribution. In the present case, this amounts to assuming that a wage subsidy program will not affect the distribution of wage offers part from the mean shift, i.e., no "extra" effects due to a substitution of labor for capital. For small programs this assumption seems tenable.

The issue also arises of how accurately this shift in the distribution is perceived by individuals. If it is fully perceived, then reservation wages rise by a fraction $\alpha/\alpha + \theta$ of the increase in the mean. This increase in reservation wages leads to lengthier search, and, consequently, the effect on duration of unemployment is lessened. Since some wage subsidy plans (e.g., jobs credit) work in a manner that may not be obvious to individuals, we present estimates of the effect on duration assuming full reservation wage change (panels A and B), and no reservation wage change (panel C).

In contrast to a UI subsidy, a direct wage subsidy appears to have quite significant effects on the job search process. From panels A and B we observe that a twenty percent wage subsidy would lead to an increase in reemployment earnings of about nineteen percent, and a reduction of unemployment duration of about a week, if the shift in the mean is

Table 5.5   Structural Simulations of the Effect of a Wage Subsidy Program

	% Δ in Mean Wage Offer				
	0.0	5.0	10.0	15.0	20.0
	A. Total Sample				
Duration (weeks)	43.10	42.87	42.51	42.23	42.06
% Δ in earnings	0.0	4.91	9.84	14.72	19.6
	B. Unemployed over 65 weeks				
Duration (weeks)	47.21	47.03	46.74	46.39	46.12
%Δ in earnings	0.0	4.87	9.78	14.68	19.2
	C. Duration of Unemployment with Incomplete Knowledge (weeks)				
Total sample	43.10	41.64	40.02	38.75	37.29
Unemployed over 65 weeks	47.21	45.88	44.16	42.82	41.28

completely perceived. The effect of the change in reservation wages can be seen clearly in panel C: if reservation wages did not adjust, expected unemployment duration would decrease by six weeks instead of one.

5.4 Conclusion

This paper has focused on two points—the inferences which can be obtained from structural versus reduced form analysis of the outcome of the job search process, and the effects of two subsidy programs on the job search process. In regard to the former topic, it is clear that a structural model permits a wider range of possible questions. In particular, it is possible to consider, ex ante, what the likely experience of a given cohort of job searchers will be, and, in principle, to tailor different types of programs to ease their labor market transitions.

The comparison of a UI subsidy with a wage subsidy revealed significant differences. Higher levels of UI payments led, as expected, to both longer durations of unemployment and higher reemployment earnings. Both effects were quite small, however, and, at least for low-wage workers similar to the individuals in this sample, there is little reason to believe that programs which emphasize income maintenance are likely to have much impact on the types of jobs obtained. By contrast, a wage subsidy program appears to have a significant effect on reemployment earnings, and also to lead to a moderate decline in duration. This is a one-blade-of-the-scissors result of course, and it is subject to criticism on those grounds. Nonetheless, for relatively small programs, the possibilities appear to be fruitful.

Notes

1. This result holds only for the case of constant reservation wages. The correct distribution of durations for the general use is given in equation (7) below.
2. The identification criteria amount to the following: some variable(s) must affect wage offers but must not directly affect reservation wages. Indirect effects—e.g., through the moments of the wage offer function—are permissible, indeed necessary.
3. There are other reasons why truncation could occur. Using state UI records on compensated unemployment results in a truncation of those with very short durations—less than the waiting period—and those with long durations—those whose unemployment exceeds the maximum duration period.
4. The estimates in the reduced form approach for the sample of workers not employed in sixty-five weeks are constructed simply by using the observed characteristics of the individual and the coefficients estimated from the sample of employed. No attempt is made to adjust the constant term such that the expected value of, say, duration reflects the obvious fact that the observed period of unemployment was greater than 65 weeks.

References

Classen, K. "The Effect of Unemployment Insurance on the Duration of Unemployment and Subsequent Earnings." *Industrial and Labor Relations Review* 30, no. 4 (July 1977): 438–44.

Ehrenberg, R., and Oaxaca, R., "Unemployment Insurance, Duration of Unemployment, and Subsequent Wage Gain." *American Economic Review* 66 (December 1976): 754–66.

Heckman, J. "Sample Selection Bias as a Specification Error." *Econometrica* 47 (January 1979): 153–62.

Johnson, N., and Kotz, S. *Distributions in Statistics*. Vol. 4: *Continuous Multivariate Distributions*. N.Y.: John Wiley, 1972.

Kiefer, N., and Neumann, G. "Estimation of Wage Offer Distributions and Reservation Wages," in S. Lippman and J. McCall, eds., *Studies in the Economics of Search*. Amsterdam: North-Holland, 1978, pp. 171–89.

―――. "An Empirical Job Search Model with a Test of the Constant Reservation Wage Hypothesis." *Journal of Political Economy* 87, no. 1 (February 1979a).

―――. "Individual Effects in a Nonlinear Model: Explicit Treatment of Heterogeneity in the Empirical Job-Search Model." Mimeo., February 1979.

McCall, J. "Economics of Information and Job Search." *Quarterly Journal of Economics*, February 1970, pp. 113–26.

Mortensen, D. "Job Search, the Duration of Unemployment, and the Phillips Curve," *American Economic Review* 60 (December 1970): pp. 847–62.

Neumann, G. "The Labor Market Adjustments of Trade Displaced Workers: The Evidence from the Trade Adjustment Assistance Program," in R. Ehrenberg, ed., *Research in Labor Economics*, pp. 353–81. JAI Press, 1978.

6 Layoffs and Unemployment Insurance

Frank Brechling

6.1 Introduction

In recent years researchers have paid increasing attention to the impact of the unemployment insurance system on various labor market phenomena. Two strands of research in this area can be distinguished. In the first, researchers have been concerned with the influence of unemployment benefits on labor supply and unemployment. The decision to participate in the labor force or to end a spell of unemployment rests with the individual person. Unemployment benefits are viewed as a subsidy to participation, leisure, or search, and, hence, both labor force participation and unemployment duration should increase with unemployment benefits (see Classen 1977; Ehrenberg and Oaxaca 1976; Hamermesh 1977 1978; Katz 1977).

The second strand of research has been developed from the recent work on labor contracts (see Azariadis 1975; Baily 1974; Gordon 1973). Explicit allowance is made for temporary layoffs and recalls by firms in response to changes in the demand for their output. Since laid off employees qualify for unemployment benefits, the level of benefits may well influence the pattern of layoffs and recalls. Moreover, benefit payments are financed in the U.S. by a payroll tax which typically is partially

Frank Brechling is Professor of Economics, University of Maryland.

The research for this paper was undertaken while the author was visiting the Center for Naval Analyses.

The research underlying this paper was undertaken in partial fulfillment of a contract with the U.S. Department of Labor, ASPER (No. J-9-M-6-0103). Its contents do not necessarily represent the official opinion or policy of the Department of Labor.

Kathleen Classen Utgoff and Daniel Hamermesh kindly read a previous draft of this paper. Their comments are acknowledged with gratitude.

experience rated. Experience rating means that a firm's tax rate rises (falls) in response to increases (decreases) in benefit payments to the firm's own ex-employees. Thus the higher the degree of experience rating, the higher will be the tax cost of temporary layoffs. Examples of theoretical models of a typical firm's response to changes in the unemployment insurance system are presented in the papers by Baily (1977), Brechling (1977a b), and Feldstein (1976). Although these models have not been subjected to extensive tests, relevant empirical information is presented in Brechling and Jehn (1978), Feldstein (1978), and Halpin (in press).

In this paper, an attempt is made to contribute to the second strand of research. In particular, it contains the results of empirical tests of the Baily-Feldstein type of model. For this purpose the main structure and theoretical predictions of the Baily-Feldstein model are presented summarily in section 6.2. Section 6.3 contains amendments, elaborations, and extentions of the Baily-Feldstein model. The main part of section 6.3 consists of parameterization of the experience-rating system which corresponds as precisely as possible to a system currently in use in the U.S. The empirical tests are presented in section 6.4, and section 6.5 contains the main conclusions of the paper.

The empirical evidence lends substantial support to the Baily-Feldstein type of model. In particular the parameters which determine a firm's layoff and rehire decisions seem to be strongly influenced by the degree of experience rating. It would appear, therefore, that increases in the degree of experience rating are likely to lead to substantial decreases in layoffs and, hence, in unemployment.

6.2 The Baily-Feldstein Model

Although the papers by Baily (1977) and Feldstein (1976) differ in detail and exposition, they contain substantially the same model of layoffs and unemployment insurance. Hence no distinction is made between them. Moreover, since both papers are published in eminent and readily available journals the following summary of the model is verbal, nonformal, and brief.[1]

In the Baily-Feldstein model, the firm offers its employees a long-term—say, annual—set of employment conditions. These conditions cover (1) wage rates; (2) hours worked; (3) the probability of being laid off; and (4) duration of the layoff. The total utility which the worker derives from these four items is a constraint to the firm. It is given by competitive conditions in the labor market. Thus although the firm may vary the four items in a mutually offsetting manner, the value of the total package cannot be changed by the firm which is assumed to maximize its profits subject to this constraint.

The total contract period is divided into two subperiods: In the first, the firm faces a high price for its output; in the second, a low price. Hence, both employment and hours tend to be lower in the second than in the first subperiod, and some workers are likely to be laid off at the beginning of the second subperiod. In the long run, however, these layoffs are not involuntary from the workers' point of view because the total expected remuneration contains compensation for the expected layoffs.

The introduction of an unemployment benefit system without experience rating raises the total expected remuneration of workers who are subject to layoffs, and, hence, both the workers and the firm should gain. It is important to note, however, that the gain can be realized only through layoffs, and, hence, the firm has an incentive to lay off more workers than in the absence of unemployment benefits. In other words, when there is no unemployment benefit system, firms must compensate workers for spells of layoff unemployment. With a benefit system, on the other hand, part of the compensation for layoffs is borne by the unemployment benefit system. Unemployment benefits thus lower the marginal cost of layoffs to firms.

Experience rating may offset, partially or fully, the reduction in the marginal cost of layoffs caused by unemployment benefits. For instance, if the firm were billed immediately for the benefit payments, then, in the absence of income tax on benefits, the marginal costs of layoffs would not be changed, and layoffs would be neither encouraged nor discouraged.

The above arguments can be illustrated conveniently by Feldstein's formula for the subsidy to layoffs:

$$(1) \qquad J_1 = \frac{[(1-t_b)-(1-t_y)e]b}{(1-t_y)}$$

where b is the benefit received by laid off workers per period of time, e is the proportion of b payable immediately by the firm, t_b is the tax on unemployment benefits, and t_y is the income tax rate payable on wage income. In the U.S., $t_b = 0$, so that the formula becomes $J_2 = [1-(1-t_y)e]b/(1-t_y)$. This expression shows that, even if experience rating were perfect, so that $e = 1$, the subsidy to layoffs would be positive, namely $J_3 = t_y b/(1-t_y)$. The reason is that the firm's wage compensation for layoffs is (income) taxable, while unemployment benefits are not. These tax effects would disappear only when $t_b = t_y$ so that equation 1 becomes $J_4 = (1-e)b$, which, in turn, becomes zero when $e = 1$, that is, when experience rating is perfect.

So far, attention has been confined to the impact of the unemployment benefit system upon layoffs. But the Baily-Feldstein model also yields a unique prediction for the impact of the unemployment benefit system on the level of hours worked during the second subperiod. A rise in the layoff subsidy J raises the level of layoffs, but it also raises the level of hours worked by the employees who have *not* been laid off.

The theoretical predictions of the Baily-Feldstein model can thus be stated summarily as follows: given that unemployment benefits are not (income) taxed, layoffs and average hours worked in the depressed subperiod rise with (1) ceteris paribus increases in unemployment benefits; (2) ceteris paribus decreases in the degree of experience rating; and (3) ceteris paribus increases in the tax rate on wage income.

It should perhaps be pointed out that one prediction of the Baily-Feldstein model depends crucially on the assumption that the composition of the long-term compensation package changes in response to changes in unemployment benefits. This assumption is attractive and plausible, especially for a long-run analysis. It may be, however, that in some industries competition in the labor market does not generate the kinds of responses that are obtained by Baily and Feldstein. What happens, for instance, if the firm's compensation package is independent of unemployment benefits? In the papers by Brechling (1977a b), this assumption was made. It leads to the following intuitively plausible results: when the system is experience rated, then an increase in unemployment benefits generates a *rise* in the marginal tax costs of layoffs, and, hence, a *decline* in the optimal level of layoffs. An increase in the degree of experience rating also raises the marginal tax costs and, hence, as in the Baily-Feldstein model, lowers optimal layoffs. In other words, an increase in unemployment benefits leads to a rise in layoffs in the Baily-Feldstein model, but to a reduction in layoffs in the Brechling model. But increases in the degree of experience rating reduce layoffs in both types of models. Since the real world may well be a mixture of the Baily-Feldstein and Brechling models, the impact of unemployment benefits on layoffs may not be as strong as that of experience rating.[2]

6.3 Extensions of the Model

In this section, two amendments of the Baily-Feldstein model are described and discussed. The first refers to the duration of temporary layoffs, and the second to the precise nature of experience rating. Let us deal with the two amendments in turn.

6.3.1 Amendments for the Duration of Temporary Layoffs

In the Baily-Feldstein model, the price for the firm's output drops to some low level at the beginning of the second subperiod and remains at that level until the end of the subperiod. In response, the firm lays off some employees for the entire subperiod, after which presumably they are recalled. In other words, the duration of layoffs for workers who do not search for and obtain jobs at other firms is assumed to equal the second subperiod.

It should be realized, however, that the layoff subsidy J can be obtained by the firm not only by laying off more employees but also by lengthening the layoff duration of a given number of layoffs, unless the layoff duration exceeds the maximum unemployment benefit period. Hence, if the firm does have some control over the layoff duration, this duration must be expected to increase with increases in the level of unemployment benefits and with decreases in the degree of experience rating.

It would appear that a relatively minor change in the structure of the Baily-Feldstein model should make the layoff duration a choice variable for the firm. Suppose, for instance, that the firm holds inventories which could be accumulated in the first subperiod and decumulated in the second subperiod. In these circumstances, the following conjecture has intuitive appeal: a rise in unemployment benefits or a fall in the degree of experience rating should induce the firm to raise its production at the beginning of the first subperiod, accumulate inventories, lay off some employees before the beginning of the second subperiod and, thereafter, decumulate inventories. In this case, the layoff duration for at least some laid off workers is likely to exceed the second subperiod. Since the main focus of this paper is empirical rather than theoretical, the above conjecture has not been examined formally. It is simply hypothesized that, since firms have an inducement to lengthen the layoff duration in response to a rise in the layoff subsidy, some firms actually do so. Hence the average layoff duration is expected to react positively to increases in unemployment benefits and negatively to increases in the degree of experience rating.

6.3.2 Amendments for Experience Rating Provisions

The second amendment to the Baily-Feldstein model consists of a precise parameterization of the experience-rating provisions. In the Feldstein (1976) treatment, for instance, the degree of experience rating is summarized by one parameter, the proportion e of benefit payments charged to the firm. Actually the relevant laws do not fix e but another set of parameters, so that observed levels of e are likely to be endogenous in the firm's decision process.

Several systems of experience rating are currently in use in the U.S. The reserve ratio method is, however, the most common system, used in thirty-two states. The ensuing theoretical discussion as well as the later empirical analysis is confined entirely to the reserve ratio method.

Under the reserve ratio method of experience rating, each firm is assigned an account in the state unemployment insurance system. The balance in this account changes in response to tax inflows and benefit outflows. Formally:

(2) $$B_t - B_{t-1} = \tau_t m - b_t$$

where B_t is the firm's balance at the end of period t, τ is the tax rate, m is the tax base or taxable payroll, and b are the benefit payments which are charged to the firm. All flows are measured per calendar year, and, for the sake of simplicity, B_t, m, and b_t are normalized for the level of employment, so that they measure balance, taxable payroll, and benefits *per employee*. When equation 2 is divided by m, its left-hand side represents changes in the reserve ratio:

(3) $$R_t - R_{t-1} = \tau_t - \frac{b_t}{m}$$

where R_t is the reserve ratio at the end of period t.

The essence of the reserve ratio method of experience rating consists of a link between τ_t and R_{t-1} which is given by the tax schedule. A typical such schedule is presented in figure 6.1. The unbroken Line (*A-B-C-D-E-F*) is described fully by five parameters: NEGTAX, MAXTAX, SLOPE, MINTAX and MINRES. Let us discuss them in turn.

NEGTAX is the tax rate which applies to firms with a negative balance, that is along (*A-B*).

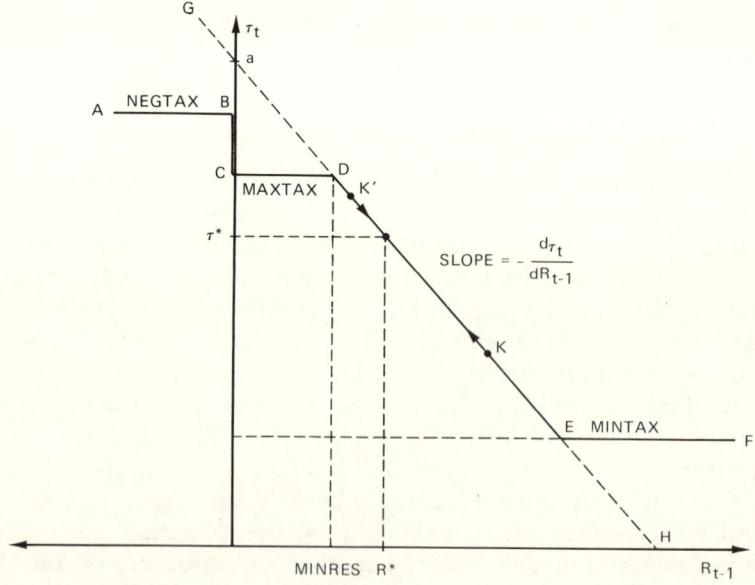

Figure 6.1 Typical Tax Schedule

MAXTAX is the highest tax rate applicable for firms with positive balances along (C-D).

SLOPE measures the slope of the line (D-E). Actually there are a large number of small steps along (D-E) which have been approximated by a straight line.

MINTAX is a critical low tax rate at which the tax schedule becomes horizontal, namely along (E-F).

MINRES is the minimum reserve ratio at which the sloped part of the tax schedule begins.

All five parameters are necessary and sufficient for a complete description of the schedule. Moreover, each may change ceteris paribus. The laws of the thirty-two states with the reserve ratio method of experience rating determine the tax schedules which imply the above five parameters. Moreover, the parameters vary automatically with the aggregate balance in a state's unemployment insurance fund. When the fund level falls below certain trigger levels, the parameters are changed so as to ensure increased tax flows, and vice versa.

The next question is: how do changes in the above five parameters affect the degree of experience rating? To answer this, let us begin by assuming that the tax schedule has no kinks or steps, so that it is sloped throughout like the line (G-H) which has its intercept at a. The tax rate τ_t can then be expressed as a simple function of R_{t-1}:

(4) $$\tau_t = a - s\, R_{t-1}$$

where s = SLOPE. Note that s is measured as a positive number: a rise in s means that the slope of the function gets steeper. When equations 3 and 4 are combined, a simple first-order difference equation is obtained:

(5) $$R_t = (1-s)\, R_{t-1} + a - \frac{b_t}{m}$$

Since s is always smaller than unity (typically $s \simeq .3$), equation 5 is stable in the sense that it approaches $R^* = R_t = R_{t-1}$ for any constant $a - (b_t/m)$. The steady state reserve ratio is given by:

(6) $$R_t^* = \frac{1}{s}(a - \frac{b_t}{m})$$

which, in turn, implies:

(7) $$\tau_t^* = \frac{b_t}{m} \text{ or } \tau_t^*\, m = b_t$$

Thus, in the steady state, tax inflows just equal benefit outflows, and, hence, the balance and reserve ratio do not change.

The dynamic pattern described by equation 5 depends crucially on autonomous changes in the average benefit payments per employee. $b_.$

The latter is equal to the product of (a) the firm's layoff rate; (b) the average duration of layoffs; and (c) unemployment benefit per period of time. Increases in one or more of these three variables lead to an increase in b and, hence, raise benefit outflows in relation to tax inflows.

Suppose, for instance, that the reserve ratio and tax rate are at K in figure 6.1. If R_t^* and τ_t^* are the relevant steady state values, then K represents a point at which benefit outflows exceed tax inflows, so that R_{t-1} is falling and τ_t is rising. During the transition, the firm's balance is reduced. Conversely, if the firm is initially at K', then tax inflows exceed benefit outflows and hence the firm's reserve ratio must rise and the tax rate must fall. During the transition period the balance is built up.

Suppose now that there is a cyclical pattern in b_t: let it be high in recessions and low in booms. Consequently the firm's balance is run down in recessions and built up in booms. But since τ_t and R_{t-1} always move toward a position where benefit outflows equal tax inflows, the firm's tax payments tend to equal benefit outflows, when both are summed over a sufficiently long period of time. In this limited sense, a tax schedule without kinks or steps and a nonzero slope would ensure full experience rating.

So far, however, neither benefit outflows nor tax inflows have been discounted. Once discounting is introduced, the speed with which the tax rate adjusts to benefit outflows becomes important. Suppose, for instance, that the firm increases its layoffs, thereby raising b_t. If, in response, tax rates rise very slowly, then the tax cost of the layoffs is payable in the distant future and its discounted value is quite small. Conversely, if the firm reduces b_t and tax rates fall very slowly, the discounted value of the future tax savings may be minimal. The speed with which the tax rate adjusts to benefit outflows depends on two factors: (1) the discrete lag of τ_t behind R_{t-1}, which seems to be necessary for administrative purposes, and (2) the speed at which the reserve ratio R_t moves toward its steady state value R_t^*. As is evident from equation 5, this speed depends crucially on the slope of the tax schedule(s). For the sake of realism, let us confine attention to the case in which $0 < s \leq 1$. As s rises from zero toward unity, the dependence of R_t on the state variable R_{t-1} decreases, and, hence, the relative importance of b_t increases. When $s = 1$, R_t becomes independent of R_{t-1}:

$$(8) \qquad R_t = a - \frac{b_t}{m} = R_t^*$$

and hence:

$$(9) \qquad \tau_t = \frac{b_{t-1}}{m} = \tau_{t-1}^*$$

so that the reserve ratio R_t is invariably at the steady state value which is appropriate for period t, while the tax rate τ_t is the steady state value which is appropriate for period $(t-1)$. Given that the discrete lag of τ_t behind R_{t-1} is necessary for administrative purposes, $s = 1$ represents the fastest reaction of the tax rate to changes in benefit flows. It represents the highest achievable degree of synchronization between benefit outflows and tax inflows.

The following important conclusion has thus been reached. If the tax schedule has no kinks or steps and has a negative slope throughout, then in the long run a firm's tax inflows equal its benefit outflows. But tax inflows lag behind benefit outflows. The speed with which taxes adjust to benefits depends on the slope of the tax schedule. As s rises from zero to unity this speed increases. The degree of experience rating thus reaches a maximum when $s = 1$. At the other extreme, when $s = 0$, the tax rate is independent of benefit outflows so that the degree of experience rating is zero.

Unfortunately the existence of steps and kinks in actual tax schedules necessitates some revision of the above simple conclusion. Let us, therefore, analyze the effects of ceteris paribus changes in all five parameters, NEGTAX, MAXTAX, SLOPE, MINTAX, and MINRES.

An increase in NEGTAX is illustrated in figure 6.2a. It simply raises the step which occurs at $R_{t-1} = 0$. This change can be interpreted as an increase in the average slope of the schedule in its upper range, and, hence, an increase in the degree of experience rating. In other words, firms now have an increased incentive to avoid NEGTAX and thus an increased incentive to reduce benefit outflows.

An increase in MAXTAX is shown in figure 6.2b. Two effects of this change can be distinguished. First, the step at $R_{t-1} = 0$ is reduced and this leads to a reduction in the average slope of the schedule in its upper range. This reduces the degree of experience rating. Second, firms which initially are at MINTAX between E and E' are now shifted, at least temporarily, to the sloped part of the schedule between G and E' and this increases the degree of experience rating. Thus a rise in MAXTAX leads to a decrease in the degree of experience rating in the upper range of the tax schedule and to an increase in the lower range.

Next consider an increase in SLOPE which is illustrated in figure 6.2c. Again two effects can be distinguished. First, for firms that are initially located between D and G the tax schedule becomes steeper, and, hence, the degree of experience rating is increased. Second, firms initially located between G and E are now moved (at least temporarily) to MINTAX and cease to be experience rated. Thus, between D and G the tax becomes more experience rated and between G and E it becomes less experience rated.

An increase in MINTAX is shown in figure 6.2d. It unambiguously reduces the degree of experience rating because firms that are located initially between E' and E are no longer experience rated. A rise in

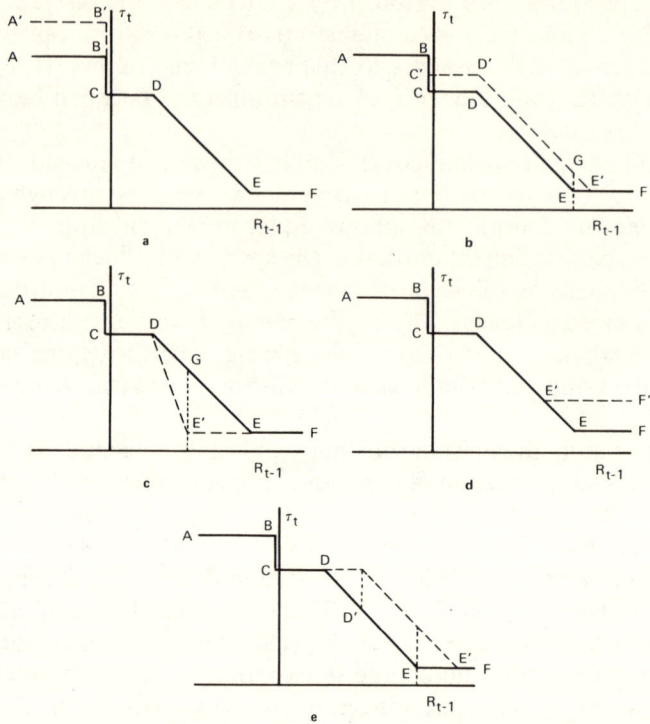

Figure 6.2 Increases in NEGTAX, MAXTAX, SLOPE, MINTAX, and MINRES

MINTAX thus reduces the range of tax rates over which experience rating applies.

Finally, a rise in MINRES is illustrated in figure 6.2e. Again the impact on experience rating is ambiguous. Firms initially located between D and D' cease to be experience rated at least temporarily. Firms initially located between E and E', on the other hand, are moved to the sloped part of the schedule and therefore become experience rated.

This concludes the discussion of the two extensions to the Baily-Feldstein model. According to the first, the layoff duration is treated as a variable which responds positively to increases in unemployment benefits and negatively to increases in the degree of experience rating. The second extension concerns the parameterization of experience rating. It has been related to the parameters of the tax schedule for the reserve ratio method. The degree of experience rating is related positively to NEGTAX and negatively to MINTAX. MAXTAX, SLOPE, and MINRES also tend to influence the degree of experience rating, but a priori argument does not yield unambiguous sign predictions.

6.4 Empirical Evidence

This section contains some relevant empirical evidence on the relationship between the parameters of the unemployment insurance system and layoffs, rehires, hours, and layoff duration. First, the theoretical predictions are restated summarily; second, the data are discussed and the results presented.

The theoretical arguments in sections 6.2 and 6.3 have generated the prediction that layoffs, hours, and layoff duration should all rise with increases in unemployment benefits and with decreases in the degree of experience rating. Since the flow of temporary layoffs may be measured either by layoffs or by rehires, the above prediction applies also to rehires. The prediction can be made specific by using the parameters of the tax structure. Thus, the four dependent variables—layoffs, rehires, hours, and layoff duration—should: (1) increase with increases in unemployment benefit rate; (2) decrease with increases in NEGTAX and; (3) increase with increases in MINTAX. Their responses to changes in MAXTAX, SLOPE, and MINRES may be positive or negative. Further, in view of the qualifying comments at the end of section 6.2, the impact of unemployment benefits may be weak. The empirical research underlying this paper has been designed to test these specific propositions.

Since the models discussed in sections 6.2 and 6.3 describe the behavior of individual firms, the data on layoffs, rehires, hours, and layoff duration should ideally also refer to individual firms. Unfortunately, however, no such micro data are readily available. Consequently the data used in the actual computations are aggregates. Specifically, layoff rates, rehire rates, and average weekly hours refer to averages in industry-state-year categories. Further, since no information on layoff duration is readily available, the duration variable is average unemployment duration (in weeks). Unemployment duration, average unemployment benefits (weekly in dollars), and the tax parameters NEGTAX, MAXTAX, SLOPE, MINTAX, and MINRES all refer to state-year categories. The years covered are 1962–69, and the states are all reserve ratio states. But for some industry-state-year categories not all relevant data are available, and, hence, these categories have been omitted. The number of observations is 170 for total manufacturing, and for two-digit industries it varies between 126 and 48 with a mean of about 96. All the data are readily available from *Employment and Earnings* and various publications of the Federal Unemployment Insurance Service.

For the purposes of estimation the following specific assumptions and amendments have been made.

1. Unemployment benefits are calculated typically as a fraction of previous earnings up to a certain limit. Hence, a state's benefit liberality should be measured, not by absolute benefits but by benefits in relation to

wage rates. For this reason the straight-time hourly wage rate was introduced as an additional explanatory variable. This procedure has some obvious disadvantages, and it is to be hoped that at some future date it will be replaced by the use of a set of parameters which describe benefit liberality.

2. The influence of all the explanatory variables upon the four dependent variables is assumed to be linear.

3. An additional explanatory variable is COVERAGE which is the ratio of employees covered by unemployment insurance to total employees. This variable has been included to take account of the fact that layoffs, rehires, and hours refer to total employment while the other variables refer only to covered employment.

4. Since the four dependent variables fluctuate cyclically, annual intercept dummies have been included as explanatory variables.

Now that we have stated the theoretical predictions and discussed the data used in the empirical analysis, let us now turn to an examination of the empirical results. Table 6.1 contains the regression coefficients when layoffs, rehires, hours, wage, and coverage refer to total manufacturing. Let us discuss, in turn, the influence of the various parameters of the unemployment insurance system.

1. BENEFITS have a positive but weak influence upon layoffs and duration and none on rehires and hours. This may be owing to the reasons given at the end of section 6.2. But this weak result may also be due to multicollinearity. The simple coefficient of correlation between wage and benefits is 0.82. This may have caused the standard errors of both variables to be large.

2. NEGTAX has a strong negative influence upon all four dependent variables. This finding lends substantial empirical support to the theoretical argument that a ceteris paribus increase in NEGTAX increases the degree of experience rating and, hence, reduces all four dependent variables.

3. MAXTAX has a strong positive influence on all four dependent variables. The joint impact of NEGTAX and MAXTAX suggests that the average slope of the tax schedule in its upper range is an especially important determinant of the degree of experience rating.

4. SLOPE has a positive influence which is weak for layoffs but quite strong for the other three dependent variables. In terms of the theoretical arguments in section 6.3, the positive relationship can be interpreted as follows: as SLOPE increases, some firms cease to be experience rated, and their reaction must be stronger than that of firms which remain on the sloped part of the schedule and thus face an increase in the degree of experience rating.

5. The influence of MINTAX is positive and quite strong for layoffs, rehires, and duration and weakly negative for hours. The theory predicts

Table 6.1 Regression Coefficients for total Manufacturing (*t*-statistics in parentheses)

Independent Variable	Mean Value	Dependent Variable			
		Layoffs	Rehires	Hours	Duration
		1.449	1.262	41.12	11.18
WAGE	2.490	.2556 (1.78)	−.0657 (.63)	−.1082 (.38)	.1329 (.28)
BENEFITS	36.20	.0136 (1.37)	.0047 (.66)	−.0068 (.35)	.0486 (1.51)
NEGTAX	3.452	−.2398 (3.68)	−.1113 (2.37)	−.3011 (2.34)	−.6810 (3.22)
MAXTAX	2.899	.2391 (3.00)	.1929 (3.35)	.6541 (4.15)	.5202 (2.01)
SLOPE	.3237	.1998 (.6472)	.6054 (2.72)	3.458 (5.67)	2.3846 (2.38)
MINTAX	.4731	.1474 (1.84)	.1286 (2.23)	−.2276 (1.44)	1.0264 (3.96)
MINRES	3.535	.0146 (.66)	−.0229 (1.43)	−.0571 (1.30)	.1308 (1.82)
COVERAGE	.9941	−12.884 (4.84)	−8.401 (4.37)	−30.446 (5.79)	−6.721 (.78)
DUM 63		−.1985 (1.35)	.0072 (.07)	.1458 (.50)	−.2491 (.52)
DUM 64		−.2475 (1.69)	−.0252 (.24)	.3064 (1.06)	−.3512 (.74)
DUM 65		−.4253 (2.91)	−.1532 (1.45)	.6055 (2.10)	−1.0128 (2.13)
DUM 66		−.4940 (3.14)	−.0741 (.65)	1.1739 (3.78)	−1.8601 (3.65)
DUM 67		−.4899 (3.00)	−.0607 (.51)	.3745 (1.16)	−1.9971 (3.77)
DUM 68		−.7873 (4.59)	−.1417 (1.14)	.5113 (1.51)	−1.7286 (3.10)
DUM 69		−.8390 (4.69)	−.2518 (1.95)	.3197 (.90)	−2.0440 (3.52)
Constant		13.514 (5.20)	9.344 (4.97)	69.793 (13.59)	16.055 (1.90)
R^2		.440	.358	.559	.428

an unambiguous positive sign. Hence, the empirical evidence lends some support to the theory.

6. The influence of MINRES is not iniform. It is strong only for duration in which case it is positive.

7. COVERAGE has a very strong negative impact on layoffs, rehires, and hours, and a weak one on duration. There are two possible explanations of this strong effect. In the first place, it might be argued that extensions of the unemployment insurance system reduce layoffs, rehires, and hours among *newly covered* employees. If this interpretation is accepted, then the coefficients of COVERAGE constitute fairly strong prima facie evidence against the Baily-Feldstein model. In the second place, it might be argued that COVERAGE simply corrects for the fact that layoffs, rehires, and hours refer to total employment, while the unemployment insurance parameters apply to only covered employment. Let X be such a parameter and let $f(X)$ be the layoff rate for covered employees and α that for uncovered employees. It can then be shown easily that the total layoff rate is the weighted average of the covered and uncovered rates $f(X)$ COVERAGE $+ \alpha(1\text{-COVERAGE})$, so that the linear effect of COVERAGE is negative. A complete test of this proposition would, however, require that COVERAGE be used multiplicatively with the other unemployment insurance parameters. The fact that duration, which refers only to covered employees, is not affected by COVERAGE lends some support to the second explanation.

8. The annual dummy variables reflect the well-known cyclical pattern in labor turnover, hours, and unemployment: as the economy moves into a boom, layoffs, rehires, and duration decline and hours rise.

Table 6.2 contains the number of positive and negative coefficients as well as the number of significant coefficients for the layoff, rehire, and hours equations run on date for sixteen two-digit manufacturing industries. Since duration is not available by industry, its equation is not included. Further, the reader is reminded that BENEFITS refers to benefits in the state as a whole and not to those paid in the industry.

By and large the disaggregated data reflect the same pattern as the aggregate ones. BENEFITS, MAXTAX, and MINTAX still seem to have predominantly positive coefficients. The influence of NEGTAX is still strongly negative. Disaggregation has led to a fair number of negative signs for SLOPE. Moreover, disaggregation has much weakened the strong negative effect of COVERAGE, especially for rehires and hours.

The strong and consistent negative influence of NEGTAX is especially encouraging because it is incompatible with the argument that high labor turnover rates cause high tax schedules. As already mentioned, in most states the laws provide for automatic increases in the entire tax schedule as the state unemployment insurance fund falls. It might be argued,

Table 6.2 Signs and Significance of Regression Coefficients for 16 Two-Digit Manufacturing Industries

	Layoffs				Rehires				Hours			
	Pos		Neg		Pos		Neg		Pos		Neg	
	Tot	Sig	Tot	Sig	Tot	Sig	Tot	Sig	Tot	Sig	Tot	Sig
WAGE	8	3	8	6	7	6	9	6	4	4	12	9
BENEFITS	10	8	6	1	9	4	7	3	12	3	4	3
NEGTAX	2	0	14	11	4	0	12	6	4	2	12	6
MAXTAX	13	6	3	1	10	5	6	4	7	7	9	5
SLOPE	5	1	11	5	7	5	9	3	11	5	5	2
MINTAX	9	5	7	2	11	6	5	3	8	4	8	5
MINRES	9	2	10	5	9	3	7	4	10	4	6	3
COVERAGE	6	2	10	5	9	3	7	4	10	3	6	2

Note: A significant coefficient is one with a t-statistic in excess of 1.5 (all t-statistics are treated as positive numbers).

therefore, that a rise in layoffs may cause a rise in benefit payments, a fall in the state fund and, hence, a rise in the tax schedule. This argument would not, however, generate a *fall* in NEGTAX.

Another interesting aspect of the empirical results appears in the duration equation. Hitherto, unemployment duration has been investigated primarily in terms of unemployment benefits and personal characteristics. As mentioned in the introduction, the papers by Classen (1977) and Ehrenberg and Oaxaca (1976) are excellent examples of this type of research. The evidence in table 6.1 suggests, however, that duration is much more responsive to the tax parameters than to BENEFITS. All five tax parameters, NEGTAX, MAXTAX, SLOPE, MINTAX and MINRES have a significant impact on duration. This evidence is consistent with a theory according to which duration is controlled to a significant extent by firms through their recalls of temporarily laid off workers.

This concludes the presentation of the empirical results. In view of the fact that the unemployment insurance tax constitutes a relatively small proportion of the payroll, the empirical results seem quite strong. NEGTAX has a consistently strong negative impact on layoffs, rehires, hours, and duration. MINTAX and BENEFITS have predominantly positive effects. All three effects are unambiguous predictions of the theory. Two other parameters of the tax structure, MAXTAX and SLOPE, tend to have significant effects on the four dependent variables. Thus the results seem to be quite consistent with a Baily-Feldstein type of model. Even if this kind of model should be refuted by future evidence, it seems clear that many strong empirical associations exist among labor market phenomena and the parameters of the unemployment insurance system.

6.5 Conclusions

In this paper an attempt has been made to examine the relationship between layoffs and the unemployment insurance system. The starting point of the analysis has been the Baily-Feldstein model according to which both layoffs and average hours worked increase with (1) increases in unemployment benefits, and (2) decreases in the degree of experience rating of the unemployment insurance tax. This model has been extended by letting the layoff duration be endogenous and by parameterizing experience rating. The empirical examination of the relationship between layoffs, rehires, hours, and unemployment duration as dependent variables and the parameters of the unemployment insurance system as explanatory variables has yielded very encouraging results. The strongest impact is that of NEGTAX, the tax rate which applies to firms with a negative balance in the unemployment insurance fund. A rise in NEGTAX reduces layoffs, rehires, hours, and unemployment duration.

Although the empirical results have been encouraging, they also suggest further research. In particular, it seems desirable to have a better parameterization of benefit liberality than has been used in this paper. Further, it may be necessary to model explicitly the determination of the parameters of the unemployment insurance tax.

The implications of the research findings are fairly obvious. Increases in NEGTAX tend to reduce strongly both layoffs and unemployment duration. The approximate elasticities of these two relationships are .55 and .21, respectively, so that a rise in NEGTAX of ten percent (from, say, 3.4 to 3.74) might reduce layoff unemployment by as much as seven percent. Moreover, increases in NEGTAX would improve the financial viability of the unemployment insurance system on two counts: tax inflows would rise and benefit outflows would fall because of the reduced layoff unemployment.

It is not claimed that the empirical research underlying this paper is more than a first attempt at discovering potentially important relationships. Thus, while the results are most encouraging, no finality is claimed for them at this stage.

Notes

1. In a recent paper Dale Mortensen presents a generalized version of the Baily-Feldstein model and shows that under theoretically standard conditions layoffs will not occur in the Baily-Feldstein model. See: Mortensen; "On the Theory of Layoffs." Discussion Paper No. 322, Center for Mathematical Studies in Economics and Management Science, Northwestern University, March 1978.

2. It should also be pointed out that the shifting and redistribution of both the unemployment benefits and the unemployment tax is likely to follow a possibly complex dynamic path.

Comment   Daniel S. Hamermesh

Brechling's work is an important contribution to the analysis of the effects of unemployment insurance (UI) and, more generally, to the economics of labor market policy. It takes the analysis two steps forward. First, and most important, Brechling shows how the structure of the experience-rated tax that finances UI can be parameterized in an empirically fruitful way. This is a major step forward, both because of the closer link forged between the constraints facing employers and their behavior, and because Brechling is one of the first even to consider the empirical effects of this tax. Bypassing simplistic approaches—for example, allowing the effective tax rate alone to reflect the degree of experience rating, an approach that has been used in studying the effects of UI benefits on unemployment until recently[1]—he has advanced the literature by moving directly to modeling and testing the institutional details of this tax.

The second contribution is the analysis of how the tax structure can affect the duration of temporary layoff employment. Implicitly, Brechling conducts a "horse race" between the UI tax parameters and the weekly UI benefit in explaining intertemporal variations in layoff rates. While I have some problems with the formulation of this race —particularly with the hobbles placed on the benefit variables in this sweepstakes—the role of imperfect experience rating in affecting the duration of unemployment spells has not been pointed out before.

While Brechling's intuition about the effects of the individual tax parameters on layoff duration seems correct, formal modeling of their role would be worthwhile verification. The Baily-Feldstein model contains one simple parameter (the fraction e of layoff costs paid by the firm through higher UI taxes). Imposing a complicated set of five tax parameters implies that the firm faces different constraints on its profit-maximizing behavior at different times, depending upon its past layoff experience. In other problems of this sort, the effects of changes in these constraints on choice variables are often counterintuitive, mainly because of the nonlinearities or discontinuities of the constraints.[2]

Modeling the experience-rated UI tax by a set of five parameters is important, but this particular set is not unique. For example, the reserve ratio at which the minimum tax rate becomes applicable—call it MAXRES—could have been used in place of SLOPE. Alternatively, MAXRES and SLOPE could have been used in place of MINRES to describe the tax structure completely along with the other three parameters. Obviously, if we measure the tax structure perfectly, the particular set of parameters chosen is immaterial. However, partly because of the

---

Daniel S. Hamermesh is Professor of Economics, Michigan State University, and Research Associate, National Bureau of Economic Research.

steps in the tax function between MAXRES and MINRES, but also because of administrative problems in assigning tax rates to firms—both problems that can be characterized as errors in variables—we do not measure the tax structure exactly. The empirical work would thus be far more convincing if each of the alternative parameterizations were used in the layoff and other regressions to test whether the interesting results are merely an artifact of the particular parameterization Brechling has chosen.

The perennial bugaboo of any empirical work on UI (or indeed any social insurance program in the U.S.) is the burden of the payroll tax that finances the program. Empirical work even in the area of the flat rate payroll tax for OASDHI is weak; on the experience-rated UI tax it is nonexistent. If the tax is not shifted at all, or if only the average tax rate in a labor (product) market is shifted backward (forward), Brechling is correct in ignoring the shifting problem in analyzing the effects of this tax. If, though, firms correctly perceive the results of their layoff actions and are able to shift their own tax costs at least partly onto labor or to consumers of their products, tax shifting will moderate the effects of taxes implicit in Brechling's theoretical discussion. Especially in the horse race between the tax parameters and an appropriate parameterization of benefits, the shifting issue should be considered. That the Baily-Feldstein model ignores it is no argument for ignoring it here.

Perhaps the most important problem with the theory and empirical work is the dynamic simultaneity between layoffs and the parameters of the UI tax structure facing the individual firm. If the layoff rate in year t increases because of some exogenous shock, benefit payments rise and the entire tax schedule facing firms in year $t+1$ will be higher. Thus a random error in year t will be correlated with each of the parameters in year $t+1$ because of the existence of multiple tax schedules in each state. This correlation induces a complicated form of simultaneity bias into the equations Brechling estimates. To take account of this problem and provide better estimates of the effects of the tax parameters on layoffs, rehires, etc., a simultaneous model that includes the determination of the tax parameters themselves as functions of past years' layoffs and benefit payments should be estimated.

That this point is not merely a minor econometric quibble is shown by the substantial variation in tax rates within many states as the overall state fund balance changes. For example, in 1974, in New York, the highest tax rate in effect (NEGTAX) was 3.0 percent, yet on the highest schedule the rate was 5.2 percent. The corresponding figures for Massachusetts were 2.9 and 5.1 percent. With the shocks that occurred in 1974 and 1975, these higher tax rates in fact became effective in 1976. The variation in the tax parameters over time is of roughly the same magnitude as interstate variation, suggesting that the dynamic feedback effect should be modeled.

Some specific estimation problems should be considered in any further work on UI financing and its effects. The COVERAGE variable produces very strange results—an effect on layoffs of -13 percentage points (the variable's mean is only 1.4), and on hours worked of -30 hours per week. While the paper goes to some lengths to rationalize these findings, they are far better rationalized by looking at the structure of the UI system. In manufacturing in the 1960s, coverage was nearly universal, as shown by the mean of this variable, .994. While the data are such that the COVERAGE measure could exceed one, it is likely that most of the variation in this measure is accounted for by several outliers whose layoff experience happens to be correlated with this variable.

Apart from the simultaneity problems noted above, the regression results appear convincing. However, it is well known that in most states firms with negative balances (for which NEGTAX is applicable) are in construction and certain seasonal manufacturing industries, while those to which the minimum tax rate (MINTAX) applies are in services, trade, and stable manufacturing industries. Recognizing this, we should observe that interstate variations in variables like MAXTAX and NEGTAX should be reflected in differences in turnover rates mostly in industries like autos, food processing, and lumber—seasonal industries. Similarly, variables like SLOPE and MINTAX should be most important in industries like trade, industries that unfortunately are not included in Brechling's regressions. A strong test of the hypothesis would involve constraining the coefficients of the variables describing taxes at the lower reserve ratios to be zero in seasonal industries, and those at the high end (SLOPE, MINTAX) to be zero in nonseasonal industries. If both constraints are rejected, that would indeed be impressive.

This suggests an interpretation of Brechling's strong results for NEGTAX and MAXTAX, and the relatively weak ones for the other parameters, particularly SLOPE and MINTAX. Manufacturing generates above-average benefits relative to manufacturing payrolls.[3] That being the case, manufacturing firms are in most cases on that part of the tax structure where the parameters applicable to firms with low reserve ratios are relevant. That it is these tax parameters that appear significant in regressions explaining layoff and other behavior in manufacturing is not surprising; the other parameters simply do not form part of the set of constraints affecting profit-maximizing behavior in this industry.

While the results clearly show that experience rating matters, the implicit size of its effects are too large to credit. For example, if the value of NEGTAX were changed from its minimum in the sample, 2.7 percent, to its maximum, 5.4 percent, the change in the layoff rate would be $-.65$, nearly half the mean of the layoff rate. Even simulating the effect of a change from the mean of NEGTAX to its maximum produces a reduction in layoffs of .47, one-third of the layoff rate. Results that imply that changing one parameter of a tax that has not exceeded 1.5 percent of payrolls since 1950 would reduce layoffs by one-third strain credulity severely.

Perhaps the most important result of Brechling's work is its implications for the political economy of the social insurance scheme. Nearly all of the recent empirical work by economists has focused on benefits and implied that the deleterious effects of the system could be removed by such steps as shortening potential duration or taxing benefits. Brechling's study suggests that much of the same improvement can be effected instead by improving the experience rating in the UI tax. Changes on the benefit side are likely to be hard to implement, as workers nearly unanimously see such changes as harmful to their interests. Improvements in experience rating, on the other hand, are clearly perceived by many employers (generally larger firms with stable work forces) as beneficial, and appear not to concern workers. Accordingly, the results of the study should provide an intellectual basis for a reform of UI that would be effective in keeping the program financially sound while removing some of its unfortunate side effects.

Notes

1. The usual technique has been to include the weekly benefit payment and the wage prior to unemployment as separate variables or in ratio form (see Ehrenberg and Oaxaca 1976; Classen 1977). More recently, Hamermesh (1979) has parameterized the structure of benefits to include amount, potential duration, and qualifying requirements.

2. For example, in the analysis of the effects of the availability of UI benefits on labor supply, we find that eligibility requirements induce a discontinuity in the budget constraint facing the household with unusual results on the choice of hours within some range of hours (see Hamermesh 1980).

3. Becker (1972: 14–15) finds that in nine of the ten states for which data were available, the cost rate—benefit payments as a percent of taxable payrolls—in manufacturing in 1967 exceeded the average for the state.

References

Azariadis, C. "Implicit Contracts and Underemployment Equilibria." *Journal of Political Economy,* November/December 1975.

Baily, M. "Wages and Employment under Uncertain Demand," *Review of Economic Studies,* January 1974.

―――. "On the Theory of Layoffs and Unemployment." *Econometrica,* July 1977.

Becker, J. *Experience Rating in Unemployment Insurance: Virtue or Vice.* Kalamazoo: W. E. Upjohn Institute, 1972.

Brechling, F. "The Incentive Effects of the Unemployment Insurance Tax," in R. Ehrenberg, ed., *Research in Labor Economics.* JAI Press, 1977a.

———. "Unemployment Insurance Taxes and Labor Turnover: Summary of Theoretical Findings." *Industrial and Labor Relations Review,* July 1977b.

Brechling, F., and Jehn, C. "The Unemployment Insurance Tax and Labor Turnover: An Empirical Analysis." CRC 349, Public Research Institute, Center for Naval Analyses, 1978.

Classen, K., "The Effect of Unemployment Insurance on the Duration of Unemployment and Subsequent Earnings." *Industrial and Labor Relations Review,* July 1977.

Ehrenberg, R. and Oaxaca, R. "Unemployment Insurance, Duration of Unemployment, and Subsequent Wage Gain." *American Economic Review,* December 1976.

Feldstein, M. "Temporary Layoffs in the Theory of Unemployment." *Journal of Political Economy,* October 1976.

———. "The Effect of Unemployment Insurance on Temporary Layoff Unemployment." *American Economic Review,* December 1978.

Gordon, R. J. "The Welfare Costs of Higher Unemployment." *Brookings Papers on Economic Activity,* 1973(1).

Halpin, T. "The Effect of Unemployment Insurance on Seasonal Fluctuations in Employment." *Industrial and Labor Relations Review,* forthcoming.

Hamermesh, D. S. *Jobless Pay and the Economy.* Baltimore: John Hopkins University Press, 1977.

———. "Entitlement Effects, Employment Decisions and Unemployment Insurance." *Economic Inquiry* 17 (July 1979).

———. "Unemployment Insurance and Labor Supply." *International Economic Review* 21 (October 1980).

Katz, A., ed. "The Economics of Unemployment Insurance: A Symposium." *Industrial and Labor Relations Review,* July 1977.

7 Employment in Construction and Distribution Industries: The Impact of the New Jobs Tax Credit

John Bishop

The New Jobs Tax Credit (NJTC) offers a tax credit of fifty percent of the first $4200 of wages per employee for increases in employment of more than two percent over the previous year. Economic theory predicts that such a tax credit should stimulate employment, decrease hours worked per week, and reduce product prices of the subsidized industries. A time series analysis of the construction, retailing, and wholesaling industries finds strong support for these hypotheses. Our results suggest that the NJTC was responsible for 150,000–670,000 of the more than 1-million increase in employment that occurred between mid-1977 and mid-1978 in the construction and retailing industries. Similar analysis indicates that by June 1978, NJTC had produced roughly a 1 percentage point reduction in the margin between retail and wholesale prices of commodities that saved consumers $1.9–$3.6 billion over the course of the previous year.

7.1 Introduction

This paper examines the effect of the NJTC provision of the 1977 Tax Reduction and Simplification Act on employment demand and pricing policies in the construction, trucking, wholesaling, and retail sectors of the economy. Employing 22.7 million workers in 1976, these industries

John Bishop is Project Associate, Institute for Research on Poverty, University of Wisconsin.

The research reported here was supported by Grant No. 51-55-73-04 from the Employment Training Administration of the Department of Labor and by funds granted to the Institute for Research on Poverty of the University of Wisconsin, Madison, by the Department of Health, Education, and Welfare. John Geweke and Bob Haveman provided helpful comments on previous drafts. The opinions expressed and any remaining errors are the responsibility of the author.

provided 26 percent of the nation's jobs and 27 percent of the hours worked by all persons engaged in production.

Time series studies of employment demand have neglected these industries, despite their importance and the availability of reasonably good monthly data on input and output prices, wages, employment, hours worked, and sales or output. Wages tend to be low: average earnings in the retail sector are two-thirds the national average; construction earnings are only slightly lower than that average, but vary greatly. A large share of the nation's low-earning workers is employed in these industries—in 1970, 45 percent of teenagers, 21 percent of black males, and 23 percent of women.

Because the life of capital equipment is short and rates of labor turnover are high, the response of construction and distribution to changes in input prices induced by tax policy may be speedier than in the rest of the economy. NJTC places a $100,000 cap on the amount of subsidy each firm may receive, and one would expect the most noticeable response to it to occur in industries dominated by small and medium sized firms like construction and the distribution sector.

The data reported here are consistent with the hypothesis that firms in the construction and distribution industries have responded to NJTC by increasing employment, of part-time workers especially, and by reducing prices. The point estimates of the increase in employment that the credit had stimulated by March 1978 generally lie in the neighborhood of 400,000, with a band of uncertainty of ± 180,000. A 400,000-job stimulus is roughly one-third of the growth in employment that these industries were experiencing between April 1977 and April 1978. Point estimates of the decline in the margin between the retail price of commodities and manufacturers' wholesale prices suggest that by April 1978 the credit had reduced the consumer price index for commodities by slightly less than one percentage point.

Section 7.2 outlines the problem that employment subsidies are designed to address and describes the structure of the currently operating marginal employment incentive. Section 7.3 discusses how a firm should respond to such an incentive and selects three hypotheses for testing at the industry level. Section 7.4 describes the estimating equations and the methods of testing the hypotheses. Section 7.5 reviews the data and section 7.6 presents and discusses the results. In section 7.7, we review the limitations of the study and suggest some fruitful areas for research.

7.2 Background

Over the past six years, overall unemployment has averaged 6.8 percent, nonwhite unemployment 12.2 percent, and teenage unemployment

17.5 percent. This discouraging unemployment record has led both economists and politicians to search for new ways to stimulate the employment of inexperienced and disadvantaged workers. Martin Baily and James Tobin (1977) suggested that, by focusing the employment stimulus on the lower-skilled, less-experienced workers, it may be possible to lower the rate of unemployment at which inflation accelerates (NAIRU, the nonaccelerating inflation rate of unemployment).

One approach is to expand public service employment for young unskilled workers. The cost per job created, however, is high; and it is in any case doubtful that in the long run public service employment results in large net additions to total employment. An additional problem is that the public sector is highly skill-intensive. The proportion of workers with at least one year of college is twice as high in the public as in the private sector (45% vs. 22%).

These difficulties have led to programs whose objective is to create additional jobs for unskilled and inexperienced workers in the private sector. WIN and JOBS are examples of programs that have attempted to induce the private sector to hire the disadvantaged by offering employers a subsidy to hire workers in their target groups. They have not, however, proved very effective.

Most employers that hire target group workers for whom a subsidy is available neglect even to apply for the money (Hamermesh 1977), apparently because of the paperwork involved in applying for the subsidy. A further disadvantage of this approach seems to be that the subsidy adheres to specific individuals. Employers may feel that eligibility for the subsidy signals that the job applicant is likely to be a worker of low productivity—leading to the paradox that the programs may in fact lower the subsidized worker's chances of getting a good job.

A third approach is to subsidize employment generally. First proposed by Nicholas Kaldor in 1936, this approach has more recently been refined and analyzed by Fethke and Williamson (1977) and Kesselman, Williamson, and Berndt (1977). These analyses suggest that by paying the subsidy only for increases in employment over a threshold level based on a firm's past employment—that is, by designing a so-called marginal employment subsidy—it is possible to achieve rather large increases in employment at rather limited cost to the government. Independently, several influential members of Congress (Senator Lloyd Bentsen and Representatives Barber Conable and Al Ullman among them) were thinking along similar lines and introduced bills implementing this marginal employment subsidy approach.

President Carter's January 1977 tax reduction recommendations contained a nonmarginal wage bill tax credit. The House Ways and Means Committee substituted a marginal employment subsidy for the president's proposal; this, after being somewhat modified by the Senate, was passed and signed into law as part of the Tax Reduction and Simplification Act of 1977.

This law provided businesses with a tax credit against corporate or personal income tax liability for expansions in employment in 1977 or 1978.

> The credit is 50 percent of the increase in each employer's wage base under the Federal Unemployment Tax Act (FUTA) above 102 percent of that wage base in the previous year. The FUTA base for a year consists of wages paid up to $4,200 per employee. . . .
>
> The employer's deduction for wages is reduced by the amount of the credit. Therefore, although the maximum gross credit for each new employee is $2,100, the effective credit ranges from $1,806 (for a taxpayer in the 14-percent tax bracket) to $630 (for a taxpayer in the 70-percent bracket).
>
> The total amount of the credit has four limitations: (1) the credit cannot be more than 50 percent of the increase in total wages paid by the employer for the year above 105% of the previous year, (2) the credit must be no more than 25% of the current year's FUTA wages, (3) the credit for a year cannot exceed $100,000 and (4) the credit cannot exceed the taxpayer's tax liability. Credits which exceed tax liability for a year may be carried back for 3 years and carried forward for 7 years. [Joint Committee on Taxation 1977]

The requirement that the total wages paid rise by at least five percent was designed to ensure that NJTC was based on actual increases in employment rather than artificial increases in unemployment insurance wages (for example, an employer could increase unemployment insurance wages by dividing full-time jobs into part-time or part-year jobs). The requirement that the credit not exceed twenty-five percent of the FUTA wages limited the amounts of credit that new and rapidly expanding businesses could receive. (The tax credit for each newly hired handicapped worker was 60% of the first $4,200 of wages paid, with no limit on the total amount of subsidy. This paper does not analyze the effects of the credit for the handicapped.)

In 1977, its first year of operation, $2.358 billion of NJTC credits were claimed on a total of 614,000 tax returns. In 1978, its second and final year of operation, $4.513 billion of credits were claimed on a total of 1,142,000 tax returns. Since the firm's deductions for wages must be reduced by the amount of the credit, revenue costs (assuming no direct effects on before-tax profits) were approximately $1.4 billion in 1977 and $2.7 billion in 1978. Although roughly one-third of the returns claiming a credit were corporate returns, two-thirds of the dollars claimed were on these returns. Since the credits due to a partnership or subchapter-S corporation may show up on more than one individual return, the total number of businesses claiming the credit in 1978 is likely to have been closer to 1 million than 1.14 million. This would imply that approximately twenty-eight percent of the nation's 3.5 million employers claimed the credit in 1978. A lower-bound estimate of the number of workers whose employment received subsidy can be obtained by dividing the dollars of credit claimed by $2,100, the maximum credit an employer can receive for one worker. This calculation implies that at least 1.1 million employees were subsidized in 1977, and at least 2.15 million in 1978. By comparison, total private nonagricultural employment grew 2.8 million in 1977 and 3.6 million in 1978.

7.3 The Likely Impact of NJTC

Key features of NJTC are that it is (a) a fixed proportion of earnings up to a rather low maximum; (b) marginal; and (c) temporary. Each of these features has important consequences. The first feature focuses the employment stimulus on low-wage, part-time, part-year workers, a group that currently suffers from very high unemployment rates. The second feature, that the subsidy is based on a threshold employment level defined by last year's employment, makes possible a high rate of subsidy at low cost to the treasury; it also restructures the relationship between the marginal and average costs of existing firms and between the average costs of new and existing firms. The third feature, that the subsidy expired at the end of 1978 and has an eligibility threshold that is updated each year to reflect last year's change in employment, tends to make it an "automatic destabilizer."

7.3.1 Employment

The first crucial feature of NJTC is that it is paid on only the first $4,200 of earnings of each extra worker. Among full-time, full-year workers, therefore, NJTC works to the advantage of low-wage workers because the proportionate subsidy of their wages is greater. NJTC also tends to provide a proportionately larger subsidy of part-time and temporary employment.

Since members of minority groups, women, and teenagers predominate in all three types of employment—low-wage, part-time, and part-year—NJTC should, as a consequence, target the employment stimulus on groups that currently experience very high rates of unemployment.

7.3.2 Price Inflation

The impact of the marginal employment subsidy on the pricing policies of firms is of major importance. If the subsidy is immediately passed on to consumers, the employment stimulus will be larger because the lower price will cause an expansion in demand for real output. This once-and-for-all reduction in the price of output will also temporarily reduce inflation. How large these effects will be depends on how firms set prices.

Tax incidence theory tells us that the size of the price reduction induced by the subsidy depends upon the nature of the market and the slopes of the demand and supply curves. If industry demand is defined as $P_d = B + bQ$ for $b < 0$, and the supply curve as $P_s = A + \alpha Q - S$ for $\alpha > 0$, then the impact of a subsidy S on price in a competitive industry is $dP/dS = b/(b - \alpha)$. An industry's long-run supply curve depends on the average costs of production of new entrants and the incremental total costs of expansion by existing firms. If there are no factors specific to the industry (i.e., the price of factors supplied to the industry does not depend on that industry's output), then the long-run supply curve should be quite flat ($\alpha \approx 0$). Thus, except for agriculture and mining, dP/dS should be closer to 1 than to zero. In the long run, shocks to demand should have only minor effects on price; and changes in costs of production will be passed on to the consumer almost completely. In the long run, prices will behave as if they were set according to a standard markup on normal average costs.

Normal average cost pricing is also a popular theory of short-run pricing behavior and currently predominates in certain lines of econometric work on inflation (Nordhaus 1974). For competitive industries like retailing and services, the basis for using this theory to predict short-term pricing behavior is that rates of entry and exit are very high and that since most firms operate with substantial excess capacity, marginal costs do not increase as sales rise. For firms in oligopolistic industries, one of the primary theoretical justifications for setting prices administratively according to a normal average cost rule is limit price theory. According to this theory, prices in an oligopolistic industry are set in order to forestall or minimize entry of new competitors into the industry. Prices are therefore set below the average costs of new entrants and adjusted up or down as these costs change. To the extent that changes in the normal average costs of existing firms approximate changes in the costs of entry, normal average costs will be good predictors of short-term pricing behavior.

A permanent marginal employment subsidy with a fixed threshold changes the relationship between the average costs of existing firms and the average costs of new entrants. The fact that new firms receive a subsidy on all their workers rather than just a few will give them a cost advantage, even though the subsidy per worker is half the standard amount. Existing firms that choose to expand by bringing out a new product line or opening an establishment to serve a new market will also have a cost advantage over firms that are already serving that market. Such marginal employment subsidy would cause the limit price that would otherwise forestall entry of a new firm to decline by substantially more than the average costs of existing firms.

New firms compete at a substantial disadvantage, because they lack an established reputation with customers, have inexperienced managers, and need to start from scratch in recruiting and training a labor force. The advantages that marginal employment subsidies would give new firms are not likely to outweigh these disadvantages completely. When the costs of energy, materials, and capital are taken into account, the advantage produced by NJTC was only four percent in manufacturing, three percent in retailing, and 4–8 percent in services. Relative to the current environment, a permanent NJTC with fixed threshold could be expected to provide an important stimulus to the formation of new firms and the expansion of small ones.

A permanent marginal employment subsidy with a fixed threshold and no upper limit on the subsidy per firm might, therefore, reduce prices by more than it reduces the average costs of existing firms. It is somewhat more difficult to predict, however, whether the temporary and constrained NJTC credit of the 1977 Tax Reduction and Simplification Act will have a substantial impact on prices.

The $100,000 maximum on the credit offered any one firm limits the size of the subsidized expansion to forty-eight workers for existing firms and ninety-six for new firms. The expiration date means that a new firm cannot plan on receiving a subsidy for more than the first two years (i.e., for a maximum of 192 workers). As a result, the credit will be of only minor help to entrants into industries with scale economies that require firms to employ many more than that. Almost fifty percent of all private wage and salary workers are in firms that employ more than five-hundred workers. In many cases, however, the large firms compete directly with small firms in certain segments of their business. NJTC should be more effective in such situations. Computer software, auto parts manufacture, and steel wholesaling and fabrication are examples of this type of industry. In these markets the invigorated competition coming from small, fast-growing firms may compress everyone's margins and reduce the share of the market served by large firms.

The fact that permanent increases in employment receive a NJTC subsidy only in the first year also lowers the impact of the subsidy on average costs of production over a ten-year horizon. This feature will limit the credit's effect in lowering the entry-forestalling price. It also means, however, that the potential entrant can be sure he will get the credit even if his attempt at entry fails. If he fails to make profits, the credit (which can be carried forward for 7 years) is still worth something to potential purchasers of business.

7.3.3 The Hypotheses

The list of ways in which we might expect NJTC to change firm behavior is quite long. Work that used to be contracted out, such as cleaning, maintenance, accounting, etc., might be done internally. If deferred maintenance can be done by new hiring of additional workers, we would expect it to be completed before January 1979. Where manufacturing firms have low wages and high turnover, there might be a build-up of the inventory of finished goods. Large firms that are no longer subsidized on the margin by NJTC might contract work out to firms that are eligible for NJTC; the negotiated price for that work would, as a result, be lower. Groups of workers that were avoided because of their high turnover rates might now become especially desirable.

In the empirical work of this chapter, however, only three hypotheses will be examined:
1. Employment will rise
2. Hours worked per week will fall
3. Prices will fall

Behavior will change only if the firm is aware of the subsidy and can increase its tax credit by increasing employment. Small firms tend to be unaware of the credit (only 30 percent of firms with 1–10 employees had heard of it by February 1978). Firms with over 2,000 employees will generally have hit the $100,000 cap without having to change their behavior. Consequently industries dominated by medium-sized firms should respond more than industries composed wholly of either small or large firms.

7.3.4 Other Studies of the Impact of NJTC

Two other studies have found evidence that is consistent with the hypothesis that NJTC had a substantial impact on employment in 1977 and 1978, and that the tax revenue lost per job created was under $5,000.

The first study (McKevitt 1978) is based on a mail questionnaire survey of a sample of the membership of the National Federation for Independent Businesses (NFIB). The first survey to ask questions about NJTC was conducted in January 1978. Of the employers responding, 43% knew about NJTC and 1.4% reported that the credit had influenced them to hire extra workers (the number averaged 2.0 per firm). The April survey found that 51% knew of NJTC's existence and that 2.4% had increased hiring by an average of 2.3 employees as a result. In the July 1978 survey, 58% were aware of the credit and 4.1% of the firms reported that they had increased hiring as a result. An increase in employment of 2.3 employees by over 4% of all employers is not a small response. If the NFIB survey is representative, and other firms are not hurt by the expansion of subsidized firms, these responses imply that in the second quarter of 1978 there were more than 300,000 extra jobs directly created as a result of NJTC at a tax expenditures of roughly $6,500 for each job created. The NFIB firms seem to be more aware of the credit's existence, but not to be more likely to respond that they are increasing employment because of the credit. A Bureau of the Census survey of a stratified random sample of firms found that, in February 1978, 2.4% of firms reported being aware of the credit and making a conscious effort to increase employment because of it. This contrasts with NIFB's findings of a 1.4% response the previous month and a 2.4% response two months later. Thus the census survey indicates that, if anything, the NFIB survey is a conservative indicator of employer response to NJTC.

Another study (Perloff and Wachter 1978) is based upon the survey conducted by the Bureau of the Census. Perloff and Wachter compared rates of employment growth between 1976 and 1977 for firms that knew about the credit and those that did not. Holding employment size, class, region, form of organization, type of industry, and the growth rate of sales constant, they found that the employment of firms that had heard of the credit before February 1978 had grown three percent faster. Firms that reported they made a conscious effort to expand employment because of the credit grew nine percent faster than firms that knew about the credit but did not report making any special effort. If one were to assume that NJTC caused the three percent higher growth of the small and medium-sized firms that knew about the credit (about a quarter of total employment is in these firms) and left the rest of the economy unaffected, the total number of extra jobs in 1977 would be roughly 700,000. Tax expenditure per job created would be $2,000 per job. Since NJTC had not passed Congress until almost half the year had passed, effects of this magnitude for 1977 are large indeed. Perloff and Wachter pointed out that some firms may learn about the credit because they are growing fast or because they are generally more aware of opportunities to expand their business. Consequently, they suggest that their results should be viewed "as an upper bound on the short-run impact of this program."

Studies like those just reviewed are measuring the differential impact of NJTC across firms, not the net impact of NJTC on the total economy. If NJTC is to have any impact on total employment, it must first change the employment level of individual firms. These two studies provide some support for the hypothesis that firms did change their behavior because of NJTC. However, since firms compete with each other in both labor and product markets, the increases of employment in subsidized firms may cause decreases of employment in their unsubsidized competitors. Alternatively an NJTC-induced expansion by one firm may cause that firm's suppliers to expand as well. The direction of NJTC's impact on nonsubsidized firms cannot be signed a priori, for it depends upon the relative size of offsetting effects. We suspect, however, that the first effect is larger than the second. If so, simple extrapolations from measured impact on firms to impacts on the economy will exaggerate the true impact. Most of the displacement effects that may bias estimates of net job creations when the firms are the unit of observation are netted out when the industry is the unit of observation. A study that uses aggregate industry data to test for the impacts of NJTC would seem to have an important contribution to make.

7.4 Specifications of the Model

In a world of perfect information, no inventory, and zero adjustment costs, optimal levels of employment and hours depend solely on current prices and sales. In a world of imperfect information, inventory holding, and adjustment costs, the firm's optimal employment and hours in period t depends upon the realized level of employment in period $t-1$ and upon anticipated levels of sales and input prices in both current and future periods.

$$(1) \qquad E_t = f(S^e, \frac{W^e}{P^e}, \frac{Q^e}{P^e}, E_{t-1})$$

where S, W, P, and Q denote sales, wages, output prices, and input prices respectively, and the e superscript denotes a vector of anticipations of future values, based on all information available up to time t.

When the observable lagged values of S, W, P, and Q are used in an estimating equation, lag distributions will vary, not only because adjustments to different stimuli take different amounts of time but also because the expectation formation process for each variable will have different lag structures.

Since the information set used to predict future values of a particular variable may include other variables in the model, coefficients on lagged values of sales or wages may not follow a regular pattern. The primary objective of this study is to obtain unbiased measures of NJTC's impact on employment and prices. Imposing regularity conditions on the lag structure might bias our estimates of the NJTC's effect. Consequently, estimating techniques are employed that produce free estimates of the lag structure.

Since $E_{t-1}, E_{t-2}, \ldots$, etc., are themselves a function of lagged values of S, W, P, and Q, we may substitute the lagged dependent variable out of the equation. Since expectations about P may be formed very differently from expectations about W and Q, the most general way to write our equation in terms of observable, contemporaneous, and lagged values is

$$(2) \qquad E_t = f(S, W, P, Q)e^{u_t}$$

where S, W, P, Q denote vectors containing current and lagged values of the variable.

Econometric studies of labor demand often estimate their models under some rather strong maintained hypotheses, many of which have recently received severe criticism. Clark and Freeman (1977) find that for manufacturing, the data reject the constraint that the rental cost of capital and real wage rates has equal but opposite effects on employment demand. Constraints requiring identical lag structures across variables have also been found to be inconsistent with the data (Sims 1972 1974; Clark and Freeman 1977).

Estimates of systems of demand equations that have included materials and energy inputs typically reject the weak separability of materials and energy from capital and labor (Berndt and Wood 1975; Gollop 1974). This rejection implies that the correct specification of a labor demand function contains the prices of materials and energy. Since the prices of materials may be correlated with the cost of capital or wage rates, estimates of labor demand functions derived from a value-added production specification are likely to be biased.

A number of other potentially troublesome maintained hypotheses, relating to the exogeneity of industry sales and wage rates in regressions predicting employment, will be tested. Sims (1972) has shown that, under fairly general conditions, a test of the hypothesis that coefficients on future values of the wage rate or on sales are all zero can be regarded as a test of the hypothesis that the equation is in fact structural. Rejection of this hypothesis will be taken as evidence for simultaneity, and the equation will be reestimated using two-stage least squares (2SLS). Potential exogeneity problems with the price of output are eliminated by treating P as a function of nominal input prices and solving P out of the model.

Our models were estimated under two alternative sets of maintained hypotheses. The relative wage model assumes that the information set used in generating expectations about future input price ratios is limited to current and lagged information about input price ratios. This specification implies that a simultaneous five percent increase in all input prices will leave current and all future employment levels unchanged. Although the tests for exogeneity that were applied to this model were rejected for some industries, there was no attempt to apply 2SLS using this model, because to do so would have involved simultaneously instrumenting all input prices.

The second, somewhat more general, specification is the nominal input price model. Using nominal input prices rather than price ratios as regressors means that we are dropping the assumption that the information set is limited to input price ratios. Firms are certainly aware of the history of nominal prices. Rational behavior implies that expectation formation takes into account the noise-to-signal ratio of a series, and this, in turn, implies that the time pattern of response to each nominal input price should be estimated separately. In this model we choose not to impose the constraint that the coefficients on input prices sum to zero, because errors in measurement of the rental price of capital and of price indexes for consumable materials and business services are likely to be larger than errors in measurement of wholesale prices and wage rates (especially in the disaggregated retail industry models). Imposing this constraint would increase the likelihood of transmission of a bias arising from an error in variables to the wage coefficients. (Clark and Freeman 1977 demonstrate this for simple cases.) If we are wrong, and the constraint should have been imposed, we lose efficiency only.

All the variables in these models except for seasonal dummies, time trends, and NJTC are expressed as logarithms. The estimating form of the relative wage model is:

$$E = \beta_0 + \beta_1 T + M\beta_2 + TM\beta_3 + \beta_4 \text{ NJTC} + S_1\beta_5 + S_2\beta_6$$
$$+ (Q - W)\beta_7 + (R - W)\beta_8 + \beta_9(\bar{P}_k - \bar{W}) + e$$

The estimating form of nominal price model is:

$$E = \alpha_0 + \alpha_1 T + M\alpha_2 + TM\alpha_3 + \alpha_4 \text{ NJTC} + S_1\alpha_5 + S_2\alpha_6$$
$$+ W\alpha_7 + Q\alpha_8 + R\alpha_9 + e$$

T = a time trend

M = a vector of monthly seasonal dummies

TM = time trends on the seasonal dummies

NJTC = measure of knowledge of NJTC

S_1 = a row vector of current and lagged measures of output for the entire industry

S_2 = a row vector of current and lagged measures of the subindustry's output

W = a row vector of current and lagged hourly rates of compensation in the industries

Q = a row vector of current and lagged prices of the industry's intermediate inputs

R = a row vector of current and lagged rental costs of capital specific to the industry

$\bar{P}_k - \bar{W}$ = a three-year average of the ratio of capital goods prices to wage rates

The basic model assumes that anticipations of present and future values of sales and prices are based on the previous three-year record of these variables. The sales, wage rate, and intermediate input price variables are represented by their current value, with averages for the previous four quarters and half-yearly averages going a further two years back in time.[1]

Cost of capital is represented by four variables: an average for the previous twelve months and this same variable lagged one, two, and three years.[2]

7.5 Data

For the construction industry, the output variable is construction put in place, deflated by an interpolated National Income Accounts (NIA) deflator for structures. For the retail industry, aggregate output is defined as retail sales, deflated by the consumer price index (CPI) for commodities. Industry-specific output measures for the disaggregated segments of the retail industry are retail sales for that segment of the industry deflated by the appropriate components of the CPI. For trucking, the output variable is a seasonally adjusted index of the volume of general freight hauled by class 1 and 2 common carriers of property. For wholesaling, we use the sales of merchant wholesalers deflated by the CPI for commodities. For trucking and wholesaling, only partial coverage of the industries is provided by these indexes, and the data on employment and hours and those on retail or wholesale sales are obtained from separate samples of firms. When industry subaggregates are being used, sampling error in the industry-specific sales variable can become a serious problem. Consequently, models predicting employment in trucking, wholesaling and disaggregate retail industries contain the additional scale variable of current and lagged total retail sales.

Indexes of the rental cost of capital services in the construction, trucking, and retail industries were calculated. The appendix details our data sources and assumptions. The main features of the resulting calculations are summarized in table 7.1. In the first three rows are tabulated present values (at a 10% discount rate) of the depreciation deductions allowed on equipment used by retail firms. Note that these present values have increased (from 41.7¢ to 72¢ per dollar invested) as tax lives have shortened. The liberalization of depreciation rules and the investment tax credit have lowered the rental on capital goods (rows 4–7). For retail corporations the rental cost of equipment fell from .278 in 1950 to .224 in 1978. Corporate rental costs for trucks fell from .44 in 1950 to .373 in 1978. Rentals in 1978 are almost equal to those that would prevail if there was no taxation of business income or complete expensing of all investment costs in the first year (compare the first and last columns of rows 4–7).[3]

The retail industry's compensation per hour of work has risen in current dollars to 4.7 times its level in 1950 (see bottom row). The price of other inputs has not been rising quite as rapidly so their relative cost has been declining. An index of the relative rise in labor costs (the log of the wage deflated by a price index of the competing input) is tabulated in

Table 7.1   History of the Tax Treatment of Capital and of Relative Input Prices

	1950:01	1955:01	1960:01	1965:01	1972:01	1975:01	1978:03
A. Present value of deprec. deduct. for:							
1. Structures	.287	.445	.508	.508	.508	.508	.508
2. Retail equipment	.417	.580	.644	.698	.720	.720	.720
3. Trucks	.799	.849	.849	.908	.951	.951	.951
B. Implicit rental cost of:	No tax						
4. Structures—corporate	.094	.170	.164	.159	.158	.158	.158
5. Equipment—corporate	.207	.288	.288	.245	.235	.235	.224
6. Equipment—proprietorship	.207	.237	.245	.222	.224	.221	.213
7. Trucks—corporate	.37	.439	.447	.447	.398	.382	.382	.373
C. Log ratio of retail wage to:							
8. Wholesale price of cons. fin. goods	0	.157	.329	.505	.731	.612	.703
9. Price of business serv. and materials	0	.128	.261	.415	.591	.501	.533
10. Price of capital goods	0	.042	.058	.136	.211	.176	.206
11. Rental cost of capital	0	.155	.217	.497	.717	.657	.747
D. Nominal compensation in retail	1.00	1.294	1.619	1.953	2.967	3.672	4.701

Note: The assumptions and data sources used to calculate the present value of the depreciation deduction on one dollar of investment (Z) and the implicit rental cost of capital (R_t) are described in the appendix. Rows 8–11 present the log of the ratio of nominal hourly compensation in the retail sector to the price of the other factor inputs in this sector.

$$\log \frac{W_t}{W_{1950.1}} \div \frac{P_t}{P_{1950.1}}$$

In the bottom row, $W_t/W_{1950.1}$ = index of the nominal rate of hourly compensation in retailing.

rows 8–11. Relative to the wholesale price of consumer finished goods, wages had risen in 1972 to 2.1 (antilog .731) times their 1950 level. The price explosion following the Yom Kippur War, however, lowered real wages by nearly twelve percent in three years to 1.84 times their 1950 level. Since then, real wage rates have recovered somewhat to 2.02 times their 1950 level. Relative to the price of business services and consumable materials or to the price of capital equipment, wages have risen much less dramatically. Between 1950 and 1978 wage rates rose only twenty-three percent faster than an index of plant and equipment prices. The increasingly favorable tax treatment of capital investment has meant, however, that the price of efficiency units of capital services has lagged behind the prices of the equipment and buildings that provide those services. As a result, wage rates (the price of labor services) have doubled relative to the price of capital services.

Most studies of the effect of tax incentives on firm behavior assume that factor demand responds to the after-tax cost of the variable. Studies of investment incentives imbed a multiplicity of tax provisions in a single variable for the rental cost of capital. To construct this cost of capital variable, assumptions must be made about (1) the appropriate market interest rate; (2) how expectations of output and capital goods prices are formed; (3) the level and timing of knowledge of tax incentive provisions; and (4) the nature of the firm's expectations about changes in tax provisions. Inferences about the effect of specific tax provisions are based on the role the tax provision has in determining rental cost and the magnitude and significance of the rental cost variable. The inevitable errors in constructing the rental cost variable bias both the coefficient on rental cost and the policy simulations that are derived from that coefficient. Studies applying this methodology to labor demand attempt to measure the wage elasticity of employment. Hamermesh (1976) has recently reviewed these studies and predicts that a marginal wage subsidy of NJTC's generosity would have a substantial impact upon employment. The assumptions necessary to draw such an inference are considerable, however: (1) Employers must know of NJTC's existence and provisions and believe the credit will not be extended beyond 1978. (2) Employers cannot be subject to income effects, for the income effects of wage rate changes and a marginal wage subsidy are very different. (3) Elasticities based on historical responses to anticipated and permanent changes in before-tax wage rates must correctly predict the response to an unanticipated temporary change in a tax provision. Policy simulations of this kind are useful (Bishop and Lerman 1977; Hamermesh 1977), but they cannot be conclusive.

Where it is feasible, direct measurement of the effects of a tax provision is to be preferred. This is what we propose to do in this paper. Since our primary purpose here is to provide a powerful test of the effects of

NJTC, the specification of this variable is important. The effect of the tax credit is likely to be very different from the effect of an equivalent change in the wage rate. NJTC is capped, temporary, and marginal; it requires that the firm have tax liability if it is to receive benefits. In February 1978, more than half of all firms were unaware that the credit existed, and many of those that had heard of it wrongly thought themselves to be ineligible.

In February 1978, a census bureau survey asked a large sample of firms whether they had heard of the tax credit and, if so, when they had heard of it. Large firms were much more likely to have heard of the credit and to have heard of it immediately after its passage in May 1977. Using a distribution of retail employment categorized by size of firm, we estimated the proportion of retail employees that were in firms that knew about the credit for each month of 1977 and 1978. (Firms employing more than a thousand workers were excluded from this calculation.)

It was assumed that once a firm knows about the credit its response will be distributed over the following six months. The NJTC variable is, therefore, an average over the past six months of the proportion of firms (weighted by employees) that knew about the credit. The firms that reported hearing of the credit before it was passed were assumed to have waited until passage before responding. Defining the NJTC variable in this way means that, although the House passed a bill with the credit in early March, we are assuming that anticipation of that credit was not responsible for any part of the spring 1977 upswing in employment.

The NJTC variable had a value of .057 in June 1977, and rose at an average rate of .0424 per month. By March 1978 it had achieved the value of .435. In June 1978 its value was .572. Multiplying the coefficient on NJTC by .435 provides our estimate of the credit impact on the March 1978 value of a dependent variable. Note that this specification implies an assumption that almost the entire impact of the credit on the average level of employment will occur in 1978 rather than 1977, although in fact it might have had important impacts on the level of employment in November and December 1977.

7.6 Results

7.6.1 Employment Models

Relative input price model regressions using three-year-distributed lags on sales, wages, the rental rate on capital, and materials input prices are presented in table 7.2. Corresponding nominal input price model regressions are presented in table 7.4. The two-state least-squares results for construction and retail aggregates are presented in table 7.5. All the results reported are for models estimated with data transformed to correct for serial correlation of residuals. The estimate of ρ used to correct

Table 7.2 Equations Predicting Employment: Sums of Coefficients of Relative Wage Model

	NJTC	Sum of Wage Coefficients					Capital		Sales		Ind. Sales 3 Yr	Total Ret. Sales 3 Yr	σ_e	ρ	DW
		1Q	1 Yr	2 Yr	Total	Other Inputs	Rental Rate	Price	1Q	1 Yr					
Retail and wholesale household data	.094 (.055)	.176	.102	−.631	−.420	—	+.595	−.581	.230	.667	1.153	—	.0117	.62	2.02
	.068 (.041)	−.199	−.430	−.482	−.295	+.574	+.307	−.507	.288	.626	.897	—	.0117	.50	1.76
Retail established data	.048* (.026)	+.150	+.127	−.187	−.232	—	+.165	−.367	.273	.563	1.013	—	.0041	.78	2.08
	.045* (.028)	+.074	.097	−.229	−.488	+.313	+.157	−.371	.264	.558	.995	—	.0040	.78	2.15
Eating and drinking (64–78:03)	−.025 (.06)	−.087	−1.310	−2.63	−3.10	+3.88	+.873	−1.948	.158	.693	−1.316	2.532	.005	.15	1.809
Apparel (52–78:03)	.0125** (.064)	−0.202	.62	.182	−.162	−.0196	+.330	−.660	.329	.514	.6034	.682	.013	.27	2.03
Other retail (61–78:03)	.0727** (.0266)	.014	−.223	−.148	−.038	−1.124	+.296	0	.253	.481	.091	.815	.003	.42	1.602
Food (61–78:03)	.112** (.037)	−.134	.064	.076	−.707	−.6903	−0.177	0	.213	.659	−.035	.998	.005	.45	1.602

Table 7.2 (continued)

| | NJTC | Sum of Wage Coefficients ||||| Capital ||| Sales || Ind. Sales | Total Ret. Sales | | | |
		1Q	1 Yr	2 Yr	Total	Other Inputs	Rental Rate	Price	1Q	1 Yr	3 Yr	3 Yr	σ_e	ρ	DW
General merchandise (52–78:03)	−.054 (.0417)	−.221	−.288	−.355	−.28	−.796	+.339	0	0.403	.658	.909	0.141	.0089	.41	1.92
Furniture (61–78:03)	.122** (.026)	.167	.084	−.412	−.488	−.315	+0.702	.568	.1624	.37	.597	−.23	.003	.28	1.89
Wholesale (52–78:03)	.007 (.021)	−.088	−.149	−.417	−.296	+.346	−.228	−.445	.126	.303	−.019	.275	.0031	.715	1.51
Construction est. (52–78:03)	.230** (.082)	−.283	−.128	−.321	+.285	+.224	−.674	—	.254	.355	.176	0	.0154	.789	1.71

Note: All input prices are entered as ratios to the wage. This imposes the constraint that an equal percentage change in all input prices leaves employment levels in all future periods unchanged. The lag structures on all variables go back 3 years.
Columns 2–5 are the negative sum of the coefficients on the wage rate variables starting with the contemporaneous coefficients and including all lags back to the indicated one.
Columns 6–8 are the sum over the full three-year period of the lag structure of the coefficients on other input prices—wholesale prices of goods sold, rental cost of capital, and the price index for plant and equipment.
Columns 9–10 sum the coefficients on both sales variables—subindustry retail sales and total retail sales—starting with the contemporaneous coefficients and including all lags back to the indicated one.
Columns 11 and 12 are the sum of the full three-year period of the coefficients on subindustry sales and total sales, respectively.
The standard error appears in parentheses under the NJTC coefficient.
Significant levels * $.05 \geq p \geq 0.1$ ** $.01 \geq p$.

Table 7.3 The Impact of NJTC on Employment under Alternative Specifications of the Relative Wage Model

Industry	Time Period	Employment 1977 (000)	Coefficient on NJTC		
			3-Yr Lag	2-Yr Lag	1.5-Yr Lag
Eating and drinking	61–78:03	3,854	−.025	−.054	−.006
t-value			−.41	−1.08	−.19
(σ_e)			(.0050)	(.0059)	(.0066)
Apparel	52–78:03	821	.0125	.028	.067
t-value			.20	.63	1.67
(σ_e)			(.013)	(.013)	(.014)
Other retail	61–78:03	4,021	.073	−.028	−.026
t-value			2.74	−1.24	−1.57
(σ_e)			(.0029)	(.0035)	(.0041)
Food	61–78:03	2,116	.112**	.113**	.184**
t-value			3.04	3.44	5.25
(σ_e)			(.0048)	(.0057)	(.0072)
General merchandise	52–78:03	2,541	−.054	−.035	.051
t-value			−1.28	−.953	1.35
(σ_e)			(.0089)	(.0094)	(.0107)
Furniture	61–78:03	551	.122**	−.024	−.018
t-value			4.73	−1.47	−1.14
(σ_e)			(.0031)	(.0045)	(.005)
Wholesaling	52–78:03	4,389	−.012	−.014	.045**
t-value			−.54	−.68	2.20
(α_e)			(.0032)	(.0033)	(.0037)
Trucking	61–78:03	1,131	+.128	−.037	−.010
t-value			1.67	.96	−.27
(σ_e)			(.0073)	(.0081)	(.0084)
Constr. (estab. data)	52–78:03	3,844	.230**		
t-value			2.81		
(σ_e)			(.0154)		
Increase in employment by March 1978 (000)		474			

Note: Derivation of these series is described in the appendix. Underneath the coefficient is first the t-statistic for testing the null hypothesis of no effect and then the standard error of the regression (in parenthesis).

Table 7.4   Employment in Construction and Distribution Industries: Nominal Input Price Models with 3-Year Lags

	NJTC	Sum of Coefficients on Hourly Compensation				Materials Price	Rental Cost of Plant & Equipment	Sales			Ind. Sales 3 Yr	Total Ret. Sales 3 Yr	σ_e	ρ	DW
		1Q	1 YR	2 YR	Total			1Q	1 Yr						
Construction estab. data	.065 (.104)	−.230	.701	.237	−.638	1.162	−.235	.531	.745		.947	0	.0143	.818	1.98
Retail & wholesale household data	.041 (.071)	−.795	−.583	.700	.092	.623	−.143	.274	.741		1.017	0	.0122	.657	2.00
Retail estab. data	.067** (.034)	.187	.475	.402	−.171	.343	−.159	.286	.515		.777	0	.0043	.846	2.24
Eating & drinking	.250** (.066)	.122	−.447	−.580	.054	.526	−.218	.387	.605		−.515	1.275	.0060	.584	1.54
Food	−.044 (.031)	−.005	−.339	−.126	−.106	.497	−.116	.091	.414		.506	.206	.0046	.616	1.89
Apparel	−.119 (.052)	−.095	−.590	−.780	−.653	.728	.019	.318	.406		.007	.900	.0140	.387	2.04
Furniture & appliance	−.001 (.033)	.183	−.070	−.400	−.665	.014	.538	.212	.605		.267	.915	.0041	.663	1.73

Table 7.4 (continued)

	NJTC	Sum of Coefficients on Hourly Compensation				Materials Price	Rental Cost of Plant & Equipment	Sales		Ind. Sales 3 Yr	Total Ret. Sales 3 Yr	σ_e	ρ	DW
		1Q	1 YR	2 YR	Total			1Q	1 Yr					
General merchandise	.073 (.062)	-.163	-.337	-.296	-.151	-.344	.390	.379	.615	1.020	-.126	.0092	.575	2.09
Other retail	.053* (.027)	-.037	.078	.476	-.355	.142	.185	.173	.474	-.487	1.668	.0036	.510	1.49
Wholesaling	.007 (.028)	.165	.143	.174	.089	.135	-.200	.147	.324	.203	.273	.0032	.774	1.49
Trucking	-.013 (.061)	-.317	-.200	.097	.085	-.533	.223	.377	.523	.984	-.514	.0072	.408	1.83

Note: Columns 2–5 are the sum of coefficients on the wage rate starting with the contemporaneous coefficients and including all lags back to the indicated one, i.e., $1Q = \alpha_t + a_{-1}$
Columns 6–7 are the sum over the full three-year period of the coefficients in other input prices. Derivation of rental cost of capital is described in appendix.
Columns 8 and 9 sum the coefficients on both sales variables back to the indicated lag.
Columns 10 and 11 are the sum for the full three-year period of the coefficients on subindustry sales and total sales, respectively.
Significance levels * $.05 \geq p \geq .01$ ** $.01 \geq p$

Table 7.5   Comparison of Ordinary Least-Squares (OLS) and Two-Stage Least-Squares (2SLS) Models of Employment, Nominal Input Price Model

		Wage				Material Price	Capital Rent	Sales		Ind. Sales			
	NJTC	1Q	1 YR	2 YR	Total			1Q	1 YR	3 YR	σ_e	ρ	DW
Construction													
OLS													
Employment Household data	.095 (.152)	−.744	−.114	.59	−.477	.672	−.075	.521	.767	.799	.0251	.722	1.89
Estab. data	.065 (.104)	−.230	.701	.237	−.638	1.162	−.235	.531	.745	.947	.0143	.818	1.98
Man hours	−.046 (.138)	.100	.99	.009	−.701	1.273	−.283	.598	.891	1.068	.0280	.580	2.17
2SLS													
Employment Household data	.199+ (.133)	−.371	1.089	.369	−.351	.518	−.039	.485	.677	.659	.0265	.668	1.70
Estab. data	.174* (.098)	−.944	1.133	.259	−.614	1.064	−.196	.556	.771	.959	.0148	.820	1.89
Man hours	.048 (.131)	−.330	1.283	.241	−.800	1.235	−.206	.591	.977	1.140	.0287	.601	2.14

Table 7.5 (continued)

| | NJTC | Wage | | | | Material Price | Capital Rent | Sales | | Ind. Sales 3 YR | σ_e | ρ | DW |
		1Q	1 YR	2 YR	Total			1Q	1 YR				
Retail													
OLS													
Employment Household data	.041 (.071)	−.795	−.583	.118	−.490	.622	.016	.274	.743	1.019	.0122	.657	2.00
Estab. data	.067** (.034)	.187	.476	.407	.288	.342	−.159	.287	.516	.778	.0043	.845	2.24
2SLS													
Household data	.056 (.067)	−1.200	−.706	.115	−.491	.691	−1.96	.298	.751	1.050	.0123	.657	2.01
Estab. data	.069** (.032)	.094	.415	.390	−.164	.364	−.170	.29	.518	.792	.0043	.846	2.26

Note: Derivation of these series is described in the appendix.
Double 2SLS involves applying two-stage least squares to the data twice. In the first application we assume that w at all lags is endogenous. This produces a consistent estimator of $\hat{\rho}$ which is used to transform the data. 2SLS is then applied to the data a second time, assuming only the current w endogenous.
Significance levels ** $.01 \geq p$ * $.05 \geq p > .01$

Table 7.6 Impact of New Jobs Tax Credit on Employment in the Nominal Input Price Model

Industry	Time Period	Employment 1977 (000)	Coefficient on New Jobs Tax Credit		
			3-Yr Lag	2-Yr Lag	1.5-Yr Lag
Construction (household) data	51:02–78:03	3,844	.095	.124	.194†
t-value			.62	.89	1.43
(σ_e)			(.0251)	(.0261)	(.0263)
Construction (estab. data)	51:02–78:03	3,844	.065	.149†	.190**
t-value			.63	1.57	2.06
(σ_e)			(.0143)	(.0147)	(.0148)
Retail and wholesale (household data)	51:02–78:03	18,292	.041	.002	.012
t-value			.57	.03	.21
(σ_e)			(.0121)	(.0122)	(.0122)
Retail (estab. data)	51:02–78:03	13,903	.067**	.016	.044†
t-value			1.96	.55	1.56
(σ_e)			(.0043)	(.0044)	(.0046)
Eating & drinking	58:02–78:03	3,854	.250**	.161**	.127**
t-value			3.79	3.43	3.90
(σ_e)			(.0059)	(.0064)	(.0065)
Food	58:02–78:03	2,116	−.044	.036	.089†
t-value			1.40	1.24	1.51
(σ_e)			(.0046)	(.0051)	(.0053)
Apparel	52:02–78:03	821	−.119	−.125	−.122
t-value			2.27	2.59	2.56
(σ_e)			(.0140)	(.0140)	(.0140)

Furniture & appliance	58:02–78:03	551	−.001	−.035	−.049
t-value			.02	1.67	2.41
(σ_e)			(.0041)	(.0042)	(.0043)
General merchandise	52:02–78:03	2,541	.073	−.004	.050
t-value			1.18	.08	1.05
(σ_e)			(.0092)	(.0099)	(.0170)
Other retail	61:02–78:03	4,021	.053*	−.007	−.016
t-value			1.94	.52	1.22
(σ_e)			(.0026)	(.0029)	(.0031)
Wholesaling	51:02–78:03	4,389	.007	−.007	.019
t-value			.27	.36	1.00
(σ_e)			(.0032)	(.0033)	(.0035)
Trucking	58:02–78:03	1,131	−.013	−.006	.029
t-value			.21	.18	.93
(σ_e)			(.0072)	(.0076)	(.0078)
Life insurance	61:02–78:03	519	.019	−.014	−.001
t-value			.55	.66	.03
(σ_e)			(.0030)	(.0039)	(.0041)
Increase in Employment by March 1978 in Construction and Distribution (000)					
Using detailed indust. model			566	471	581
Using estab. data aggregates			441	334	580
Using household data			398	225	379

Note: Derivation of these series is described in the appendix.
All models were estimated with the same ρ correction. Underneath the coefficient on NJTC is first the t-statistic for testing the null hypothesis of no effect and then the standard error of the regression (in parentheses).
Significance levels ** .01 ≥ p   * .05 ≥ p > .01   † .10 ≥ p > .05

the data is presented in the second to last column of the tables. The Durbin Watson statistic is for the regression using the transformed data and is therefore a test for second-order serial correlation of the residuals.

The elasticity of employment with respect to sales is indicated in columns 9–12 of table 7.2, columns 8–11 of table 7.4, and columns 8–10 of table 7.5. The elasticity of employment with respect to changes in wage rates or input prices is presented in columns 2–8 of table 7.2 and columns 2–7 of tables 7.4 and 7.5. The response of employment to a change in an input price depends on how long a time there has been to react. The elasticity of response after a change has been maintained for three months is given by the column headed 1Q. The responses after 1, 2, and 3 years are given respectively in columns 3, 4, and 5 of table 7.2. Note that with a freely estimated lag structure, the high degree of colinearity between wage rates in adjacent quarters produced rather jagged lag structures. The sum of coefficients for all lagged values of a variable is a more stable parameter than sums for only part of the estimated lag structure.

Our focus is on the NJTC variable, however. Most of the coefficients are positive. In the relative input price model, we may reject at the .05 level or better the hypothesis that NJTC has had zero or negative effects on employment for the construction industry and the industry subaggregates for apparel, food, furniture, and other retailing. In the nominal input price model, statistically significant, positive coefficients on the NJTC variables are obtained for eating and drinking places and for other retailing. Tables 7.3 and 7.6 summarize the sensitivity of the NJTC coefficient to reductions in the length of the lags on all variables. At the bottom of these tables we sum the effects implied by each industry equation across industries, to obtain for March 1978 a total effect for the industries studied. For the relative wage model, the estimates of employment stimulus are 470,000 for the preferred three-year lag. In the nominal input price model of table 7.6, estimates of employment stimulus range between 225,000 and 585,000. During this period employment rose 1,140,000 in these industries and roughly 3,800,000 in the nation as a whole. These results are consistent with the observation that between 1977:II and 1978:II rates of employment growth in both construction and retailing substantially exceeded the rates of output growth. For example, while the growth rate of construction put in place was 4.5 percent over this period, the growth rate of employment was 8.2–9.9 percent and that of man-hours was 10.4 percent. Even in retailing, where cyclical increases in sales are typically handled without hiring extra workers, employment growth—3.4 percent in household data and 4.0 percent in establishment data—outpaced the 3.0 percent growth of deflated retail sales.

Table 7.7   **Impact of NJTC on Hours Worked per Week in Construction and Distribution (Nominal Compensation Model)**

	1.5-Yr Lag	2-Yr Lag	3-Yr Lag
Construction	.034	.041	.022
t-value	.77	.90	.40
(σ_e)	(.0166)	(.0167)	(.0167)
Retail[a]	−.028*	−.021**	−.049**
t-value	3.66	2.83	2.58
(σ_e)	(.0033)	(.0031)	(.0026)
Eating & drinking[a]	−.002	−.039	−.101
t-value	.07	.94	1.49
(σ_e)	(.0059)	(.0059)	(.0055)
Food	−.027*	−.032*	−.023
t-value	1.77	1.81	1.02
(σ_e)	(.0048)	(.0048)	(.0047)
Apparel	−.005	−.006	.008
t-value	.22	.31	.32
(σ_e)	(.0067)	(.0067)	(.0066)
Furniture	−.061*	−.064*	−.088
t-value	3.95	4.26	3.76
(σ_e)	(.0056)	(.0053)	(.0034)
General merchandise	−.079*	−.030	.023
t-value	3.72	1.31	.74
(σ_e)	(.0060)	(.0057)	(.0055)
Other retail	.006	.024	−.021
t-value	.58	2.42	.89
(σ_e)	(.0036)	(.0031)	(.0028)
Wholesaling	.017	.023	.013
t-value	1.86	2.33	1.10
(σ_e)	(.0032)	(.0031)	(.0026)
Trucking	.004	.029	−.105*
t-value	.17	1.34	2.31
(σ_e)	(.0080)	(.0076)	(.0072)
Life insurance	−.013	.027	−.080
t-value	.66	1.13	1.73
(σ_e)	(.0060)	(.0052)	(.0040)

Note: Derivation of these series is described in the appendix.
Underneath the NJTC coefficient is first the t-statistic for testing the null hypothesis of no effect and then the standard error of the regression (in parentheses).
[a]64–78:03
Significance levels ** $.01 \geq p$ * $.05 \geq p > .01$

Hours

Table 7.7 presents coefficients on NJTC in regressions predicting the log of hours worked per week. Coefficients are consistently negative in retailing. Statistically significant negative coefficients are obtained for the retail aggregate and for food, furniture, and general merchandising. The coefficient in the construction hours equation may be biased by simultaneity. The man-hours 2SLS regression reported in table 7.5 has a considerably smaller coefficient than the corresponding employment equation. When one takes into account the reduction in average hours worked per week that the New Jobs Tax Credit seems to be producing in the retail sector, the percentage increase in man-hours worked is likely to be only half the percentage increase in employment.

7.6.2 Retail Price Models

In competitive industries like those studied, reduced marginal costs imply reduced prices. To test this relationship, the monthly rate of change of the retail price was regressed on current and lagged changes in a number of industry cost variables—wage rates; wholesale price of the product; the price of materials, services, and energy consumed by the distribution sector; the rental price of capital; and excise taxes—as well as on the unemployment rate, seasonal dummies, and trends on the seasonal dummies. The sums of the coefficients on the input price terms reported in columns 5–8 of table 7.8 have a pattern that is reasonable. The restaurant and tavern industry has the largest wage coefficients, and the elasticity of retail price with respect to the wage rate is approximately equal to the share of distribution sector labor compensation in the total costs of the industry. In retail sectors where payroll is a smaller (10%–20%) share of total costs, the sum of the wage coefficients is smaller. The elasticity of the retail price with respect to wholesale prices of the goods being sold is high in sectors with low retail markups (food) and lower in sectors with high markups (furniture). The impact of the rental cost of the plant and equipment used by the distribution sector is uniformly low. The coefficients on the price of energy, materials, and business services do not seem to follow any pattern.

The coefficient on CONTROLS measures the response of the yearly rate of change of prices to the eighteen-month period of controls running from August 1971 to January 1973. When price controls are phased out, retail margins should return to their former level, so the CONTROLS variable becomes midly negative during Nixon's phase 3 (1973) and more strongly negative during phase 4 (1974). Although most of the coefficients are not statistically significant, it is certainly remarkable that they are all negative. The statistically significant coefficient in the food away from home regression suggests that the controls may have succeeded in compressing the margins of companies like MacDonald's and Denny's. A rising unemployment rate also seems to compress retail sector margins. The unemployment variable is the average monthly proportionate rate of increase or decrease in the unemployment rate of prime-age males over the previous 6–9 months. The coefficients imply that a doubling of the unemployment rate compresses the retail margins of furniture by .8 percentage points and of food away from home by 1.1 percentage points.

Estimates of the impact of NJTC on retail margins in our preferred model are given in column 1 of table 7.8. Table 7.9 reports the NJTC coefficients, the standard errors of the coefficient, and the regression standard error for alternative specifications of the model. The NJTC variable in the price change equations is the first difference of the NJTC variable used in the unemployment and hours equations. Column 2 presents the coefficients for a model which excludes the price of consumable inputs and business services. Column 3 presents the results when there are no trends on the seasonal dummies. Column 4 presents the results for a model which restricts lags to six months. Beginning in January 1978 there was a rapid escalation of food prices. Column 5 presents estimates which exclude this period and which therefore measure NJTC's impact during the first eight months. For nonfood commodities and restaurant meals, the retail trade margin is negatively and significantly related to the timing of NJTC knowledge. Between May 1977 and June 1978 nonfood commodity retail prices rose 4.73 percent while wholesale prices of nonfood, consumer finished goods were rising by 6.56 percent. This discrepancy of 1.83 percentage points is quite close to the NJTC effect of 2.2 percent ($.038 \times .572 \times 100$) estimated by the preferred model (column 1). The observed decline in the margin is particularly surprising given recent increases in the relative price of imported consumer goods. (Imported products, it should be noted, are included in retail but not wholesale price indexes.)

The payroll of the distribution sector is less than twenty percent of the retail price of the commodities sold to consumers. Only in the restaurant and tavern industry does payroll approach thirty percent. Consequently, there is only a limited amount of room for reductions in prices in response to a subsidy of payroll costs.

Among the subsectors, the pattern of coefficients is consistent with a priori expectations. For example, the large negative NJTC coefficients in the restaurant industry equation suggest that in this low skill, intensive sector the 8%–12% policy-induced reduction in marginal costs resulted in a 1.1 percent decline in output price during the twelve-month period. Estimates for moderately wage intensive retail industries (apparel, furniture) indicate that the 5%–7% reduction in marginal costs induced here is associated with a smaller .5 percent reduction in prices over the period. In contrast, the small-margin, non-wage-intensive retail food industry has a

Table 7.8   Equations Predicting the Rate of Change of Retail Prices of Commodities

					Sum of Coefficients on						
	NJTC	Sales Tax	CONTROLS	Δ Log Unemp.	Wage	Wholesale Price	Service & Mat. Price	Rental on Capital	σ_e	ρ	DW	R^2
Food away from home	−.036** (.013)	1.0	−.015* (.007)	−.016** (.003)	.332	.243	.122	.137	.0017	0	1.87	.723
Nonfood commodities	−.038** (.015)	.93* (.515)	−.001 (.009)	−.003 (.005)	.186	.539	.040	.044	.0020	0	1.88	.755
Apparel	−.017 (.022)	1.0	−.006 (.012)	−.008 (.006)	.049	.625	.075	−.005	.0029	0	1.93	.841
Furniture	−.016 (.017)	1.0	−.003 (.009)	−.011** (.005)	.087	.459	.306	.102	.0015	.41	1.79	.559
Food	.046 (.039)	1.0	−.022 (.023)	.001 (.011)	−.030	.720	.509	−.044	.0054	0	2.51	.700
All commodities	−.018 (.017)	1.32** (.574)	−.006 (.009)	−.0002 (.005)	.274	.684	−.004	−.035	.0002	0	2.23	.733

Note: Derivation of these series is described in the appendix.
The price index for commodities excluded prices of owner-occupied housing. In the disaggregated equations (1, 3, 4, and 5) the coefficient on the state and local excise tax rates was constrained to be 1. The sales tac variable in the equation for all commodities and nonfood commodities includes federal excise taxes.
All models were estimated for 53:03–78:06 except Furniture, which was estimated for 58:03–78:06. Standard errors are located in parentheses underneath variables that do not have freely estimated lag structures.
Significance levels ** .01 ≥ p   * .05 ≥ p > .01

Table 7.9 Impact of NJTC on the Margin between Retail and Wholesale Prices under Alternative Models

	1-Yr Distributed Lag					
	Trends on Seasonals		No Trends with Q	6-Month Lag Trends with Q	1-Yr lag Trends with Q
CPI Component	with Q	w/o Q			
Food away from home					
σ_B	−.036**	−.037**	−.032**	−.033**	−.051**
	.013	.012	.013	.013	.018
(σ_e)	(.0017)	(.0017)	(.0017)	(.0018)	(.0017)
Nonfood commodities					
σ_B	−.038**	−.038**	−.031*	−.038**	−.049**
	.015	.015	.016	.015	.020
(σ_e)	(.0020)	(.0021)	(.0022)	(.0020)	(.0020)
Food at home					
σ_B	.051	.041	.051	.051	.011
	.039	.038	.040	.038	.059
(σ_e)	(.0053)	(.0053)	(.0052)	(.0052)	(.0053)
All commodities					
σ_B	−.018	−.019	−.013	−.018	−.036
	.016	.016	.017	.016	.022
(σ_e)	(.0022)	(.0022)	(.0023)	(.0022)	(.0022)
Reduction in consumer costs between 6/77 and 6/78 (in billions)					
All commodity regressions	3.4	3.6	2.4	3.4	2.5
Disaggregated regressions	2.8	3.3	1.9	2.8	2.3

Note: Derivation of these series is described in the appendix.
The standard error of the coefficient and the regression are located beneath the coefficient. Models 1–4 estimated on monthly data 1953:03 to 1978:06. For model 5, sample period ends 1978:01. Weights for Q are based on the 1967 input-output table, which includes gasoline, electricity, telephones, containers, cellophane packaging, supplies, insurance, auto repair, and legal fees.
Significance levels ** $.01 \geq p$ * $.05 \geq p > 0.1$

nonsignificant positive coefficient, reflecting the fact that incremental employment in this sector tends to contribute more to the quality than to the volume of output.

The final rows of table 7.9 indicate the reduction of consumer costs due to NJTC-induced compression of the distribution margin implied by the equations. The estimated cost savings of $1.9–$3.6 billion in the first twelve months after passage of the credit can be compared with total NJTC claims of $2.4 billion in 1977 and $4.5 billion in 1978.

7.7 Caveats and a Research Agenda

This study finds considerable evidence for the hypothesis that in the construction and distribution industries NJTC had the effects on employment, hours worked per week, and prices that would be predicted by economic theory. The point estimates of the size of these effects—400,000 extra jobs in construction and distribution and one percentage point reduction in the margin between retail and wholesale prices of commodities—seem to imply that the program succeeded in achieving some of its goals.

Our findings must be viewed as preliminary, however, for they are based on only twelve months of experience with the program and on outcomes in industries that employ only thirty-five percent of all private nonagricultural workers. Perhaps the NJTC variable is capturing other exogenous forces that are inducing contemporaneous employment increases and price decreases in the sectors studied. And, if that is the case, perhaps improved specifications would reduce the impacts attributed here to NJTC. Longer or shorter lags, adding the price of energy, or assuming a once-and-for-all shift in the time trend during 1974, do not, however, cause major reductions in the NJTC coefficients. There may, nevertheless, be other factors at work, and the conclusion that NJTC is having major effects on employment and prices must remain tentative until better data or more periods of observation become available.

Further evidence on the impact of NJTC can be obtained by studying a greater variety of industries. The cap on the credit means that industries dominated by large firms—e.g., aluminum, metal mining, autos, insurance—do not receive significant benefits. NJTC should either leave employment in these industries undisturbed or cause them to lose workers to the more favored industries. Examining the employment and pricing behavior of these industries would thus simultaneously sharpen our tests of NJTC's impact and measure any across-industry displacements that may be occurring. Good price, wage rate, and output data are essential if the methodology used in this paper is to be applied to other industries. The necessary data are available for mining, manufacturing, transportation, and ultilities, and studies of these industries should be high on the research agenda.

This paper has not attempted to measure the effects of NJTC on output or wage rates. The efficacy of marginal wage subsidies cannot be evaluated, however, without knowing how they influence output and wage rates. One of the primary arguments for marginal wage subsidies is that they can induce an employment expansion while simultaneously putting downward pressure on prices. If, however, they induce wage increases and most of the inertia in the wage-price spiral is wages chasing wages, NJTC could cause the underlying rate of inflation to accelerate rather than decelerate. Three types of issues must be investigated: (1) What is the impact effect of NJTC on the wage rates of industries that benefit from the credit? (2) Does the impact effect observed in these industries induce catch-up wage increases in other industries? and (3) Do the wage adjustments induced by NJTC accelerate the underlying rate of wage inflation or are they once and for all shifts of relative wage rates?

Output effects are also extremely important, for if the total economy's real output has not increased, aggregate social welfare will almost certainly have declined. Empirical studies of NJTC output effects will be difficult to do, however. In most industries the output measures available do a very poor job of capturing changes in quality or service mix. Measures of the quantity of other factor inputs used are also generally unavailable. Under these circumstances it is hard to envision how it will be possible to make definitive statements about wage subsidy impacts on total factor productivity. In the retail industry, for instance, the extra workers hired because of a wage subsidy might carry packages to a customer's car, contact delinquent credit customers more quickly, take inventory or clean the store more frequently, substitute for deliverymen as arrangers of product displays, or allow the store to remain open longer hours. None of these responses will raise total sales of the retail sector. Nevertheless, the extra workers have allowed the firm either to reduce other costs or to improve the quality of the service provided. The data limitations mean that results of any studies of productivity impacts will have to be interpreted cautiously.

Making wage rates and output endogenous is desirable for still another reason. The models we have used to estimate the impact of NJTC take output and wage rates as given. If NJTC raises output, our measure of its employment effect will understate the true impact. To the extent that NJTC raises wage rates and wage rates have a negative short-run impact on employment, our measure of employment effects will overstate the true impact.

Research is also needed on (1) the sensitivity of wage subsidy impacts to the stage of the business cycle; (2) the optimal timing of the initiation and cancellation of such a subsidy; and (3) the long-term response of business to a predictable countercyclical manipulation of this policy instrument. Temporary programs have a way of becoming permanent, so it is important to understand how the response of firms and the economy will change if the program becomes permanent. The temporary nature of NJTC certainly reduced employer awareness of and responses to it. If a marginal wage subsidy were permanent, this program would eventually disappear. On the other hand, a permanent credit would not induce firms to build up inventories, as NJTC may have done. If, in a permanent marginal NJTC, the threshold of eligibility were revised periodically to reflect more recent employment experience, raising current employment would reduce the future expected subsidy, thus inducing a smaller response (Bishop and Wilson 1980).

Appendix

Calculation of Rental Price of Capital Indexes

The rental price of capital services for the ith industry is given by:

$$R_i = P_{ki}\left[\tau_p + \frac{(1 - uz - k + uzk')}{(1 - u)}(\delta_i + r - \dot{P}^e_{ki})\right]$$

P_{ki} = price of investment goods used by the ith industry

τ_p = property tax rate on business property

u = effective tax rate on business income (depends upon form of organization)

z = present value of depreciation deductions

k = statutory rate of the investment tax credit

k' = statutory rate of the investment tax credit during the period of the Long amendment, when firms were required to subtract the investment tax credit from their depreciation base

δ = rate of replacement

r = nominal rate of return

$\dot{P}^e_{ki}$ = expected rate of price appreciation of capital goods

This formula was separately applied to the corporate and noncorporate business sector. The share of corporate business in each of our industries was estimated from the 1967 Statistics of Income by calculating the share of the total business receipts of proprietorships, partnerships, and corporations in the industry that went to corporations with more than $25,000 in profits. This share is 75 percent in wholesaling, 66 percent in retailing, 47 percent in eating and drinking places, and 72 percent in trucking. The business receipt ratio of 68 percent for construction was adjusted to 60 percent to reflect the greater importance of subcontracted work in large, corporately held construction firms.

The rental price used in the equations is a composite of rental prices for structures and for equipment. Estimates of gross stocks of plant and equipment for each industry were taken from Fawcett's "Development of Capital Stock Services by Industry Sector." Updates of the time series of effective tax rates and present values of depreciation deductions for nonresidential structures published in Christensen and Jorgenson (1973) were graciously provided by L. Christensen.

For each period, 1947–54, 1954–62, 1962–71, 1971–78, separate present values of depreciation deductions were calculated for four types of trucks, two types of construction equipment, two types of office and business equipment, and office furniture. It was assumed that between 1954 and 1962, twenty percent of new investment continued to be depreciated by straight line methods. Since January 1, 1959, small businesses have been able to write off immediately twenty percent of the value of new investments in equipment with a tax life of six or more years. It was assumed that lack of knowledge and the $4,000 cap per joint return caused only half the proprietorships and partnerships to claim this deduction, and the present values of office furniture and business equipment depreciation deductions were adjusted accordingly. The timing of changes in depreciation policy was taken to be the date of announcement for the administrative liberalizations of 1962 and 1971 and the date of enactment for legislated changes. Effective rates of property taxation were taken from Christensen and Jorgenson (1979).

The seven percent investment tax credit was part of the revenue act which became law October 16, 1962. The date of the Long amendment's repeal was February 26, 1964. As an antiinflationary measure, the credit was suspended from October 10, 1966, to March 1967, and from April 19, 1969, to August 15, 1971. The period of the Long amendment is therefore taken to be 1962:11 through 1964:02. The periods of suspension are defined as 1966:10 through 1967:02 and 1969:05 through 1971:07. The value of the tax credit was raised to ten percent by the tax reduction act enacted on March 29, 1975. Bischoff has recommended that the effective rate of the investment tax credit be adjusted downward to reflect the lower rate available on short-lived equipment and on equipment purchased by utilities. Our assumptions are that for fixed producers' durable equipment, retail and wholesale industries were eligible for 6/7 of the statutory rate of the credit. Corporations were assumed to receive a tax credit of 3/7 of the statutory rate for trucks and 4/7 of the statutory rate for construction equipment. Because proprietorships and small corporations face lower marginal tax rates, they will prefer the higher tax credit that they receive for reporting a five-year lifetime for trucks and equipment to the speedier depreciation deductions that a three-year lifetime provides. This option is provided by the Asset Depreciation Range System; we assume that such firms exercise it, and we adjust the value of depreciation deductions and the investment tax credit (2/3 of the statutory rate) to reflect it.

We assume that real, after-tax rates of return (nominal after-tax returns minus expected capital gains on plant and equipment) are equated across industries, and are constant over time. The average of the after-tax, real rates of return given in Christensen and Jorgenson (1979) for 1947 through 1969 is five percent for corporations and 4.8 percent for noncorporate business. We adopt five percent as our assumed real rate of return.

Price indexes for nonresidential structures were obtained from the Data Resources Data Bank. Wholesale price indexes for trucks were adjusted for the federal excise tax and used as the price index for trucking equipment. The wholesale price index for construction equipment was used in construction. The price index for nontransport producers' durable equipment in wholesale and retail industries is an average of wholesale price indexes adjusted for state and federal excise tax changes. The components of this are office and store machines equipment ($wt = .30$), office furniture ($wt = .35$), and general purpose machinery ($wt = .35$). For retailing, replacement rates of .044 for plant and .157 for nontransport equipment were provided by Gollop and Jorgenson. Replacement rates for trucks and construction equipment were .32 and .2858, respectively.

In both 1963 and 1967, forty-one percent of the retail and wholesale industry's purchases of new equipment were from the motor vehicles and equipment industry. The replacement rate for trucks is twice that of other nontransport producers' durable equipment. Using this fact we calculate motor vehicles to be 25.8 percent of the industry's stock of equipment.

Notes

1. For instance the vector $W = (W_t, W^q, W^q_{-3}, W^q_{-6}, W^q_{-9}, W^s_{-12}, W^s_{-18}, W^s_{-24}, W^s_{-30})$ where $W^q = \sum_{i=1}^{3} \frac{W_{t-i}}{3}$ and $W^s = \sum_{i=1}^{6} \frac{W_{t-i}}{6}$

The one exception is that the sales variable specific to the industry whose employment is being predicted has the first three months of the lag structure entering individually rather than as a quarterly average.

2. $R = (R, R_{-12}, R_{-24}, R_{-36})$ where $R = \sum_{i=1}^{12} \frac{R_{t-i}}{12}$

3. V. Smith (1963) has shown that investment incentives when there is no taxation of business income are identical to those prevailing when investment is experienced in the first year.

References

Baily, M. N., and Tobin, J. "Direct Job Creation, Inflation and Unemployment," in John Palmer, ed., *Creating Jobs*. Washington: The Brookings Institution, 1978.

Berndt, E. R., and Wood, D. O. "Technology, Prices, and the Derived Demand for Energy." *Review of Economics and Statistics*, August 1975, pp. 259–68.

Bishop, J. "The General Equilibrium Impact of Alternative Antipoverty Strategies," *Industrial and Labor Relations Review*, Vol. 32, No 2 (January 1979).

Bishop, J. and Lerman, R. "Wage Subsidies for Income Maintenance and Job Creation." *Job Creation: What Works?* pp. 39–70.

Bishop, J. and Wilson, C. "The Impact of Marginal Employment Subsidies on Firm Behavior." Paper Given at the Brookings Conference on Categorical Wage Subsidies, April 1980.

Christensen, R., and Jorgenson, D. W. "Measuring Economic Performance in the Private Sector," in Milton Moss, ed., *The Measurement of Economic and Social Performance*, pp. 233–351. New York: National Bureau of Economic Research, 1973.

Clark, K. B., and Freeman, R. B. "Time Series Models of the Elasticity of Demand for Labor in Manufacturing." Discussion Paper No. 575. Harvard Institute of Economic Research, Harvard University, Cambridge, Massachusetts, 1977.

Fair, R. C. *The Short-run Demand for Workers and Hours*. Amsterdam: North Holland, 1969.

Fawcett, J. *Development of Capital Stock Series by Industry Sector*. Executive Office of the President, Office of Emergency Preparedness, 1973.

Fethke, G. C., and Williamson, S. H. "Employment and Price Level Effects of a Variable Base Wage Credit." Department of Economics, University of Iowa, 1977.

Gollop, F. M. "Modeling Technical Change and Market Imperfections: An Econometric Analysis of U.S. Manufacturing, 1947–1971." Ph.D. Thesis, Harvard University, 1974.

Geweke, J. "Wage and Price Dynamics in U.S. Manufacturing: New Methods in Business Cycle Research." Proceedings from a Conference, Federal Reserve Bank of Minneapolis, October 1977.

Hamermesh, D. S. "Econometric Studies of Labor Demand and Their Application to Policy Analysis." *Journal of Human Resources* 11, No. 4 (Fall 1976): 507–25.

———. "Indirect Job Creation in the Private Sector: Problems and Prospects." Paper Prepared for the Brookings Conference on Job Creation, April 7–8, 1977.

Johnson, G. E., and Blakemore, A. E. "Estimating the Potential for Reducing the Unemployment Rate Consistent with Non-Accelerating Inflation: Methodology Issues." Discussion Paper, Council of Economic Advisors, March 1978.

Kesselman, J. R.; Williamson, S. H.; and Berndt, E. R. "Tax Credits for Employment Rather than Investment." *American Economic Review* 67, No. 3 (June 1977).

Lucas, R. E., Jr. "Econometric Policy Evaluation: A Critique," in Karl Brunner and Allan H. Metzler, eds., *The Phillips Curve and Labor Markets*. Amsterdam: North-Holland, 1976.

Mc Kevitt, J. Testimony before the Senate Finance Subcommittee on Administration of the Internal Revenue Code and Select Committee on Small Business, July 26, 1978.

Nadiri, M. I., and Rosen, S. *A Disequilibrium Model of Production*. New York: National Bureau of Economic Research, 1967.

Nordhaus, W. D. "Recent Developments in Price Dynamics," in Otto Eckstein, ed., *The Econometrics of Price Determination*. Conference Sponsored by the Board of Governors of the Federal Reserve System, 1974.

Perloff, J. M., and Wachter, M. L. "The New Jobs Tax Credit: An Evaluation of the 1977–78 Wage Subsidy Program." *American Economic Review* 69, No. 2 (May 1979): 173–79.

Popkin, J. "Consumer and Wholesale Prices in a Model of Price Behavior by Stage of Processing." *Review of Economics and Statistics* 56 (November 1974): 486–501.

Sims, C. A. "Money, Income, and Causality." *American Economic Review* (September 1972): 540–52.

———. "Output and Labor Input in Manufacturing." *Brookings Papers on Economic Activity*. March 1974, pp. 695–728.

Smith, V. L. "Tax Depreciation Policy and Investment Theory." *International Economic Review* 4 (January 1963): 80–91.

Stern, I. "Interindustry Transactions in New Structures and Equipment, 1967." *Survey of Current Business*. U.S. Department of Commerce, Bureau of Economic Analysis, September 1975.

Young, A. M. 1978. "Students, Graduates, and Dropouts in the Labor Market, October 1977." *Monthly Labor Review* 101, No. 6 (June 1978): 46.

8 Black Economic Progress after 1964: Who Has Gained and Why?

Richard B. Freeman

After decades of little or no economic progress relative to whites, black Americans made substantial advances in the job market after 1964 and, to a lesser extent, in earlier post–World War II years. Studies based on diverse data sets and analytic models report sizable declines in traditional discriminatory differences in the 1960s—declines which appear to have been maintained in the seventies (see Weiss and Williamson 1972; Freeman 1973; Welch and Smith 1975; Hall and Kasten 1973; Welch 1973; Hauser and Featherman 1975b). While some may (and some have) objected to my 1973 characterization of the gains as "dramatic," heralding the "decline of market discrimination," it is clear that beginning in the 1960s the job market for black Americans diverged sharply from the historic pattern of persistent and unchanging black-white differentials.

The change in the market raises many important questions about the economic well-being of black Americans and the economics of discrimination in a market economy. On the one hand are questions regarding the nature of black economic gains—their magnitude, incidence, and permanence. On the other side are questions of causality—of the effect of factors like governmental antidiscriminatory activity and social programs on the demand for and supply of black labor. Because of the complexity of major social changes, the controversy over programs like affirmative action, and the importance of reductions in discriminatory differences to the United States, questions regarding the nature and cause of black economic progress in the post–World War II period have generated

---

Richard B. Freeman is Professor of Economics, Harvard University, and Research Associate, National Bureau of Economic Research.

This research was supported by a grant from the Hoover Institute.

considerable scholarly work and discussion and will undoubtedly generate more in the future.

This study used three types of evidence to analyze the nature and cause of black economic progress in post–World War II years: aggregate evidence on the timing and incidence among skill groups of changes in the relative earnings or occupational position of blacks; cross-sectional evidence on the family background determinants of the socioeconomic achievement of blacks; and information from company personnel offices regarding personnel policies toward black (and other) workers affected by civil rights legislation.

Section 8.1 summarizes aggregate evidence on the timing of black economic gains and on the incidence of gains by demographic and skill groups. It finds that gains have been concentrated in the post-1964 period; have not dissipated in the 1970s despite high rates of unemployment; and have been largest among more educated or skilled workers, younger workers, and female workers. Section 8.2 examines the effect of family background factors on black educational, earnings, and occupational attainment. It finds that young blacks from more advantaged family backgrounds have made especially large gains in the market, to such an extent that family background has become a much more important determinant of black socioeconomic position than in the past. As a result of the decline in black-white economic differentials and the enhanced impact of family background on black educational and economic attainment, *background differences appear to have become a more important impediment than market discrimination to attainment of black-white economic parity among the young*. Section 8.3 turns to the issue of causality. It argues that the timing and incidence of gains and the information on company personnel and employment practices supports the proposition that governmental antibias activity played a major role in the change in the job market. The evidence from company studies is given great weight in evaluating causality.

8.1 Measuring Black Economic Gains

Analysis of the nature of black economic gains depends at least in part on the statistical measures used to evaluate the economic status of blacks relative to the economic status of whites. In this paper I am concerned with patterns of *labor market discrimination* and choose measures of relative economic status designed to reflect market discrimination. In the framework of the standard economic analysis of discrimination, discriminatory differences will be defined as differences in wages, employment, or occupational attainment between otherwise comparable workers that can be traced to the effect of prejudiced employers, employees, unions, or consumers on the demand for labor. The conceptual experiment which measures such discrimination would be to change the race (religion, sex, etc.) of the individual and observe what happens to his economic position. A possible practical experiment would be to present employers with a set of job applications from workers that differ solely in, say, their race and find out who would in fact be hired. Discrimination could be inferred from a deviation in the selection process from that predicted by random sampling. In the absence of such experiments, discriminatory differences will be measured as a "residual" from comparisons of economic position corrected for productivity-related or income-related characteristics,[1] including diverse measures of prelabor market factors. Since labor market discrimination involves shifts in demand schedules, which depend on ratios of productivities and wages, the analysis will concentrate on relative rather than absolute economic differentials between blacks and whites. Since individuals rather than families are employed in the job market, the analysis will deal solely with measures of the economic position of individuals, and not with family incomes.

8.1.1 The Decline in Discriminatory Differences

Evidence that the labor market position of black Americans improved significantly after 1964, and to some extent earlier, is substantial and growing. Aggregate statistical measures of individual incomes or occupational position reveal a sizable "twist" in the trend line for the incomes and occupational attaintment of blacks relative to the income or occupational attainment of whites after 1964 (Freeman 1973; Vroman 1974; Masters 1975). Cross-sectional and longitudinal data, available from computer tapes on thousands of individuals, corroborate this finding. Comparisons of earnings functions estimated with data from the Census of Population of 1970 with earnings functions estimated with data from the Census of Population of 1960 show a sharp drop in the effect of race on earnings (Welch and Smith 1975). Detailed investigation of the National Longitudinal Survey (NLS) has found the occupational position of young black men entering the market after 1964 to be essentially the same as that of young whites with similar premarket background characteristics (Hall and Kasten 1973). The 1973 Occupational Change in a Generation (OCG) survey has shown marked advances in the relative position of blacks, particularly those aged 25–34, compared with the comparable 1962 survey (Hauser and Featherman 1975b). Several studies oriented toward other labor market problems have found that the traditionally large negative impact of being black on economic status has become much smaller than in the past (Viscusi 1976; Epstein 1977; Astin 1978; and Wise, 1980). Finally, in contrast to earlier studies which showed that blacks had relatively small gains from additional schooling (Hanoch 1967; Weiss 1970), evidence for the late 1960s shows a marked convergence in the return to black and white male investments in schooling, especially among the young (Weiss and Williamson 1972; Welch 1973; Freeman 1974a).

Some of the statistical evidence on the improved labor market position of black (or nonwhite)[2] workers is given in table 8.1, which records ratios of the income or earnings of nonwhite workers to the income or earnings of white workers. Columns 1 and 2 give ratios for 1949 (except where noted) and for 1959, respectively; column 3 gives ratios for 1964, when the Civil Rights Act was passed but prior to its becoming effective; column 4 records ratios for 1969, the peak year of the late sixties boom; while column 5 records ratios for the latest year for which data are available. Because the Bureau of the Census did not publish incomes by race and occupation or by race and age until 1967 and did not ask for "usual weekly earnings" until then, the figures for those categories in the 1964 column relate, as noted in the table, to 1967.

Columns 6 and 7 present average annual changes in the ratios for the period preceding 1964 and the period following 1964. In the rows where data are not available until 1967, the pre-1964 changes cover the period 1949-59 while the post-1964 changes are from 1967 to the final year. If, as seems reasonable, declines in market discrimination move income ratios toward an asymptote of unity, annual percentage point changes can be expected to decline over time.[3] Hence, any acceleration in rates of change should be viewed as evidence (all else the same) of significant structural change in the market.

Rows 1-5 present figures for male workers, decomposed by occupation, education, and age. Rows 6-9 treat women. As the average female income ratios approach unity by the end of the period and exceed unity within disaggregate skill groupings by the early 1970s (Freeman 1973), I have not decomposed these earnings ratios into the detailed groups used for men.

There are three basic findings in the table. First, contrary to the fears of several analysts that the advances of the late 1960s were due to cyclical rather than more fundamental market changes (see Freeman 1973), the gains in the relative income of blacks did *not* erode through the severe recession of the mid-seventies. Indeed, except for the figures in row 1, the data give little evidence of deceleration in the rate of gain after 1969. Of particular interest is the large increase in the ratio of black to white median usual weekly earnings from 1969 to 1976, which suggests that black wage rates rose rapidly even when unemployment was sizable. Among women, the income ratios rise sharply in the seventies to approach unity by 1976.

The second finding of the table is that in *all* of the comparisons given, the rate of increase in the black-white income ratio is greater after 1964 than before 1964, despite the fact that the "income gap" to be closed tends to be smaller in the latter period. Larger increases post-1964 are a

Table 8.1 The Ratio of the Earnings of Nonwhites or Blacks to the Earnings of Whites or All Workers and Annual Changes in the Ratios, by Sex, 1949–76[a]

Variable	Earnings					Annual Changes in Earnings in Ratios	
	Pre-1964			Post-1964		Pre-1964 to "1964"	"1964" to
	1949	1959	"1964"	1969	1976	"1964"[b]	1975[c]

Males							
1. Median wages & salaries							
all workers	.50	.58	.59	.67	.70	0.6	0.9
year-round and full-time workers	.64[d]	.62	.66	.69	.75	0.1	0.8
2. Median "usual weekly earnings"	—	—	.69[e]	.71	.78	—	1.0
3. Median income, by age, all workers (1949–59) and year-round and full-time workers (other years)							
20–24	.66	.64	.70[e]	.82	.82	−0.2	1.3
25–34	.60[f]	.61[f]	.75[e]	.72	.81	0.1	0.7
45–54	.54	.55	.66	.64	.67	0.1	0.1
4. Median income, all workers (1949, 1959) and year-round and full-time workers (other years) by occupation							
Professionals	.57	.68	.69[e]	.73	.84[g]	1.1	2.6
Managers	.50	.57	.64[e]	.60	.72[g]	0.7	1.1
Craftsmen	.63	.66	.71[e]	.74	.78[g]	0.3	1.0
Operatives	.72	.70	.78[e]	.80	.84[g]	−0.2	0.9
Service Workers	.78	.76	.75[e]	.77	.84[g]	−0.2	1.3
Laborers	.81	.83	.73[e]	.88	.85[g]	0.2	1.7
5. Median income or mean earnings for young men 25–29 years old, by education							
high school graduates	.73	.70	—	—	.77	−0.3	0.4
college graduates	.67	.70	—	—	.94	0.3	1.4
Females							
6. Median wages & salaries							
all workers	.40	.53	.58	.79	1.01	1.8	3.6
year-round and full-time workers	.57[d]	.66	.69	.82	.94	1.3	2.1
7. Median "usual weekly earnings"	—	—	.80[e]	.83	.94	—	2.0

[a] Lines 1, 2, 6, and 7 give the ratios of the earnings of nonwhites to the earnings of whites. The data for 1969 and 1959 in all of the other lines give the ratios of the income of nonwhites to all workers. The remaining data give the incomes of blacks relative to the incomes of all workers.
[b] The data in lines 3–5 are from 1949 to 1959.
[c] The data in lines 2–5 and 7 begin with 1967 as the initial year.
[d] Data relate to 1955.
[e] Data relate to 1967.
[f] Data are for 25–29-year-olds.
[g] Data are for 1974 since *median* incomes by occupation and race were not published after 1974.

necessary "first fact" (other factors held fixed) for any case to be made regarding the impact on the job market of the diverse antibias activities which became intense in the mid-sixties.[4]

Third, with regard to incidence, the income ratios in table 8.1 reveal markedly different rates of progress for various groups of black workers. Among men, greater gains were made by younger black workers than by older black workers with, for example, the income ratio for 20–24-year-old full-time and year-round workers rising by twelve percentage points from 1967 to 1976 compared with almost no change for those aged 45–54. Greater gains were also made by the more highly qualified, such as professionals, managers, and (to a lesser extent) craftsmen. Perhaps most importantly, the income ratios in row 6, which focus on persons with the same education and age, show larger gains for young black college graduates than for young black high school graduates. In 1976, 25–29-year-old black male college graduates earned almost as much as white male college graduates. The ratio of black to white earnings for college men was much higher than that for young high school graduates, a result which contrasts markedly with that found in earlier years (Hanoch 1967). Studies of other data sets also find that better-educated and young black men obtained greater advances in the post-1964 period than did less-educated and less-skilled older workers (see Welch and Smith 1975). Black women, as noted earlier, had especially large gains in relative income, due in part to their movement from household service jobs to factory and clerical positions (Freeman 1973).

Table 8.2 turns to evidence on the occuational attainment of black and white workers. The occupation data have two advantages in analysis. First, occupation may be a more permanent indicator of economic status than incomes, which tend to be sensitive to cyclical ups and downs and other transitory fluctuations. Second, unlike income comparisons, which could be biased by investments in newly available opportunities to attain higher lifetime income streams,[5] occupation is likely to reflect the result of relatively enduring movements into higher or lower-paying jobs. Even if the income gains of black men had slackened in the seventies (which does not appear to be the case), evidence of continued occupational advance might be taken as indicative of continued declines in discriminatory differences.

The position of blacks in the occupational structure is measured in two ways in the table. Rows 1 and 2 record ratios of fixed income weighted indexes of the value of the nonwhite and white occupational structures. These are calculated by weighting the proportion of nonwhite or white persons in an occupation by the median income of all men or women in the occupation reported in the Census of Population of 1960. When the job distribution of nonwhites shifts toward higher-income occupations relative to the occupational distribution of whites, these statistics will

Table 8.2   **The Relative Occupational Position of Nonwhite Workers and Changes in Position, 1950–77**

Group	Position				Annual Change in Position	
	1950	1964	1969	1977	1950–64	1964–77
Ratio of Nonwhite to White Index of Occupational Position[a]						
1. Male	.76	.80	.84	.89	0.3	0.7
2. Female	.49	.69	.80	.92	1.4	1.8
Relative Penetration into Selected Jobs[b]						
3. Professionals, male	.39	.45	.48	.64	0.4	1.5
4. Managers, male	.22	.22	.28	.43	0.0	1.6
5. Managers, male college graduates only	.42	.41	.49	.72	0.0	2.4
6. Craftsmen, male	.41	.58	.68	.72	1.2	1.1
7. Professionals, female	.47	.60	.70	.89	0.9	2.2
8. Clericals, female	.15	.33	.55	.72	1.3	3.0

Source: Rows 1 and 2: U.S. Department of Labor 1977 table 19; 1975 table 22; U.S. Bureau of the Census 1953 table 11. Rows 3–5: U.S. Bureau of Labor Statistics 1965 table J; 1970 table J; 1978 table K; U.S. Bureau of the Census 1953 table 11.
[a]Index calculated as ratio of $\Sigma_i \alpha_{ij} w_i$ for blacks ($j=1$) and whites ($j=2$) where α_{ij} = share of workers in the jth group in occupation i and W_i = median income of all workers in 1959.
[b]Percent nonwhites employed in the occupation/percent whites employed in the occupation.

rise, and conversely. During the period covered, the data show a marked improvement in the relative occupational position of nonwhites, particularly after 1964. From 1964 to 1969 the ratio of occupational indexes rises by .04 points for nonwhite men and .11 points for nonwhite women; from 1969 to 1977, the increases were .05 and .12 points, respectively. Overall, the rate of nonwhite advance accelerated by 0.4 points for both sexes after 1964. For men, it increased by 0.7 points per annum in the post-1964 period compared with 0.3 points per annum in the earlier period. For women it increased by 1.8 points per annum from 1964 to 1977 compared with 1.4 points from 1950 to 1964.

The second measure of the relative occupational position of nonwhites is the "relative penetration ratio." This is defined as the ratio of the proportion of all nonwhite workers in an occupation to the proportion of all white workers so employed. When it is unity, nonwhites and whites are equally represented in an occupation; when it is below one, nonwhites are less than proportionately represented, and conversely when it is above one. The statistics in rows 3–8 show a marked post-1964 improvement in the relative proportion of nonwhites in the "good" jobs covered in the table and indicate that the movement continued, in some instances at an accelerated rate, into the 1970s recession. Among men, the rate of advance into professional and managerial jobs accelerates sharply between 1964–69 and 1969–77. Of particular importance is the large flow of nonwhite male college graduates into managerial positions in the latter period, presumably the result of changes in education and career training induced by new opportunities (Freeman 1977a).

The apparently strong "new market" for high-level black workers is pursued in table 8.3, which presents data relating to the relative income of selected groups of highly educated or skilled black workers. Rows 1 and 2 show that among Ph.D.'s and faculty, blacks earned roughly as much as comparable whites in 1973, which contrasts sharply to long-standing patterns of market discrimination. The evidence in row 3 shows that the starting pay of black male college graduates was roughly equal to the starting pay of white male college graduates as early as 1969, a finding corroborated through 1973 by analysis of the NLS. Row 4 gives approximate earnings ratios from a recent American Council on Education survey of graduates,[6] where it was reported that for recent college graduates, "blacks can command higher salaries than whites . . . as a result of strong affirmative action pressures on business and industry" (Astin 1978: 155). Any explanation of the improved market for black workers must come to grips with the pattern of change in which young and more-qualified men appear to have made especially large gains relative to other black men.

Table 8.3   The Ratio of the Earnings of High-Qualified Black Workers to High-Qualified White Workers in the Late 1960s and Early 1970s

1. Ph.D.'s (1973)	
Total	1.01
Physical science	0.95
Social science	1.12
Engineers	1.02
2. Faculty (1973)	
Initial	.93
"Adjusted" for quality[a]	1.00–1.07
3. Starting bachelors (1969)	
Howard, civil engineering	1.00
Howard, business fields	.97
North Carolina A & T, engineering	.92
Texas Southern, MBA	1.07
4. Bachelors, 1 year after degree (1974)	
Business	≈1.13
School teaching	≈1.36

Source: Line 1: National Science Foundation, 1974, p. 141.
Line 2: Tabulated from American Council on Education, 1972–73 survey of teaching faculty, as reported in Freeman 1977a, table 3.
Line 3: Freeman 1974b, table 3-3.
Line 4: Astin 1978: 154–57.
[a]There is a range of estimates depending on what characteristics are adjusted for. The lower estimated excludes type of institution employed as a characteristic.

There are two basic conclusions to be reached from this review of black economic progress. First, the advances in the 1960s and to some extent earlier which motivated my 1973 Brookings paper (Freeman 1973) *have not been eroded* by the weakened job market of the 1970s and thus cannot be readily attributed, as some argued, to the late 1960s boom. More is involved than simple cyclical patterns. Second, the rate of black economic advance has varied significantly by sex, education, age, and skill groups. Black women attained approximate parity with white women having similar skills, though both groups trail white men by considerable amounts. Among men, where sizable economic differences remain overall, the differences declined most and/or became smallest among the highly educated and skilled. Large advances were made by the young, especially those going on to higher education, possibly because the young were not hampered by past discriminatory practices and human capital investment decisions, which effectively "lock" experienced personnel into particular career paths and seniority ladders from which change is difficult.

8.2 Changed Social Mobility Patterns and Discriminatory Differences among Young Men

The extent and incidence of economic advance among young black men is examined in greater detail in this section with data from the National Longitudinal Survey (NLS) (see U.S. Department of Labor 1970), which contains information on the labor market position, family background, and diverse other variables for about 5,200 young men. The analysis concentrates on the family background determinants of educational and labor market attainment and on the contribution of background factors to differences between blacks and whites in years of schooling, earnings, and occupational position. For the purpose of determining whether there have been changes in mobility patterns, the effect of background factors on young men in the NLS sample is compared with the effect of background factors on older men from the comparable NLS survey of 45–59-year-olds in 1966 (on the assumption that the socioeconomic status of the older men was essentially determined years earlier) and with the results of studies covering the pre-1964 period.

The principal finding is that, in contrast to the pattern of social mobility before 1964, when family background was found to have relatively small effects on black achievement and when only a modest fraction of black-white economic differences could be attributed to the "burden of background,"[7] in the late 1960s background factors became an important determinant of black socioeconomic advancement and the major cause of economic differences between black and white young men. The implication is that *blacks from more advantaged backgrounds made greater gains in the market than those from less advantaged backgrounds.*

8.2.1 Measures of Socioeconomic Position

This study examines the effect of family background and other variables on four measures of individual socioeconomic achievement: years of schooling; weekly earnings; annual earnings; and an index of occupational position, the median income of male workers in the individual's three-digit occupation in 1969. The weekly earnings variable (obtained by division of yearly earnings by weeks worked over the year) is designed to measure rates of pay,[8] while the yearly earnings variable depends on time worked over the year as well as on the rate of pay. The index of occupational position uses the same incomes for blacks and whites in an occupation despite differences in earnings within occupations, so as to focus on occupational attainment.

8.2.2 Measures of Family and Other Background Variables

The following variables are used to measure family background:[9]

1. Years of schooling of the head of the parental family, which is entered in regressions explaining the individual's years of schooling but not in regressions explaining labor market attainment, since parental education appears to affect individuals through school rather than directly.

2. Living in a one parent/female home at age fourteen, a 0–1 dummy variable entered to control for differences in the economic resources between households which include a male head and those which do not and for the possible effect of the absence of a male "role model" on the young.

3. The occupational attainment of the head of household at age fourteen, measured by the logarithm of the median income of male workers in the three-digit occupation in which the parent worked, as given in the U.S. Census of Population of 1960.[10] Because black workers have traditionally been paid lower than whites in the same occupation, the occupational attainment of black parents is measured by nonwhite median incomes while that of white parents is measured by total median incomes. Measuring parental status in this way yields larger differences between the family backgrounds of blacks and whites than those obtained in sociology studies which use the same figure for the occupations of black parents and the occupations of white parents.[11] Separate indicators for blacks and whites provide a closer fix on *economic* differences between them, as opposed to differences in socioeconomic status.

4. Three indicators of household reading resources when the individual was fourteen years old: magazines; newspapers; and library cards, entered to try to capture some of the more explicit activities or resources by which family background influences the young. While by no means optimal, these measures provide some indication of activities in the home beyond the crude standard measures of parental schooling and occupation.

In addition to the measures of family background, the calculations also contain measures of the region and type of residence of the person at age fourteen.[12] These measures are entered because of the traditional importance of "regional background" in black-white economic differences due in part to the extraordinary discrimination in schooling in the South (Welch 1973; Freeman 1974b), especially in rural areas.

The NLS data reveal sizable black disadvantages in each of the background variables. In the young male sample the parents of blacks averaged 7.9 years of schooling, whereas the parents of whites averaged 10.5 years. The log of the median income of the occupation of parents of blacks was 7.7 compared with 8.5 for the parents of whites. Forty percent of the young blacks were from one parent/female homes at age fourteen compared with twelve percent of the young white men. Forty-five percent of the black youth reported having magazines in their homes compared with eighty percent of white youth. Sixty-nine percent of the blacks reported the presence of newspapers compared with ninety-two percent of the whites. Forty-seven percent of the black youth reported having library cards compared with seventy-four percent of white youths.[13] In terms of the regional variables, young blacks were more likely to have been brought up in the South and in rural areas than young whites.

The sizable differences between the family background resources of young blacks and whites suggest that, if background factors "matter" in attainment, they are likely to be a major cause of economic inequality. To what extent does the educational and labor market attainment of young blacks and young whites depend on background factors?

8.2.3 Background and Schooling

Table 8.4 presents least-squares estimates of the effect of family background and region and type of residence on the years of schooling of young black and white men and, for comparison, estimates of the effect of these variables on the years of schooling of older black and white men as well. Since measures of household reading resources are unavailable for the older men, these variables have been excluded from the calculations; their effect on the attainment of the young is analyzed separately in table 8.6. Because many of the young men in the NLS were still enrolled in school in 1969, the year for which the analysis was conducted, they could not report their final years completed. The attainment of these men was estimated by the number of years they "expected to complete." Experiments with other methods of estimating years completed, ranging from limiting the sample to the out of school population to assigning the enrolled their current years, were also made, with results similar to those given in the table.[14]

The principal finding is that in contrast to the large racial differences in the effect of family and regional background factors on years of schooling found in pre-1964 data (Duncan 1968) and in the older male NLS sample, there are at best only slight differences in the effect of family and regional background variables on the years of schooling of young black versus young white men.

With respect to family background, what stands out in the table is the differential effect of parental occupation on the attainment of blacks and whites in the young male sample compared with its effect in the older male sample. Whereas among older men, the coefficients on parental

Table 8.4   Regression Coefficients and Standard Errors for the Effect of Background Factors on Years of Schooling of Black and White Men Aged 17–27 and 48–62[a]

	Young Men		Older Men	
	Black	White	Black	White
1. Mean years of schooling and standard deviation of years	11.5(3.1)	13.2(2.9)	6.8(3.7)	10.3(3.3)
2. Coefficients on parental status variables				
Parental years of schooling	.20(.03)	.31(.01)	.23(.04)	.30(.02)
Parental occupational status[b]	.84(.21)	.57(.12)	.52(.32)	1.37(.22)
Residence in one parent/female Household at age 14[c]	−.71(.19)	−.83(.15)	−.67(.35)	−.44(.21)
3. Coefficients on region of residence at age 14[c]				
Northeast	.04(.36)	.16(.13)	.42(1.07)	−.10(.21)
South	.13(.32)	−.35(.13)	−1.84(.83)	−.68(.21)
West	.10(.52)	−.15(.15)	2.21(1.53)	−.29(.34)
North Central	—	—	—	—
4. Coefficients on type of residence at age 14[c]				
Rural	−.50(.29)	−.20(.14)	−1.56(.65)	−.49(.26)
Small town	.39(.27)	−.04(.13)	−.28(.64)	.18(.22)
Small city	.09(.58)	.09(.19)	1.38(2.49)	.09(.49)
Suburb	.15(.30)	−.11(.15)	.20(.67)	.03(.28)
Large city	—	—	—	—
5. Coefficients for other variables				
Age	−.10(.03)	.00(.01)	−.16(.04)	−.07(.02)
Constant	4.8	4.7	12.9	.2
6. R^2	.180	.204	.268	.296
7. Size of sample[d]	1,024	3,235	471	1,408

Source: Calculated from NLS data tapes for young men and for older men in 1969.
[a]Regressions for older men relate to 1966. Regressions for young men relate to 1969. For young men who are enrolled in school in 1969, years of schooling were estimated on the basis of the years of schooling they expect to complete, as described in text.
[b]Parental occupational position measured by median male income of three-digit occupation in 1959. Income figures for all men used for whites; nonwhite incomes used for blacks. Data taken from U.S. Bureau of the Census (1963), tables 25, 26.
[c]Age 15 for men aged 48–62.
[d]The largest loss in the sample occurred because a relatively sizable number failed to report their parents' education. For results with a sample that excludes parental education see Freeman (1976).

occupation, as well as on parental years of schooling, are smaller for blacks, among the young, parental years of schooling have a smaller effect on blacks than on whites but parental occupation has a *larger* effect. Given the differences in the coefficients on the two variables, it is necessary to "average" the coefficients in some way to evaluate whether background factors have a more or less powerful effect on young blacks than on young whites. One reasonable way to form such an average is to multiply the regression coefficients by their standard deviations in the sample, divided by the standard deviation of years attained, and sum the resultant β weights to get the effect of a standard deviation increase in each. With this metric, family background is estimated to have about the same effect on the years of schooling of young blacks and young whites: the one-standard-deviation changes alter schooling by .46 standard deviations for whites versus .40 standard deviations for blacks.[15]

The estimated coefficients on the region and size of place of residence dummy variables also reveal striking changes between the younger and older male samples, with the enormous deterrent effect of southern and regional locale on black schooling in the older male sample (-1.8 years for the South and -1.6 years for rural residence versus the deleted group), dropping to insignificance among younger men (.13 years for southern residence and $-.5$ years for rural residence). Among whites, there is a smaller decline in the negative effect of southern and rural residence on years of schooling between the young male and older male samples. Presumably because of the decline in the discriminatory allocation of school resources in the rural South, the "burden" of southern and rural background was greatly reduced for blacks until it became about the same as for whites.

Analysis of the converging effect of family background factors on the years of schooling of blacks and whites between the time when the younger men were educated and the time when the older men were educated can be pursued by focusing on the effect of parental education and occupation on what has become the "cutting edge" in investment in education decisions—enrollment in college. Accordingly, I estimated the effect of the family and regional background variables treated in table 8.4 on the probability of going to college, using the logistic probability model $P = 1/(1 - \exp \Sigma \beta_i X_i)$, where P = the probability of going to college and X_i are the explanatory factors. In this functional form, the effect of X_i on P is $dP/dX_i = \beta_i P(1-P)$, so that the same parametric relation (β_i) implies different changes in probabilities depending on the starting point. The advantage of this functional specification over the linear probability model is that it correctly bounds the estimated P between 0 and 1 and takes account of the binomial structure of the errors.

The results of the logistic curve estimation are summarized in table 8.5, in terms of the coefficients and standard errors for the logistic curve

Table 8.5 Estimated Logistic Curve Parameter and Standard Error on Probability of Going to College

Family Background Variables	Young Men Black	Young Men White	Older Men Black	Older Men White
Years of schooling of parent	.13 (.02)	.17 (.01)	.17 (.04)	.19 (.01)
ℓn of median income of men in parent's 3-digit occupation	.52 (.22)	.51 (.10)	.03 (.33)	.81 (.17)

Source: Freeman 1976, table 3.
ℓn of median income calculated from the same median income measures as in table 8.4.

parameters on the years of schooling of parents and on their occupational attainment. These calculations show little difference in the impact of parental years of schooling or parental occupational attainment on the logistic curve parameters for young blacks and for young whites but show that the parental occupation variable has a much greater effect on older whites than on older blacks. This confirms the findings of a much smaller difference between the effects of background on black and white attainment among younger and older men.

Table 8.6 examines the effect of adding the "household reading resource" variables to the years of schooling regressions for the young men. Columns 1 and 3 record the coefficients on parental occupational status and parental years of schooling from table 8.4, while columns 2 and 4 give the coefficient on those variables and on the presence of magazines, newspapers, and library cards. The decline in the coefficients on parental occupation and years of schooling upon addition of the new variables provides some indication of the extent to which the traditional back-

Table 8.6 Regression Coefficients and Standard Error of Estimates of the Effect of Parental Occupation, Years of Parental Schooling, and "Household Reading Resources" on Years of Schooling of Young Black and Young White Men, 1969

	Young Black Men (1)	Young Black Men (2)	Young White Men (3)	Young White Men (4)
1. Index of parental occupational status	.84(.21)	.61(.20)	.57(.12)	.36(.12)
2. Years of parental schooling	.20(.03)	.15(.03)	.31(.01)	.25(.02)
3. Magazines in the home (yes = 1)		.81(.20)		.68(.13)
4. Newspapers in the home (yes = 1)		1.12(.23)		.92(.19)
5. Library card in the home (yes = 1)		.80(.21)		.99(.11)

Note: Regression coefficients in columns 1 and 3 are taken from table 8.4. Regression coefficients in columns 2 and 4 are based on regressions of years of schooling on the variables in table 8.4 plus the three dummy variables for household reading resources. The sample sizes are the same as in table 8.4.

ground variables operate through provision of an environment with reading materials.

The calculations show that the household reading resources significantly influence educational attainment and are an important intervening factor in the link between family background and educational attainment. The coefficients on parental education are reduced by 2–3 standard errors, and the coefficients on parental occupation are reduced by 1–2 standard errors, by addition of the new variables. Crude though the calculations are, they suggest a potentially important role for household reading resources as a determinant of years attained and as a major intervening variable in the usual background-education relation. They direct attention to the absence of reading material in black homes (which might be ameliorated by special school programs) as a likely cause of differences in years attained among the young in the 1960s.

8.2.4 The Gap in Educational Attainment

Despite the significant increase in black educational attainment in the post–World War II period and the sharp influx of blacks into college in the late 1960s (Freeman 1977a, chapter 2), a substantial difference remains among the young in the NLS sample in 1969. To what extent do differences in schooling among the young reflect differences in family background? Have background differences, which traditionally were found to explain only a modest proportion of the black-white educational gap (Duncan 1968), become an important deterrent to attainment of equality in years of schooling between the groups?

Estimates of the contribution of family background differences to the difference in years of schooling of blacks and whites can be obtained by multiplying the estimated regression coefficients from tables 8.4 and 8.6 by the average difference in the level of the background variables. Formally, if $\hat{a}_i$ is the estimated impact of X_i on years attained, and $\bar{X}_{iB}$, $\bar{X}_{iW}$ are the mean levels of X_i for blacks and whites respectively, the contribution of differences in X_i to the gap can be estimated as $\hat{a}_i(\bar{X}_{iB} - \bar{X}_{iW})$ and the contribution of all relevant variables as $\sum_i \hat{a}_i(X_{iB} - X_{iW})$. Since the regressions treat blacks and whites separately, there are two sets of coefficients for the calculations, $\hat{a}_i$ from the equations for blacks and $\hat{a}_i$ from the equations for whites.

Table 8.7 summarizes the results of such calculations using regression coefficients from both the equations for blacks and the equations for whites. Row 1 gives the absolute differences in years attained. Row 2 records the percentage contributions of each of the family background factors to the difference in years attained, obtained by dividing $\hat{a}_i(\bar{X}_{iB} - \bar{X}_{iW})$ by the absolute difference in years attained. Row 3 gives the sum of the percentage differentials attributed to family background, while row 4 records the percentage contribution of the differences in the

Table 8.7 Estimates of Percentage Contribution of Differences in Background Characteristics to Differences in Years of Schooling of Black and White Men

	Based on Years of Schooling Equations for Blacks			Based on Years of Schooling Equations for Whites		
	Older Men (1)	Young Men (2)	(3)	Older Men (4)	Young Men (5)	(6)
1. Difference in years of schooling of persons of the same age	3.7	1.6	1.6	3.7	1.7	1.7
2. Percentage contribution to differences in years of schooling of differences in:						
a) parental occupational status	16	44	31	41	24	21
b) parental years of schooling	16	31	25	22	47	41
c) residence in one parent/female home	3	6	6	3	12	12
d) household reading resources	—	—	44	—	—	41
3. Percentage contribution to differences in years of schooling of all family background factors (sum of 2a–2d)	35	81	106	66	83	100
4. Percentage contribution of differences in region and type of place of residence	14	−6	−6	14	12	6
5. Percentage contribution of all background factors (3 + 4)	49	75	100	80	95	106

Note: Estimates of the contribution of factors to the observed differences were obtained by the following procedure. Let $\hat{a}_i$ = regression coefficient for the effect of variable i on years of schooling; Δx_i = differences between the mean value of variable i for blacks and the mean value of variable i for whites. Then the percentage contribution of the ith variable is $\hat{a}_i \Delta x_i$/data in row 1.
Figures for columns 1 and 2 and for columns 4 and 5 obtained using regressions reported in table 8.4. Figures for columns 3 and 6 based on regressions summarized in table 8.6.
Years of schooling differences have been adjusted for the effect of age by multiplying the difference in the mean ages of blacks and whites by the coefficient on age in the schooling equations. As age has a positive effect on years of schooling in the equation for blacks but not in the equation for whites, this adjustment produces a smaller difference in the analysis based on the equations for blacks than in the analysis based on the equations for whites.

distribution of blacks and whites by region and type of place. The figures in columns 1, 2, 4, and 5 show that family background factors are a much more important cause of black-white differences in years of schooling among young men than among older men, indicative of considerable change in social mobility patterns. The differences are particularly marked when the regression coefficients from the black schooling equations are used to weight the different factors. According to columns 1 and 2, for example, only thirty-five percent of the difference between the years of schooling of older black men and older white men is attributable to family background factors, whereas eighty-one percent of the difference between younger black and white men is attributable to family background factors. This reflects in large part the increased effect of background factors in the schooling attainment equations for blacks between the two samples.

In contrast to the increased importance of differences in family background, the table shows sizable reductions in the impact of differences in the distribution of persons by geographic area. This is largely owing to the convergence in the coefficients on the geographic variables between blacks and whites shown in table 8.4.

Columns 3 and 6, based on regressions which include household reading resources as explanatory variables, show that essentially *all* of the difference in educational attainment between young black and white men in 1969 can be attributed to family background factors. Even with the family resources excluded, 80 + percent of the difference is accounted for by background factors. Similar findings are reported by Epstein (1977) using the NLS for the high school class of 1972 and by Hauser and Featherman (1975a) in their analysis of the 1972 OCG data file. For young black men the disadvantages in family background have become *the* deterrent to attainment of parity with whites in years of school completed.

8.2.5 Background and Labor Market Attainment

To analyze the effect of family and other background variables on the labor market position of men, the three measures of market attainment described earlier—hourly earnings, yearly earnings, and the median income of men in the individual's three-digit occupation—were regressed on the family and regional and size of place variables used earlier and on years of work experience. For young men, years of experience are calculated using a complex algorithm designed to measure, as well as possible, actual time worked.[16] For older men, years of experience are measured by two variables: years of tenure in a job, and age minus years of schooling minus 5. The parental years of schooling variable was deleted from the analysis after preliminary calculations showed that it had little effect on the labor market position of individuals.[17] Years of schooling of the individual were first excluded from the regressions to obtain estimates of the full or reduced form impact of background factors and then included an additional measure of "prelabor market" determinants of labor market position. In the regressions for young men, those still enrolled in school were deleted from the calculations.

Table 8.8 summarizes the results in terms of the estimated coefficients on the log of the index of parental occupational standing. It shows a marked difference between the effects of parental occupation on the labor market position of young blacks and whites and older blacks and whites. Among the older men, the background variable has a much smaller and generally negligible effect. This is consistent with the traditional finding in the sociology literature (Duncan 1968) that parental status has a more modest effect on the attainment of blacks than on the attainment of whites. Among younger men, by contrast, the coefficients on the background variable for blacks are sizable and significant in all of the calculations. In the hourly earnings regressions and in the occupational status regressions the coefficients in the black equations are roughly comparable in magnitude to the coefficients obtained in the equations for whites. In the annual regressions, however, the coefficient on black parental occupation is still noticeably smaller than the coefficient on white parental occupation.

Table 8.8   Regression Coefficients and Standard Errors of Estimates for the Impact of the Log of Parental Occupational Status on the Log of Weekly Earnings, Annual Earnings, and Occupational Status for Young and Older Men, by Race, 1969

Dependent Variable and Group	Black	White
Hourly earnings		
Young men	.17(.09)	.16(.05)
Older men	.02(.05)	.22(.03)
Annual earnings		
Young men	.09(.03)	.18(.02)
Older men	.04(.03)	.13(.02)
Index of occupational status		
Young men	.20(.07)	.23(.04)
Older men	.03(.06)	.24(.03)

Note: The regressions include the following control variables: 3 dummy variables for region of residence at age 14; 5 dummy variables for type of place of residence at age 14; dummy variable for living in one parent/female home at age 14. These variables are described in table 8.4.

In addition the regressions include measures of years of work experience: for younger men, years of experience are determined by an algorithm based on weeks worked in each year since 1966 and on years since first postschool job; for older men, years of tenure with current employer and years since leaving school minus 5 are used to measure experience.

Parental occupational status is measured as the log of income in the parents' three-digit occupation as described in the text.

The sample sizes are: young black men, 634; young white men, 1,607; older black men, 947; older white men, 2,131. The samples are restricted to persons not enrolled in school in 1969 and reporting data for all of the variables in the regressions.

Index of occupational status is measured by the log of the median income in the individual's three-digit occupation in 1969, as reported in the U.S. Bureau of the Census (1973c), tables 16 and 17.

As there are no apparent life cycle changes in the effect of family background factors on the attainment of individuals,[18] the greater coefficient obtained for young blacks would appear to reflect a trend over time in social mobility patterns, with young black men from more advantaged homes making greater economic advances in the job market than those from less advantaged homes. Presumably as a result of the decline in market discrimination, the pattern of social mobility among blacks seems to have converged toward that found among whites. Since Duncan found little effect of background on black labor market attainment in 1962, moreover, *the change appears to have occurred in the period of intense antibias activity and of sizable black economic advance relative to whites.*[19] In contrast to the past, when "stratification within the Negro population (was) less severe than in the white" (Duncan 1968: 88), what sociologists call "intergenerational status transmission" has become quite similar for young persons in the late 1960s.

8.2.6 Background versus "Residual Discrimination"

Given that family background has become more important in black economic attainment and that black-white economic differences have diminished, differences in the background resources of blacks and whites can be expected to explain a greater fraction, and "residual market discrimination" to explain a lesser fraction, of racial economic differences now than in the past.[20]

Table 8.9 presents calculations which confirm both of these expectations. Row 1 gives estimates of the log differences in occupational position, weekly earnings, and yearly earnings of young and older black and white men, adjusted for differences in years of experience. Rows 2 and 3 estimate the percentage contribution of differences in background variables to the differences in labor market position using the procedure described on p. 00—that is, by multiplying differences in the mean value of the explanatory variables by the regression coefficient estimate of their impact on attainment.

The effect of differences in parental occupational position on differences in labor market position are given in row 2 using the regression coefficients from table 8.8. The effect of differences in a "full" set of prelabor market variables—parental occupational position, region and type of place of residence, and years of schooling—are given in row 3, using coefficients obtained by including the person's years of schooling in the regressions of table 8.8. Row 4 estimates the extent of "residual" discrimination, defined as the log differential not attributed to differences in the background variables and in schooling. Columns 1–6 use regression coefficients from attainment equations for blacks while columns 7–12 use regression coefficients from attainment equations for whites.

Table 8.9 Estimated Percentage Contributions of Parental Occupational Status and Prelabor Market Factors to Economic Differences between Blacks and Whites and Estimated Residual Market Discrimination, Young and Older Men, 1969[a]

	Log Difference between Blacks and Whites, Adjusted for Years of Work Experience[b] (1)	Percentage of Differences Due to Differences in Parental Occupational Status[c] (2)	Percentage of Differences Due to Differences in Prelabor Market Factors[d]				Residual Market Discrimination (7)
			Parental Occupational Status (3)	Region and Type of Place of Residence (4)	Years of Schooling (5)	Prelabor Market Factors (3+4+5) (6)	
		Based on regression equations for black workers					
1. Index of occupational position							
Young men	.20	40	25	15	40	80	.04
Older men	.30	13	7	17	27	51	.15
2. Log of weekly earnings							
Young men	.23	36	28	36	24	88	.03
Older men	.62	3	−3	31	24	52	.32
3. Log of yearly earnings							
Young men	.44	39	27	34	11	72	.12
Older men	.66	4	−5	36	18	49	.34

Based on regression equations for white workers

1. Index of occupational position							
Young men	.19	79	47	53	11	111	−.02
Older men	.30	47	17	43	10	70	.09
2. Log of weekly earnings							
Young men	.27	41	26	33	30	89	.03
Older men	.62	37	13	40	11	64	.22
3. Log of yearly earnings							
Young men	.41	49	22	39	10	71	.12
Older men	.68	37	12	41	10	63	.25

[a]Estimates of the contributions of factors to the observed differences obtained by the following procedure: Let $\hat{a}_i$ = regression coefficient for the effect of variable i on the dependent variable; Δx_i = difference between the mean value of variable i for blacks and the mean value of variable i for whites. Then the percentage contribution of the ith variable is $\hat{a}_i \Delta x_i$/data in column 1.

[b]The figures adjusted for years of experience differ for young blacks and young whites because of different regression coefficients in the equations for blacks and whites and sizable differences in years of experience. One reason for the different years of experience is differences in age: sixty-two percent of blacks in the sample are below twenty-three years of age compared with fifty percent of whites. Another reason is that blacks experience more instability in employment than whites, thereby accruing less experience. Years of experience have a large effect on annual earnings but not on hourly earnings or on the index of occupational standing.

[c]Based on regression coefficients presented in table 8.8.

[d]Based on regression coefficients obtained by adding years of schooling of the individual to the regressions of table 8.8.

What stands out in the table is the dominant role of premarket factors in accounting for black-white economic differentials among the young, compared with the modest role of these variables in explaining economic differences among older men. With the regression weights from the attainment equations for blacks, differences in parental occupation account for forty percent of the difference in occupational attainment between young black and white men, for thirty-six percent of the difference in hourly earnings, and for thirty-nine percent of the difference in yearly earnings. By comparison, differences in parental occupational attainment make only a negligible contribution to differences in the labor market position of older black and white men. With the regression weights from the white attainment equations, the results are less dramatic but similar.

The calculations for the full set of prelabor market factors show that, as expected, differences in these factors have become more important deterrents to the attainment of black-white economic parity among the young than residual market discrimination. The black attainment equations attribute 72%–88% of the differences among the young to differences in prelabor market factors, the white attainment equations 71%–111%. By contrast, in the older male sample, with either set of the attainment equations, the contribution of background factors to economic differences is noticeably lower.

The final column of the table records the "residual" difference in the dependent variables which may be attributable to market discrimination. It shows strikingly lower discriminatory differences between young blacks and whites than between older blacks and whites, with virtually no differentials among the young in occupational position or in weekly earnings. Large discriminatory differentials do however remain in yearly earnings, which highlights the importance of differences in time worked in causing black-white economic differences among the young.

We conclude that, while residual market discrimination has not disappeared, the changing job market of the 1960s reduced the importance of residual discrimination in economic inequality between young blacks and whites and made disadvantages in prelabor market factors, particularly family background resources, a more important cause of economic inequality. The decline in the importance of discriminatory differences and heightened role of family background raises a host of new questions for policy regarding black-white economic differences. What responsibility should the society take for helping blacks to overcome long-run disadvantaged backgrounds? Since part of the background disadvantage of blacks results from past discrimination, do they merit special compensatory or redistributive programs? If the developments delineated in this section persist, these issues may come to the fore in the debate on how to eliminate economic differences between blacks and whites.

8.3 Why?

What factors underlie the improvement in the relative economic position of black workers found in this and in other studies?

From the perspective of the basic economic analysis of demand and supply, the observed increases in the relative income and occupational status of blacks could be due, ceterus paribus, either to increased demand for black labor relative to white labor or to shifts in the supply of black labor relative to white labor.

On the demand side, the principal force likely to have increased demand for black labor was the intense antibias activity which followed the Civil Rights Act of 1964 and which caused significant changes in corporate recruitment and personnel policies. Prior to the act, there was no federal law against discrimination and no serious effort to increase minority or female employment in sectors of severe underrepresentation. Beginning in March 1965, the Equal Employment Opportunities Commission (EEOC), which was set up by Title VII of the act, became increasingly active; EEOC annual reports show that expenditures rose from modest amounts to $55 million by 1975, while cases handled increased from about nine thousand in 1966 to seventy-seven thousand in 1975. Following Executive Order 11246, the Office of Federal Contract Compliance (OFCC) and related agencies exerted considerable pressure on enterprises to develop affirmative action programs to increase minority and female employment. Most important, from the mid-1960s to the early 1970s federal courts interpreted the law in ways that tended to favor active equal employment and affirmative action programs. In the mid-1970s, however, a change in the tone of decisions is evident.[21] At the state level, the activities of state fair employment practice commissions (FEPC) grew markedly, in part because of EEOC deferral of cases to state agencies: state FEPC expenditures grew from about $2 million in 1964 to about $34 million in 1975 (see Freeman 1977a).

On the supply side, two very different sets of factors have been suggested as contributing to the improved economic status of blacks. Some have cited increases in the quality of schooling afforded blacks, which have been immense over the long run (Welch and Smith 1975). While there is no denying the long-term improvement in the relative quality of black schooling (see Welch 1973; Freeman 1974a), many have argued that changes in quality of schooling have made only a modest contribution to the post-1964 changes in black earnings (Kneisser, Padilla, and Polachek 1978a b; Akin and Garfinkle 1980; Padilla, n.d.; Levin 1978; Freeman 1977a). Others have hypothesized that the gains in black economic status are the result of a decline in black labor force participation rates allegedly due to expanded social programs, which reduced the relative quantity of black labor and removed those with especially low earnings from the work force (Butler and Heckman 1977). While there is no denying the decline in black participation rates, the evidence does not support the argument that welfare-induced changes in the relative supply of black labor caused relative earnings to rise. First, the black population has increased more rapidly than the white population, so that the ratio of nonwhite workers to white workers has *increased*, rather than decreased since 1964,[22] which would reduce rather than increase relative earnings by causing a movement down rather than up the demand curve. Second, there is no evidence that the lower tail of the black earnings distribution diminished,[23] as would be expected if the earnings increase were due to withdrawal of low earners, and no evidence that labor force withdrawal is closely linked to expansion of welfare payments over time.[24]

This section shows that the evidence on the timing and incidence of gains, while not ruling out potentially important supply side effects, are consistent with an explanation of black economic gains post-1964 that stresses the role of national antibias activity in raising the demand for black labor. Because of the problems in interpreting limited time series, which underlies controversies over the causal forces at work, the section also reviews evidence on the effect of the law on company personnel and employment practices. This evidence makes it difficult to gainsay the impact of federal equal opportunity and affirmative action pressures on employer behavior.

8.3.1 Evidence on Timing

Since the national antibias effort was initiated following passage of Title VII of the Civil Rights Act of 1964, a sine qua non for any case to be made regarding the impact of that effort is that increases in the ratio of black to white economic position be greater post-1964 than prior to 1964. Such a pattern was found in tables 8.1 and 8.2, but must be viewed solely as suggestive. There may be other correlated patterns of change that commenced in the mid 1960s. To see whether there is, in fact, a statistically significant post-1964 improvement in the relative economic position of blacks which could be attributed to changes in demand or whether the post-1964 changes are due to other measurable factors, measures of the relative economic position of blacks were regressed on an indicator of federal antibias activity and several other factors that might cause the relative economic position of blacks to improve (see table 8.10). The dependent variables, measured in logarithmic form, are: the median wage and salary earnings of nonwhite workers relative to white workers from 1948 to 1975; the median wage and salary earnings of nonwhite workers employed full-time year-round to the earnings of comparable white workers from 1955 to 1975; the ratio of the fixed weight index of the occupational position of nonwhite workers to the index for white workers from 1958 to 1975.

The explanatory variables are:

TIME, a time trend which takes the value 1 in the first year of the regression and increases by one unit in each succeeding year. This variable is designed to control for overall trends in the relative earnings of nonwhites.

CYCLE, a business cycle indicator which is obtained as the deviation of the log of real gross national product from its trend level.

EEO, real cumulated expenditures by the equal employment opportunity agency per nonwhite worker, measured in log units, with the value 1 used for the period prior to the Civil Rights Act of 1964, and the value of cumulated real spending per nonwhite plus 1 in later periods.[25] This variable is essentially a post-1964 trend variable, which has the value 0 until 1965, when the act became effective and which trends upward thereafter. It is to be viewed as an indicator of the shift in demand for the period and *not* as a measure of the effectiveness of the EEOC or of any specific governmental activity. If in the future the pattern of demand should change owing, say, to court rulings reducing the efficacy of the affirmative action effort, a more complex variable would be required.

RED, the ratio of the median years of schooling of nonwhite workers to the median years of schooling of white workers, entered to control for the increased educational attainment of nonwhite relative to white workers. Because this variable has a very strong trend, however, its effect cannot be readily distingusihed from TIME. It is entered only in a limited number of equations.

REMP, the log of the ratio of nonwhite employment to white employment, which is designed to test for the possibility that changes in relative earnings are due to movements along a relative demand schedule as a result of shifts in supply. Since relative employment is endogenous, the coefficient on REMP is estimated by instrumental variables, with the following instruments: the ratio of the nonwhite population to the white population and the two social welfare programs which are alleged to reduce supply (Butler and Heckman 1977): Aid to Families of Dependent Children (AFDC) payments and unemployment compensation.

RPART, the log of the ratio of the nonwhite participation rate to the white participation rate. This variable is entered to test the possibility that the reduction of the ratio of nonwhite to white participation rates raised the ratio of nonwhite earnings relative to white earnings by removing nonwhites with low earnings from the work force. Since relative participation rates are endogenous, the effect is estimated by instrumental variables, with the two social welfare program measures used as instruments.

Regressions for men are given at the left-hand side of the table, while regressions for women are presented at the right-hand side. All of the variables except the relative employment and participation rates are the

Table 8.10 Regression Coefficients and Standard Errors for the Effect of Variables on the Log of the Ratio of Nonwhite to White Earnings and Occupational Position, 1948–75[a]

Measure of Relative Economic Position	Constant	Male Workers							
		TIME	CYCLE[b]	EEO	RED	REMP[c]	RPART[d]	R^2	DW
1. Median wages & salaries, 1948–75	−.55	−.001 (.002)	.42 (.23)	.08 (.01)				.83	2.32
2. Median wages & salaries of year-round and full-time workers, 1955–75	−.49	.003 (.002)	−.40 (.17)	.03 (.01)				.87	2.19
3. Occupation index, 1958–75	−.33	.003 (.002)	.10 (.05)	.02 (.004)	.08 (.14)			.99	2.31
4. Median wages & salaries, 1948–75	1.98	.005 (.005)	.33 (.30)	.12 (.03)	.84 (.80)	−.97 (.74)		.82	2.45
5. Median wages & salaries, 1948–75	−.25	.004 (.003)	.42 (.30)	.12 (.06)	−.48 (.55)		1.07 (2.52)	.82	2.41
6. Median wages & salaries of year-round and full-time workers, 1955–75	2.24	−.011 (.011)	−.92 (.38)	.04 (.02)	.49 (.58)	1.28 (.91)		.88	2.05
7. Median wages & salaries of year-round and full-time workers, 1955–75	−.95	−.006 (.009)	−.82 (.39)	.07 (.05)	.81 (.74)		2.47 (2.33)	.87	1.99

			Female Workers					
Constant	TIME	CYCLE[b]	EEO	RED	REMP[c]	RPART[d]	R^2	DW
−.96	.022 (.002)	.34 (.32)	.13 (.02)				.97	1.85
−.70	.019 (.004)	−.48 (.27)	.05 (.02)				.96	1.30
−.97	−.001 (.005)	.12 (.10)	.07 (.01)	.66 (.25)			.99+	2.03
1.09	.025 (.016)	.52 (.36)	.12 (.02)	.008 (.81)	1.12 (.66)		.98	1.89
−1.66	−.014 (.025)	−.011 (.46)	.12 (.04)	1.78 (1.22)		−.97 (1.62)	.98	2.22
−6.25	.055 (.056)	−.20 (.65)	−.08 (.17)	−1.26 (2.12)	−3.29 (3.85)		.93	1.70
−1.68	.030 (.025)	−.71 (.39)	.21 (.14)	−.08 (.99)		3.24 (2.85)	.97	2.00

Source: See appendix.
[a]Dependent variables are the log of the relative economic status of nonwhites to whites.
[b]CYCLE obtained as residual from regression: $GNP = 6.14 + \frac{.035T}{(.001)}$; $R^2 = .99$ where GNP = log of GNP in 1972 dollars.
[c]Log ratio of nonwhite to white employment, instrumented on log ratio of nonwhite to white population 16 and over (male or female); AFDC payment; unemployment compensation per person.
[d]Log ratio of nonwhite to white labor participation rates instrumented on AFDC payment; unemployment compensation per person.

same for the two groups; those variables relate to men or women, respectively.

Rows 1–3 record the results of least-squares regressions of the three measures of relative economic position on TIME, CYCLE, and EEO. If the post-1964 changes in the relative economic position of blacks were due to past trends or cyclical changes rather than to post-1964 antibias activity, the coefficient on the EEO variable would be insignificant while the other variables would dominate the calculations. If, by contrast, post-1964 changes in the relative economic position of blacks were in fact due to post-1964 antibias activity, the coefficient on the EEO variable would be significant and positive.

The regressions comparing the economic position of nonwhite men with that of white men accord the EEO indicator a positive significant coefficient in each case. The regressions comparing the economic position of nonwhite with white women tell a similar story for women, with the EEO variable obtaining a highly significant coefficient on the median wages and salaries of all workers and on the index of occupational position but a much smaller and less significant coefficient in the regression for the year-round and full-time workers. Because the ratio of the earnings of nonwhite women working year-round and full-time to the earnings of white women working year-round and full-time became relatively high in the 1960s, the small estimated effect of EEO on year-round and full-time relative earnings could result from the particular functional form used, which requires that the EEO variable (and other variables) have the same effect on relative earnings even when the potential asymptote of equality is approached. An alternative, more appropriate functional form when earnings ratios approach 1.00 is the logistic or log odds ratio, which allows for differential effects of variables depending on the level of the nonwhite-white differential. Regressing the log odds ratio of nonwhite to white earnings of year-round and full-time women on the independent variables yields:

Log odds ratio of Median Wages & Salaries of Year-Round and Full-Time Women, 1955–1973

$$= -.11 + .036\text{TIME} - 9.34\text{CYCLE} + .61 \text{ EEO}$$
$$(.025) \qquad (1.78) \qquad (.14)$$
$$R^2 = .94$$
$$d.w. = 1.35$$

With the logit specification, the t-statistic on the EEO variable is 5.0, compared with the value of 2.2 in row 2. The reason for the increased significance of the EEO variable is that the logit form requires, all else the same, slackened growth in the ratio of earnings as it rises toward unity and "attributes" the continued increase in the ratio in the 1970s to the EEO variable. Comparable regressions with log odds ratio of other dependent variables show that the logit form generally yields stronger results on the EEO variable, presumably for the same reasons.

An additional experiment is to compare, as some civil rights activists have suggested, the position of nonwhite women with that of white men rather than with another group protected by the law, white women. Regressions of log (earnings of nonwhite women/earnings of white men) on EEO, TIME, and CYCLE, yield the following regression coefficients and standard errors on EEO: for median wages and salaries, .16(.02); for median salaries of year-round and full-time workers, .07(.02).

The possible effect of changes in relative supplies due to expanded social welfare programs on relative earnings is estimated in rows 4–7, using two-stage least-square regressions, along lines set out by Butler and Heckman.[26] Rows 4 and 6 examine the effect of the relative employment of nonwhite workers (REMP) on relative earnings. If the increased relative earnings of blacks are due largely to movements up a demand curve caused by expanded welfare programs rather than to increased demand for black labor post 1964, the relative employment measure should obtain a negative coefficient in the regressions and "knock out" the EEO indicator. Rows 5 and 7 examine the effect of the ratio of nonwhite to white participation rates (RPART) on relative earnings. If the main reason for increased median earnings of blacks was the removal of low wage earners from the working population, the relative participation variable would obtain a negative coefficient in the regression and "knock out" the EEO indicator. All of the calculations include the ratio of nonwhite to white median years of education to make sure that the changes under study are not due to increased demand for black labor owing to increased education. The effects of relative employment and relative participation rates are estimated, as noted previously, by instrumental variables. Given the limited variation in the time series, however, there is good reason to be leary of the regression estimates, as they are making great demands on weak data.

The resultant calculations for male workers tend to support the demand shift hypothesis and to reject the supply shift explanation of improvements in the ratio of black to white earnings. In all of the calculations the EEO variable obtains a positive sign, while the coefficients on relative employment or participation have insignificant positive signs in three or four cases and an insignificant negative sign in one case. Relative years of schooling, which trends upward over time, has an insignificant positive or negative coefficient in the regressions. The positive signs on REMP or RPART in three out of four cases do not, of course, mean either that the labor demand curve is wrongly shaped or that low wage workers were not withdrawing from the labor force, but rather that these factors have too weak an effect in the time series to be discerned. The data reject the model based on supply shifts.

For women, the picture is more complex. With relative median wages and salaries as the dependent variable in rows 4 and 5, we find that relative employment has a positive coefficient while the relative participation rates obtain a negative insignificant coefficient, which again rejects the supply shift story. By contrast, the coefficient on the EEO variable remains sizable and significant. When the relative median wages and salaries of year-round and full-time workers are the dependent variable, however, results are mixed: the relative employment variable obtains the expected negative coefficient and "knocks out" the EEO variable, while the relative participation variable obtains a positive sign and does not remove a significant EEO effect. Since the ratio of the earnings of year-round and full-time workers is close to unity, however, the result on the relative employment term could reflect improper functional form. Regressing the logit of relative earnings of year-round and full-time workers on the variables in row 6 yields a positive coefficient on EEO and a positive coefficient on REMP.[27]

All told, with the exception of the regression for females in row 6, the calculations show that the supply side factors neither explain the post-1964 gains nor eliminate the indicator of post-1964 equal employment activity from the regressions.[28]

The time series data in table 8.10 can, it should be stressed, be analyzed in other ways. In earlier work Vroman (1974) and Masters (1975) used simple post-1964 trend variables to pick up the presumed shift in demand for black labor following the initiation of EEO activity and obtained positive coefficients on their post-1964 variable. Similar results in the post-1964 trend can be obtained using the data underlying table 8.10. Since the EEO indicator is essentially a post-1964 trend, results with the trend measure must, of necessity, give similar statistical findings.[29] Burstein has developed a more complex model, including measures of changes in taste, and found that his additional variables also left a sizable positive coefficient to a measure of post-1964 EEO activity.

While it is still possible that some unmeasured factor that changed sharply after 1964 is, in fact, the true causal force, it is difficult to say what that other factor might be. In the absence of contrary evidence, the data appear consistent with a demand side explanation of black economic gains post 1964. But as the time series really consists of only a single fact—namely, that black economic gains were more rapid after 1964 when serious federal antibias activity commenced than before 1964— other types of evidence should also be examined to minimize the chances of misinterpreting the causes of observed changes.

8.3.2 Evidence on Regional Incomes

Because time series changes in the ratio of nonwhite to white incomes by region have occasionally been viewed as running counter to a demand shift explanation of black economic progress post 1964, it is of some value to examine regional patterns of change. While the regional evidence is not one-sided, regressions comparable with those in table 8.10 suggest that the regional changes are also broadly consistent with the demand hypothesis. For male workers, the regressions given in figure 8.1 show that the EEO indicator has a very sizable positive coefficient in the South, where discrimination was most severe, and obtains smaller positive coefficients in the Northeast and north central areas. The data for the West (where less than 10 percent of blacks are located) run counter to the demand hypothesis.

For women, the picture is quite different, though for an interesting reason. In the South, the calculations for the median incomes of all women yield a large significant positive EEO coefficient, but in the Northeast, north central region, and West, the coefficients on the EEO variable for earnings are negative. In each of these regions, however, the ratio of nonwhite to white median incomes for women *exceeded* unity long before 1964: the ratio exceeded unity in 1956 in the Northeast; in 1959 in the north central region; and in 1961 in the West. *As measured by these data, there was no nonwhite-white income inequality among women to be remedied by EEO*, and thus no reason to expect a positive coefficient on the variable. For the two regions where sufficient data exist on the incomes of year-round and full-time workers to merit investigation, the South and the Northeast, the EEO variable obtains a significant positive coefficient. The rejection of the demand hypothesis when the nonwhite/white income ratio exceeds unity and "acceptance" of the hypothesis when the nonwhite/white income ratio is below unity, and the strong EEO effects in the South where discrimination has been most severe, lend additional support to the hypothesis. These results suggest that the positive coefficients on EEO do in fact reflect declines in discrimination rather than some correlated general shift in demand for black labor.

8.3.3 Evidence on Incidence

One additional type of evidence which can be used to evaluate alternative explanations of the post-1964 economic gains of blacks is information on which groups of black workers made the most significant progress. The analysis in this and in other studies indicates that the largest relative economic gains were won by young black men, by highly educated and skilled black men, by those from more advantaged family backgrounds, and by black women. This pattern of incidence is consistent with the demand shift hypothesis.

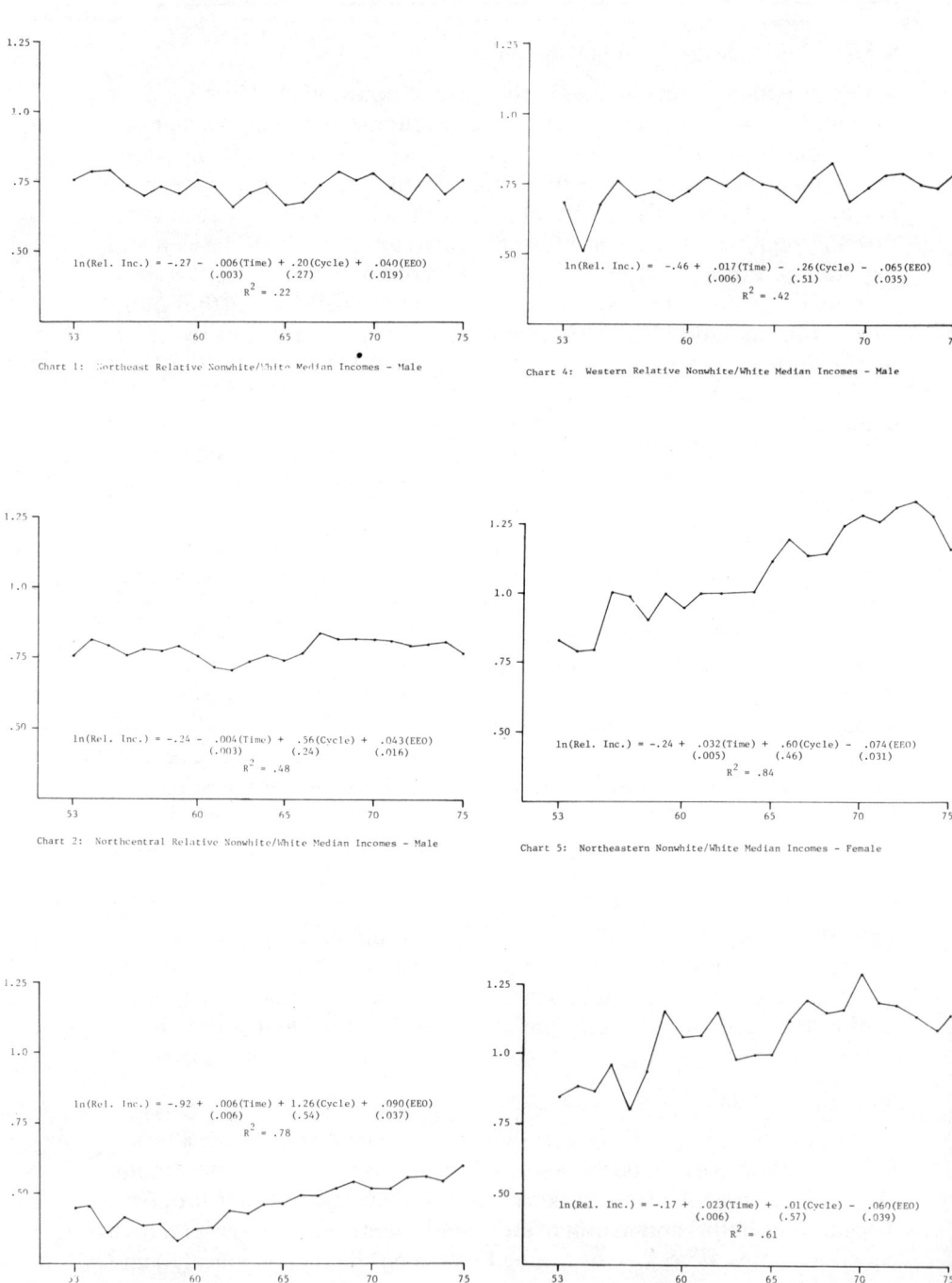

Figure 8.1 Ratio of Nonwhite to White Median Incomes

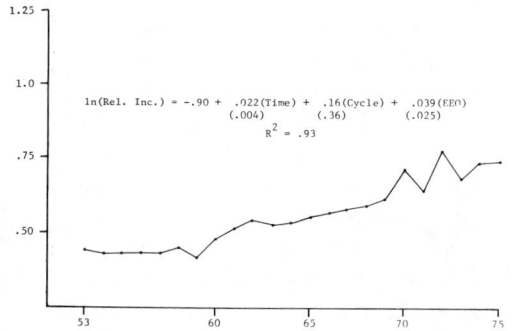

Chart 7: Southern Relative Nonwhite/White Median Incomes - Female

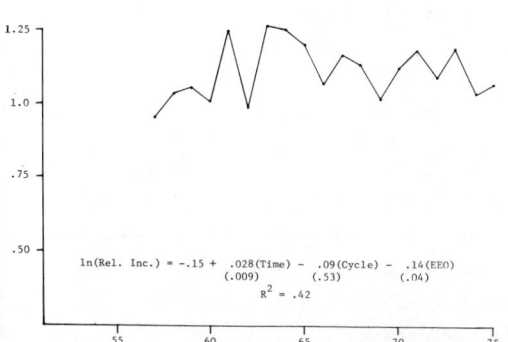

Chart 8: Western Relative Nonwhite/White Relative Incomes - Female

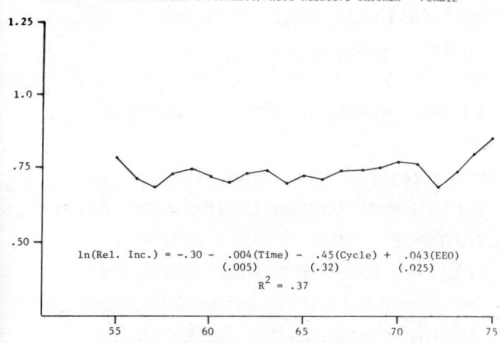

Chart 9: Northeast Relative Nonwhite/White Median Incomes of Full-Time, Year-Round Male Workers

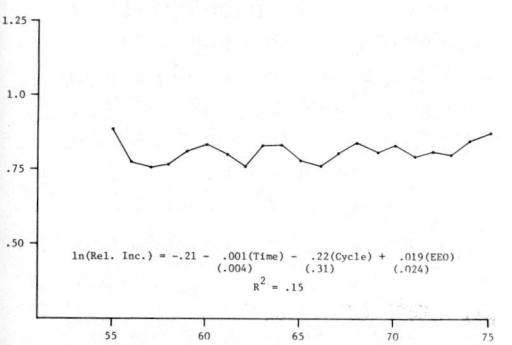

Chart 10: Northcentral Relative Nonwhite/White Median Incomes of Full-Time, Year-Round Male Workers

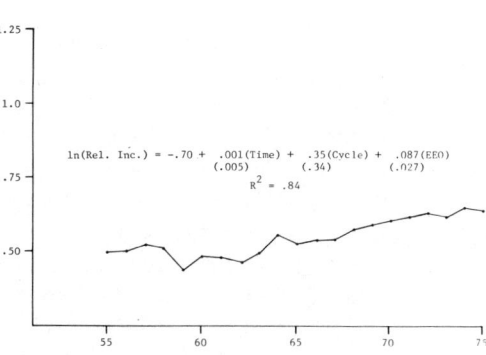

Chart 11: Southern Relative Nonwhite/White Median Income of Full-Time, Year-Round Male Workers

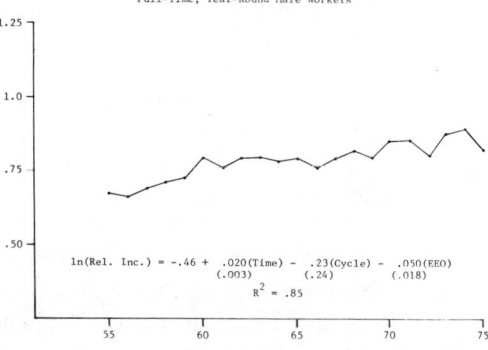

Chart 12: Western Relative Nonwhite/White Median Incomes of Full-Time, Year-Round Male Workers

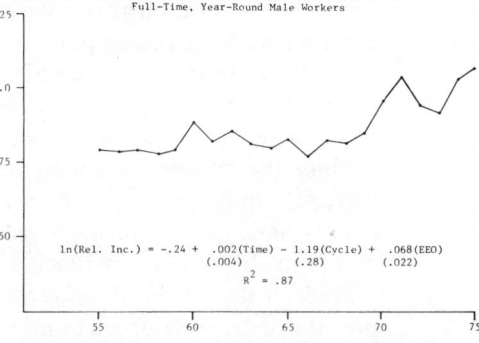

Chart 13: Northeastern Relative Nonwhite/White Median Incomes of Full-Time, Year-Round Female Workers

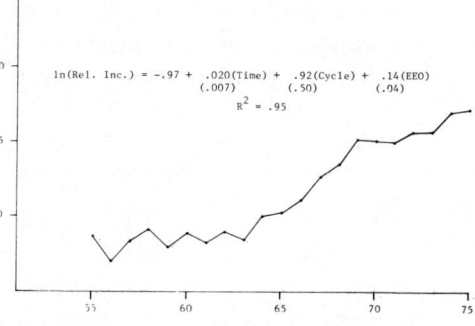

Chart 14: Southern Relative Nonwhite/White Median Incomes of Full-Time, Year-Round Female Workers

Changes in demand for black labor due to declines in discrimination or other factors can be expected to have differential effects on groups of workers depending on their position in the labor market. Larger or more immediate impacts are likely for groups of workers with flat age-earnings profiles, such as women, as opposed to workers whose earnings depend greatly on investment in skill and cumulated experience, such as older men; for groups of workers just entering the job market, such as young men; and for those in relatively short supply, such as the more skilled and educated. Given the length of training required for higher-level jobs, the supply of black workers to those jobs is likely to be inelastic, so that increases in demand are likely to yield greater income increases than in lower-skill occupations where labor supply is more elastic. Finally, to the extent that affirmative action pressures are concentrated in occupations where blacks are relatively underrepresented, the actual shifts in demand are likely to be more pronounced in high-level occupations.

The tendency for young black men from more-advantaged homes to make greater progress in the market than those from less-advantaged backgrounds can be interpreted as the result of both demand and supply forces. On the demand side, if we assume that the prime impediment to "normal" social mobility patterns in the black community was the severe discrimination against highly educated and skilled blacks, especially the lack of opportunities for managerial and professional employment in national businesses, the change in demand could be expected to create social mobility patterns comparable to those in the white community. On the supply side, young persons from the more-advantaged homes are presumably more likely to have the educational resources and personal skills which make them more adept at responding to new opportunities than those from less-advantaged homes.

Since the number of young and educated or skilled black workers has increased in the period under study, it is difficult to explain the incidence of economic gains in terms of an autonomous decline in supply. Improvements in the quality of black schooling, on the other hand, may have played a role in the rate of advance. Among college students, for example, the increased opportunities for young blacks in the higher educational system and in the job market led many to enroll in primarily white national colleges and universities, as opposed to the traditional black colleges of the South. Since the national institutions offer higher-quality education than the primarily black colleges, there was undoubtably an improvement in the quality of black college graduates in the period. This improvement was in large part induced by the same civil rights and antibias activities as the changes in the job market and should not be viewed as an autonomous development (Freeman 1977a, chapter 3).

8.3.4 Evidence from Personnel Departments and Studies of Company Employment

The most telling evidence on the effect of antibias activities on demand for black labor and thus on black economic progress post 1964 comes from studies of the personnel and employment practices of individual companies. Such evidence is critical in evaluating the role of demand forces in black economic progress post 1964 for two reasons. First, the appropriate statistical materials, while useful, do not by themselves provide information on the actual activities of employers, and thus permit alternative interpretations, as evidenced in the controversy over causality. Second, in the absence of widespread changes in company personnel practices, it is difficult to see how antidiscrimination policies could cause sizable aggregate effects, given the small number of workers likely to benefit in specific antidiscrimination cases.

The evidence that personnel policies have, in fact, been greatly altered by federal equal employment opportunity and affirmative action pressures is overwhelming. In the market for young college graduates there was a remarkable upsurge in corporate recruitment visits to the traditionally black colleges of the South, with accompanying hiring of graduates whose previous opportunities were limited to segregated professional services, especially teaching. In 1960 almost no firms recruited from the traditionally black southern colleges; in 1965 a sampling of colleges averaged 50 recruitees per school; in 1970, they averaged 277 recruitees (Freeman 1977a: 35). A 1976 Bureau of National Affairs (BNA) survey of personnel and industrial relations executives documents the far-reaching impact of the federal equal employment pressures on corporate labor market behavior. According to the BNA (1976: 1) "Equal Employment Opportunity (EEO) Programs complete with Affirmative Action Plans (AAP) are viewed as 'a fact of life' by nearly all employers, and the personnel function has changed in a variety of ways as a result of the government's efforts to enforce the employment provisions of the act." As table 8.11 documents, in the BNA sample eighty-six percent of the companies have formal EEO programs: ninety-six percent of those subject to OFCC regulations have AAP's; sixty-three percent have been investigated under Title VII. Most of the firms in the survey report changing their selection procedures (line 3) and introducing special recruiting programs (line 4) for minority workers. One third of the companies have made EEO achievements a criterion in performance appraisals of managers while many also initiated special training programs. The attention given by personnel officials to the "Uniform Guidelines on Employee Selection Procedures (1978)" and its predecessor

Table 8.11 Evidence of Changes in Personnel Practices Due to EEO

	% of Companies
1. Have *formal* EEO program	86
Including affirmative action plan	
(of those subject to OFCC regulations)	96
2. Have had investigation or other action under Title VII	63
3. Changes in selection procedures for EEO reasons:	60
Testing procedures	39
Revised job qualifications	31
Application forms	20
Recruiting techniques	19
4. Special recruiting programs	
For all minority workers	69
For minorities in professional/managerial positions	58
5. Programs to ensure EEO policies are implemented	
Communications on EEO policy	95
Follow-up personnel or EEO office	85
Training sessions on EEO	67
Periodic publications of EEO results	48
EEO achievements included in performance appraisals	33
6. Special training programs	
For entry-level jobs	16
For upgrading	24
For management positions	16

Source: Bureau of National Affairs 1976; lines, 1, 2, table 9, p. 15; line 3, table 3, p. 4; line 4, table 1, p. 2; line 5, table 6, p. 9; line 6, table 5, p. 8.

guidelines; the weekly publication of a fair employment practices newsletter; the creation of the Equal Employment Advisory Council to advise businesses about equal employment issues; and diverse other activities make it clear that *governmental EEO and AAP pressures have revolutionized personnel and employment selection practices*. Unless company personnel policies are totally ineffective or a complete sham, there would appear to be a substantial upward shift in demand for black labor as a result of these changes. This type of evidence provides a strong prior justification for evaluating aggregate data on black economic progress.

Studies of the effect of federal contract compliance pressures on employment of blacks by individual companies also yield results consistent with the demand shift hypothesis. In the earliest such study, Ashenfelter and Heckman (1976) estimated that the federal pressures raised black male employment in specific companies by 12.9 percent. Burman (1973), using different modeling procedures, estimated that OFCC pressure caused an increase in black employment in companies of 5.6 percent. Later work by Heckman and Wolpin (1976) estimated that the federal pressures raised black male employment in specific companies by 10.4 percent. Only the study by Goldstein and Smith (1976) did not find such effects. Since none of the studies allows for "spillover" effects, by which one company's policies are altered as a result of pressures from a neighboring enterprise, or for the effects of the EEOC, of state fair employment practices commissions, or of court cases, these figures are likely to understate the full effects of the changes induced by such pressures.

In sum, while by no means definitive, or ruling out other factors, the evidence on timing, on incidence, and on company personnel and employment practices suggests that at least some of the post-1964 black gains resulted from increases in demand for black labor induced, at least in part, by programs designed to accomplish that purpose. Imperfect though it is, the evidence indicates that the national antibias effort has contributed to black economic progress. As far as can be told from the data, if Title VII were repealed and equal employment efforts ended, the rate of black advancement would fall.

8.4 Conclusion

The improvement in the relative economic position of blacks documented here and elsewhere does not mean that sizable gains have been obtained in all dimensions of economic well-being or that black-white economic differences are likely to disappear in the future.

For one, the relative economic position of the black family did not improve as rapidly as that of individual earners, in large part because of the continued increase in the relative number of female-headed homes.

Second, the enormous prelabor market disadvantage of blacks—the burden of coming from families and neighborhoods of low socioeconomic conditions which fail to provide the background resources that facilitate economic success—remains. In the 1970s black youngsters trail whites greatly in a wide variety of background resources which, discrimination aside, can be expected to produce black-white labor market differences ranging 10–20 percent. These differences cannot, by their nature, be eliminated by antibias policy in the labor market and promise continued racial income inequalities into the foreseeable future.

Third, large groups of black workers—notably, experienced men—have benefited only modestly from the decline in job market discrimination. Because many "male occupations" require considerable investment in skill and cumulated experience and often have lengthy formal seniority promotion ladders, these men face the problem not simply of equal opportunity today but of making up the deficit of education and work skills of the past. Perhaps most striking, the labor force participation rate of experienced black men has declined sharply, perhaps as a result of the growth in female-headed families among blacks, and of Social Security disability insurance and related welfare programs. Whatever the causal connections, the fact is that the job market position of a large group of black workers has been only modestly improved by reducing market discrimination.

Fourth, the initial gains for young blacks in the period may dissipate over time, if discrimination in promotions reduces their advance in corporate hierarchies. While their lifetime income would still be higher than in the past, the extent of the gains would be less striking than if young blacks maintain their relatively strong starting position compared with young whites.

Fifth, unemployment remains a much more serious problem in the black than in the white community, particularly among younger persons.

The common thread running through most of the problem area—family income and composition, the burden of poor backgrounds, and the lack of sharp progress among older black male workers—is that simply ending job market discrimination and guaranteeing equal employment opportunity have not achieved black-white parity and are unlikely to. Other programs or activities (private as well as or instead of public) are needed.

Appendix   **Data for Time Series Analysis**

Year	GNP ($ millions)	CPI (X 100)	AFDC ($ per person)	UNCOMP ($ per person)	EEOC Spending ($1,000s)	Post 1964 Trend
1948	487.700	72.1000	20.9200	19.0300	0.0	0
1949	490.700	71.4000	21.7000	20.4800	0.0	0
1950	533.500	72.1000	20.8500	20.7600	0.0	0
1951	576.500	77.8000	22.0000	21.0900	0.0	0
1952	598.500	79.5000	23.4500	22.7900	0.0	0
1953	621.800	80.1000	23.2000	23.5800	0.0	0
1954	613.700	80.5000	23.2500	24.9300	0.0	0
1955	654.800	80.2000	23.5000	25.0400	0.0	0
1956	668.800	81.4000	24.8000	27.0200	0.0	0
1957	680.900	84.3000	25.4000	28.2100	0.0	0
1958	679.500	86.6000	26.6500	30.5800	0.0	0
1959	720.400	87.3000	27.3000	30.4100	0.0	0
1960	736.800	88.7000	28.3500	32.8200	0.0	0
1961	755.300	89.6000	29.4500	33.8000	0.0	0
1962	799.100	90.6000	29.3000	34.5600	0.0	0
1963	830.700	91.7000	29.7000	35.2700	0.0	0
1964	874.400	92.9000	31.5000	35.9200	0.0	0
1965	925.900	94.5000	32.6500	37.1900	3,875.00	1
1966	981.000	97.2000	36.2500	39.7500	4,245.00	2
1967	1,007.70	100.000	39.5000	41.2500	5,947.50	3
1968	1,051.80	104.200	42.0500	43.4300	7,887.50	4
1969	1,078.80	109.800	45.1500	46.1700	11,260.0	5
1970	1,075.30	116.300	49.6500	50.3400	14,792.5	6
1971	1,107.50	121.300	52.3000	54.0200	19,592.5	7
1972	1,171.10	125.300	54.1000	56.7500	27,500.0	8
1973	1,233.40	133.100	56.9500	59.0000	38,200.0	9
1974	1,210.70	147.700	65.5000	64.2400	49,740.5	10
1975	1,191.70	161.200	72.4100	70.3900	61,706.2	11

| | Labor Force Participation Rates (%) | | | | Population (in thousands) | | | |
| | Male | | Female | | Male | | Female | |
Year	White	Non-white	White	Non-white	White	Non-white	White	Non-white
1948	86.5000	87.3000	31.3000	45.6000	45,211.5	4,784.65	47,763.6	5,307.02
1949	86.4000	87.0000	31.8000	46.9000	45,506.9	4,816.09	48,305.0	5,366.73
1950	86.4000	85.9000	32.6000	46.9000	45,871.5	4,854.48	48,843.6	5,358.21
1951	86.5000	86.3000	33.4000	46.3000	44,966.5	4,758.98	49,404.2	5,395.25
1952	86.2000	86.8000	33.6000	45.5000	44,945.5	4,755.76	49,976.2	5,320.88
1953	86.1000	86.2000	33.4000	43.6000	45,893.1	4,857.30	50,673.7	5,954.13
1954	85.6000	85.2000	33.3000	46.1000	46,448.6	4,933.10	51,222.2	5,685.46
1955	85.4000	85.0000	34.5000	46.1000	47,067.9	5,034.11	51,843.5	5,776.57
1956	85.6000	85.1000	35.7000	47.3000	47,586.4	5,122.21	52,361.3	5,852.01
1957	84.8000	84.3000	35.7000	47.2000	48,138.0	5,190.98	52,997.2	5,957.63
1958	84.3000	84.0000	35.8000	48.0000	48,730.7	5,288.09	53,667.6	6,052.08
1959	83.8000	83.4000	36.0000	47.7000	49,399.8	5,383.69	54,322.2	6,138.36
1960	83.4000	83.0000	36.5000	48.2000	50,050.3	5,596.38	55,263.0	6,367.22
1961	83.0000	82.2000	36.9000	48.3000	50,585.5	5,676.40	56,010.8	6,492.75
1962	82.1000	80.8000	36.7000	48.0000	51,073.1	5,777.23	56,727.5	6,656.25
1963	81.5000	80.2000	37.2000	48.1000	52,029.4	5,891.52	57,596.8	6,817.05
1964	81.1000	80.0000	37.5000	48.5000	52,889.0	5,981.25	58,741.3	6,977.32
1965	80.8000	79.6000	38.1000	48.6000	53,712.9	6,099.25	59,658.8	7,127.57
1966	80.6000	79.0000	39.2000	49.3000	54,059.5	6,201.26	60,464.3	7,296.14
1967	80.7000	78.5000	40.1000	49.5000	54,574.9	6,299.36	61,488.8	7,482.82
1968	80.4000	77.6000	40.7000	49.3000	55,415.4	6,416.23	62,466.8	7,667.34
1969	80.2000	76.9000	41.8000	49.8000	56,340.4	6,548.76	63,622.0	7,867.47
1970	80.0000	76.5000	42.6000	49.5000	57,516.2	6,773.86	64,565.7	8,111.11
1971	79.6000	74.9000	42.6000	49.2000	58,795.2	6,969.29	65,701.9	8,337.39
1972	79.6000	73.7000	43.2000	48.7000	60,213.6	7,238.80	67,194.4	8,724.84
1973	79.5000	73.8000	44.1000	49.1000	61,192.4	7,527.10	68,120.2	9,103.87
1974	79.4000	73.3000	45.2000	49.1000	62,324.9	7,776.26	69,008.8	9,435.84
1975	78.7000	71.5000	45.9000	49.2000	63,381.2	8,019.58	70,159.0	9,745.93

Black Economic Progress after 1964: Who Has Gained and Why?

	Median Wage & Salary Income ($)				Median Years of Schooling			
	Male		Female		Male		Female	
Year	White	Non-White	White	Non-white	White	Non-white	White	Non-white
1948	2,711.00	1,615.00	1,615.00	701.000	10.4000	6.80000	12.0000	7.70000
1949	2,735.00	1,367.00	1,615.00	654.000	10.5000	6.90000	12.0000	7.80000
1950	2,982.00	1,828.00	1,698.00	626.000	10.6000	7.00000	12.0000	7.90000
1951	3,345.00	2,060.00	1,855.00	781.000	10.7000	7.10000	12.1000	8.00000
1952	3,507.00	2,038.00	1,976.00	814.000	10.8000	7.20000	12.1000	8.10000
1953	3,760.00	2,233.00	2,049.00	994.000	10.9000	7.30000	12.1000	8.20000
1954	3,754.00	2,131.00	2,046.00	914.000	11.1000	7.50000	12.1000	8.40000
1955	3,986.00	2,342.00	2,065.00	894.000	11.2000	7.60000	12.2000	8.60000
1956	4,260.00	2,396.00	2,179.00	970.00	11.4000	7.80000	12.2000	8.80000
1957	4,396.00	2,436.00	2,240.00	1,019.00	11.5000	7.90000	12.2000	9.00000
1958	4,596.00	2,652.00	2,364.00	1,055.00	11.7000	8.10000	12.2000	9.20000
1959	4,902.00	2,844.00	2,422.00	1,289.00	11.9000	8.30000	12.2000	9.40000
1960	5,137.00	3,075.00	2,537.00	1,276.00	12.0000	8.50000	12.2000	9.70000
1961	5,287.00	3,015.00	2,538.00	1,302.00	12.0000	8.70000	12.3000	10.1000
1962	5,462.00	3,023.00	2,630.00	1,396.00	12.1000	9.00000	12.3000	10.5000
1963	5,663.00	3,217.00	2,723.00	1,448.00	12.1000	9.30000	12.3000	10.7000
1964	5,853.00	3,426.00	2,841.00	1,652.00	12.2000	9.70000	12.3000	10.8000
1965	6,188.00	3,563.00	2,994.00	1,722.00	12.2000	10.0000	12.3000	11.1000
1966	6,510.00	3,864.00	3,079.00	1,981.00	12.3000	10.0000	12.4000	11.2000
1967	6,833.00	4,369.00	3,254.00	2,288.00	12.3000	10.2000	12.4000	11.5000
1968	7,291.00	4,839.00	3,465.00	2,497.00	12.3000	10.7000	12.4000	11.7000
1969	7,859.00	5,237.00	3,640.00	2,884.00	12.4000	10.8000	12.4000	11.9000
1970	8,254.00	5,485.00	3,870.00	3,285.00	12.4000	11.1000	12.5000	12.1000
1971	8,550.00	5,754.00	4,046.00	3,480.00	12.5000	11.4000	12.5000	12.1000
1972	9,190.00	6,261.00	4,218.00	3,944.00	12.5000	11.7000	12.5000	12.2000
1973	9,969.00	6,927.00	4,441.00	3,978.00	12.5000	11.9000	12.5000	12.3000
1974	10,745.0	7,617.00	4,863.00	4,751.00	12.5000	12.0000	12.5000	12.3000
1975	11,296.0	8,296.00	5,204.00	5,062.00	12.6000	12.1000	12.6000	12.4000

	Employment (in thousands)				Median Wage & Salary Income Year-Round, Full-Time Workers ($)			
	Male		Female		Male		Female	
Year	White	Non-white	White	Non-white	White	Non-white	White	Non-white
1948	37,778.0	3,935.00	14,382.0	2,272.00	—	—	—	—
1949	37,116.0	3,788.00	14,485.0	2,318.00	—	—	—	—
1950	37,770.0	3,778.00	15,079.0	2,302.00	—	—	—	—
1951	37,885.0	3,906.00	15,808.0	2,346.00	—	—	—	—
1952	37,774.0	3,913.00	16,238.0	2,283.00	—	—	—	—
1953	38,526.0	3,986.00	16,400.0	2,490.00	—	—	—	—
1954	37,847.0	3,772.00	16,110.0	2,378.00	—	—	—	—
1955	38,721.0	3,903.00	17,113.0	2,438.00	4,458.00	2,831.00	2,870.00	1,637.00
1956	39,366.0	4,013.00	17,899.0	2,521.00	4,710.00	2,912.00	2,958.00	1,637.00
1957	39,343.0	4,013.00	18,109.0	2,606.00	4,950.00	3,137.00	3,107.00	1,866.00
1958	38,592.0	3,831.00	18,022.0	2,591.00	5,186.00	3,368.00	3,225.00	1,988.00
1959	39,493.0	3,972.00	18,512.0	2,652.00	5,456.00	3,339.00	3,306.00	2,196.00
1960	39,755.0	4,148.00	19,095.0	2,779.00	5,662.00	3,789.00	3,410.00	2,372.00
1961	39,588.0	4,067.00	19,324.0	2,765.00	5,880.00	3,883.00	3,480.00	2,325.00
1962	40,016.0	4,160.00	19,682.0	2,844.00	6,025.00	3,799.00	3,601.00	2,278.00
1963	40,428.0	4,229.00	20,194.0	2,911.00	6,277.00	4,104.00	3,723.00	2,368.00
1964	41,114.0	4,359.00	20,808.0	3,024.00	6,497.00	4,285.00	3,859.00	2,674.00
1965	41,844.0	4,496.00	21,601.0	3,147.00	6,814.00	4,367.00	3,960.00	2,713.00
1966	42,330.0	4,588.00	22,689.0	3,287.00	7,164.00	4,528.00	4,152.00	2,949.00
1967	42,834.0	4,646.00	23,528.0	3,366.00	7,512.00	5,069.00	4,394.00	3,363.00
1968	43,411.0	4,702.00	24,340.0	3,467.00	8,014.00	5,603.00	4,700.00	3,677.00
1969	44,048.0	4,770.00	25,470.0	3,614.00	8,876.00	6,158.00	5,168.00	4,231.00
1970	44,157.0	4,803.00	26.025.0	3,642.00	9,373.00	6,598.00	5,490.00	4,674.00
1971	44,499.0	4,746.00	26,217.0	3,658.00	9,801.00	6,928.00	5,749.00	5,181.00
1972	45,769.0	4,861.00	27,305.0	3,767.00	10,786.0	7,548.00	6,131.00	5,320.00
1973	46,830.0	5,133.00	28,448.0	3,999.00	11,633.0	8,363.00	6,544.00	5,772.00
1974	47,340.0	5,179.00	29,281.0	4,136.00	12,343.0	9,082.00	7,025.00	6,611.00
1975	46,204.0	4,947.00	29,429.0	4,124.00	13,216.0	10,168.0	7,614.00	7,505.00

Source: 1. Income figures are from U.S. Bureau of the Census (1949–76).
2. Employment and labor force are from U.S. Department of Labor (1978b), with figures for 1948–53 estimated on the basis of reported unemployment rates and civilian labor participation rates assuming that the nonwhite share of the population aged 16 and over remained at its 1954 level.
3. AFDC payments and unemployment compensation obtained from Butler and Heckman (1977).
4. EEOC spending obtained from annual reports of the agency.
5. Median years of schooling obtained from U.S. Department of Labor (1978a), table B-9, with missing years obtained by interpolation and extrapolation.

Notes

1. The best tests of discrimination would be in areas where individual productivity is measurable, such as athletics. The "productivity" of academic faculty can be at least crudely measured by numbers of publications, as in Freeman (1977a, chapter 8).

2. Some of the published data refer to nonwhites. As about ninety percent of nonwhites are black, it is legitimate to use data on nonwhites to make inferences about the position of blacks. In the test I use the term black except where data specifically refer to nonwhites.

3. With an asymptote of unity, the ratio of the earnings of black workers to the earnings of white workers might be fit by a logistic growth curve:

$$R = 1/(1 - \exp at)$$

where R = ratio of earnings
   t = time, to measure trend over time
   a = logistic curve parameter

With this functional form, $dR/dt = aR(1 - R)$ so that dR/dt falls as R approaches unity.

4. 1964 is chosen as the year in which to break the data because the Civil Rights of 1964, which made discrimination in employment on the basis of race illegal, became effective on March 1, 1965. Hence 1964 is the appropriate year for estimating before/after effects.

5. If young blacks made less investments in the on-the-job training relative to young whites, black gains in incomes would be overstated. Conversely, if young blacks made greater investments in on-the-job training relative to young whites, black gains would be understated.

6. The ratios are termed approximate because the published survey data are based on small samples.

7. The finding that family background factors do not greatly affect the socioeconomic position of blacks was first developed by Duncan, who used data for 1962, a year just preceding the Civil Rights Act of 1964, and thus providing valuable "before" data for before/after analyses.

8. The NLS does have direct questions on rates of pay, but an examination of these data suggested that except for hourly workers there were considerable reporting problems. Hence the weekly earnings data were used.

9. In the younger male NLS sample the questions relating to background refer to the position of the individual at age fourteen. In the older male NLS sample the questions refer to the position of the individual at age fifteen. For heuristic purposes, I refer to the position of persons at age fourteen throughout the text, although the older male data relate to age fifteen.

10. In one parent/female homes, a potential problem with the use of the median income of men is that male incomes are unlikely to be a good measure of the economic position of the family. To deal with this, the interaction between the measure of occupational attainment of the head of the household and the dummy variable for one parent/female homes was added to some calculations, but the interaction variable obtained small and insignificant coefficients, suggesting that a dummy variable for the one parent/female home suffices to measure the differences in resources between those homes and homes with two parents. For example, in the equations for years of schooling the interaction variables obtain a coefficient and standard error of $-.19(.31)$ for whites and $.09(.43)$ for blacks. The results in the text exclude the interaction variable.

11. The difference in the parental occupation of young blacks and of young whites obtained from using the median income of nonwhites for blacks and the median wage of all men for whites is 0.8 ln points. The difference obtained from using the median income of all men for both groups is about half as large.

12. The region of residence at age fourteen was not reported in the young male sample and was inferred from region where the individual went to high school or (for those not reporting region of high school attendance) current residence.

13. The differences in these background variables in the older male NLS were also sizable. Among older men, the parents of blacks had 5.1 years of schooling compared with 7.8 for the parents of whites; the log of the occupational status was 7.2 for blacks compared with 8.3 for whites; 39 percent of the blacks were brought up in houses without a male head compared with 19 percent of the whites.

14. For example, the effect of the parental occupation index on the years completed by persons out of school was .48 for young whites and .80 for young blacks, which are comparable figures to those in table 8.4.

15. If we take account of the greater impact of the one parent/female home on whites than on blacks the difference is increased marginally.

16. The algorithm adds weeks worked in a year/52 to an initial estimate of years of experience obtained from data on year of first post-school job.

17. The problem of potential sample selection problems due to inclusion or exclusion of persons not reporting parental education is discussed in detail in Freeman (1976), where all calculations are estimated on two samples, one excluding those not reporting parental education, and one including those not so reporting.

18. Duncan, Featherman, and Duncan (1972) obtain roughly similar family background regression coefficients for occupational status of the first job and occupational status of current job for various cohorts. Their cross-sectional analysis of the OCG surveys of 1962 and 1973 also reveals no clear patterns of change in the impact of father's or son's occupation by age groups.

19. The Hauser-Featherman (1975b) analysis of the OCG surveys yields results consistent with a change over time interpretation of the NLS cohort differences: their analysis shows essentially no effect of parental occupation on son's occupation among 25–34-year-old blacks in 1962 compared with a sizable effect in 1973, much like that for nonblacks.

20. If differences in background variables had become smaller over time, background might not become a more important contribution to racial economic inequality. In fact, comparison of the differences in background measures among young men reported on p. 00 with those among older men reported in note 12 shows no such decline.

21. The changed attitude of courts toward affirmative action is evinced in several successful reverse discrimination suits by those injured by affirmative action and in charging burdens of proof in showing discrimination.

22.

	Ratio of Black and Other Workers to White Workers Aged 16 and Over		
	1964	1976	Change
Labor force participants	.1258	.1299	.0041
Employed persons	.1192	.1213	.0021

Source: U.S. Department of Labor (1978) table A-3, p. 140–141, pp. 158–159.

23. Specifically, one might expect a decline in the lower tail of the wage and salary distribution if large numbers of low wage earners left the job market. In fact, no such pattern is observed, at least from 1968 to 1974. Among black men, for example, the ratio of the lower quintile of the wage and salary distribution to the median was .28 in 1968 when the labor participation rate was .78, and .28 in 1974 when the participation rate was .73. U.S. Bureau of the Census (1969) No. 66, table 54, p. 124 and U.S. Bureau of the Census (1975), No. 101, table 72, p. 146.

24. Regression of nonwhite male and female participation rates on AFDC payments and unemployment compensation payments, years of schooling (educ.) TIME, CYCLE, and EEO spending yields the following:

ln (LFP of Nonwhite Men)
$$= 6.06 + .005(\text{TIME}) + .06(\text{CYCLE}) + .04(\text{AFDC})$$
$$(.004) \qquad (.05) \qquad (.05$$
$$- .08(\text{Unemp.Comp.}) - .35(\text{Educ.}) - .012(\text{EEO}) \qquad R^2 = .99$$
$$(.06) \qquad\qquad (.11) \qquad\quad (.009)$$

ln (LFP of Nonwhite Women)
$$= 5.03 + .022(\text{TIME}) + .49(\text{CYCLE}) + .05(\text{AFDC})$$
$$(.012) \qquad (.15) \qquad (.11)$$
$$- .31(\text{Unemp.Comp.}) - .12(\text{Educ.}) + .019(\text{EEO}) \qquad R^2 = .87$$
$$(.17) \qquad\qquad (.28) \qquad\quad (.018)$$

25. This is a better measure than the comparable variable used in my 1973 Brookings paper (Freeman 1973). In that paper I failed to note that the ratio of expenditures to numbers of nonwhites was below unity in the first two years after passage of Title VII, which in log form produces a negative value for the variable. This *biases* results against finding a positive EEO effect. It should be stressed that the cumulated EEO variable is roughly comparable to a trend variable beginning in 1965.

26. These results differ greatly from those reported by Butler and Heckman (1977), who performed regressions identical to those in rows 5 and 7 over slightly different years. The reason for the differences is that Butler and Heckman inadvertently used data with several keypunch errors. I want to thank them for providing me with the data and helping to obtain a corrected set.

27. In the logit form the results are:

Log odds ratio of median earnings
$$= 42.1 + .034\text{TIME} - 8.77\text{CYCLE} + 1.07\text{EEO}$$
$$(.28) \qquad (3.28) \qquad\quad (.85)$$
$$- 1.02\text{RED} + 21.09\text{RPART} \qquad R^2 = .94 \qquad d.w. = 1.84$$
$$(11.2) \qquad (19.53)$$

28. Related regressions for median incomes, which depend on non-labor-market earnings as well as on wages and salaries, yield roughly comparable results, with most but not all of the calculations giving large positive coefficients on the EEO variable and insignificant positive or negative coefficients on the relative supply variables. The logit form generally yields higher EEO effects. Related regressions using other measures of EEO activity also yield comparable results. See Freeman 1978; Burstein 1978.

29. It is also possible that the passage of the Civil Rights Act caused a once-and-for-all increase in the relative earnings of blacks. If this were the case, a dummy variable that takes the value 1 in 1965 (or 1964) and each year thereafter would capture the effect. Addition of such a dummy variable to the regessions does not support the hypothesis of a once-and-for-all jump in relative black earnings.

References

Akin, J. S., and Garfinkle, I. "The Quality of Education and Cohort Variation in Black-White Earnings Differentials" *AER* 70, no. 1 (March 1980): 186–91.

Ashenfelter, O. and Heckman, J. J. "Measuring the Effect of an Antidiscrimination Program," in Orley Ashenfelter and James Blum, eds. *Evaluating the Labor Market Effects of Social Programs*. Princeton: Industrial Relations Section, Princeton University, 1976.

Astin, A. *Four Critical Years*. Josey-Bass, 1978.

Bureau of National Affairs. "Equal Employment Opportunity: Programs and Results." Personnel Policies Forum Survey 112. Mar.1976.

Burman, G. "The Economics of Discrimination: The Impact of Public Policy." Ph.D. Thesis, University of Chicago, 1973.

Burstein, P. "Equal Employment Opportunity Legislation and the Income of Women and Nonwhites." Unpublished MS., Yale University, August 1978.

Butler, R., and Heckman, J. J. "Government's Impact on the Labor Market Status of Black Americans: A Critical Review," in Industrial Relations Research Association, *Equal Rights and Industrial Relations*, pp. 235–81. Wisconsin, 1977.

Duncan, O. "Inheritance of Poverty or Inheritance of Race?" in D. P. Moynihan, ed. *On Understanding Poverty*, pp. 85–110. New York: Basic Books, 1968.

Duncan, O.; Featherman, D. L.; and Duncan. B. *Socioeconomic Background and Achievement*. New York: Seminar Press, 1972.

Epstein, W. *Schooling and Occupation Decisions*. Ph.D. Thesis, Harvard University, 1977.

Farley, R., and Hermailin, A. "The 1960s: A Decade of Progress for Blacks?" *Demography* 9, no. 3 (1972): 353–70.

Freeman, R. "The Changing Labor Market for Black Americans." *Brookings Papers on Economic Activity*, 1973.

———. "Labor Market Discrimination: Analysis, Findings and Problems," in M. Intriligator and D. Kendrick, eds., *Frontiers of Quantitative Economics*, chap. 9. Amsterdam: North-Holland, 1974a.

———. "The Changing Labor Market for Minorities," in M. Gordon, ed., *Higher Education and the Labor Market*, chap. 3. N.Y.: McGraw-Hill, 1974b.

———. "Socioeconomic Mobility and Black-White Economic Differences in the New Market for Black Labor." Revision of Harvard Institute of Economic Research Study Paper No. 377, 1976.

———. *Black Elite: The New Market for Highly Qualified Black Americans*. N.Y.: McGraw-Hill, 1977a.

———. "A Premium for Black Academicians?" *Industrial and Labor Relations Review*, January 1977b.

———. "Time Series Evidence on Black Economic Progress: Shifts in Demand or in Supply?" Harvard Institute of Economic Research Discussion Paper 362, July 1978.

Goldstein, M., and Smith, R. S. "The Estimated Impact of the Anti-Discrimination Program Aimed at Federal Contractors." *Industrial and Labor Relations Review* 29 (July 1976): 523–43.

Griliches, Z. "Wages and Earnings of Very Young Men." *Journal of Political Economy*, June 1976.

Hall, R., and Kasten, R. "The Relative Occupational Success of Blacks and Whites." *Brookings Papers on Economic Activity* 3 (1973): 781–98.

Hanoch, G. "An Economic Analysis of Earnings and Schooling." *Journal of Human Resources* 2 (1967): 310–29.

Hauser, R. M., and Featherman, D. L. "Equality of Access to Schooling: Trends and Prospects." Center for Demography and Ecology Working Paper No. 75–17. Madison: University of Wisconsin, 1975a.

―――. "Racial Inequalities and Socioeconomic Achievement in the U.S., 1962–1973." Institute for Research on Poverty Discussion paper No. 275–75. Madison: University of Wisconsin, 1975b.

Heckman, J. J., and Wolpin, K. "Does the Contract Compliance Program Work? An Analysis of Chicago Data." *Industrial and Labor Relations Review* 29 (July 1976): 544–64.

Kneisser, T.; Padilla, A.; and Polachek, S. "Racial Differences in Earnings over the Business Cycle." Econometric Society Meetings, August 1978b.

―――. "The Rate of Return to Schooling over the Business Cycle" *JHR* 18, no. 2 (Spring 1978a): 264–77.

Levin, H. M. "Education and Earnings of Blacks in the Brown Decision." Stanford University, September 1978.

Lewis, W. A. "The Road to the Top is through Higher Education Not Black Studies." *New York Times Magazine*, 11 August 1969.

Masters, S. "Black-White Income Differentials," in *Empirical Studies and Policy Implementation*. Academic Press, 1975.

Meyer, R., and Wise, D. "High School Preparation and Early Labor Market Experience." MS. National Bureau of Economics Research Working Paper, 1980.

Moynihan, D. P. "The Schism in Black America." *The Public Interest*, Spring 1972, pp. 3–24.

National Science Foundation. "Characteristics of Doctoral Scientists and Engineers in the U.S." 1978.

Padilla, A. "Race and Economics: A Human Capital Inquiry." Unpublished MS.

U.S. Bureau of the Census. *Current Population Survey: Consumer Income*. Series P60. Washington, D.C., 1949–76.

―――. *Census of Population 1950: Education*. Series PL–5B. Washington, D.C., 1953.

———. *Census of Population, 1960: Occupational Characteristics*. Series PC2–7a. Washington, D.C., 1963.
———. *Statistical Abstract of the United States, 1971*. 92d Ed. Washington, D.C., 1971.
———. *Census of Population, 1970: Occupational Characteristics*. Series PC2–7B. Washington, D.C. 1973a.
———. *Current Population Reports: The Social and Economic Status of the Black Population in the U.S., 1972*. Series P–23, no. 46. Washington, D.C., 1973b.
———. *Census of Population 1970: Occupational Characteristics*. Series PC2–7A. Washington, D.C., 1973c.
U.S. Bureau of Labor Statistics. Educational Attainment of Workers. Special Labor Force Report. Washington, D.C., 1960–77.
U.S. Department of Labor. Manpower Administration. *Employment and Earnings*. Washington, D.C., January 1975.
———. *Handbook of Labor Statistics 1976*. Bulletin 1905. Washington, D.C., 1977.
———. *Career Thresholds*. Manpower Administration Research Monograph No. 16, 1978a.
———. Employment and Training Report of the President 1977. Washington, D.C., 1978b.
Viscusi, W. K. *Employment Hazards: Investigation of Market Performance*. Ph.D. Thesis, Harvard University, 1976.
Vroman, W. "Changes in Black Workers' Relative Earnings: Evidence for the 1960s," in G. Von Furstenberg, ed., *Patterns of Racial Discrimination*, vol. 11, chap. 11. Lexington, Mass.: Heath-Lexington, 1974.
Weiss, L., and Williamson, J. "Black Education, Earnings and Interregional Migration: Some New Evidence." *American Economic Review*, 62 (June 1972): 372–83.
Weiss, R. "The Effect of Education on the Earnings of Blacks and Whites." *Review of Economics and Statistics*, May 1970.
Welch, F. "Black-White Returns to Schooling." *American Economic Review* 63, no. 5 (March 1973): 893–907.
Welch, F., and Smith, J. "Black/White Male Earnings and Employment: 1960–1970." U.S. Department of Labor Publication R–1666–DOL, June 1975.

9 Risk Shifting, Statistical Discrimination, and the Stability of Earnings

Herschel I. Grossman and
Warren T. Trepeta

9.1 Introduction

This paper develops possible theoretical explanations for the observed racial differential in stability of earnings. Most research on racial factors in the labor market has focused on observed differences in the average earnings of whites and blacks in the United States. However, some authors have also recognized the existence of a racial differential in earnings stability over business cycles. For example, Wohlstetter and Coleman (1972) observe that year-to-year percentage changes in median family income and median income of persons were roughly parallel to business cycles and greater in absolute values for nonwhites than for whites from 1947 through 1967. Deviations from trend of percentage changes in median family income and median income of persons were much greater for nonwhites than for whites over that period.

In order to address these observations, this paper draws together two recent theoretical developments in labor economics: the theory of the risk-shifting function of labor contracts (see, for example, Azariadis 1975; Baily 1974; Grossman 1977; and Stiglitz 1974), and the theory of statistical discrimination (see, for example, Arrow 1972, 1973; and Phelps 1972). A central idea developed in the paper is that statistical discrimination can generate distortions in market behavior—for example, different competitive equilibria for intrinsically identical groups, as

---

Herschel I. Grossman is Professor of Economics, Brown University and Research Associate, National Bureau of Economic Research.
Warren T. Trepeta is staff economist, Federal Reserve Board, Washington, D.C.

The National Science Foundation, a W. Randolph Burgess Fellowship, and the Brookings Institution have supported this research. Dennis Carlton and James Brown have given helpful comments.

suggested by Arrow (1973) and Starrett (1976). The theoretical analysis focuses specifically on the distortions in worker behavior that can result from statistical discrimination in the market for risk-shifting arrangements, and shows how the nature of these distortions depends on interactions between the price of risk shifting and the average reliability of workers and on the presence or absence of intrinsic differences in the attitudes of different groups of workers toward reliability.

The theory of the risk-shifting function of labor contracts develops what can be denoted as a Knightian view of the entrepreneur and the firm. In this view, certain individuals, either because they are intrinsically less timid or because they have substantial wealth which facilitates asset diversification, exhibit less risk-averse behavior than the average person. The equilibrium structure of a market economy finds these individuals specializing in the entrepreneurial role, forming firms, and employing labor services. According to the theory, this systematic difference between firms and their workers with regard to risk aversion leads to long-term contractual commitments in which firms absorb risk that would otherwise be borne by workers.

Several recent papers noted above apply this view to an analysis of risk associated with variations in the value of worker output. Specifically, these papers suggest that labor contracts explicitly or implicitly involve two transactions: (1) firms pay workers for the productivity of labor services; (2) risk-averse workers purchase from less risk-averse firms insurance against fluctuations in earnings that would result, in the absence of such insurance, from variations in the value of worker output. The insurance arrangement involves (1) a premium payment by the worker, which takes the form of an excess of the value of the worker's product over his earnings when the value of his product is high; and (2) an indemnity to the worker, which takes the form of an excess of the worker's earnings over the value of his product when it is low. This arrangement shifts risk to the firm and facilitates the stabilization of worker consumption, making it unnecessary for the worker to accumulate a large store of assets for that purpose.

The point of departure for the present analysis is the observation that once the value of worker output is known, either the employer or the worker has an incentive to default on a risk-shifting agreement. If the value of worker output is low, employers can obtain short-run gains by temporarily lowering wages to take advantage of cheaper substitute labor. If the value of worker output is high, workers can make themselves better off in the short run by demanding a temporary wage increase or by quitting their jobs to take advantage of more lucrative opportunities available elsewhere. The term "reliability" refers here to an individual's propensity to forego short-run gains to comply with an existing risk-shifting agreement. The analysis below focuses on default behavior—that is, "unreliability"—on the part of workers.

In choosing between default and reliable behavior, a worker considers the short-run increase in consumption that he can obtain by defaulting and weighs it against a variety of incentives for reliability. These incentives include such factors as moral aversion to default, the value of a good reputation for reliability in facilitating future risk-shifting arrangements, and the preservation of claims to deferred compensation, such as nonvested pensions. The present paper abstracts, for simplicity, from considerations other than the moral factor. The analysis assumes, critically, that this moral aversion to default varies among workers, but that it is typically finite. Specifically, for a given high value of his product, whether a particular worker will evince reliable behavior depends on both the strength of his moral aversion to default and the terms of his existing risk-shifting arrangement, particularly the excess of the value of his product over his contractual earnings. Further research will deal with such related considerations as the effect on worker behavior of a relation between individual work history and the terms of risk-shifting arrangements, and the interplay between cyclical risk shifting, on which the present discussion focuses, and changes in productivity over the life cycle. A general point worth noting is that, mainly because of the subjective motivation aspect of labor services, these examples of incentives for reliable behavior all involve extralegal considerations.

As essential assumption for the analysis is that employers do not know the moral characteristics of individual workers and, consequently, are unable to identify and avoid hiring unreliable workers. This informational imperfection means that, in order to avoid expected losses in risk-shifting arrangements, employers can offer to absorb risk only on terms that reflect their beliefs about the proportion of workers who will behave reliably.[1]

Employers adjust these beliefs, and, thus, the terms of risk-shifting arrangements, on the basis of their actual observations of average worker reliability. However, as noted above, the terms of risk-shifting arrangements affect individual choice between reliable behavior and default. This interaction between employer beliefs and worker behavior creates a possibility for multiple competitive equilibria—that is, there may be more than one employer estimate of average reliability such that worker behavior will be induced that will confirm employer beliefs and be invulnerable to competitive attempts to increase expected profits by marginal adjustments in the terms of risk shifting.

The employers' inability to determine an individual's reliability before hiring also makes it likely that employers engage in statistical discrimination. Specifically, if workers are distinguished by characteristics that employers can observe easily, such as race and sex, and if employers believe that such identifiable groups of workers differ with respect to average reliability, competition will cause employers to take an individual's observable characteristics into account when making risk-shifting arrangements. Consequently, different identifiable groups will make risk-shifting arrangements on different terms.

Whether or not employer beliefs about the average reliability of identifiable groups are correct, describing this employer behavior as discriminatory seems appropriate because individuals who may be equally reliable receive different treatment. The use of the term "statistical" to describe discrimination in this context reflects the fact that employer behavior is based on belief in the existence of empirical correlations between reliability and the observable characteristics of workers, rather than, for example, on taste or distaste for those characteristics.

Given the interaction between employer beliefs about reliability and worker behavior, statistical discrimination generates two important implications regarding differences in the stability of earnings of different groups. First, if the market for risk-shifting arrangements possesses multiple equilibria, then even if two identifiable groups are identical with respect to the distribution of aversion to default among their members, they can exhibit persistent differences with respect to reliability, the terms on which they shift risk to employers, and stability of earnings. Second, if two identifiable groups differ with respect to the distribution of aversion to default among their members, then in equilibrium they can differ more or less with respect to actual reliability than they would if employers pooled them and absorbed risk from both groups on terms that reflected the average reliability of the two groups combined.

In what follows, section 9.2 describes a specific analytical framework. Within this framework, section 9.3 analyzes the terms of risk-shifting arrangements and the worker's choice between reliable and unreliable behavior. Section 9.4 discusses the characteristics of equilibrium in the market for risk-shifting arrangements and derives sufficient conditions for the existence of a unique equilibrium. Section 9.5 analyzes the stability properties of equilibria when multiple equilibria exist. Section 9.6 analyzes the impact of statistical discrimination on risk-shifting arrangements. Section 9.7 analyzes the implications of more sophisticated employer behavior that takes account of the influence of the terms of risk shifting on worker reliability. Section 9.8 contains a summary of the main results and briefly discusses the implications of the theoretical analysis for a program of empirical research.

9.2 Analytical Framework

Consider a labor market in which, as discussed above, employers and workers differ in their attitudes toward risk. Specifically, employers compose a large class of identical individuals who behave as if they were risk neutral. In other words, their utility is a linear function of consumption, and, thus, they are indifferent between a constant consumption stream and a fluctuating consumption stream that has the same average value. In addition, these employers have a deserved reputation for complete reliability, which means that they never fail to comply with the risk-shifting agreements that they have made.

Workers, in contrast, compose a large class of individuals whose degree of risk aversion is identical and positive. In other words, their utility is a concave function of consumption, and, thus, they prefer a constant consumption stream to a fluctuating consumption stream that has the same average value. In addition, worker utility functions reflect an exogenous moral aversion to default, which is finite, differs among individuals, and is distributed such that, given the terms on which risk shifting takes place, some workers behave reliably and some do not.

The class of workers is divisible into large groups according to observable characteristics such as race and sex. Each such group has a reputation for average reliability. The analysis in the next three sections focuses on transactions between the employers and one such group of workers. The reputation for reliability of this group is such that employers believe that a proportion $\hat{R}$ of the group will comply with the risk-shifting agreements that they make, where $0 \leq \hat{R} \leq 1$.

In order to focus on the importance of risk shifting, the analysis ignores the technological aspects of the organization of production. Such factors as the advantages of team production, firm-specific human capital, costs of adjusting employment, and mobility costs surely influence both the organization of production and the form of optimal long-term agreements between firms and workers. However, the present analysis considers only the role played by firms in absorbing risk that their employees otherwise would bear. Specifically, the analysis assumes that each individual in the economy would be equally productive whether he chose to be an independent producer, an employer, or an employee. In other words, the assumed technology makes production solely an independent activity. In addition, the analysis abstracts from interpersonal differences in productivity. Thus, the value of output is perfectly correlated across individuals.

The value of per capital output, denoted by X, is the product of the number of units of output per capita and, if this output is not directly consumed, the exchange ratio between consumption goods and produced output. Either or both of the factors in this product can be subject to variation. Specifically, assume that the actual value of X is determined at periodic intervals by serially independent drawings from an exogenously determined population. The interval between these drawings defines a unit of time. The population of X is such that

$$X = \begin{cases} X_1 \text{ with probability } \alpha_1 \\ X_2 \text{ with probability } \alpha_2 \end{cases}$$

where $X_2 > X_1 \geq 0$, $\alpha_1 + \alpha_2 = 1$, and $0 < \alpha_1 < 1$. Thus, X_2 characterizes a good state of nature and X_1 characterizes a bad state of nature. The expected value of per capita output, denoted as $\bar{X}_{av}$, is $\alpha_1 X_1 + \alpha_2 X_2$.[2]

Another convenient simplification is that individuals have no alternative uses, such as direct production of consumption goods or leisure activities, to which to devote their time. This assumption enables the analysis to avoid analyzing employment schedules, which would involve variations in the amount of time devoted to the production of marketable output, and to focus on the earnings schedules stipulated in labor contracts. Grossman (1978) analyzes the determination of employment schedules in labor contracts involving risk shifting.

9.3 The Decisions of Workers and Firms

9.3.1 The Worker Consumption Schedule

A worker consumption schedule under a risk-shifting arrangement is a vector (w_1, w_2), where $w_1(w_2)$ is the worker's earnings if X turns out to equal $X_1(X_2)$. Given (w_1, w_2), the worker receives an insurance indemnity equal to $(w_1 - X_1)$ if the bad state of nature occurs, and $\alpha_1(w_1 - X_1)$ is the worker's expected indemnity per period. Alternatively, the worker is obliged to pay an insurance premium equal to $(X_2 - w_2)$ if the good state occurs, and $\alpha_2(X_2 - w_2)$ is the worker's expected premium payment per period if he complies with the insurance arrangement. The worker's expected premium per period is zero if he is unreliable. Thus, if a worker complies with an insurance agreement, he is effectively charged, on average, a price of $\alpha_2(X_2 - w_2)/\alpha_1(w_1 - X_1)$ units of consumption in the good state per unit of indemnity consumption received in the bad state. Let Q denote this price.

A reliable worker, when entering into an employment agreement, takes Q and the distribution of X as given, and selects (w_1, w_2) to maximize expected utility $\alpha_1 u(w_1) + \alpha_2 u(w_2)$, subject to the budget constraint $Q = \alpha_2(X_2 - w_2)/\alpha_1(w_1 - X_1)$ and the nonnegativity constraints $w_1 \geq X_1$ and $w_2 \geq 0$, where $u(w)$ is the worker's concave utility function. The constraint $w_1 \geq X_1$ rules out the possibility that these individuals might try to play the entrepreneurial role, in which they have no reputation for reliability. This maximization involves the first-order condition $u'(w_1) = Qu'(w_2)$, which in turn implies worker demand schedules for consumption in the good and bad states.

For consumption in the bad state, we have $w_1 = \max [f(Q), X_1]$ and $f[u'(X_1)/u'(X_2)] = X_1, f(1) = \bar{X}$, and $f'(Q) < 0$. According to this demand schedule, as long as Q is less than the ratio of the marginal utilities of X_1 and X_2, each worker desires to reduce his risk by contracting for w_1 to exceed X_1. As Q decreases, his desired level of w_1 increases. If Q is equal to unity, he wants w_1 to equal the average value of per capital output, which, according to his budget constraint, is equivalent to making w_1 equal to w_2 and thereby avoiding all risk. As noted above, we assume that unreliable workers demand consumption in state 1 according to the same schedule.

For consumption in the good state, we have

$$w_2 = \min [g(Q), X_2] \text{ and } g[u'(X_1)/u'(X_2)] = X_2$$

$$g(1) = \bar{X}, \text{ and}$$

$$g'(Q) \gtreqless 0 \text{ as } RRA(w_1) \equiv \frac{-w_1 u''(w_1)}{u'(w_1)} \lessgtr \frac{w_1}{w_1 - X_1}$$

The variable $RRA(w_1)$ denotes the coefficient of relative risk aversion that characterizes a worker's utility function at consumption level $w_1 = f(Q)$. Note that for a decrease in Q the income and substitution effects on w_1 are both positive, whereas the income effect on w_2 is positive and the substitution effect on w_2 is negative. Consequently, the net effect of a change in Q on w_2 depends on the size of $RRA(w_1)$ relative to $w_1/(w_1 - X_1)$. This result reflects the familiar proposition that the strength of an income effect depends on the shape of the utility function and on the quantity currently demanded of the item whose price is changing. Note further that, given $x_1 > 0$, $g'(Q)$ can be negative only if $RRA(w_1)$ exceeds one.

9.3.2 The Determination of Q

Let $\hat{P}$ denote the number of units of consumption that employers expect to receive from workers in the good state of nature per unit of indemnity consumption paid out to workers in the bad state of nature. Assume, for simplicity, that $\hat{P}$ is equal to unity in competitive equilibrium. This assumption implies that aggregate worker demand for consumption in the bad state does not exceed the value of aggregate output in the bad state. See Grossman (1977) for a fuller discussion of the determination of the equilibrium price for risk shifting.

If employers expect some workers to default on a risk-shifting agreement—that is, if $\hat{R}$ is less than unity—this anticipated unreliability drives a wedge between $\hat{P}$ and Q. Specifically, given $\hat{R}$ and w_2, employers expect to receive a premium equal to $\hat{R}(X_2 - w_2)$ from a representative worker in the good state, and $\hat{R}\alpha_2(X_2 - w_2)$ is the expected premium per worker per period. Employers expect to pay indemnity equal to $(w_1 - X_1)$ per worker in the bad state, and $\alpha_1(w_1 - X_1)$ is the expected indemnity payment per worker per period. Thus,

$$Q = \frac{\alpha_2(X_2 - w_2)}{\alpha_1(w_1 - X_1)} = \frac{\hat{P}}{\hat{R}}$$

where $0 \leq \hat{R} \leq 1$. This relation indicates that, to expect a given $\hat{P}$, employers must charge workers a higher price for indemnity consumption as their estimate of worker reliability decreases. Finally, this section assumes that employers form their belief about the proportion of workers who are reliable by observing the proportion of workers who actually behave reliably, denoted by R, and that this learning process involves gradual adjustment of $\hat{R}$ in the direction of R. Section 9.7 below considers the possibility that employers take account of the fact that the terms of risk-shifting arrangements affect worker reliability.

9.3.3 The Choice between Reliability and Unreliability

As discussed above, a worker who has entered a risk-shifting arrangement has an incentive to default on the arrangement when the good state of nature occurs. Specifically, if the worker threatens to leave his employer or actually quits to work elsewhere in the good state of nature, he can obtain X_2, the full value of his product, rather than w_2, the lower consumption which he has agreed to accept under the risk-shifting arrangement. Thus, a worker who chooses default over reliable behavior obtains an increase in utility from consumption equal to $u(X_2)$ minus $u(w_2)$. However, given his moral aversion to default, if the ith worker behaves unreliably, he suffers a loss of utility, denoted by A_i with $A_i \geq 0$. Thus, assuming, for simplicity, that A_i is independent of the terms of the risk-shifting arrangement, unreliable behavior produces a net change in utility equal to $u(X_2) - u(w_2) - A_i$. A worker chooses to behave unreliably (reliably) if this net change is positive (negative or zero).

Aversion to default varies among individuals. Assuming A_i to be distributed in the worker population with cumulative distribution function $H(A_i; Z)$ where Z is a vector of parameters of the distribution function, then the aggregation of individual choices between reliability and unreliability yields the following functional relation for the proportion of workers who behave reliably:

$$R = 1 - H[u(X_2) - u(w_2); Z] \equiv R(w_2; Z)$$

For the moment, we can suppress the vector Z, which plays no role in the analysis until section 9.7. The assumption that A_i is nonnegative implies that $R(X_2) = 1$, and the nature of the cumulative distribution function and the utility function implies that $R'(w_2) \geq 0$. Finally, fairly weak restrictions on the form of $H(A_i)$—for example, uniformity or approximate normality—imply that $R''(w_2) \leq 0$, either everywhere or at least for sufficiently high values of w_2.

9.4 Equilibrium in the Risk-Shifting Market

Informational equilibrium involves a value of $\hat{P}$ equal to unity, and an employer estimate of worker reliability and a corresponding vector of worker consumption that induces worker default behavior that confirms employers' beliefs concerning reliability. Thus, an informational-equilibrium vector of worker consumption has the property that (w_1, w_2) maximizes worker utility, given Q, where $Q = 1/\hat{R}$, and $\hat{R} = R(w_2)$. An informational equilibrium is also a competitive equilibrium if it is invulnerable to attempts by employers to increase expected profits by experimenting with marginal adjustments in Q.

Figure 9.1 depicts one example in which the market for risk-shifting arrangements possesses a unique informational equilibrium, which is also a competitive equilibrium. The locus labeled $R = R(w_2)$ depicts the relevant segment of the functional relation between actual worker reliability and consumption in the good state. As indicated above, the depiction of

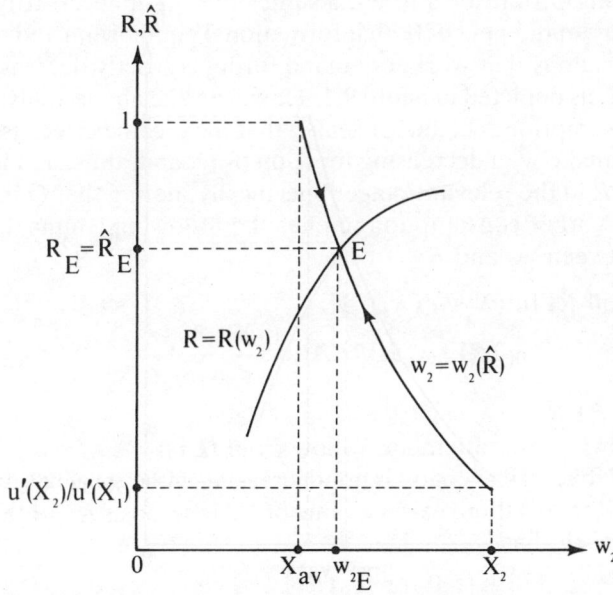

Figure 9.1 Unique Equilibrium. $w_2'(\hat{R}) < 0$ for all $R \in [u'(X_2)/u'(X_1), 1]$

this segment as concave seems reasonable. The locus labeled $w_2 = w_2(\hat{R})$ represents the relation between worker demand for consumption in the good state and the estimate of worker reliability held by employers, for all $\hat{R} \varepsilon [u'(X_2)/u'(X_1), 1]$—that is, for all $Q \varepsilon [1, u'(X_1)/u'(X_2)]$. As depicted in this example, the negative slope of this locus implies that the negative substitution effect on w_2 of an increase in $\hat{R}$ (decreases in Q) outweighs the positive income effect.

Point E in figure 9.1 represents competitive equilibrium. At point E, $\hat{R}$ equals $\hat{R}_E$ and workers choose to receive consumption w_{2E} in the good state. Note that consumption in the bad state, w_{1E}, can be calculated by substituting the coordinates of point E into the worker's budget constraint. At point E, the locus $w_2 = w_2(\hat{R})$ intersects the locus $R = R(w_2)$ indicating that w_{2E} induces a proportion of workers R_E to behave reliably, such that $R_E = \hat{R}_E$, thereby confirming employer beliefs concerning reliability.

If, either as an initial condition or as a result of employer experimentation, $\hat{R} \neq \hat{R}_E$, workers choose $w_2 \neq w_{2E}$. These values of w_2 induce values of R, according to the schedule $R = R(w_2)$, such that $R \neq \hat{R}$. Consequently, employers revise R, in accordance with the assumed learning process. This learning process moves the system toward point E along the locus $w_2 = w_2(\hat{R})$, as indicated by arrows attached to that locus.

An essential question is whether informational equilibrium and competitive equilibrium in this market generally are unique. Given that R is nondecreasing with respect to w_2, a sufficient, but unnecessarily strong, condition for uniqueness of both informational equilibrium and competitive equilibrium is that worker demand for w_2 is strictly decreasing with respect to R, as depicted in figure 9.1. However, the above analysis of the worker consumption schedule revealed that the income effect associated with Q can make w_2 a decreasing function of Q, and, thus, an increasing function of $\hat{R}$ in the relevant range. Specifically, noting that $Q = 1/\hat{R}$, the analysis of worker consumption implies the following lemma about the relation between w_2 and $\hat{R}$:

(L1) For all $\hat{R} \varepsilon [u'(X_2)/u'(X_1), 1]$

$$w_2'(\hat{R}) \gtreqless 0 \text{ as } RRA(w_1) \gtreqless \frac{w_1}{w_1 - X_1}$$

where $w_1 = f(1/\hat{R})$.

The following useful lemmas follow from (L1).

(L2) If relative risk aversion is nondecreasing with respect to consumption, then either (a) there exists a value of $\hat{R}$, denoted as $\hat{R}^*$, $\hat{R}^* \varepsilon [u'(X_2)/u'(X_1), 1]$, such that

$$w_2'(\hat{R}) \begin{cases} >0 \text{ for } \hat{R} \varepsilon (\hat{R}^*, 1] \\ =0 \text{ for } \hat{R} = \hat{R}^* \\ <0 \text{ for } \hat{R} \varepsilon [u'(X_2)/u'(X_1), \hat{R}^*) \end{cases}$$

or (b) $w_2'(\hat{R}) < 0$ for all $\hat{R} \varepsilon [u'(X_2)/u'(X_1), 1]$.

(L3) If relative risk aversion is nondecreasing with respect to consumption, then

$$w_2'(\hat{R}) < 0 \text{ for all } \hat{R} \text{ for which } w_2(\hat{R}) \varepsilon (\bar{X}, X_2)$$

To understand L2 and L3, recall that $w_2[u'(X_2)/u'(X_1)]$ equals X_2, whereas $w_2(1)$ equals $\bar{X}$, which is less than X_2. Therefore, for some values of $\hat{R} \varepsilon [u'(X_2)/u'(X_1), 1]$, the substitution effect of an increase in $\hat{R}$ on w_2 must dominate the income effect, implying that $w_2'(\hat{R})$ is negative. Furthermore, if relative risk aversion is constant or increasing, the income effect is always increasing in size relative to the substitution effect. Thus, there can exist at most one value of $\hat{R}$, denoted by $\hat{R}^*$, for which the two effects are exactly offsetting and for which $w_2'(\hat{R})$ equals zero. Moreover, the substitution effect dominates and $w_2'(\hat{R})$ is negative for all $\hat{R} \varepsilon [u'(X_2)/u'(X_1), \hat{R}^*)$, whereas the income effect dominates and $w_2'(\hat{R})$ is positive for all values of $\hat{R}$ above $\hat{R}^*$. Furthermore, since $w_2(1)$ equals $\bar{X}$, $w_2'(\hat{R}) \geq 0$ implies $w_2(\hat{R}) \leq \bar{X}$.

Taken together, L1, L2, and L3 imply proposition P1 about equilibrium in the market for risk-shifting arrangements.

(P1) Nondecreasing relative risk aversion is a sufficient condition for uniqueness of informational and competitive equilibrium in conjunction with either of the following conditions:

(a) $RRA(\bar{X}) \leq \bar{X}/(\bar{X} - X_1)$ or

(b) $R(\bar{X}) \leq u'(X_2)/u'(X_1)$

To understand the first part of P1, recall that when $\hat{R}$ equals one, workers select the consumption schedule $(w_1, w_2) = (\bar{X}, \bar{X})$. Thus, according to L1, the sign of $w_2'(\hat{R})$ at $\hat{R} = 1$ depends on the value of $RRA(\bar{X})$. Specifically, if $RRA(\bar{X})$ is less than (equal to) $\bar{X}/(\bar{X} - X_1)$, then $w_2'(\hat{R})$ is negative (zero) when $\hat{R}$ equals one. If, in addition, relative risk aversion is nondecreasing, then, by L2, $w_2'(\hat{R})$ is negative for $\hat{R} \varepsilon [u'(X_2)/u'(X_1), 1)$.

To understand the second part of P1, refer to figure 9.2. The locus labeled $w_2 = w_2(\hat{R})$ again depicts the demand for w_2. The shape of this locus reflects two assumptions: (1) Relative risk aversion is nondecreasing, implying, by L3, that the demand locus is negatively sloped for $w_2 \varepsilon (\bar{X}, X_2)$; (2) $RRA(\bar{X}) > \bar{X}/(\bar{X} - X_1)$, implying, by L2, that the demand locus has a positive slope for $\hat{R} \varepsilon (\hat{R}^*, 1]$. The locus labeled $R = R(w_2)$ again depicts the relevant segment of the reliability function. If, as shown, $R(\bar{X}) \leq u'(X_2)/u'(X_1)$, then the reliability function necessarily lies below the locus $w_2 = w_2(\hat{R})$ for $w_2 \leq \bar{X}$. Furthermore, since the reliability function is nondecreasing on the interval $(\bar{X}, X_2)$, whereas the demand locus is negatively sloped on this interval, the two loci intersect once and only once at point E.

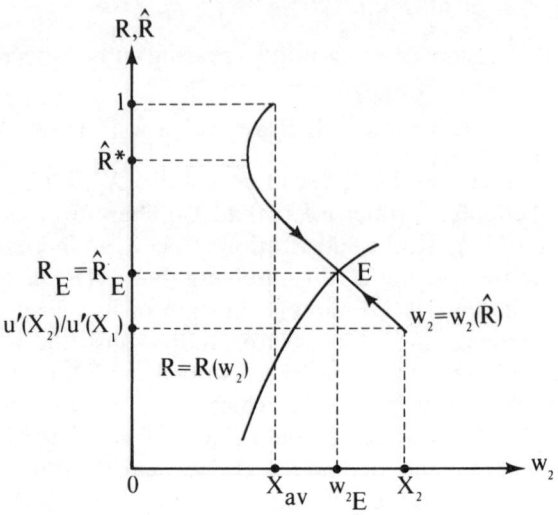

Figure 9.2 Unique Equilibrium, $R(\overline{X}) < u'(X_2)/u'(X_1)$

The analysis of worker consumption also implies proposition P2 about equilibrium.

(P2) The following condition is sufficient for uniqueness of informational and competitive equilibrium:

$$R'(w_2) \le \frac{R}{X_2 - w_2} \text{ for all } w_2 \varepsilon [0, X_2]$$

This condition says that worker reliability decreases slowly as w_2 falls from X_2 to zero. To understand P2, note that, given this restriction on the reliability function, the existence of more than one equilibrium would imply that worker demand for w_1 remains constant or increases with respect to its relative price Q, for some range of Q less than $u'(X_1)/u'(X_2)$. However, the income and substitution effects of an increase in Q both serve to reduce worker demand for w_1.

9.5 Dynamics of the Market for Risk Shifting in the Presence of Multiple Equilibria

The results of the previous section imply that if the market for risk-shifting arrangements exhibits multiple informational and competitive equilibria, then all of the following conditions hold:

(a) The demand for w_2 is not strictly decreasing for $\hat{R} \varepsilon [u'(X_2)/u'(X_1), 1]$,

(b) $R'(w_2) > R/(X_2 - w_2)$ for some $w_2 \in [0, X_2]$, and

(c) $R(\bar{X}) > u'(X_2)/u'(X_1)$, if relative risk aversion is nondecreasing with respect to consumption.

The analysis in this section assumes that these conditions hold and focuses on the stability properties of informational equilibria and the relation between informational equilibrium and competitive equilibrium.

Figure 9.3 depicts a situation in which the market for risk-shifting arrangements possesses three informational equilibria. If $\hat{R}$ initially equals $\hat{R}_E$, $\hat{R}_F$, or $\hat{R}_G$, then worker behavior confirms employer beliefs concerning reliability, and the market remains in informational equilibrium at point E, F, or G, respectively. As in earlier figures, arrows attached to the locus labeled $w_2 = w_2(\hat{R})$ indicate the direction in which learning moves the market along this locus.

The informational equilibrium at point F is locally unstable. Specifically, if $\hat{R}$ is marginally greater than $\hat{R}_F$ initially, then $R > \hat{R}$, and learning moves the market away from point F toward point E. Alternatively, if $\hat{R}$ is marginally less than $\hat{R}_F$ initially, then $R < \hat{R}$, and learning moves the market away from point F toward point G.

Because informational equilibrium at point F is locally unstable, it is not a competitive equilibrium. Specifically, it is vulnerable to individual firms' experimentation with a value of $\hat{R}$ that is marginally greater than

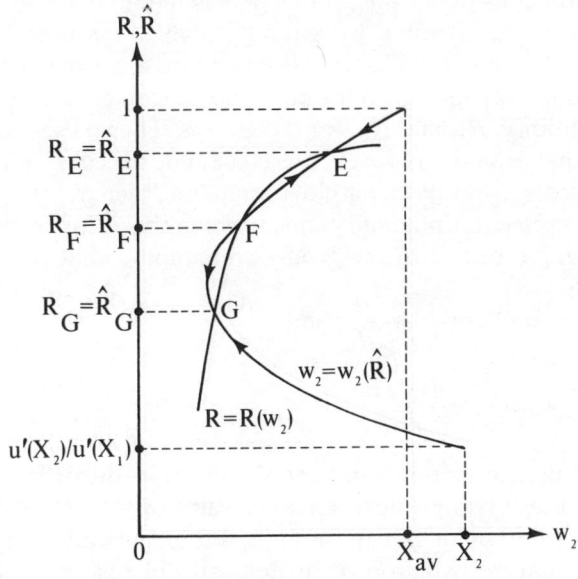

Figure 9.3   Multiple Equilibria

$\hat{R}_F$. Suppose that $\hat{R}$ were to equal $\hat{R}_F$ initially, yielding informational equilibrium at point F. If a firm were then to experiment with a slightly higher $\hat{R}$ and a correspondingly lower price of indemnity consumption, it would (1) find $R > \hat{R}$; (2) earn positive profits; and (3) attract workers away from other firms. All firms would have an incentive to raise $\hat{R}$ and lower Q. Thus, experimentation of the sort described would move the market toward point E.

The informational equilibria at points E and G are locally stable, and thus are competitive equilibria. Specifically, they are vulnerable to neither learning on the part of employers nor to marginal experimentation by individual employers.

Points E and G, however, are not globally stable. Moreover, the competitive equilibrium at point G is vulnerable to experimentation with much different beliefs by firms. Specifically, if the market were initially in competitive equilibrium at point G, and if firms were to experiment with values of $\hat{R}$ other than $\hat{R}_G$ but less than $\hat{R}_F$, worker behavior would disconfirm beliefs and learning would return the market to competitive equilibrium at G. However, if firms were to experiment with values of $\hat{R}$ greater than $\hat{R}_F$, they would attract workers away from other firms and learning would move the market toward competitive equilibrium at point E.

9.6 Statistical Discrimination

This section considers transactions between employers and two large groups of workers, denoted by W and B, which, as noted above, are distinguished by an easily observable characteristic, such as race. Statistical discrimination means that employers form separate estimates of average reliability, $\hat{R}_W$ and $\hat{R}_B$, for the groups. The analysis assumes, for simplicity, that employers revise these estimates according to the same learning process. Moreover, employers equate $\hat{P}$ across groups by charging a group a price for indemnity consumption that is inversely related to the employers' estimate of the group's reliability—that is,

$$Q_W = \frac{\hat{P}}{\hat{R}_W} = \frac{1}{\hat{R}_W} \text{ and}$$

$$Q_B = \frac{\hat{P}}{\hat{R}_B} = \frac{1}{\hat{R}_B}$$

Statistical discrimination can have the effect of distorting the market behavior of these two groups, but the nature of the possible distortion depends on whether or not the groups are intrinsically different. One possibility is that the two groups are identical with respect to the distribution of aversion to default among their members. In this case, given the assumption that all workers have the same degree of risk aversion, if employers do not engage in statistical discrimination, but instead charge all workers the same Q based on the average reliability of the total labor force, or if the market for risk shifting has a unique competitive equilibrium, the observed behavior of the two groups in this market in competitive equilibrium will be indistinguishable. However, if multiple competitive equilibria are possible and if employers practice statistical discrimination, then, depending on initial conditions, the two groups in competitive equilibrium can exhibit different average reliability, shift risk to employers on different terms, and experience different stability of earnings, even though they possess the same propensity to default for a given w_2. For example, referring to figure 9.3, if $\hat{R}_W > \hat{R}_F$ and $\hat{R}_B < \hat{R}_F$ initially, then group W attains the superior competitive equilibrium at point E while group B attains the inferior competitive equilibrium at point G. Furthermore, group B can move to E only if firms undertake major experiments with $\hat{R}_B > \hat{R}_F$.

An alternative possibility is that groups W and B actually differ with respect to the distribution of aversion to default among their members. Specifically, let K be a positive constant, and assume that,

$$R_B(w_2) = R_W(w_2) - K$$

In this case, if employers do not engage in statistical discrimination, both W and B workers select the same w_2, and the difference between R_W and R_B equals K. However, if employers practice statistical discrimination, the behavior of the two groups in competitive equilibrium can differ by more or less than K. Figures 9.4 and 9.5 illustrate these possibilities. Both diagrams assume that competitive equilibrium is unique.

In figure 9.4, competitive equilibrium for both groups occurs where w_2 is increasing with respect to $\hat{R}$. In this case, the difference between R_W and R_B is R_{EW} minus R_{EB}, which is clearly greater than K. Statistical discrimination magnifies the exogenous behavioral differences between groups.

In figure 9.5, competitive equilibrium for both groups occurs where w_2 is decreasing with respect to $\hat{R}$. In this case, the difference between R_W and R_B is clearly smaller than K. Statistical discrimination narrows the differences between groups. Furthermore, in both this case and the previous case, given K, the absolute magnitude of the difference between K and R_{EW} minus R_{EB} is greater as reliability is more responsive to changes in w_2, and as worker demand for w_2 is more sensitive to changes in $\hat{R}$.

9.7 More Sophisticated Employer Strategy

The preceding analysis assumes that employers do not take account of the dependence of worker reliability on the terms of risk-shifting arrangements. In other words, employers behave as if R were an exogenous

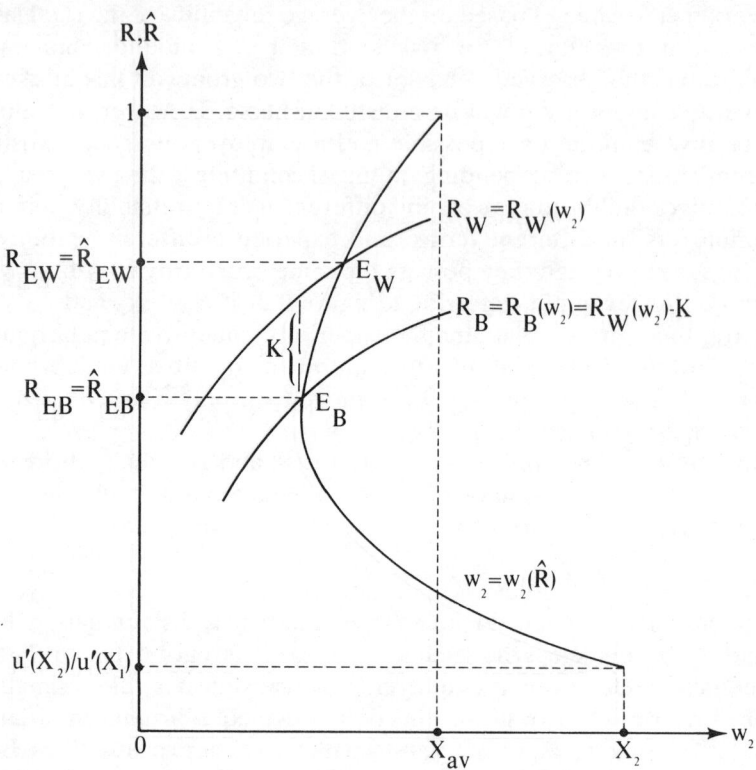

Figure 9.4 Statistical Discrimination Magnifies Differences between Groups

variable, rather than determined by the function $R(w_2;Z)$. However, such simplistic behavior may not be realistic. After witnessing changes in worker reliability that are positively correlated with changes in w_2, employers would tend to realize that R is endogenous and to adopt a more sophisticated strategy for setting Q that takes account of the functional dependence of R on w_2.

This section analyzes the implications of such a strategy. However, in order to retain an element of informational imperfection, the analysis allows the employers to be less than fully informed about the relation between R and w_2. This possible ignorance is embodied in an implicit belief, denoted by $\hat{Z}$, about the vector of parameters Z that describe the distribution of aversion to default. Thus, the employers' estimate of average reliability is given by

$$\hat{R} = R(w_2; \hat{Z})$$

In addition, the analysis assumes that employers revise their beliefs about the distribution of aversion to default in response to any observed error in their estimate of average reliability, and that this learning process involves adjustment of $\hat{Z}$ toward Z in response to any discrepancy between R and $\hat{R}$. Note that this learning process need not produce full information concerning the relation between R and w_2. Because $R(w_2;\hat{Z})$ is not a one-for-one function of $\hat{Z}$, for any given value of w_2, equality between $R(w_2;\hat{Z})$ and $R(w_2;Z)$ does not imply that $\hat{Z}$ is equal to Z. (See Trepeta 1981 for a fuller discussion of this problem as well as the other issues raised in this section.)

The main behavioral consequence of employers' taking account of the dependence of R on w_2 is that they do not allow workers to choose any amount of indemnity for the bad state at a fixed level of Q. Instead, employers offer workers a schedule of quantity and price given by the functional relation

$$Q = 1/R(w_2;\hat{Z}) \equiv Q(w_2;\hat{Z}) \text{ with } Q'(w_2;\hat{Z}) \leq 0$$

The worker, when entering into an employment agreement, takes this relation between Q and w_2 as given. Thus, the worker's problem now is to

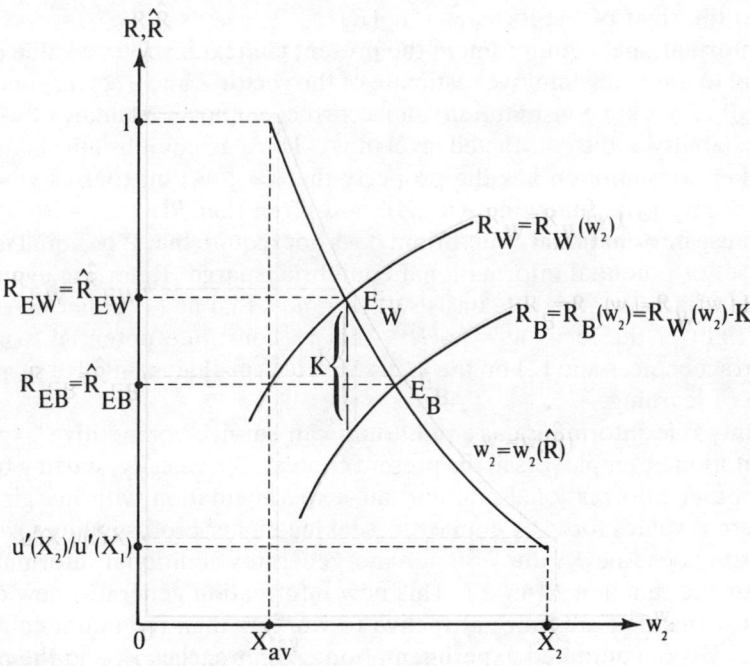

Figure 9.5 Statistical Discrimination Narrows Differences between Groups

choose (w_1, w_2) to maximize $\alpha_1 u(w_1) + \alpha_2 u(w_2)$, subject to the budget constraint $Q(w_2; \hat{Z}) = \alpha_2(X_2 - w_2)/\alpha_1(w_1 - X_1)$, and the nonnegativity constraints $w_1 \geq X_1$ and $w_2 \geq 0$.

This maximization involves the first-order condition

$$u'(w_1) = \frac{Q(w_2; \hat{Z}) \, u'(w_2)}{1 + (X_2 - w_2) Q'(w_2; \hat{Z})/Q(w_2; \hat{Z})}$$

If, as in the analysis of the preceding sections, employers were to set Q independently of w_2, the worker would treat Q' as being equal to zero, and this first-order condition would reduce to the first-order condition of section 9.3, $u'(w_1) = Q u'(w_2)$. However, in the present context, when employers adjust Q to allow for the effect of w_2 on R, the worker takes $Q'(w_2; \hat{Z})$ to be negative. In that case, the worker chooses (w_1, w_2) such that $u'(w_1)$ is larger than $Q(w_2; \hat{Z}) \, u'(w_2)$. In other words, if the purchase of an additional unit of indemnity raises the price of all intramarginal units, the marginal cost of indemnity for the individual worker exceeds its price. Consequently, the worker would associate with a chosen value of Q a lower value of w_1, and a higher value of w_2, than he would choose for that value of Q if Q were independent of w_2.[3] Referring to earlier diagrams, worker choices in the present context can occur anywhere on or to the right of the locus $w_2 = w_2(\hat{R})$.

Informational equilibrium in the present context involves a value of $\hat{P}$ equal to unity, an employer estimate of the vector Z and a corresponding vector of worker consumption, and a correct employer estimate of worker reliability at the contracted level of w_2. Thus, an equilibrium vector of worker consumption has the property that (w_1, w_2) maximizes worker utility given the function $Q(w_2; \hat{Z})$, and given that $R(w_2; \hat{Z}) = R(w_2; Z)$. Because informational equilibrium does not require that $\hat{Z}$ be equal to Z, the set of potential informational equilibria is large. Referring again to earlier diagrams, this set consists of all points that lie (1) either on or to the right of the locus $w_2 = w_2(\hat{R})$—that is, constitute potential worker contract choices and (2) on the locus $R = R(w_2)$—that is, involve suspension of learning.

Only one informational equilibrium can survive competitive experimentation by employers in the present context. Specifically, starting from any other informational equilibrium, experimentation with marginally different values for $\hat{Z}$ by employers seeking higher profits induces workers to choose new values for w_2 and generates additional information about the function $R(w_2; Z)$. This new information generates new contract forms that are more attractive to workers than the initial equilibrium. Given continued experimentation, $\hat{Z}$ approaches Z, and the market converges to the unique competitive equilibrium, which involves the vector of worker consumption that maximizes worker utility subject to the full information price schedule $Q(w_2;Z)$. When the market reaches competitive equilibrium, employers may not have full knowledge about the vector Z; they may, therefore, undertake some further experimentation. However, additional information about Z would not generate new contract forms more attractive to workers than the contract at competitive equilibrium.

9.8 Summary and Implications for Empirical Research

This paper has analyzed the stability of workers' earnings in a context where employers, who are less risk averse than workers, absorb from workers risk that is associated with fluctuations in the value of worker product. The terms on which employers stabilize workers' earnings depend on employers' estimates of worker reliability, which is defined as the propensity of workers to comply with risk-shifting agreements that they make. The analysis has assumed that employers adjust their estimates of worker reliability if new observations on reliability disconfirm prior beliefs. In addition, the analysis has assumed that worker reliability depends on the terms of risk-shifting arrangements, as well as on workers' exogenous attitudes toward default on contractual commitments. A basic result is that the two-way interaction between employer beliefs and worker reliability can generate multiple informational equilibria—that is, more than one employer estimate of worker reliability can be self-confirming. However, in order for more than one equilibrium to be competitive—that is, invulnerable to individual firms' competitive experimentation with marginally different beliefs—employers must behave as if worker reliability is exogenous, and the degree of worker risk aversion and the distribution of aversion to default must obey specific restrictions.

An important implication of this result is that, if employers engage in statistical discrimination, identifiable worker groups that are identical with respect to risk aversion and the distribution of attitudes toward default among their members can exhibit different reliability and experience different stability of earnings in competitive equilibrium, simply because employers initially believe that the groups differ with respect to reliability. However, the nature of the necessary conditions suggests that such an outcome is unlikely. Nevertheless, even if intrinsically identical groups approach the same competitive equilibrium, a historical legacy of discrimination could persist for many years. Specifically, the speed with which groups approach competitive equilibrium depends on such factors as the frequency with which new data on reliability become available to employers, which depends in turn on the frequencies of industry-specific and general business cycles. Discrimination in the market for risk-shifting arrangements could take decades to disappear because cycles in demand have a duration of many months.

The analysis has also shown that statistical discrimination can either magnify or narrow intrinsic behavioral differences between groups. Specifically, if identifiable groups of workers differ with respect to the distribution of aversion to default among their members, then they will exhibit different average reliability when allowed to enter risk-shifting arrangements on the same terms. However, if employers absorb risk from the groups on different terms, on the basis of a belief that the groups differ with respect to reliability, the reliability differentials between groups in competitive equilibrium may be greater than, equal to, or less than those that would exist in the absence of statistical discrimination.

The foregoing analysis suggests that if statistical discrimination by employers in the market for risk-shifting arrangements contributes to the racial differential in stability of earnings, and if employers' beliefs about worker reliability are correct, then whites behave more reliably on average than blacks. A basic test of the theory would be to determine whether such a difference in reliability actually exists, in the form of a racial differential in the quit rate in periods of high aggregate demand. Unfortunately, accessible data do not readily provide evidence on this issue. However, work on this question continues and some tentative inferences from the data may be possible.

The preceding analysis shows that average reliability differences between worker groups could result either from intrinsic differences in the distribution of attitudes toward default or from initial differences in employer beliefs about reliability. If reliability differences do exist, another important and difficult empirical problem would be to determine the source of these differences.

Notes

1. If unreliable workers were naive, they might reveal their intention to pay nothing for indemnity income by seeking agreements that provide very large earnings when the value of worker product is low. In contrast, the present discussion implicitly assumes that unreliable workers demand indemnity income as if they plan to act reliably, dissembling their true intentions in order to avoid exclusion from risk-shifting arrangements. For a further discussion of dissembling behavior, see Grossman (1979).

2. The analysis also assumes that consumption goods and produced output are the only commodities in the economy. Specifically, there are no investment goods, and neither consumption goods nor produced output is storable. These assumptions imply that, in aggregate, current consumption is equal to the value of current output, and that, in aggregate, the economy cannot smooth out its consumption stream by varying either its accumulation of investment goods or its commodity inventories. Allowing for either invest-

ment goods or commodity inventories would make the analysis both more realistic and more complex, but would probably not change the main conclusions regarding the market for risk-shifting arrangements.

3. Jaffee and Russell (1976) use a similar framework to analyze the terms of loan agreements in a competitive credit market. In their model, lenders expect the default rate among borrowers to be positively related to the amount owed, and they make the interest rate an increasing function of the amount owed. Consequently, the actual loan size associated with any interest rate is smaller than borrowers would demand if they could obtain loans of any size at that interest rate. Jaffee and Russell denote this outcome as "credit rationing." Moreover, Jaffee and Russell assume that lenders know precisely the relation between the default rate and the terms of loan agreements. The present discussion extends their analysis to allow for the possibility that imperfect lender (employer) understanding of borrower (worker) default behavior can generate multiple informational equilibria.

Comment   Dennis W. Carlton

This is an interesting and instructive paper. It combines ideas from the literature on statistical discrimination with those from the literature on contracts. It also makes some headway in analyzing the important issue of default behavior. A major finding of the paper is that the existence of multiple equilibria could help explain the lower earnings of blacks relative to whites.

The paper makes very simple assumptions. Such an approach has both virtues and costs. One virtue is that the essential ideas can be presented clearly and quickly. One cost is the possibility that relaxation of some of the assumptions could fundamentally alter some of the model's conclusions.

Some of the assumptions could probably be relaxed without changing the main results of the model, though the model would become more complicated. For example, firms could be allowed to "cheat" workers through layoffs when the value of the marginal product of a worker fell below price. Firms and workers could acquire reputations for reliability. I suspect that the better the information the less likely multiple equilibria become. Firms could require advance payments (or investment in job-specific skills) to be returned only to nonquitting workers. If the worker's loss from quitting always equals or exceeds the wage gain from quitting, no contracts will be broken. I believe that these relaxations can be made in such a way as to make the model more realistic but still allow for (though reduce) the possibility of multiple equilibria.

My main criticism is that the paper emphasizes the case where firms take quit rates as independent of the wage. Even in the simple model in the first part of the paper this assumption cannot hold exactly; otherwise unreliable workers would choose as high a payoff as possible in the

Dennis W. Carlton is Professor of Economics, University of Chicago Law School.

favorable state and as low a payoff as possible in the state in which they quit. The authors rule out this case by assumption—but it is clearly awkward to maintain on the one hand that firms do not realize that wages are correlated with quit rates but on the other hand that unreliable workers do not choose high payoffs in the good state and low payoffs in the bad state because firms will use wage choices to infer quit probabilities (i.e., reliability).

Assuming that firms do not realize that wage rates affect the behavior of labor supply strikes me as unrealistic. If firms realize that the supply of labor depends on wages they offer, then the problem of characterizing equilibrium reduces to the problem of choosing wages w_1 and w_2 so as to maximize expected utility subject to the budget constraint

$$\alpha_1(w_1 - X_1) + \alpha_2 R(w_2)(w_2 - X_2) = 0$$

where α_i = probability of state i, w_i = wage paid in state i, X_i = amount produced in state i, and $R(w_2)$ = probability that a worker quits in unfavorable state given a wage w_2. In this formulation, firms recognize that the quit rate R will change as wage w_2 changes. The budget constraint guarantees zero expected profits for firms. The equilibrium (w_1, w_2) will be a tangency—in (w_1, w_2) space—between the indifference curves and the budget constraint. It is a simple exercise to show under the assumptions of the model that along an indifference surface $d^2w_2/dw_1^2 > 0$, while along the budget constraint $d^2w_2/dw_1^2 < 0$. This means that there can be at most one tangency between the indifference curves and the budget constraint—hence we obtain a unique equilibrium. The possibility of explaining black-white earning differentials as arising from multiple equilibria vanishes. I find it disturbing that relaxing what appears to be an overly restrictive assumption fundamentally changes one of the model's results.

I therefore doubt that much of the black-white earnings inequality can be attributed to the multiple equilibria story. Nevertheless the model is a rich one with many empirical applications. For example, the model makes predictions about the relation of wage rates and reliability, and about quit rates in booms. I would encourage the authors to analyze these issues with their insightful model.

References

Azariadis, C. "Implicit Contracts and Underemployment Equilibria." *Journal of Political Economy* 83 (December 1975): 1183–1202.

Arrow, K. "Models of Job Discrimination," in A. H. Pascal, ed., *Racial Discrimination in Economic Life*, pp. 83–102. Lexington, Mass.: Heath, 1972.

———. "The Theory of Discrimination," in O. Ashenfelter and A. Rees, eds., *Discrimination in Labor Markets*. Princeton, N.J.: Princeton University Press, 1973.

Baily, M. N. "Wages and Employment under Uncertain Demand." *Review of Economic Studies* 41 (January 1974): 37–50.

Grossman, H. I. "Risk Shifting and Reliability in Labor Markets." *Scandinavian Journal of Economics* 79, No. 2 (1977): 187–209.

———. "Risk Shifting, Layoffs, and Seniority." *Journal of Monetary Economics* 4 (November 1978): 661–686.

———. "Adverse Selection, Dissembling, and Competitive Equilibrium." *Bell Journal of Economics* 10 (Spring 1979): 336–343.

Jaffee, D. M., and Russell, T. "Imperfect Information, Uncertainty, and Credit Rationing." *Quarterly Journal of Economics* 90, (November 1976): 651–66.

Phelps, E. S. "The Statistical Theory of Racism and Sexism." *American Economic Review* 62 (September 1972): 659–61.

Starrett, D. "Social Institutions, Imperfect Information, and the Distribution of Income." *Quarterly Journal of Economics* 90 (May 1976): 261–84.

Stiglitz, J. "Incentives and Risk Sharing in Sharecropping." *Review of Economic Studies* 41 (April 1974): 219–55.

Trepeta, W. T. "Reliability and the Racial Differential in Income Stability." Ph.D. Thesis, Brown University, 1981.

Wohlstetter, A., and Coleman, S. "Racial Differences in Income," in A. H. Pascal, ed., *Racial Discrimination in Economic Life*, pp. 3–81. Lexington, Mass.: Heath, 1972.

10 Signaling, Screening, and Information

Michael Spence

10.1 Introduction

In the past seven years, a variety of models that focus upon the informational aspects of labor markets have been developed. The starting premise of most of these models is that while individuals differ in their abilities with respect to various kinds of jobs, these differences are not immediately evident to the employer, either at the time of hiring, or even soon thereafter. Jobs and income are allocated on the basis of imperfect indicators or surrogates for productive capability or potential. Education has been the focus of much of the discussion, it being one of the bases for entry into job categories and for salary levels. There are, however, other potential sources of information about employees in labor markets. Previous work history, previous salary, the very fact that an individual is in a particular labor market, criminal and service records, medical history are all potential sources of information.

The collection of models is variously referred to as signaling and screening. The literature in the area of signaling attempts several objectives. One is the construction of rigorous models in which the equilibrium content of a potential signal is explained and explored. A second is the identification of the implications of the existence of signaling for market performance and the allocation of individual resources. A third consists of an attempt to identify the empirical magnitude of the signaling effects, if any, especially with respect to education. A fourth area concerns the concept of equilibrium that is employed and some related problems with the existence of equilibria. A fifth broad area deals with the policy implications of signaling and screening. These may include discrimina-

Michael Spence is Professor of Economics, Harvard University.

tion, job mobility, efficiency in the area of education, aspects of the problem sometimes (and misleadingly) referred to as privacy, the effects of training programs, and licensure.

The goals of this paper are to survey and extend in certain areas the analysis of signaling and screening. Except in the earlier sections which are expository, I have tried to set out versions of the models that would lend themselves to empirical testing and the application of data. I have also attempted to explore in a limited way the implications of results of regressions of earnings on education and "ability," depending upon assumptions about the underlying structure of the model. The paper tries to present a more complete and balanced view of the welfare aspects of signaling. Later sections discuss, sometimes briefly, some of the policy areas that I mentioned above. Conclusions must be tentative, as the empirical work upon which the policy implications are partially based is not yet complete. I am afraid that this latter discussion may appear rather disjointed, perhaps a necessary consequence of the state of development of the subject.

10.2 The Signaling Model and Alternatives

Let me begin by reviewing a variety of models that are in some sense competitive hypotheses. It is convenient to do this with numerical examples, leaving to a later section the problem of putting the models in an empirically more usable form. The main point of this analysis is to convey the idea that at least three rather different models have very similar-looking equilibria, and that, using data one can reasonably be expected to have, they are difficult to distinguish. They differ not in their predictions about resource allocation, but rather in the welfare implications of the pattern of resource allocation that develops. What appears below are three polar cases, the signaling model, the rationing model, and the human capital model. It is possible to have a debate about whether these terms have been used historically to refer to the phenomena I have in mind, and it might be fairer to refer to them as A, B, and C. Those who find the terms misleading can so translate.

Let us assume that there are two groups of people in an employable population. The people have different productivities in different jobs. Each group can invest in education. The costs, monetary and psychic, of education differ from the two groups. For group 1, e years of education cost $c_1 e$ dollars. For group 2, the cost is $c_2 e$ dollars. It is assumed that $c_2 < c_1$. The proportion of people in group 1 is a_1. The proportion in group 2 is $a_2 = 1 - a_1$. Let us assume that there are two jobs. Let $f_{ij}(e)$ be the productivity of some of group i in job j with education e. There are a variety of assumptions that one can make about the magnitudes of the $f_{ij}(e)$. These will appear in the sequence of models that follow. In fact, this is what distinguishes the models from each other.

The models have certain assumptions in common. Employers observe education, but not productivity, directly, and make job decisions on the basis of education. People of a given level of education are offered the job where their expected productivity is highest. Further, they are offered a salary equal to their expected productivity, conditional on the education level. Finally, these expected productivities are accurate. That is to say, the salaries at each education level correspond exactly to the average productivity of people in that education group. Individuals optimally invest in education, given the costs and the above-mentioned salary and job offers. These investment decisions determine the average productivities for each education level, which in turn determine the job and salary offers. I shall assume that individuals maximize income net of signaling costs. Preferences with respect to jobs are ignored, though their introduction would produce no qualitative changes in the results. These then are the common features of the models.

10.2.1 Pure Signaling

Assume that $f_{ij}(e)$ does not depend upon e and further that $f_{i1} = f_{i2} = f_i$ for groups $i = 1, 2$. Define e^* to be a number which satisfies the inequalities

(1) $$\frac{f_2 - f_1}{c_1} < e^* < \frac{f_2 - f_1}{c_2}$$

Here, it is assumed that $f_2 > f_1$, and that $c_2 < c_1$. The equilibrium in the model is as follows. The salary offer is f_1 if $e < e^*$, and f_2 if $e \geq e^*$. Group 1 rationally invests $e = 0$, while group 1 sets $e = e^*$. Salaries correspond to average productivities because group 2 (at $e = e^*$) has productivity f_2 and group 1 (at $e = 0$) has productivity f_1. The model is referred to as pure signaling because education does not contribute to productivity and because productivity of all jobs is the same.

The equilibrium is summarized in table 10.1. The single most important property of the equilibrium is that the private and social returns to education differ. As a result, the second group overinvests in education. The optimum would require $e = 0$ for both groups. But then group 2 would not be distinguished. Salary would be $\alpha_1 f_1 + \alpha_2 f_2$ for everyone. That would benefit group 1 but not group 2. In the pure signaling case, education is invested in because it distinguishes people, thereby redistributing (rather than increasing) the product and income.

10.2.2 Pure Human Capital

Assume that $f_{ij}(e) = f(e)$ for both groups and both jobs. Neither the job nor the type of person affects productivity. Let $f(0) = f_1$ and $f(e^*) = f_2$. Assume that e satisfies the inequalities in (1) above. The equilibrium for this model is much like that for the signaling model. It is summarized in table 10.2. The difference between this model and the signaling model

Table 10.1   **Signaling**

	Productivity $e=0$	Productivity $e=e^*$	Schooling Cost	Salary	Education Expenditure
Group 1	**f_1**	**f_1**	c_1	f_1	0
Group 2	f_2	**f_2**	c_2	f_2	$c_2 e^*$

Note: Bold face figures indicate equilibrium productivities.

Table 10.2   **Human Capital**

	Productivity $e=0$	Productivity $e=e^*$	Schooling Cost	Salary	Education Expenditure
Group 1	f_1	f_2	c_1	f_1	0
Group 2	f_1	f_2	c_2	f_2	$c_2 e^*$

lies in the off-diagonal terms in the productivity part of the table, and therefore in the welfare implications. Here salary offers at different levels of education reflect different productivities. The equilibrium is efficient, meaning that each person or group invests in the correct amount of education. I assume the choice is restricted to $e=0$ and $e=e^*$. Education is productive. People invest in it differentially because the costs vary over people. But that is the desired outcome.

There is an alternative version of the model that deserves mention. It could be that $f_{ij}(e)$ does vary with i. If the employer could directly observe an individual's type, or productivity, then he would put a group i person with education e in a job where j maximizes $f_{ij}(e)$. Individuals would then optimize by selecting e to maximize

$$\max_j f_{ij}(e) - c_i e$$

The results would again be efficient.

10.2.3 The Rationing Model

In the previous models, we have concentrated on the type of person and the educational level as a determinant of productivity. Here, we turn to the job. Suppose that $f_{ij}(e) = f_j$ so that productivity depends on the job, but not the type of person or the education level. Assume that the proportion of jobs of type 2 is a_2 and that $f_2 > f_1$. The fact that the proportion of jobs of type 2 is a_2 is rigged to make the model work. Later, I shall discuss rationing in a more general setting.

The equilibrium in this model is summarized in table 10.3. Once again, it has the observable attributes of the equilibria in the previous two

Table 10.3   **Rationing**

	Productivity		Schooling		Education
	Job 1	Job 2	Cost	Salary	Expenditure
Group 1	f_1	f_2	c_1	f_1	0
Group 2	f_1	f_2	c_2	f_2	$c_2 e^*$

models. But here education is being used to ration high-productivity jobs so the group with the lower costs of education does not get them. If jobs were randomly assigned to people, output and total incomes would be the same, but the education costs would be avoided. People could be paid either f_1 or f_2, depending upon the job they draw, or the average $a_1 f_1 + a_2 f_2$. As in the signaling model, education investment redistributes income without changing the size of the pie.

The rationing model is incomplete without an explanation of the reason why higher-productivity jobs might be scarce, or at least have higher salary offers attached to them. Certainly, the usual notion of expansion and contraction until productivities are equated at the margin has been dropped. It is not difficult to see that certain kinds of jobs in hierarchical productive organizations are not easily duplicated. This would tend to suggest that there is a difficulty in defining the notion of productivity, and perhaps some concomitant arbitrariness in the salaries and incomes attaching to certain kinds of jobs. The salary structure might be maintained for incentive purposes. The idea that salaries in part attach to jobs does not fit into conventional theory easily, and whether or not it is true is an open question. If it is, then the jobs have to be rationed, and costly investments might be one basis for the rationing.

10.2.4 Productive Information

The information carried by signals in the market can be socially productive if it improves the quality of decisions with respect to jobs or training. Assume that f_{ij} does not depend on e. But let us assume that $f_{12} = f_{21} = g$, and that $f_{22} > f_{11} > g$. Under these considerations, there is a benefit to ensuring that group 1 ends up in job 1 and group 2 ends up in job 2. The equilibrium involves the same investments in education and incomes as in the pure signaling model. It is summarized in table 10.4. As before, the incentive for investing in education is to distinguish different types of people. But, the information is productive, because the types of people are differentially productive. Without the signal, the best that could be accomplished is the maximum of $a_1 f_{11} + a_2 g$ and $a_1 g + a_2 f_{22}$, both of which are lower than the output $a_1 f_{11} + a_2 f_{22}$ realized with the signal. Of course, the signals have a cost and the cost does not necessarily justify the increase in output. The best signaling outcome occurs when

Table 10.4   Information Productive

	Productivity Job 1	Productivity Job 2	Schooling Cost	Salary	Education Expenditure
Group 1	f_{11}	g	c_1	f_{11}	0
Group 2	g	f_{22}	c_2	f_{22}	$c_2 e^*$

$e^* = (f_{22} - f_{11})/c_1$. In that case, the signaling equilibrium increases net income (net, that is, of signaling costs) if

$$g < a_2[(1 - c_2/c_1) f_{22} + (c_2/c_1) f_{11}]$$

The value of the signals, therefore, decreases as g increases, and increases with a_2, f_{22}, f_{11}, and c_2/c_1. I should add that in doing this calculation, I have assumed that $a_1 f_{11} + a_2 g$ is larger than $a_1 g + a_2 f_{22}$. A similar formula holds for the opposite assumption.

Notice that if $f_{22} = d_{11}$, the signaling equilibrium could not be sustained. Group 2 would set $e = 0$ and hence not be distinguished. In this case, it would benefit everyone if group 2 were paid $w_2 > f_{22} = f_{11}$ and if, as a result, group 1 were paid $w_1 < f_{11} = f_{22}$. In fact, this kind of noncompetitive salary could be advantageous even if $f_{22} < f_{11}$, at least over a certain range.

10.2.5 Inducing Efficient Investment in Education

The signaling effect can be beneficial in providing the correct incentives to invest in education, when the latter is productive. Assume that $f_{ij}(e) = f_i(e)$, so that jobs are not relevant. Assume further that $f_1(0) = f_2(0)$ and that $f_1(e^*) < f_2(e^*)$. Let $f(e^*) = a_1 f_1(e^*) + a_2 f_2(e^*)$, the average of the productivities at $e = e^*$. Finally, assume that because of education costs, it is efficient for group 1 so to invest. The equilibrium is depicted in table 10.5. Once again, it has the properties discussed under previous models. Moreover, the equilibrium is efficient.

However, there is another possible type of equilibrium. Suppose that the salary offer for e^* were $f(e^*)$, the average. This might induce group 1 to invest in the signal, in which case we would have an equilibrium, but it would be inefficient. Group 1 would be overinvesting. Similarly, such a salary offer might induce group 2 to set $e = 0$. That also would be an

Table 10.5   Efficient Investment and Information

	Productivity $e = 0$	Productivity $e = e^*$	Schooling Cost	Salary	Education Expenditure
Group 1	$f_1(0)$	$f_1(e^*)$	c_1	$f_1(0)$	0
Group 2	$f_2(0)$	$f_2(e^*)$	c_2	$f_2(e^*)$	$c_2 e^*$

equilibrium and would be inefficient in the other direction. The point here is that education signals productivity and thus provides the returns that induce efficient levels of investment in education—or at least it can.

10.2.6 Some General Remarks

One could go further with these models. There is no reason to assume that the signaling, human capital, and rationing effects are mutually exclusive. In fact, they are unlikely to be. The point I want to make is that market outcomes with quite different normative properties appear similar, in terms of the observable variables, education levels, and average productivities or outputs. To distinguish among them, one has to observe the off-diagonal entries in the tables above. These productivities result when groups have levels of education and jobs that differ from the equilibrium levels.

10.3 Signaling, Human Capital, and Ability

In this section, I should like to set forth a version of the model containing signaling and human capital that can be adapted to empirical work on the determinants of individual productivity. Let y be the number of years of schooling and let n be the ability that is relevant to the determination of individual productivity. Productivity is determined by education and ability according to the function

$$s = ny^\alpha$$

Here, s denotes productivity.

Education is costly, and the costs vary over individuals. Let us assume that y years of schooling cost a person of type z, $C(y, z) = y/z$ dollars, or at least that that is the monetary equivalent of the cost. Productivity is to be interpreted as an average and discounted output over the expected life of the individual. The present value of salary is $W(y)$. Individuals select schooling to maximize $W(y) - y/z$ by setting

$$W'(y) = \frac{1}{z}$$

The parameters n and z are distributed in the employable population.

To complete the model, we must characterize the joint distribution of n and z. The assumption is that

$$n = \frac{z^\varepsilon}{K(\varepsilon)} u$$

where u is independent of z and has a mean of one. Further, it is assumed that $K(\varepsilon)$ is the expected value of z^ε, so that

$$K(\varepsilon) = E(z^\varepsilon)$$

As a result, the expected value of n, given z, is

$$N(z) = \frac{z^\varepsilon}{K(\varepsilon)}$$

The unconditional expected value of n is one. The parameter ε is the elasticity of the conditional mean with respect to z. Thus we can vary the power of the signal by varying ε, and the noisiness by varying the dispersion of u.

The model can now be completed. In equilibrium for every y,

(2) $\qquad E(s/y) = W(y)$

From (1) y is determined by z. Thus (2) becomes

(3) $\qquad y^\alpha N(z) = W(y)$

or simply

(4) $\qquad \dfrac{y^\alpha}{K(\varepsilon)}[W'(y)]^{-\varepsilon} = W(y)$

The solution to this first-order differential equation gives the family of equilibrium salary schedules. I shall assume that when $n = 0$, $y = 0$. This is the equilibrium with the least overinvestment in education (see Riley 1975a for a discussion). Thus the solution, upon integrating (4), is

$$W(y) = \left(\frac{1+\varepsilon}{\alpha+\varepsilon}\right)^{\frac{\varepsilon}{1+\varepsilon}} K(\varepsilon)^{-\frac{1}{1+\varepsilon}} y^{\frac{\alpha+\varepsilon}{1+\varepsilon}}$$

This is the equilibrium salary schedule in the market. The elasticity of salary with respect to schooling is $(\alpha + \varepsilon)/(1 + \varepsilon)$. It contains a term involving ε, the elasticity of productivity with respect to schooling. The signaling effect and ε are the same thing. Signaling occurs when ability and the costs of schooling are negatively correlated, or, more precisely, when the expected value of ability falls as education costs rise.

The model can be solved for investment in schooling, productivity, and net income, for each type of individual. An individual is characterized by n and z or, equivalently by u and z. Table 10.6 reports these quantities for the signaling case (i.e., the situation in which productivity is not directly observed by employers) in column 1. Schooling and net income do not depend upon y. Productivity does. The average value of productivity is formed by setting $u = 1$ in the productivity figure. That is equal to the gross income (before schooling costs) for individuals of type z.

In column 2 of table 10.6, I have reported, for comparative purposes, the values of the relevant variables for the case where market information is perfect, so that schooling does not serve as a signal. Here, u appears in all the expressions, because investment in schooling depends upon n.

The third column reports the ratio of the first two columns. It is the second column divided by the first. I want to focus on the third column for the moment.

There is a tendency to overinvest in schooling. The term $[(\alpha+\alpha\varepsilon)/(\alpha+\varepsilon)]^{1/1-\alpha}$ is less than 1. Thus the ratio is less than one until u gets above its mean which is one. However $u^{1/1-\alpha}$ is convex in u. Therefore those with high levels of u may underinvest in schooling by large amounts. This is worrying, since these are talented people who happen to have high schooling costs. If there were a mechanism for identifying them, the efficiency of the market could be improved. Figure 10.1 depicts the relation between the ratio R and u.

Note that if $u \equiv 1$ so there is no noise, then everyone overinvests in schooling, which is the conventional conclusion. Here I want to emphasize that there is the further problem of the distribution of investments associated with variations in productivity, not correlated with schooling costs.

The second row of table 10.6 contains productivity figures. The constant term in the ratio is again less than one. However the shape of $u^{\alpha/1-\alpha}$ depends on α. It can be convex or concave. If α is small, the ratio as a function of u is concave. The productivity of those with high u will not differ from the optimum by as much as it will if α is large. Thus the performance of output depends in part on the elasticity of productivity with respect to education. Figure 10.2 illustrates the relationship for the case $\alpha < 1/2$.

Next consider net income. The term $(1+\varepsilon)[(\alpha+\alpha\varepsilon)/(\alpha+\varepsilon)]^{\alpha/1-\alpha}$ can be shown to be greater than one.[1] The ratio as a function of u is depicted in

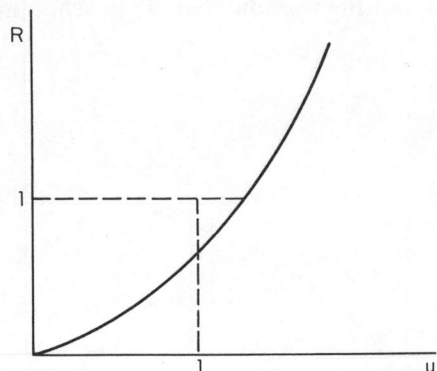

Figure 10.1

Table 10.6 Schooling, Productivity, and Net Income with and without Perfect Information

Variable	(1) Employer Does Not Observe Productivity Directly	(2) Employer Does Observe Productivity Directly
Schooling	$K^{\frac{1}{\alpha-1}}\left(\frac{\alpha+\varepsilon}{1+\varepsilon}\right)^{\frac{1}{1-\alpha}} z^{\frac{1+\varepsilon}{1-\alpha}}$	$\alpha^{\frac{1}{1-\alpha}} z^{\frac{1+\varepsilon}{1-\alpha}} K^{\frac{1}{\alpha-1}} u^{\frac{1}{1-\alpha}}$
Productivity	$u\, K^{\frac{1}{\alpha-1}}\left(\frac{\alpha+\varepsilon}{1+\varepsilon}\right)^{\frac{\alpha}{1-\alpha}} z^{\frac{\alpha+\varepsilon}{1-\alpha}}$	$u^{\frac{1}{1-\alpha}} K^{\frac{1}{\alpha-1}} \alpha^{\frac{\alpha}{1-\alpha}} z^{\frac{1+\varepsilon}{1-\alpha}}$
Income for individuals	$\frac{(1-\alpha)}{(1+\varepsilon)} K^{\frac{1}{\alpha-1}}\left(\frac{\alpha+\varepsilon}{1+\varepsilon}\right)^{\frac{\alpha}{1-\alpha}} z^{\frac{\alpha+\varepsilon}{1-\alpha}}$	$u^{\frac{1}{1-\alpha}} K^{\frac{1}{\alpha-1}} \alpha^{\frac{\alpha}{1-\alpha}} (1-\alpha) z^{\frac{1+\varepsilon}{1-\alpha}}$
Total net income	$\left(\frac{1-\alpha}{1+\varepsilon}\right) K^{\frac{1}{\alpha-1}}\left(\frac{\alpha+\varepsilon}{1+\varepsilon}\right)^{\frac{\alpha}{1-\alpha}} E\left(z^{\frac{\alpha+\varepsilon}{1-\alpha}}\right)$	$(1-\alpha) E\left(u^{\frac{1}{1-\alpha}}\right) K^{\frac{1}{\alpha-1}} \alpha^{\frac{\alpha}{1-\alpha}} E\left(z^{\frac{\alpha+\varepsilon}{1-\alpha}}\right)$

figure 10.3. Here the gainers are a subset below the mean. If the variance of u is zero, everyone loses. Those with high productivity relative to schooling costs lose a potentially large amount. As with schooling, the convexity of this relationship is worrying. It implies that in addition to the efficiency cost of imperfect information, there is a potentially large redistribution from the high-productivity/high-schooling-cost group to

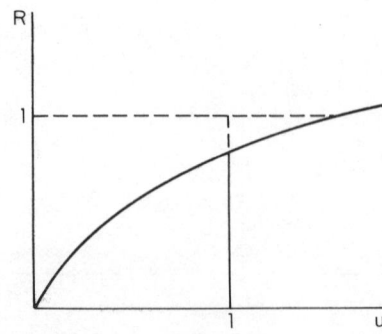

Figure 10.2 Relative Productivity Levels

(3) Ratio of Column 2 over Column 1	(4) Employer Does Not Observe Productivity Directly, but There are Optimal Taxes	(5) Ratio of Column 4 over Column 1
$u^{\frac{1}{1-\alpha}} \left[\frac{\alpha+\alpha\varepsilon}{\alpha+\varepsilon}\right]^{\frac{1}{1-\alpha}}$	$\alpha^{\frac{1}{1-\alpha}} K^{\frac{1}{\alpha-1}} z^{\frac{1+\varepsilon}{1-\alpha}}$	$\left(\frac{\alpha+\alpha\varepsilon}{\alpha+\varepsilon}\right)^{\frac{1}{1-\alpha}}$
$u^{\frac{\alpha}{1-\alpha}} \left[\frac{\alpha+\alpha\varepsilon}{\alpha+\varepsilon}\right]^{\frac{\alpha}{1-\alpha}}$	$u\,\alpha^{\frac{\alpha}{1-\alpha}} K^{\frac{1}{\alpha-1}} z^{\frac{\varepsilon+\alpha}{1-\alpha}}$	$\left(\frac{\alpha+\alpha\varepsilon}{\alpha+\varepsilon}\right)^{\frac{\alpha}{1-\alpha}}$
$u^{\frac{1}{1-\alpha}} (1+\varepsilon) \left[\frac{\alpha+\alpha\varepsilon}{\alpha+\varepsilon}\right]^{\frac{\alpha}{1-\alpha}}$	$(1-\alpha)\,\alpha^{\frac{\alpha}{1-\alpha}} K^{\frac{1}{\alpha-1}} z^{\frac{\varepsilon+\alpha}{1-\alpha}}$	$(1+\varepsilon) \left[\frac{\alpha+\alpha\varepsilon}{\alpha+\varepsilon}\right]^{\frac{\alpha}{1-\alpha}}$
$E\!\left(u^{\frac{1}{1-\alpha}}\right)\left[\frac{\alpha+\alpha\varepsilon}{\alpha+\varepsilon}\right]^{\frac{\alpha}{1-\alpha}} (1+\varepsilon)$	$(1-\alpha)\,\alpha^{\frac{\alpha}{1-\alpha}} K^{\frac{1}{\alpha-1}} E\!\left(z^{\frac{\varepsilon+\alpha}{1-\alpha}}\right)$	$(1+\varepsilon) \left(\frac{\alpha+\alpha\varepsilon}{\alpha+\varepsilon}\right)^{\frac{\alpha}{1-\alpha}}$

the remainder. If the high schooling costs are associated with variables such as family income, the discriminatory implications of imperfect information deserve attention, because they are more extreme than they would be with better information (even if there were no changes in the schooling costs themselves). To put this another way, there is an interaction effect between schooling costs and imperfect job market information

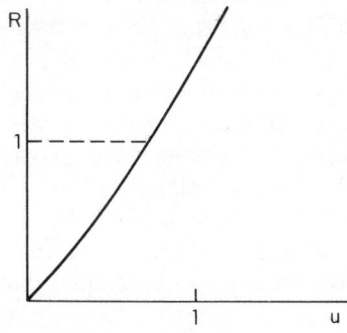

Figure 10.3   Relative Net Incomes

that imposes very high costs on high-productivity/high-schooling-cost people.

Total net income is unambiguously greater with perfect information because, in addition to the constant term that is positive, $E(u^{1/1-\alpha}) > 1$ because of the convexity of $u^{1/1-\alpha}$.

To summarize, the model captures in analytically tractable form, the signaling effect of schooling. The elasticity of productivity with respect to schooling can be adjusted parametically. The "correlation" of schooling costs and productivity is also parametrically specified. In addition to the earlier conclusions about overinvestment in education, there are distributional or discrimination problems associated with high-productivity people whose schooling costs are high, sometimes for reasons extraneous to their abilities.

Thus far, I have been using the market with perfect employer information as the standard. Such a standard may not be attainable. One can ask what the second-best alternative is, and how it compares with the market equilibrium. The second best concedes that productivity is not directly observable, so that investment in schooling cannot be sensitive to u. Nevertheless, we can tax the signaling activity so as to change the relationship between y and z. If we do this so as to maximize total net income, the results are as reported in column 4 of table 10.6.[2] Column 5 reports the ratio of column 4 to column 1, so that we have a measure of the extent to which the market outcome differs from the imperfect information, second-best outcome.

The results are quite easy to summarize. With imperfect information, we get what would be the optimal levels of investment if $u \equiv 1$, that is, if the signaling effect is removed. But the sensitivity to the random component of productivity is lost. Thus if we compare columns 3 and 5 for total net income, column 3 has two terms that are greater than one—$E(u^{1/1-\alpha})$ and $(1+\varepsilon) [(\alpha+\alpha\varepsilon)/(\alpha+\varepsilon)]^{\alpha/1-\alpha}$. Column 5 for the informationally constrained optimum has only the second term. This represents the gain from preventing average overinvestment in signaling. But the unobservability of u means that the first term is lost.

The point of this is to illustrate that imperfect information causes two problems. Investment in schooling is insensitive to the full differences across individuals in the return to investment in schooling. Second, there is a tendency to overinvest in schooling on average because the private return contains that component of ability that is correlated with schooling costs. The fact that schooling is a signal means that investment in it is partially sensitive to ability differences. This is good, but the market tends to overdo it; the second-best optimum calculation illustrates this.

If one calculates the return to schooling required to achieve the second-best optimun, it is

$$\hat{W}(y) = \alpha^{\frac{1}{1+\varepsilon}} K^{-\frac{1}{1+\varepsilon}} \left(\frac{1+\varepsilon}{\alpha+\varepsilon}\right) y^{\frac{\alpha+\varepsilon}{1+\varepsilon}} + d$$

where d is calculated so as to cause the supply side to break even. The ratio of $\hat{W}'(y)$ to $W'(y)$, the slope of the equilibrium schedule, is

$$\frac{\hat{W}'(y)}{W'(y)} = \left(\frac{\alpha+\alpha\varepsilon}{\alpha+\varepsilon}\right)^{\frac{1}{\varepsilon}} < 1$$

Hence the optimal schedule is flatter than the market equilibrium. It induces lower levels of investment in schooling. We can think in terms of taxing schooling. Let the tax schedule be $-f + ty$ where f is a subsidy, and t is the marginal tax rate. It can be shown that when

$$t = \left(\frac{\alpha+\alpha\varepsilon}{\alpha+\varepsilon}\right)^{\frac{1}{\varepsilon}} - 1$$

then the market equilibrium is efficient in the second-best, imperfect information sense.[3] Thus the optimal tax schedule for schooling is linear. The subsidy f is calculated so that the government breaks even. While the marginal tax is positive, the overall tax is negative for lower levels of schooling and positive for higher levels.

There is one related point I should like to make in this context. Consider average net income in the market (column 1, row 4, in table 10.6). It is

$$N(\alpha, \varepsilon) = (1-\alpha) K^{\frac{1}{\alpha-1}} (1+\varepsilon)^{\frac{1}{\alpha-1}} (\alpha+\varepsilon)^{\frac{\alpha}{1-\alpha}} E(z^{\frac{\alpha+\varepsilon}{1-\alpha}})$$

As we have seen, there is a signaling component of the return to schooling that incudes overinvestment. On the other hand, with imperfect information, schooling distinguishes people and therefore makes investment sensitive to at least one component of ability. One can ask which is more important. What I want to show is that

(5) $$\left.\frac{\partial N}{\partial \varepsilon}(\varepsilon, \alpha)\right|_{\varepsilon=0} > 0$$

so that at least over some range, the beneficial second effect outweighs the overinvestment cost. Or to put it another way, with imperfect information, at least some signaling is beneficial. There is in fact an optimal degree of correlation of n and z. I will confine myself to showing that inequality 5 holds.

The argument is as follows. Taking logs and differentiating, we have (with $\beta = \alpha/(1-\alpha) > 0$),

$$\left.\frac{\partial \log N}{\partial \varepsilon}\right|_{\varepsilon=0} = \frac{1}{1-\alpha} \left[\frac{\int z^\beta \log z\, h(z)}{\int z^\beta h(z)} - \int \log z\, h(z)\right]$$

We want to show that the term in square brackets is positive. Let $X = \log z$ and $r(X) = e^X h(e^X)$. It is sufficient to show that

$$\int X e^{\beta X} r(X) dx > \int X r(X) dX \int e^{\beta X} r(X) dX$$

Let $\bar{X}$ be the mean of X, that is, $\bar{X} = \int X r(X) dX$.

Then

$$\int e^{\beta X} r(X) dX = \int \bar{X} e^{\beta X} r(X) dx + \int (X - \bar{X}) e^{\beta X} r(X) dx$$
$$> \bar{X} \int e^{\beta X} r + \int (X - \bar{X})[e^{\beta \bar{X}} + \beta e^{\beta \bar{X}}(X - \bar{X})] r$$

which, by the convexity of $e^{\beta X}$, equals

$$\bar{X} \int e^{\beta X} r + \beta e^{\beta \bar{X}} \int (X - \bar{X})^2 r$$
$$> \bar{X} \int e^{\beta X} r = \int X r(X) \int e^{\beta X} r$$

Thus the term in square brackets is positive for $\beta > 0$, or equivalently $\alpha > 0$. The implication is that net income rises as ε rises starting from $\varepsilon = 0$.

Note however that when $\alpha = 0$, net income is

$$N(0, \varepsilon) = \frac{1}{K} \cdot \frac{1}{1+\varepsilon} E(z^\varepsilon) = \frac{1}{1+\varepsilon}$$

This declines in ε. The reason is that when $\alpha = 0$, the optimal investment in y is zero. Thus the presumed benefit of signaling, making investment sensitive to differences in productivity, is nonexistent when any amount of investment is inefficient, i.e., when $\alpha = 0$.

10.4 Estimating the Determinants of Productivity

In view of the preceding models, several potential problems arise in estimating the determinants of productivity using data on earnings and schooling.

The first problem is that for young workers, earnings and productivity may differ because their productivity has not been discovered. If productivity is ny^α, earnings in a sample of younger workers might be

(6) $\qquad e = \beta n y^\alpha + (1 - \beta) W(y),$

where $W(y)$ is the average return to each level of education and β is a random variable between zero and one.

If we could observe n and y, and estimated (6), the result would be

$$e = \bar{\beta} n y^{\alpha} + (1 - \bar{\beta})\, W(y),$$

where $\bar{\beta}$ is the average value of β in the sample.

This would understate the contribution of ability, and overstate that of schooling.

A second problem is that we do not measure the relevant kind of ability directly. There are surrogates, such as test scores, that may be used in isolating the effects of schooling and ability on productivity. Let me assume that earnings accurately measure productivity so that the first problem does not arise. The problem then is that we do not measure n.

Using capital letters for logs, and eliminating means and constant terms, the signaling model implies that

$$N = \varepsilon Z + U$$

and

$$Y = \left(\frac{1+\varepsilon}{1-\alpha}\right) Z$$

Then, using the equilibrium relationship

$$E = (\alpha + \theta) Y + U$$

where $\theta = \varepsilon(1-\alpha)/(1+\varepsilon)$, productivity is $E = N + \alpha Y$.

Suppose there is a measure I of ability. It can be thought of as a test score. Suppose further that we regress E on Y and I:

$$E = \gamma_y y + \gamma_I I + v$$

The estimated coefficients, for a large sample are

$$\gamma_I = \frac{\sigma_U}{\sigma_I} \frac{\rho_{IU}}{1 - \rho_{YI}^2}$$

$$\gamma_Y = (\alpha + \theta) - \frac{\sigma_U}{\sigma_Y} \frac{\rho_{YI} \rho_{IU}}{(1 - \rho_{YI}^2)}$$

Now if the variable I is correlated with N because of its correlation with Z and hence Y, so that $\rho_{IU} = 0$, then the estimated coefficient of I will be zero and the coefficient of schooling will be $\gamma_Y = (\alpha + \theta)$. The schooling coefficient picks up the productive effect and the signaling effect of schooling. The variable, I, would capture nothing because it operates through schooling; that is, it is correlated with ability because it is correlated with schooling costs. One can put this more positively. In order for the surrogate for ability not to distort the estimates, it must be positively correlated with that part of the ability variable that is not correlated with schooling or schooling cost variables.

It has been suggested that ability may be productive through its effect on the productivity of schooling. There are several interpretations that can be given to this idea. One is that ability and schooling are complementary inputs, a feature built into the model above. A second might be that the variance of U is small, so that productivity is largely determined by the ease with which the individual acquires education. One difficulty with that interpretation is that there are real cost differences over individuals related to family income and the like, which make it seem unlikely, at least to me, that the variance of U is small or zero. But that aside, a low coefficient on the surrogate ability variable is at least open to the interpretation that the surrogate variable picked up the part of ability that varies systematically with schooling cost, and that as a result its impact was already captured by the schooling variable. The measured ability variables are often test scores, where the tests were designed to predict educational performance. The conclusion that ability is not particularly important does not seem warranted.

If the variable I is perfectly correlated with U, so that it precisely captures that part of the variance in ability that is not systematically related to schooling, then the estimated coefficients will be

$$\gamma_I = \frac{\sigma_U}{\sigma_I}$$

$$\gamma_Y = (\alpha + \theta)$$

because $\rho_{IY} = 0$ in that case. Schooling continues to pick up the signaling effect. The magnitude of the coefficient on I will depend upon the relative sizes of the school-related and independent components of the variance in N. There is a direct test of this hypothesis. If U and I are perfectly correlated, then I and Y are uncorrelated, because Y and U are uncorrelated. This is testable and, for most measures of ability employed, does not hold.

The formulas above express the estimated coefficients in terms of parameters of the model. They all have unobservables in them. It remains, therefore, to consider what can be estimated with the data, and what one needs to know in order to separate the productivity and signaling effects. The answer to the second question is that one has to know the correlation coefficient between N and I. To see this, we can proceed as follows. First, from $E = N + \alpha Y$, and $N = \theta Y + U$, we can rewrite the expression for E: $E = (\alpha + \theta)Y + U$. Also, U and Y are uncorrelated, so that immediately

$$\alpha + \theta = \frac{\sigma_{YE}}{\sigma_Y^2}$$

Moreover, we can compute the variance of U and the covariance of I and U:

$$\sigma_U^2 = \sigma_E^2 - \sigma_{YE}^2/\sigma_Y^2$$

$$\sigma_{IU} = \sigma_{IE} - \sigma_{YE}/\sigma_{IY}$$

Ability is related to schooling and U by the relationship $N = \theta Y + U$. Thus, the variance of N and the covariance of N and I are

$$\sigma_N^2 = \theta^2 \sigma_Y^2 + \sigma_E^2 - (\sigma_{YE}^2/G_Y^2)$$

$$\sigma_{IN} = \theta \sigma_{IY} + \sigma_{IE} - \frac{\sigma_{YE}\sigma_{YI}}{\sigma_y^2}$$

These two relationships contain three unknowns, the variance of N, the covariance of N and I, and the parameter θ. Any one of these pieces of information would suffice to compute the other two. In particular, it is sufficient to know the correlation coefficient of N and I, to compute θ. Once θ is computed, α follows immediately.

If one could experiment, one would want randomly to assign people education levels, and then observe their subsequent earnings. In terms of the model, that would have the effect of artificially setting $\theta = 0$ and therefore ε equal to zero. The estimated coefficient of Y would then be α as desired.

10.4.1 Self-Employment

Some people are self-employed and hence not in need of signals of productivity directed at employers. One might argue that the self-employed have to signal to their consumers, as with doctors, dentists, and lawyers. But let us set that aside for the moment. If the self-employed do not have to signal, one might expect the self-employed sector to be a place where the returns to schooling are easier to observe.

Suppose that those who go into the self-employed sector know their own productivities, and invest accordingly. Suppose further, for the moment, that those who enter the self-employed sector are statistically similar to those in the non-self-employed sector. By this I mean the decision to enter the employed or the self-employed sectors is uncorrelated with schooling costs, or ability. I shall relax this assumption shortly. The question that I want to pose is, What will the average productivity at each education level look like in the self-employed sector, and how does that compare with the return in the other sector? The answer is, I think, somewhat surprising.

If people know their own productivity, they maximize $ny^\alpha - y/z$ by setting

$$n\alpha y^{\alpha-1} = \frac{1}{z}$$

Solving for z in terms of y and u, we have

$$z = \left(\frac{Ky^{1-\alpha}}{\alpha u}\right)^{\frac{1}{1+\varepsilon}}$$

Therefore, that person will have a productivity, expressed in terms of y and u, of

$$\alpha^{\frac{\varepsilon}{1+\varepsilon}} K^{-\frac{1}{1+\varepsilon}} y^{\alpha+\theta} u^{\frac{1}{1+\varepsilon}}$$

Thus, the expected or average productivity of people with education level y is

$$w^*(y) = \alpha^{-\frac{\varepsilon}{1+\varepsilon}} K^{-\frac{1}{1+\varepsilon}} y^{\alpha+\theta} E(u^{\frac{1}{1+\varepsilon}})$$

Here, $\theta = \frac{\varepsilon(1-\alpha)}{1+\varepsilon}$ as in previous sections.

Several points are of interest. First, the elasticity of the average productivity with respect to schooling contains the signaling term θ. The reason is that abilities are correlated with schooling costs and therefore with levels of schooling. It is not, therefore, surprising that that effect should appear in the averages. Second, we can compare the returns in the self-employed and the employed sectors. From a previous section, the return to schooling in the employed sector is

$$w(y) = \left(\frac{1+\varepsilon}{\alpha+\varepsilon}\right)^{\frac{\varepsilon}{1+\varepsilon}} K(\varepsilon)^{-\frac{1}{1+\varepsilon}} y^{\alpha+\varepsilon}$$

Therefore, the ratio of the two returns of average productivity is

$$\frac{w^*(y)}{w(y)} = \left[\frac{\alpha+\varepsilon}{\alpha(1+\varepsilon)}\right]^{\frac{\varepsilon}{1+\varepsilon}} E(u^{\frac{1}{1+\varepsilon}})$$

The first term is greater than one because $\alpha + \varepsilon > \alpha + \alpha\varepsilon$. On the other hand, the second term is an expected value of a concave function of u, which has a mean of one, so that it is less than one. The net effect is ambiguous. No definite relationship exists between the returns in the two sectors. If the variance of u is small, the second term is close to one and the return or average in the self-employed sector is higher than in the other sector. The elasticities of the returns are the same in each sector, independent of the relative magnitudes of the coefficients. The inconclusive results of this type of test do not therefore seem surprising.

If the allocation of people between the self-employed and the non-self-employed sectors is nonrandom, then different results may be obtained.

It is difficult to model the interaction of the two sectors rigorously, because of the complexity of the model. However, one would expect that the people who select themselves into the self-employed sector are those whose ability is high relative to the average, given the costs of education. That is to say, the self-employed are likely to be people who find schooling unattractive, so that it is better to avoid being assessed on the basis of schooling. If this process went on to its logical limit, everyone would be self-employed. But then one would have to take into account changes in productivities due to changes in factor input ratios. This is the complexity that is hard to model. But if the process does not go to its extreme, then those in the self-employed sector will have high abilities relative to education costs, and hence high ability relative to levels of schooling. Therefore, the productivity per unit of schooling will be high in the self-employed sector, though the average levels of schooling may be lower. The kind of selection process will make schooling look more productive in the self-employed sector than in the other sector. That would reflect differences in schooling costs across individuals. But it does not directly test for the presence of the signaling effect.

10.5 The Rationing Model

In an earlier section, I mentioned that jobs may contribute to productivity and that they might be scarce. If they are scarce, for whatever reason, then they will be allocated on some basis, and schooling or some other costly characteristic like experience or age might serve the purpose. Part of the return will then appear to be to the characteristic which serves as a basis for rationing. And for the individual, the return will be real as well as perceived. I should like to set out the rationing model somewhat more precisely, to illustrate it with an example, and to show that the rationing effect can be added to the signaling-human capital model discussed previously.

Suppose that there is a spectrum of jobs, indexed by their productivity J. For the time being, J is the only determinant of productivity. The distribution of jobs is $G(J)$, this being the left-hand cumulative. As before, the marginal cost of education is $1/z$, and the cumulative distribution of z is $H(z)$. The problem is to find an equilibrium income function $W(y)$. Given the income function, individuals select y to maximize $W(y) - y/z$, so that

$$W'(y) = 1/z$$

In addition, incomes must correspond to productivities, so that if a person with schooling y receives job J

$$W(y) = J$$

We now have to associate the J's and the y's. Schooling is used to ration the jobs. The people who have schooling of y or less are paid $W(y)$ or less. They therefore have productivities of $W(y)$ or less. Their number is therefore $G[W(y)]$. On the other hand, the same group has marginal costs of schooling equal to or greater than $z = 1/W'$. Thus, there are $H(1/W')$ of them, counting through the education cost distribution. For these two different tallies to be consistent, it must be true that

$$(7) \qquad G(W) = H(1/W')$$

for every level of y actually observed. That defines the equilibrium income function. As in the signaling model, there are many such functions, but I shall not dwell on that here. Differentiating (7), we have

$$W'' = -(W')^3 \frac{G'}{H'} < 0$$

so that $W(y) - y/z$ is concave, and the first order condition $W' = 1/z$ in fact yields a maximum. This holds for any distributions G and H.

The two distributions G and H determine the income function in the rationing model. As can be seen from (7), the formula is quite simple. It may be useful to illustrate the equilibrium with an example. Suppose that

$$G(J) = 1 - TJ^{-\beta} \text{ and}$$
$$H(z) = 1 - Nz^{-\gamma}$$

Here, T, N, β, and γ are parameters of the distributions. It then follows that the equilibrium income function satisfies the equation

$$W' = \left(\frac{T}{N}\right)^{\frac{1}{\gamma}} W^{-\frac{\beta}{\gamma}}$$

Its solution, assuming that $W(y) = 0$ at $y = 0$, is

$$W(y) = Cy^{\frac{\gamma}{\beta+\gamma}}$$

where the constant is $C = [(\beta + \gamma)/\gamma]^{\gamma/(\beta+\gamma)} (T/N)^{1/(\beta+\gamma)}$. An increase in T raises C because it increases the number of high-productivity jobs. An increase in N lowers C because it increases the mean level of marginal costs of education. Similarly, as β gets large, the variance in J falls, and, assuming a compensating change in the mean of J, the return to education falls, eventually reaching zero.

10.5.1 Signaling, Rationing, and Human Capital

Rationing need not function by itself. It can simply augment the returns to the signal in the market without rationing. The following model, which integrates the earlier model of signaling and human capital and the model above, will serve to illustrate. Productivity is determined jointly by ability, schooling, and the job according to

$$s = nJy^\alpha$$

The income schedule is $W(y)$. The equilibrium is defined by three relations. Schooling is rationally invested in, so that

$$W' = 1/z$$

Jobs are rationed so that

$$G(J) = H(z)$$

This connects J and z. And, finally, salaries are equal to expected productivities. Assume that the mean of n, conditional on z, is $z^\varepsilon/[K(\varepsilon)]$ as before. Then we have

$$W(y) = y^\alpha J \frac{z^\varepsilon}{K(\varepsilon)}$$

Combining these conditions, and assuming G and H are as in the numerical example above, we have

(8)
$$W(y) = \frac{y^\alpha}{K(\varepsilon)} (W')^{-\varepsilon} G^{-1} [H(1/W')]$$

or

$$W(y) = \frac{y^\alpha}{K(\varepsilon)} \left(\frac{T}{N}\right)^{\frac{1}{\beta}} (W')^{-(\varepsilon + \frac{\gamma}{\beta})}$$

This again defines the equilibrium income function. The solution to (8) is

$$W(y) = Dy^{\frac{\alpha + \phi}{1 + \phi}}$$

where D is a constant and $\phi = \varepsilon + (\gamma/\beta)$. Notice that if β is large, there is no variance in J and the rationing effect is missing. Then we have the previous model with just signaling and human capital. Rationing simply adds to the elasticity of the return to schooling.

I do not want to pursue the rationing model further here. It does not accord easily with existing microeconomic theory, and, like some of the other effects that have been discussed, it is not established empirically. On the other hand, it does seem to me that it is worth pursuing empirically and theoretically. Some things of considerable importance are rationed. I have in mind places in college, places in several different kinds of professional schools, places in legislatures and congresses, and so on. Its greatest applicability may be to organizations with elements of hierarchical structure that are not easily eliminated by the forces of supply and demand for jobs.

10.6 Contingent Contracts and the Avoidance of Signaling Costs

It has been argued that under certain conditions, employers can elicit information from potential employees by offering them a menu of contracts whose rewards are contingent upon subsequent discovery of their productive capabilities. (See Salop and Salop 1976). These devices can replace costly signals and reduce the costs of transmitting information, borne by individuals. That is to say, they are in everyone's interest, when they can function effectively. The analysis of contingent contracts has been carried out for discrete groups. But discrete numerical examples often have some special features. I should like, therefore, to develop a general model of self-selection with contingent contracts, using a large number or continuum of people of the type employed in the preceding analysis of signaling.

The idea behind self-selection through contingent contracts is relatively straightforward. It is assumed that individuals know their productivities in advance. Employers learn individual productivities after a period whose length is less than the full period of employment. Individuals are then induced to reveal their productive capability when they select a contract. The menu of contracts, somewhat roughly, consists of a set of opportunities to defer income now in favor of higher incomes later, contingent upon high productivity. The analytic task is to show that such a menu can be part of an equilibrium, and to explore what the properties of the equilibrium intertemporal wage or salary contracts are.

Let the productivity of an individual be s. Productivities are distributed in the population. Let s^* be the lowest value of s. Contingent contracts have two components. One is the initial salary, which depends upon the contract that the individual selects. While it is not necessary for the individual to report a productivity at the time of hiring, it is convenient to have him do so, for the purposes of the analysis. Let r be the productivity that the individual reports. The initial salary is $w(r)$. That salary lasts for a period at the end of which his productivity is discovered. At that point, his salary becomes a number which depends upon his productivity and the reported productivity in the previous period. Denote it by $v(r, s)$. Depending upon the length of time before the productivity is discovered, these two incomes will have different weights. By choosing the period and the discount rate for present value calculations, the present value of the income of a person of type s reporting a productivity r is

$$w(r) + dv(r, s)$$

The factor d represents the discount rate and the relative lengths of the two periods. The present value of income will be denoted $T(r, s)$, so that

$$T(r, s) = w(r) + dv(r, s).$$

There are three equilibrium conditions that must be satisfied. Individuals maximize $T(r, s)$ with respect to r, so that

$$T_r(r, s) = w'(r) + dv_r(r, s) = 0$$

Individuals must accurately report s, so that $r = s$, or

$$w'(s) + dv_r(s, s) = 0$$

for all s. That is one condition. The second is that the present value of the incomes of all people equal the present value of their output or

(10) $\qquad w(s) + dv(s, s) = (1 + d)s$

This also must hold for all s. The third is that future earnings must be sufficient to keep the individual working for the firm he contracted with. Otherwise, he might simply leave and earn s elsewhere. The assumption is that individuals cannot bind themselves to an employer forever. The condition is that

$$v(s, s), \geqq s$$

for all s.

The first question is, What are the feasible equilibrium contracts? Here I will discuss a class of them and their properties. Differentiating (10) we have

$$w'(s) + d[v_r(s, s) + v_s(s, s)] = (1 + d)$$

But because $w'(s) + dv_r(s, s) = 0$, this reduces to

(11) $\qquad v_s(s, s) = (1 + d)/d$

Consider the class of functions

$$v(r, s) = K r^a s^b - \text{constant}$$

Members of that class will satisfy (11) provided that $K = (1 + d)/ad$ and $a + b = 1$. Let the constant be w^*/d. Then

$$v(r, s) = \frac{(1 + d)}{ad} r^a s^{1-a} - w^*/d$$

With that assumption, $w(r)$ becomes, from (10)

$$w(r) = w^* - (1 + d)(1/a - 1)r$$

The present value of total income is

$$T(r, s) + \frac{(1 + d)}{a} r^{1-a} s^a - (1 + d)[1/(a - 1)]r$$

Maximizing with respect to r, we have

$$T_r = (1 + d)[(1 - 1/a) + [1/(a - 1)](s/r)^a] = 0$$

The solution to this equation is $r = s$, so that individuals do accurately report their productivity. Moreover,

$$T_{rr} = -(1+d)(1-a)\, s^a\, r^{-(1+a)} < 0$$

so that the second-order condition for a maximum is satisfied.

There remains the question of incentive to remain with the firm with whom the contract is made. The condition is that $v(s, s) \geq s$. Writing this out, we have

$$w^* \leq \left(\frac{1+d-ad}{a}\right) s$$

The right-hand side is at a minimum when $s = s^*$. Thus the largest value that w^* can have is

$$w^* = \left(\frac{1+d-ad}{a}\right) s^*$$

When w^* has this value, then the initial salary of people of productivity $s = s^*$ is

$$w(s^*) = w^* - (1+d)(1/a - 1)s^*$$
$$= s^*$$

That is to say, the initial salary of the people with the lowest productivity is s^*, their productivity. If this were not true, then they would have an incentive to report some other productivity, one that corresponded to a higher income, since they are assured s^* in future periods.

Notice that the highest starting salary is w^*, because $w(r)$ is declining in r. One might suspect that someone would report s^* in the first period and then take s later on. That will not happen for the following reason. To adopt that strategy would be to achieve a present value of income of $s^* + ds$. By playing the game, one gets $T(s, s) = (1+d)s > s^* + ds$. Thus, the strategy is not advantageous.

There are several properties of this kind of equilibrium that are worthy of comment. First, the highest starting salary is s^*. It is paid to those with the lowest productivity. Second, initial salaries decline as a function of productivity. Of course, they are made up in subsequent periods. Third, the rate of decline of starting salaries with productivity can be controlled. The rate of decline diminishes as the parameter a rises toward one. Therefore, if evening out the income streams is desirable, it can be accomplished to a limited extent with the choice of the function $v(r, s)$. And presumably the market would move in that direction.

There is another feature of the market that is of interest. Contingent contracts tend to lock people in with the firm that they initially joined. The reason is that they sacrificed income at the start for income later. But that premium for productivity later comes only from the firm that accepted the contract. This lock-in effect is stronger, the higher the productivity, because the premium increases with productivity. This feature of the equilibrium is not necessarily implausible from an empirical point of view. Intuitively, an individual may have an incentive to remain with the firm he starts with. In fact one can think of the investment in having the firm learn about one's capabilities as a form of specific human capital.

Contingent contracts have been criticized on the ground that the employer has an incentive to renege in the second period. This is a problem, especially when the individual has difficulty proving that his productivity is what he implicitly stated initially, in accepting a contract. However, in most markets reneging may not be a serious problem. Most firms are in business for an extended period. The reputation for reneging on implicit contracts of this type would impair the firm's future ability to hire high-productivity people, with a concomitant high cost.

This discussion of contingent contracts has set signaling aside. The two may interact. In particular, the contingent contracts can eliminate the inefficiency in signaling. Schooling, on the other hand, can make it possible to pay higher-productivity people more than the productivity at the bottom end, thereby reducing but not eliminating the divergences between earnings and productivity. This subject is explored in appendix A.

10.7 Occupational Licensure and Minimum Quality Standards

Occupational licensure has captured the attention of economists and regulators. It is an increasingly pervasive phenomenon, and one which affects almost every consumer in some form or other. It is a complicated subject, and has not received the sort of attention from a theoretical point of view that it deserves (but see Leland 1977). I do not have the space here to do more than set forth some of what seem to me to be the issues, and to suggest how at least some of them might be explored.

There is a tendency for most of us—perhaps with the model of medicine in mind—to think of licensure as the last step in a quality-screening process that is designed to assure competence in a profession. Such screening is thought necessary or desirable because consumers are imperfectly informed about the quality of the services that they receive. Of course, the state of being imperfectly informed has many dimensions: how imperfectly, for how long, how quickly does the consumer learn, and so on.

But licensure is a device which serves many functions, and I should like to pause briefly to comment on some of them. It can simply be the end point of a quality-screening process. It can also be the certification that the individual has acquired a certain amount of human capital and is thereby likely to be capable of producing reasonably high-quality services. And it can be both of these things together. Certainly, these are aspects of licensure in law, medicine, academia (the license is the Ph.D.), and many other professions.

Licensure is also a device for controlling the behavior of those in the profession. Performance, at least in some industries, is determined not only by ex ante competence, but also ex post effort. The threat of removal of a license in the case of poor performance, combined with some mechanism by which removal takes place, acts as an incentive to maintain performance when consumer perceptions weaken the incentive that would be provided were there perfect information. There are alternative mechanisms for taking care of poor performance. Liability is one. Strongly developed professional norms are another. Ex post control is needed in varying degrees in different professions. Academics presumably have little incentive to do poor research, although it is sometimes argued that permanent licensure in the form of tenure weakens the incentive to produce. On the other hand, there are other objectives than maintenance of job and income, objectives related to professional status and prestige. These function effectively in many professions. Indeed, a stronger professional association and stronger norms in a field like automobile repair, where it appears that fraud is a problem in part of the industry, might serve a useful purpose.

Licensure is used as a control device by the service industries. It is used to control numbers, for good or ill. It is also used to control conduct: rules against price competition and advertising have been cited as potentially adverse prohibitions, based on the ultimate threat of loss of license.

The threat of loss of license, used for whatever purpose, is more or less compelling, depending upon the industry. If entry is relatively easy, the rents not terribly high, and the initial investment in human capital not large, then the threat of removal may not carry much weight. This is especially true if licensure attaches to business and not individuals, so that the business can disappear but the individual reappear with a different corporate suit.

Licensure can serve as an ex post screen for quality (apart from effort). This may be useful if the ex ante screening either does not exist, or is imperfect.

The relative importance, and the welfare effects, of these phenomena vary from industry to industry, and depend upon a host of structural features of the market. Among them are how imperfectly informed consumers are, whether the service industry sells information as well as a service, information upon which the demand for the service is based, the human capital requirements, the degree to which ability varies and is a necessary input, and others.

It would be well beyond my current task to delve into all of these phenomena. I do believe the subject is one of considerable interest and one requiring additional work with a potentially high payoff for informing regulatory policy. In what follows, I shall focus upon some problems connected with the ex ante quality-screening aspects of the subject, since these bear some resemblance to the earlier models of signaling and rationing.

I want to consider the following constellation of factors in a first pass at the issue of licensure and minimum quality standards. Consumers value quality in a service differently, and are distributed with respect to their valuations of quality. Let quality be denoted by n. Setting a minimum quality standard $\bar{n}$ would be to screen out suppliers with $n < \bar{n}$ for some level of $\bar{n}$. Consumers value quality in dollars according to θn, where θ is distributed according to $G(\theta)$. Services of different qualities have prices $p(n)$ which depend on n. The schedule $p(n)$ will be determined as part of the equilibrium.

Given $p(n)$, consumers optimize $\theta n - p(n)$, by setting

$$\theta = p'(n)$$

At least, that is what they would do with perfect information. But I want to assume that the information is imperfect and indeed biased. To be specific, let us assume the quality n is perceived to be $a + sn$, where we might expect that $a > 0$, and $s < 1$. This would make consumers relatively insensitive to quality differences. For reasons which will be apparent shortly, the magnitude of a is immaterial, while s is an important parameter.

With imperfect information, the consumer selects n to maximize $\theta(a + sn) - p(n)$ by setting

$$\theta s = p'(n)$$

If there is a minimum quality standard $\bar{n}$, so that $n \geq \bar{n}$, then consumers maximize $\theta sn - p(n)$, subject to $n \geq \bar{n}$. The solution to that problem is the following. Let $\bar{\theta} = p'(\bar{n})/s$. If $\theta' < \bar{\theta}$, then $n = \bar{n}$, and if $\theta > \bar{\theta}$, $\theta s = p'(n)$.

10.7.1 Model 1

Suppose first that the supply of services at each level of quality n is potentially unlimited. Let $w(n)$ be the opportunity cost of being in this market for a server of quality n. The prices will be equal to $w(n)$ so that $p(n) = w(n)$. As a result of individual optimization with imperfect information, total net benefits are

$$W(\bar{n}, s) = \int_0^{\bar{\theta}} [\theta \bar{n} - w(\bar{n})] g(\theta) d\theta + \int_{\bar{\theta}}^{\infty} \{\theta n(\theta s) - w[n(\theta s)]\} g(\theta) \, d\theta$$

where $\theta s = w'[n(\theta s)]$, and $g(\theta)$ is the density function for θ.

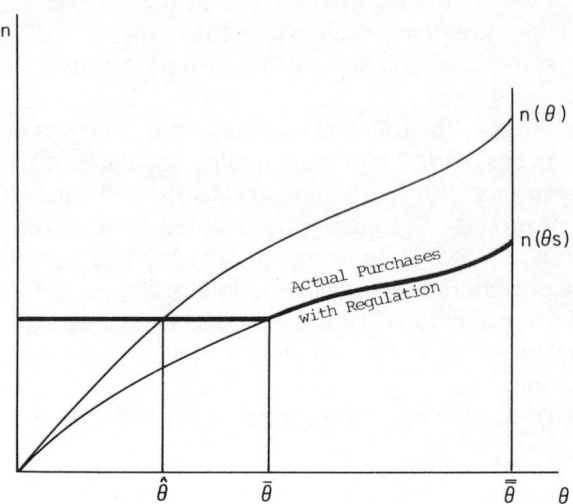

Figure 10.4

I want to establish the properties of this net benefit function, and the nature of the optimal quality standard. First, consider the relation between optimal and selected qualities, at each level of θ. The situation is depicted in figure 10.4. Here, $n(\theta)$ is the optimal n given θ, $n(\theta s)$ is the unregulated n given θ and s, and $\bar{n}$ is the minimum quality standard. $\bar{\bar{\theta}}$ is the upper level of θ. There are three groups. Those below $\hat{\theta}$ purchase too little without regulation, and now purchase too much. Those between $\hat{\theta}$ and $\bar{\theta}$ are closer to the optimum than without regulation. Those above $\bar{\theta}$ are unaffected by regulation. The tradeoff, then, is between the first and second groups. Whether regulation is desirable at all depends on the misperceptions.

One can easily verify that $\partial W/\partial \bar{\theta} = 0$. Thus the maximum of $W(\bar{n}, s)$ with respect to $\bar{n}$ occurs when

$$\frac{\partial W}{\partial \bar{n}} = F(\bar{\theta})\,[E(\bar{\theta}) - w'(\bar{n})]$$

$$= F(\bar{\theta})\,[E(\bar{\theta}) - s\,\bar{\theta}] = 0$$

where $E(\bar{\theta})$ is the expected value of θ given that $\theta \le \bar{\theta}$.
Thus the first order condition for a maximum is

$$E(\bar{\theta}) = s\,\bar{\theta}$$

Signaling, Screening, and Information

One has to be a little careful about second-order conditions, as we shall see in a moment.

Note first that when $s = 1$, $\bar{\theta}$ must be zero, or whatever the bottom end of the θ spectrum is. That means no regulation. Second, since $E(\bar{\theta})$ must cross $s\bar{\theta}$ from above at the maximum, an increase in s reduces $\bar{\theta}$ and hence the desired level of minimum quality. There can, however, be sharp jumps in the desired levels of regulation. Consider the case where $G(\theta)$ is uniform on $[0, 1]$. In that case,

$$\frac{\partial W}{\partial \bar{n}} = \bar{\theta}^2 \left[\frac{1}{2} - s\right]$$

Its sign is therefore determined by $s - (1/2)$. If $s > 1/2$, $\partial W/\partial \bar{n} < 0$ and no regulation is optimal. If $s = 1/2$, $\partial W/\partial \bar{n} = 0$ and it does not matter. And if $s < 1/2$, $\partial W/\partial \bar{n} > 0$, and the minimum standard should be above the unregulated level of n at $\theta = 1$, the upper end. The optimal $\bar{n}$ maximizes $(1/2)\bar{n} - w(\bar{n})$, and satisfies $w'(\bar{n}) = 1/2$. Everyone selects the minimum quality.

In general, the situation is depicted in figure 10.5. The line $\bar{\theta}$ lies above $E(\bar{\theta})$. For s close enough to one, $s\bar{\theta}$ also lies above $E(\bar{\theta})$, and $\bar{\theta} = 0$ is optimal. When $s = s_1$, there are two local maxima. Either could be optimal. As s falls, the second local maximum moves toward $\bar{\bar{\theta}}$. For s small

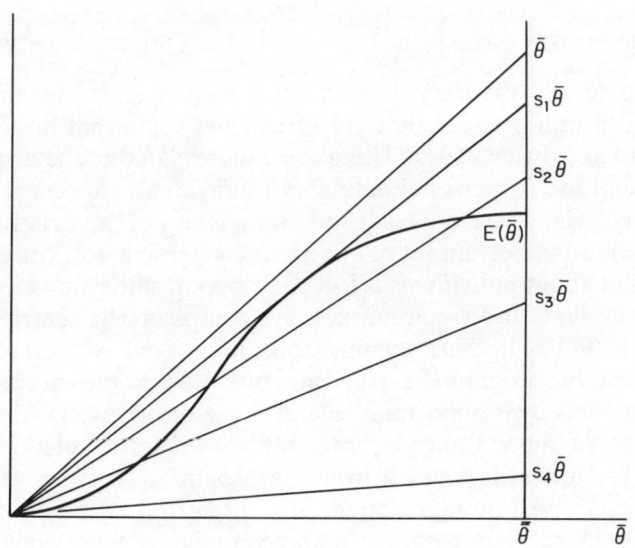

Figure 10.5

enough, $s\bar{\theta}$ lies below $E(\bar{\theta})$. Then $\bar{\theta} = \bar{\bar{\theta}}$ is optimal and $\bar{n}$ is selected to maximize $E(\bar{\bar{\theta}})\bar{n} - w(\bar{n})$, where $E(\bar{\bar{\theta}})$ is just the mean of θ.

The lessons of this analysis are two. The desirability of regulation and the appropriate level of the minimum quality standard increase with the extent to which consumers underestimate quality differentials. And, second, with the right kind of regulation, the greater the underestimates by consumers, the larger the fraction of people at the minimum quality standard.

Note also that a considerable amount of information is required to set the minimum quality. It includes costs $w(n)$, the distribution of θ, and the level of s or an assessment of the misperceptions. An alternative strategy of informing consumers might seem desirable. Indeed, it would be in the interest of at least the upper end of the quality spectrum on the supply side, because it would increase their business. It is also in the interest of the low end of the quality spectrum if regulation is the alternative. The gainers from misperceptions and regulation are those in the middle of the quality spectrum.

10.7.2 Model 2

The preceding model assumed that the supply of services at each level of n is unlimited. When that is not true, the results change. They are reported in appendix B for the reader who may be interested.

10.8 The Privacy Issue

Related to the theoretical work on signaling and screening are a collection of policy issues that are often (and somewhat misleadingly) referred to as privacy issues. These are issues related to the acquisition, storage, and use of personal data about individuals, to screen them in various markets. There are legal and moral issues of privacy. But often, too, there is an important set of questions concerning how collections of information about individuals affect their opportunities in various markets. Job markets and credit markets are conspicuously central in these discussions. Policy in this area must consider not only what information an individual has a right to keep private, but also how the exercise of that right affects his own opportunities and those of others. Distinguishing among two or more things is, after all, a symmetric relation. If you effectively distinguish yourself from me, we are, as it were, effectively distinguished, even though I might have preferred to remain undistinguished in the relevant respect. In an economic context, when an individual exercises an option either to distinguish himself, or not to be distinguished, at least on some criteria, the exercise of that option generates externalities which affect the performance of the market.

In the short space available, I cannot explore these issues completely. But I do want to make one point with respect to solutions to the privacy problem that involve optional signals, having to do with the "copyright" solution to the problem.

In view of the vastly reduced costs of collecting and transmitting personal information it has been suggested that the law should either assert or reaffirm the individual's property right in information about himself. That is to say, the individual is to be regarded as having a copyright on this information. He or she must be consulted before it is transmitted or reproduced. One virtue of such a proposal is that it provides a semiautomatic mechanism for detecting and eliminating errors. A potential defect is its administrative cost (some would regard this as a virtue—perhaps ignoring the difficult question of who would or could bear the cost).

But in addition to errors and costs, there is the central question of whether voluntary control over signals is likely to affect substantially the signals that are in fact used. I believe the answer that it will not is closer to the truth than the opposite conclusion. This is not an argument that copyright is a poor policy, but only that it may be ineffective in dealing with certain kinds of problems. In particular, it may be ineffective in preventing people from being forced to reveal personal information about themselves, and from having certain opportunities foreclosed as a result.

Consider a simple case. Individuals are asked to state their criminal records (if any) and to authorize the institution that is inquiring to check it. Individuals have the right to refuse. They may even have the right to be "considered" for a job or for credit without the answer. If everyone refused to answer, or were compelled to answer, or if the questioner were compelled not to ask, then everyone would be treated as the average. But those with no records are likely to have an incentive to answer. Given that they answered, those with arrests for misdemeanors have an incentive to answer, since they are at the top of the remainder. And, thus, with the incentives operating through those at the top of the remaining undifferentiated group, the question is answered. Refusal to answer amounts to an answer. So the right to refuse confers little benefit, either in privacy, or in opportunities in the market.

Signals that people invest in are subject to similar incentives. If a certain job or salary has an educational prerequisite, those who can afford it, or who derive sufficient benefits from education to make it worthwhile, will invest. If the initial position were one in which everyone had the same or similar educations, or appeared to, there would still be an incentive for certain people to invest further.

In the case of the criminal records, I have tried to avoid the questions of whether arrest records are legitimate, informative, or desirable sources of information. Whether they are informative is an empirical question to which I do not know the answer. The point I want to make is simply that copyrights in personal information may not solve the privacy or the market opportunity problems, if indeed there are such problems. To alter substantially the performance of the market requires collective action, though not necessarily governmental action.

In general, the incentives for signaling come from the upper end of the spectrum down. To stop this process would require collective action, since the individual incentives are to signal and be screened.

Appendix A

Contingent Contracts and the Time Profile of Earnings

In the signaling model, schooling, in addition to its contribution to an individual's productivity, served to distinguish the person by his or her ability. This occurs because the generalized costs of schooling were negatively correlated with ability and because employers could not observe productivity directly. The result was in some cases overinvestment in schooling in the sense that the private return exceeds the direct contribution to productivity.

It has been objected to the schooling-as-a-signal model that, while productivity or productive potential may not be directly observable for young workers, it will become observable to the employer over time. That raises the possibility that employers will defer wages and salaries until productivity is observed, and then reward people directly on the basis of productivity.

That by itself is not a very interesting possibility, because individuals would not necessarily be sorted out in the earlier years on the basis of their productive potential. And there may be private and social benefits to screening at the early stages of employment. These benefits may result from improved resource allocation to on-the-job training, or from better job placement. But the argument goes further to assert that there may be screening. Potential employees are not offered one deferred salary contract but several. In choosing from the menu of contingent contracts, they will signal their productive potential. Thus the information transfer at the time of hiring that occurs when schooling is a signal may also occur with selection via contingent contracts.

Contingent contracting is a possible market response to the inefficiency associated with overinvestment in schooling in the signaling case. Since the present value of earnings in the contingent contract regime is a function of *actual* productivity, the ability component of the return to education is removed. As a result, efficient levels of investment in schooling can be sustained in an equilibrium.

However, as we have seen, contingent contracts have an interesting property. They cause the time path of earnings to diverge from the path of productivity, individually and on average. Therefore, if one adopts the view that contingent contracts are a likely market response to signaling inefficiency, one would also expect that earnings would not accurately reflect the profile of the individual's productivity over time.

The purpose of this section is to illustrate how contingent contracts screen people without distorting the educational investment decision, and then to determine the extent of the divergence between earnings and productivity. Generally, earnings rise more rapidly than productivity over time. Thus if one were to use earnings as a proxy for productivity in estimating the relative contributions of schooling and on-the-job learning to productivity, one would overestimate the latter and underestimate the contribution of schooling.

The purpose of the model is to investigate the extent to which earnings are deferred from the first period to the second. Individual productivity is $S(n, y)$ where n varies continuously in the employable population. First-period earnings are $\bar{W}(y)$. In the second period, they are

$$(1+\beta) S(n, y) - \bar{W}(y)$$

Net earnings in present value terms are

$$(1+\beta) S(n, y) - c(y, n)$$

where $c(y, n)$ is the cost of y years of schooling to a person of type n. Here I assume that schooling costs depend directly on n. Let $y^*(n)$ be the optimal y for each n, and $n^*(y)$ its inverse. Let

$$G(n) = \max_y (1+\beta) S(n, y) - c(y, n)$$

The default strategy (the worker stays with the original employer for only the first period, and then goes on the open market) yields benefits of

$$\bar{W}(y) + \beta S[S(n, y) - c(y, n)]$$

Thus in a market equilibrium

(A1) $$\bar{W}(y) \leq G(n) - \beta S(n, y) - c(y, n)$$

for all y and n. In particular, the upper bound on $\bar{W}(y)$ is

$$\bar{W}(y) = \min_n [G(n) - \beta S(n, y) + c(y, n)]$$

This upper bound has two properties of interest. First, from the definition of $\bar{W}(y)$

(A2) $$\bar{W}(y) \lessgtr G[n^*(y)] - \beta S[n^*(y), y] + c[y, n^*(y)]$$
$$= S[n^*(y), y]$$

Moreover, the n that minimizes the right-hand side of (A1) is not $n^*(y)$. To see that we note that the minimizing condition is

$$(1 + \beta) S_n[y^*(n), n] - c_n(y^*, n) - \beta S_n(y, n) + c_n(y, n) = 0$$

If the solution is $n = n^*(y)$, we would have

$$S_n(y, n) + 0$$

but $S_n > 0$ so that this cannot happen. Therefore the inequality in (A2) is strict, and for everyone in the first period, earnings fall short of productivity. In fact the minimizing n is less than $n^*(y)$ since $S_n > 0$.

It follows that the slope of the earnings schedule is

$$\bar{W}'(y) = c_y[y, n(y)] - \beta S_y[y, n(y)]$$
$$> c_y[y, n^*(y)] - \beta S_y[y, n^*(y)]$$
$$= S_y[y, n^*(y)] > 0$$

One concludes that the slope of the earnings schedule as a function of y in the first period is (*a*) positive, and (*b*) greater than the marginal product of schooling in that period.

It is perhaps worth noting that nothing in the argument above relies on the assumption that schooling costs depend on n, the attribute that determines productivity. Thus the divergence of earnings and productivity over time will occur with implicit contingent contracts even when schooling costs are the same for everyone, or, in general, when they vary randomly with respect to ability. It is also to be noted that the divergence of earnings from productivity creates an incentive for people to stay with the firms that they begin with. The reason is that in the second period, earnings exceed productivity, and hence what the older worker can command on the open market.

In view of these results, a few remarks about the use of earnings data seem in order. Investment in schooling is efficient. However, the slope of the schedule of lifetime earnings (in present value terms) as a function of education overstates the productivity of schooling, because it contains the ability component. It seems worth emphasizing that this holds in spite of the appropriateness of the educational investment from an efficiency point of view. The intertemporal earnings profiles are steeper than the productivity profiles. Therefore, if earnings are taken as equal to productivity, and the time slope (with suitable controls for discounting) taken as the result of the acquisition of human capital on the job, then the return to that capital will be overestimated. In the signaling situation without contingent contracts, this problem does not arise. Earnings and productivity at each level of schooling are equal (at least on average) at each time in the life cycle. Of course there can be overinvestment in schooling because the private return contains the ability effect.

Appendix B

Quality Standards with a Limited Supply of Services

In the model in section 10.7, the supply of services at each level of quality was potentially unlimited. In this second model, the availability of quality is limited, and the supply is distributed according to $F(n)$.

The equilibrium occurs when consumers are distributed over suppliers properly, that is, proportionately. This equilibrium is much like that in the educational rationing model. However, here price is the rationing instrument. Given $p(n)$ consumers with $\theta \leq p'(n)/s$, select quality n or less. There are $G(p'/s)$ such consumers. The fraction of suppliers at quality n or less is $F(n)$. Thus in an equilibrium

$$F(n) = G\left(\frac{p'}{s}\right)$$

for all n. This defines the equilibrium schedule $p(n)$, up to a constant. I want to incorporate quality standards or licensure at the outset. That requires the following modification. If n is restricted to be equal or greater than $\bar{n}$, the relevant distribution of n is $[F(n) - F(\bar{n})]/[1 - F(\bar{n})]$. Therefore, with the quality standard, the equilibrium is defined by the two relations

(B1)   (A) $\theta = \dfrac{p'(n)}{s}$

          (B) $G(\theta) = \dfrac{F(n) - F(\bar{n})}{1 - F(\bar{n})}$

Given $\bar{n}$, the level of quality purchased by people of type θ does not depend on s, the parameter that determines perceptions. The price schedule does depend on s, and adjusts to make the equilibrium relation (B1) hold. Let

$$H(\theta, \bar{n}) = F^{-1}\{[1 - F(\bar{n})]\, G(\theta) + F(\bar{n})\}$$

The equilibrium condition (B1) is then

(B2) $n = H(\theta, \bar{n})$

Let $w(\theta) = \theta n - p(n)$. Taking the derivative with respect to θ, we have

(B3) $$\frac{dw}{d\theta} = (\theta - p')\frac{dn}{d\theta} + n(\theta)$$

$$= \theta(1-s)\frac{\partial H}{\partial \theta} + H(\theta)$$

Let $\bar{\bar{\theta}}$ be the highest level of θ, and assume it exists. Integrating (B3) we have

$$w(\theta) = w(\bar{\bar{\theta}}) + \int_{\bar{\bar{\theta}}}^{\theta}\left[v(1-s)\frac{\partial H}{\partial \theta} + H\right]dv$$

This tells us the level of dollar benefits for a person of type θ in the market. The number $w(\bar{\bar{\theta}})$ is determined by the position (as opposed to the slope) of $p(n)$. That in turn is determined by the alternate opportunities of suppliers with different levels of n. Let those alternative salaries or incomes be $w(n)$. Let $\bar{n}$ be the highest level of n. I shall assume that $p(\bar{n}) = w(\bar{n}) = \bar{w}$. This means that the level of prices is set by the highest-quality suppliers. More generally, one assumes $p(n) \geq w(n)$ for all n, and then computes the level of the schedule from that. For now, this set of constraints is assumed to bind at $\bar{n}$.

Given that assumption

$$w(\bar{\bar{\theta}}) = \bar{\bar{\theta}}\bar{n} - \bar{w}$$

We can compute the total net benefits by adding up over the $w(\theta)$. They are

(B4) $$w(\theta) = \bar{\bar{\theta}}\bar{n} - \bar{w} - \int_0^{\bar{\bar{\theta}}} g(\theta)\int_{\theta}^{\bar{\bar{\theta}}}\left[v(1-s)\frac{\partial H}{\partial \theta} + H\right]dv\, d\theta$$

$$= \bar{\bar{\theta}}\bar{n} - \bar{w} - \int_0^{\bar{\bar{\theta}}}\left[\theta(1-s)\frac{\partial H}{\partial \theta} + H\right]G(\theta)\, d\theta$$

Several things can be inferred from (B4). First, net benefits are an increasing function of s. The reason is not hard to locate. The parameter s determines the slope of the price function. Recall that

$$p'(n) = sG^{-1}\left[\frac{F(n) - F(\bar{n})}{1 - F(\bar{n})}\right]$$

But by hypothesis, the upper end of $p(n)$ is fixed. Therefore, a reduction in s flattens out the price function as shown in figure 10.6. Thus, if the upper end of the n spectrum locates $p(n)$, consumers lose and incomes in the profession rise as consumer perceptions of quality differences are blunted. The reverse holds if the bottom end of the quality spectrum locates $p(n)$. Then the situation is shown in figure 10.7. Intermediate cases are possible. In general, as s falls, the likelihood that the upper end

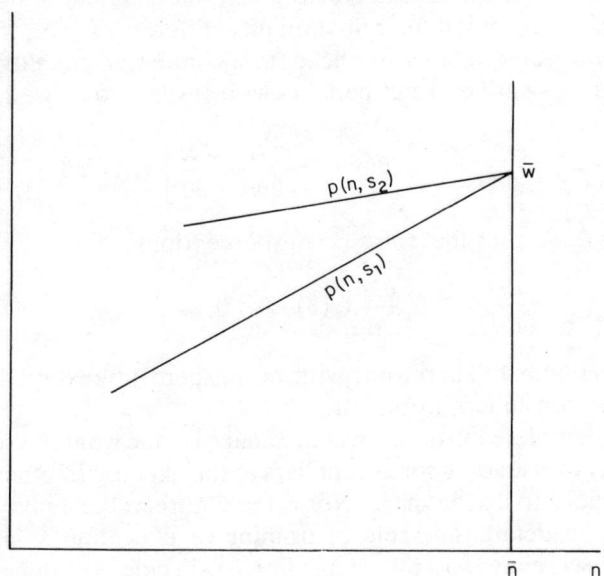

Figure 10.6

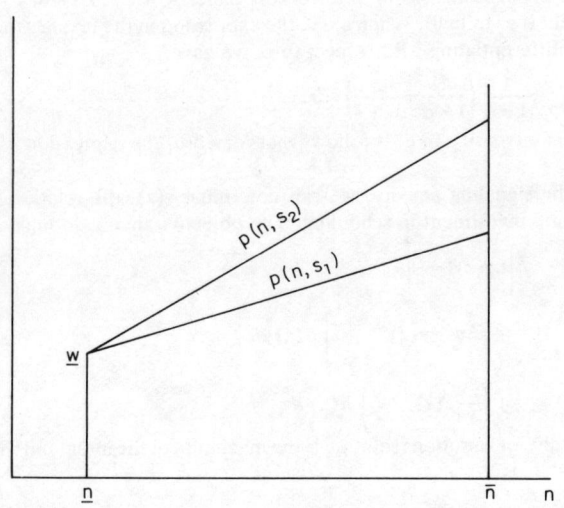

Figure 10.7

will be the binding constraint increases. These remarks hold even if consumers overestimate marginal quality differences, i.e., if $s>1$.

A second point relates to the optimal minimum quality standard. Taking the derivative of net benefits with respect to n, we have

$$\frac{dw}{d\bar{n}} = -\int_0^{\bar{\theta}} \left[\theta(1-s)\frac{\partial^2 H}{\partial \theta \partial \bar{n}} + \frac{\partial H}{\partial \bar{n}} \right] G(\theta) \, d\theta$$

Where $s=1$, so that there are no misperceptions,

$$\frac{dw}{dn} = -\int_0^{\bar{\theta}} \frac{\partial H}{\partial \bar{n}} G(\theta) \, d\theta < 0,$$

because $\partial H/\partial \bar{n} > 0$. Therefore, with no misperceptions, quality regulation makes consumers worse off.[4]

To do a complete job on the welfare analysis, one would have to specify the costs of overloading some suppliers at the expense of others. I do not have the space to do that here. Nor is the nature of the quality screening developed in detail. The role of training or education as part of that process of screening and the acquisition of specific human capital could also be developed.

Notes

This research was supported by the Department of Labor and the National Science Foundation. This paper is a revision of a working paper written in 1976.

1. The argument is as follows. When $\varepsilon = 0$, the expression in the text has the value, one. Taking logs and differentiating with respect to ε, we have

$$\frac{1}{1-\alpha}\left(\frac{1}{1+\alpha} + \frac{\varepsilon}{\alpha+\varepsilon}\right) > 0$$

Thus the term is increasing in ε. It follows that for $\varepsilon > 0$, the expression is greater than one.

2. By taxing the signaling activity, we can determine $y(z)$, the relationship between schooling costs, and investment in schooling. The objective then is to maximize

$$E\left[ny(z)^\alpha - \frac{y}{z}\right]$$

$$= \int E\left[u\frac{z^\varepsilon}{K}y(z)^\alpha - \frac{y}{z}z\right] h(z) \, dz$$

$$= \int \left(\frac{z^\varepsilon}{K}y(z)^\alpha - \frac{y}{z}\right) h(z) \, dz$$

The standard calculus of variations solution is the maximum of the integrand with respect to y for each level of z. It is

$$y(z) = \alpha^{\frac{1}{1-\alpha}} z^{\frac{1+\varepsilon}{1-\alpha}} K^{\frac{1}{\alpha-1}}$$

That, and the other variables are what is reported in table 10.6, column 4.

3. By second best, we mean simply the most efficient outcome attainable when n or u cannot be observed directly.

4. From the definition of $H(\theta)$, $\bar{n}$), we have

$$\frac{\partial H}{\partial \bar{n}} = \frac{1}{F'\{[1 - F(\bar{n})] F(\theta) + F(\bar{n})\}} \cdot F'(\bar{n}) [1 - G(\theta)]$$

which is nonnegative because $G(\theta) \leq 1$.

References

Chamberlin, G. "Education, Income, and Ability Revisited." Draft, July 1975.
Chamberlin, G., and Greliches, Z. "Unobservables and Variance Components Structure: Ability, Schooling, and the Economic Success of Brothers." *International Economic Review*, June 1975.
Greliches, Z. "The Changing Economics of Education." Harvard Institute of Economic Research Discussion Paper No. 426.
Leland, H. "Quacks, Lemons, and Licensing." University of California at Berkeley School of Business Discussion Paper, 1977.
Riley, J. "Competitive Signalling." *Journal of Economic Theory*, 1975a.
———. "Information, Screening, and Human Capital." Working Paper, Department of Economics, University of California at Los Angeles, October 1975.
Salop, J., and Salop, S. "Self-Selection and Turnover in the Labor Market." *Quarterly Journal of Economics*, 1976.
Spence, A. M. *Marketing Signalling: Informational Transfer in Hiring and Related Screening Process*. Boston: Harvard University Press, 1974a.
———. "Competitive and Optimal Responses to Signals." *Journal of Economic Theory*, 1974.
———. "Competition in Salaries, Credentials, and Signalling Prerequisites for Jobs." *Quarterly Journal of Economics*, forthcoming.
Wolpin, K. "Education and Screening." City University of New York, 1975.

11 Learning by Observing and the Distribution of Wages

Stephen Ross, Paul Taubman,
and Michael Wachter

It is well known that the more educated have higher earnings. There are several possible explanations for this fact. In the framework of the human capital model, education produces skills that are rewarded in the marketplace. Of course, part of the observed differences in earnings by education level may arise because the more educated are also more able, but such an observation is not in conflict with the human capital production model. However, some economists have gone beyond the observation that ability and earnings are correlated to argue that the only or primary role of education is to signal who are the more able.[1]

It is extremely difficult to distinguish between the human capital and signaling models based on information confined to education and its returns, though there have been several papers on the subject (see Taubman and Wales 1973; Riley 1978). When one set of empirical information is not able to distinguish theories, an obvious approach is to test the theories against other types of information. In this paper we first consider what other information about the distribution of income is available. We summarize the human capital model explanation of these additional facts. We then present an alternative model based on two assumptions; the different skills and wage changes which occur over a

---

Steven Ross is Professor of Economics, Yale University Graduate School of Management.
Paul Taubman is Professor of Economics, University of Pennsylvania, and Research Associate, National Bureau of Economic Research.
Michael Wachter is Professor of Economics, University of Pennsylvania.

The research in this paper was supported by the National Science Foundation under grant Soc 77-08568. Additional support was obtained from funds granted to the Institute for Research on Poverty, University of Wisconsin-Madison, by the Office of Economic Opportunity pursuant to the provisions of the Economic Opportunity Act of 1964.

person's life cycle do so because a firm monitors the worker's performance on a particular job. As a consequence of monitoring, the firm may alter the worker's job assignment to fit the updated evaluation of performance. Finally, we demonstrate that the observed earnings data are as consistent with our model as with the human capital model.

11.1 Background

The multitude of empirical work over the past two decades has generated many results about the distribution of annual earnings and its evolution as people age. Some of the results which are found in nearly all studies include the following:[2] (1) in general, average earnings increase with years of schooling, quality of schooling, and years of work experience; (2) the age-earnings profile slopes upward, but it does so at a decreasing rate; and (3) the variance of earnings, or of its log, is not invariant with respect to age. Often the variance of the log of earnings is U-shaped, indicating a larger dispersion for young workers and older workers. Diamond, et al. (1976), however, present some evidence that this variance decreases continuously as people age.

There are other empirical features which have been found in several studies based on specialized and as yet infrequently available samples. If these are substantiated in other samples, they should prove to be important elements in income distribution models. To begin with, the correlation between (natural log) earnings and variables such as years of schooling or IQ is lowest when years of work experience is small and increases with experience for at least the first 7–10 years of experience.[3] Second, Lillard and Willis (1977), using a nationwide random sample, find that 70%–80% of the variance in annual earnings is attributable to permanent income and that annual fluctuations about the permanent level have a serial correlation coefficient of about 0.3. Also Taubman (1975) finds that in the NBER-TH sample, the average percentage growth rate in earnings between 1955 and 1969, when the men averaged thirty-three and forty-seven years old, respectively, is the same regardless of their 1955 earnings level—except for men with the very highest and very lowest income. Diamond, et al. (1976), using Social Security data for 1957–72, find that when men are grouped by their permanent earnings level, the slopes of the age-earnings profiles are quite similar. Those with permanently low income, however, tend to reach their peak income at a slower rate.

Recently Mincer (1974) has modified and extended the human capital model to explain many features of the evolution of the distribution of annual earnings as people age. Mincer's model for earnings in year t can be written as

(1) $$\ln Y_t = bS + cK_t - I_t$$

where Y is earnings, S is years of schooling, K is the stock of on-the-job training capital, and I is investment in on-the-job training. Both K and I in equation 1 would be unobserved but denominated in units of time. K and I are assumed to differ across individuals.

Mincer explains the age profiles for natural log earnings and their variance and for correlation coefficients by changes in the level and distribution of K_t and I_t. For example, consider the variance in $\ln Y_t$ in equation 2.

(2) $$\sigma^2 \ln Y_t = b^2\sigma_S^2 + c^2\sigma_{K_t}^2 + \sigma_{I_t}^2 + 2bc\sigma_{S,K_t} - 2b\sigma_{S,I_t} - 2c\sigma_{K_tI_t}$$

Note first that this variance need not remain constant as a cohort ages since components such as $\sigma_{K_t}^2$ can change. Moreover equation 2 need not imply monotonic changes in $\sigma^2 \ln Y_t$. Consider for example three time periods. In the initial year of working, K is zero for all workers. In Mincer's so-called overtaking period, $cK_t = I_t$. Finally, in the peak period, I_t is zero. Under certain conditions all individuals will be in the overtaking period and subsequently in their peak period at the same time. In the overtaking period, $\sigma^2 \ln Y_t = b^2\sigma^2 \ln S$. The variances in the initial period will also involve the variances and covariance terms of I and K, respectively. Depending on the size of the coefficients b and c and the sign of σ_{SI_t}, $\sigma_{K_tI_t}$, and σ_{SK_t}, various age profiles for $\sigma^2 \ln Y_t$ can be generated.

In Mincer's (1975) model the time coefficient of schooling is a constant, b. The corresponding coefficient that would be estimated by ordinary least squares could change, however, because K_t and I_t would be omitted variables whose covariances with S could vary with t or age. Similarly, Mincer's model would suggest that the correlation of S with $\ln Y_t$ are functions of age.

In Mincer's work, it is generally assumed that individuals and firms always know a person's marginal product at each and every point in time, in each and every occupation, and with and without various training programs. There have been some attempts to incorporate uncertainty about future wages and/or marginal products into this framework using the expected utility approach (see, for example, Thaler and Rosen 1976; Levhari and Weiss 1974; Weiss 1972; and Fardoust 1978). We think, however, that informational uncertainty is best approached in a different fashion.

A basic problem that faces firms and individuals is matching the right person with the right job, an issue which inherently involves uncertainty. This matching process is made difficult because the particular job may not be well defined by a firm. Even if the job is defined, the requisite skills may not be easily measured in advance of hiring workers, and may not correlate well with any easily observed set of personal attributes.[4]

Recently economists have begun to examine in some detail how workers and firms solve this matching problem in the face of uncertainty. The Spence (1973) Arrow (1973) signaling model basically argues that in some instances individuals invest in signals so that firms can better distinguish among workers of different skills. Using this information, the firm separates workers into categories with differing marginal products and real wages. Inherent in much of this work is the notion that if a worker acquires a signal such as schooling, he is always thought of as a better worker and paid the average wage in that category. To make this assumption more palatable, it is argued that poor workers do not invest in the signal because the investment costs are higher for these workers.

The signaling literature appears to suggest different conclusions from the human capital model on two separate points. First, population-wide increases in investment in schooling need not lead to increases in earnings. Second, one-to-one correspondence of real wages and marginal productivity in the human capital model need not hold. Even if the signal is unbiased, under a range of assumptions, considerable latitude exists for randomness in the eventual income distribution. In models which assume that signals are biased, the randomness is considerably strengthened.

In this paper we provide a somewhat different critique of the human capital framework and, at the same time, of the signaling literature. Our model is based on the existence of an internal labor market in the firm. An important function of this market is to sort workers into jobs where they are most productive. To focus attention on the potential importance of sorting, we shall examine a model where the only function of the internal labor market is to sort workers. No on-the-job training is provided; this is a pure ability model. In our simplified model, we show that we also can explain the observed empirical facts concerning age-earnings profiles, changes in the variance of earnings, and the movements in the correlation coefficients by assuming that firms unravel the uncertainties about the abilities of the work force.

In addition, our model, as opposed to the traditional signaling model, implies that in the long run, the distribution of annual real wages may or may not ever equal marginal productivities. Moreover, the distribution of present discounted value of real wages will not equal the distribution of marginal products. If there is "incomplete" sorting, distinctions between marginal products and real wages will persist. If there is "complete" sorting, these differences will eventually disappear. How quickly these differences disappear will affect the extent to which the present discounted value of expected lifetime earnings departs from the distribution of real wages.

11.2 A Sorting Model

We assume that each worker comes to the firm with certain observable characteristics such as education and age. The exact skill of the worker is unknown, but his characteristics permit the assignment of a probability vector

$$p = <p_{1j} \ldots p_n>j; \sum_j p_i = 1; jp_i \geq 0$$

The number p_i indicates the subjective market probability that a worker is of type or skill i. A cohort of workers is defined as a group of workers with the same signal p. Workers initially enter a firm with a p derived purely from external (to the firm) characteristics. Once workers are assigned to jobs, the vector p is altered to reflect the internal labor market experience of the workers.

The firm is defined by a job technology which describes its output as a function of a job structure. This job structure is the internal labor market of the firm. For purposes of simplicity, we assume that the internal labor market is "open" in that horizontal movements across firms can occur at any point along the job structure. A "perfectly closed" internal labor market would be one where horizontal interfirm mobility was possible only at the time when workers are first choosing a firm. After the initial assignment, interfirm movement would require a "demotion" in the job structure matrix.

In an open structure the firm never pays each cohort less than its expected marginal return. Hence, on a worker with characteristics p,

$$w(p) \geq E(p)$$

where $w(p)$ denotes the wage structure. Implicit in the notation $w(p)$ is the assumption that the wage structure is functionally dependent on the workers' signals.[5]

At any point in time, the firm hires a group of workers. For simplicity we assume that these workers can be placed into a discrete number of categories where each category has a separate p. Clearly, the workers with the highest signals, e.g., the best education, will be placed in jobs with higher starting salaries. This follows from our assumption of an open internal labor market. Each firm must pay its various cohorts a wage no less than $E(p)$ or it will lose the group. This assumes, of course, that the market is rational in the way it processes information on signals p.

The basic construct of the firm is the job ladder or matrix. Firms are viewed as having a technology describing the output of particular types of workers across the job array. Suppose, for example, that there are n basic types of workers and m jobs at which workers can be employed. The symbol a_{ij} will denote the (marginal) output of a worker of type i assigned to job j.

If there were no uncertainty whatsoever about the market type, and with constant returns (or using the marginal job matrix), then the ith worker or cohort would be assigned to the job j^* with

$$\sup_j \max a_{ij} = a_{ij^*} \geq a_{ij} \text{ all } j.$$

Under competitive conditions, a_{ij^*} would also be the cohort's wage. With uncertainty, and under the conditions discussed above, the workers in the cohort would receive a wage equal to their expected product. Typically, the exact worker type is in fact unknown, and a category is defined by certain educational and personal characteristics which permit only the assignment of the probability vector p.

The expected return on a worker in this cohort in job j then is given by

$$E_j(p) = \sum_i p_i a_{ij}$$

and the firm will assign workers to the job so as to maximize this return. That is, given our assumption of an open internal labor market, workers with signal p will receive

$$w(p) = \max_j \sum_i p_i a_{ij}$$

11.2.1 Properties of the Wage Structure

The definition of the wage structure permits us to establish a close connection between wages and jobs. More specifically, the wage structure $w(p)$ contains all of the information on the job structure a_{ij} in the same way as the cost function embodies information on the firm's technology.

If we think of the job structure as representing a set A of jobs $a \varepsilon A$, then

$$w(p) = \sup_{a \varepsilon A} \sum_i p_i a_i = \sup_{a \varepsilon A} p.a.$$

Since $w(p)$ is a support function for the set A, it is well known from duality theory that the set

$$A^* = \{a \mid pa \leq w(p) \text{ for all } p \varepsilon S\}$$

contains A. Furthermore, if A is closed and convex and admits free disposal in that some of the worker's output can be thrown away, the set $A^* = A$. Even if not, the wage structure derived from A^* will be the same as that from A, and, thus, information on the wage structure alone will not permit us to infer more about the job matrix than that A^* is its convex hull.

A second property about such a wage structure is that it is a convex function of the probability vector p. Formally, for any two signals x and y

$$w\left(\frac{1}{2}x + \frac{1}{2}y\right) = \sup_{a \varepsilon A} \left(\frac{1}{2}x + \frac{1}{2}y\right) \cdot a$$

$$= \frac{1}{2} \sup_{a \varepsilon A} (xa + ya)$$

$$\leq \frac{1}{2} \sup_{a \varepsilon A} xa + \frac{1}{2} \sup_{a \varepsilon A} ya$$

$$= \frac{1}{2}w(x) + \frac{1}{2}w(y)$$

In other words, suppose an individual has a signal [1/2 1/2]; that is, he is thought to have a 1/2 chance of being a type x worker and a 1/2 chance of being a type y worker. Then his wage cannot be greater than the average of the wages for an x worker and a y worker. Indeed, under very general circumstances, as shall be shown below, the wage must be lower than the average for x and y workers. Although this may seem paradoxical in a risk neutral world, it has a simple explanation which is central to the sorting model. Knowledge that the worker is of type x or y will permit a more optimal job placement than in the 50–50 uncertain situation. For example, consider the job structure in figure 11.1. A worker with a signal [1/2 1/2] will be paid a wage of 5 and placed in J_1. In the next period, the firm will be able to tell whether a worker is an x or a y by whether he had produced 10 units of output or zero output. With this new information, the worker's signal changes to either [1 0] or [0 1]. If he produced 10, he will be labeled an x worker, left in job 1, and paid a wage of 10. If he produced 0, he will be labeled a y worker, changed to job 2, and paid a wage of 9. In either case, his wage increases.

The basic proposition, however, is not that all workers have wage increases, but rather that the average wage increases. For example, if the job structure is as shown in figure 11.2, the initial wage for the cohort is 5 and they are all placed in job 1. In the following period, the x workers receive a wage increase to 10 and the y workers receive a wage cut to 1. The average wage is 5.5 which is greater than the initial average wage. (The fact that 1/2 the workers are x while 1/2 are y follows from the assumption that the signal is unbiased. If this were not the case, the average wage could decline.)

11.2.2 Upward-Sloping Age-Earnings Profiles

The knowledge that the wage structure is a convex function of the signals permits us to derive an important result. Even in the absence of

	J_1	J_2
x	10	0
y	0	9

Figure 11.1

	J_1	J_2
x	10	0
y	0	1

Figure 11.2

any change in the intrinsic productivity of a worker over a lifetime, the market's perception of a worker's ability tends to alter with work experience. The job performance might reveal that a particular worker has been overvalued or undervalued, but on average his wage will increase over the worker's lifetime. This arises simply from the procedure of sorting workers over their lifetime.

Theorem 1: The average wage for a cohort will rise over time, i.e., age-earnings profiles rise.

Proof: Since we have assumed that the signal implies a probability vector about the true population proportion, it is sufficient to show that the expected wage increases with any initial signal. Let p^0 be the initial signal and p^1 the random signal at time 1 dependent on both p^0 and the information acquired in the first job. If a^0 is the initial job then

$$w(p^0) = \sup_{a \in A} p^0 \, a$$
$$= p^0 \, a^0$$

Now, if a worker is of type i, then let I_i denote the information such a worker gives in job a^0, and $p^1(I_i)$ be the probability vector for a worker of type i in job a^0.

It is important to realize that we do not always have full information about a worker simply by observing the worker on a job. For example, suppose in job a, that $a_1 = a_2 = , \ldots, = a_m$, i.e., all workers perform the same. The job matrix has a column of identical numbers. Clearly, if the only information is the productivity of the worker, then observing the worker in job a^0 provides no additional knowledge about the worker, and the future signal equals

$$p^1(I_i) = p^1 = p^0$$

the initial signal. It is in this case, which we call "incomplete" sorting, that the average wage is constant over time and does not increase.

In general, though, the market will obtain on-the-job information, and $I_k \neq I$ if $k = \ell$. Now, $p_k^1(I_i)$ is defined as the probability that the worker is of type k, conditional on having the information I_i. At time 0 the probability that a worker will be of type k will be given by

$$p_k^0 = \sum_i p_k^1(I_i) \, p_i^0$$
$$\equiv E\{p_k^1\}$$

Thus, p^1 must be a probability vector with expected value or, for the cohort, average value equal to p^0. This makes intuitive sense since at time 0 with p^0 the market cannot anticipate receiving information that will lead to a p^1 systematically biased from p^0; if such information were anticipated in a rational framework it would already be reflected in p^0.

The rising age-earnings profile now follows directly from the convexity of the wage function,

$$E\{w(p^1)\} \geq w(E\{p^1\})$$
$$\geq w(p^0),$$

with strict inequality if p^1 ranges over some nonlinear portion of the wage structure.

Theorem 1 verifies that the sorting, on-the-job ladder model implies the first stylized empirical observation of earnings profiles. This theorem is strikingly robust since no structure need be imposed on the job matrix. Sorting alone is sufficient to impart a positive slope to the age-earnings profile.

It is useful to define a sorting equilibrium as occurring when all workers or worker cohorts hold the identical jobs in periods $t+1$ as they did in t. The sorting process can be in equilibrium in two situations. The first, which we refer to as a complete sorting, occurs whenever all of the workers are placed optimally in the job structure. Incomplete sorting occurs when workers are not optimally placed, but the job structure does not permit further sorting. As indicated above, this results whenever a column in the job matrix has identical entries.

Let the job structure be given by figure 11.3, and suppose a type x worker belongs to a cohort whose initial signal is $p^0 = (1/2, 1/2)$. With this initial signal the cohort will be assigned to job J_1 at which all members will produce 2 units and in which no information will be obtained. The x workers in the cohort will now produce below what they could produce in job J_2. Of course, this result depends critically on the assumption that the worker knows only the initial signal p^0.

Suppose, for example, that the worker knew he was a type x, but only signaled $p^0 = (1/2, 1/2)$. Such a worker could volunteer to work for less than 2 units in job J_y to prove himself a type x. Even better, the worker could agree to a contingent on performance contract. If he produced 3 units in job J_y he would receive 2+ units with the remainder for the firm; otherwise, he would receive nothing. Nor is there any moral hazard dilemma with such a contract. Quite to the contrary, only those who

	J_1	J_2
x	2	3
y	2	0

Figure 11.3

knew themselves to be of type x would accept jobs J_y under such conditions; other workers would stay with J_x. We do encounter problems if we let the acceptance of the offer alone represent a signal, for then wages might be paid ahead of performance which would create a moral hazard. We will ignore such difficulties below, and return to our initial assumption that firms and workers have the same perception of worker signals.

11.2.3 The Diminishing Rate of Increase

The second stylized fact is that age-earnings profiles rise at eventually diminishing rates. While this hypothesis is as consistent with the job ladder model as with the human capital model, its derivation requires somewhat more structure than that required for theorem 1.

It is tempting, for example, to argue that the incremental value from additional information along the job ladder must be declining, and that wages, therefore, while rising must do so at a diminishing rate. That is, the initial jobs contribute a great deal of new information on a worker cohort, allowing for major revisions in this signal p. After several job changes, however, the new information flow decreases so that the increase in wages slows also. Although this is an attractive initial point, it is not sufficient to prove diminishing ratios of wage growth.

Suppose that the job ladder takes the form shown in figure 11.4, and that the initial signal is $p^0 = (p_x^0, p_y^0, p_z^0) = (1/2, 1/3, 1/6)$. The highest initial wage is attainable by placing this group in J_1.

$$w(p^0) = \max_{\{x, y, z\}} p^0 a$$

$$= p^0 J_x$$

$$= (1/2 \times 5) + (1/3 \times 5) + (1/6 \times 10)$$

$$= 5\ 5/6$$

If the worker produces 10 units, then he will be identified as a type z and left in J_1, but if 5 units are produced he can be either a type x or y. The x or y workers are placed on job J_2 and the z workers remain in J_1. The expected wage is thus

$$E\{w(p^1)\} = (1/2 \times 10) + (1/3 \times 0) + (1/6 \times 10)$$

$$= 6\ 2/3$$

	J_1	J_2	J_3
x	5	10	0
y	5	0	10
z	10	0	0

Figure 11.4

At time 2, all of the workers will be fully identified and placed in the correct job. Hence

$$E\{w(p^2)\} = w(p^2) = 10$$

The age-earnings profile increases at an increasing rate between periods 1 and 2. It initially increases from 5 5/6 to 6 2/3, but then it jumps to 10 in the final period.

This same job structure, though, can result in a concave age-earnings profile for a different cohort. If the initial signal is $p^0 = (1/12, 7/12, 4/12)$, then the initial job is still J_1, and $w(p^0) = (5 \times 1/12) + (5 \times 7/12) + (10 \times 4/12) = 6\ 2/3$. In the next period 4/12 of the workers remain in j_1. For those that can either be x or y workers, the optimal second job is J_3. Thus 8/12 of the workers are placed in that job. Of that group, 1/12 are misplaced; they are actually X workers and hence produce 0 in J_2. The remaining 7/12 are still in their optimal job and produce w.

$$E\{w(p^1)\} = (1/12 \times 0) + (7/12 \times 10) + (4/12 \times 10)$$
$$= 9\ 1/6$$

In the final period, all workers are again correctly placed and $w(p^2) = 10$. The age-earnings profile in this case does increase at a diminishing rate. Notice also that the job progressions are different with the two signals. For the workers that change jobs twice, the progression is from J_1 to J_2 to J_3. In the latter case, it is J_1 to J_3 to J_2.

These two examples indicate that without additional information, the job ladder provides no quantitative restrictions on the age-earnings profiles. Furthermore, even if such restrictions were put on the job structure, the issue would still be unresolved. Demonstrating that a plot of earnings against *jobs* is rising at a diminishing rate is neither necessary nor sufficient for an *age*-earnings profile to have the same shape. The reason is that the data are on *age*-earnings profiles, not *job*-earnings profiles.

By way of illustration, consider the example where $w(p^0) = 6\ 2/3$, $E\{w(p^1)\} = 9/16$, and $E\{w(p^2)\} = 10$. These points are plotted in figure 11.5. Suppose, now, that the length of time between job changes is fixed, either institutionally through sensitivity rules or by the nature of the information structure of the model. In addition, suppose that the length of time for the first move is over three times longer than that for the second. Figure 11.6 illustrates that the associated age-earnings profile is convex.

To derive an eventual leveling off of the age-earnings profile thus requires a theory of the rate at which job performance is generated.

If the bulk of the value of sorting occurred early in the worker's life span and the worker tended to remain in jobs for increasing time periods as the incremental value of sorting diminished, then the age-earnings

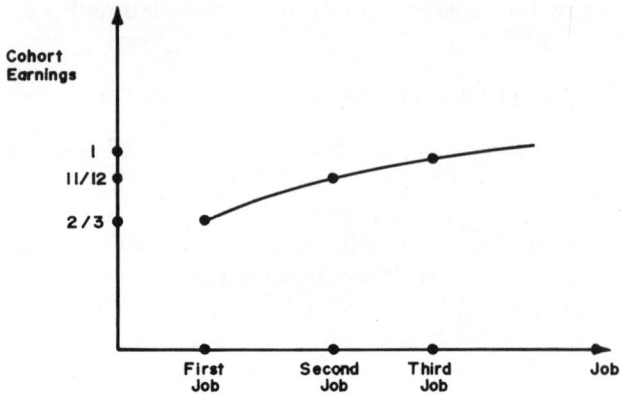

Figure 11.5   Job Earnings Profile

profile would level off. At the beginning, though, the shape of the profile would be somewhat indeterminate. If the job structure is one which has equilibrium sorting within the worker's lifetime, then the age-earnings profile must level off.

The data indicate that a cohort's age-earnings profiles become flat early in the workers' careers and that correlations of earnings with schooling increase with experience for seven to ten years and then level off. These findings are consistent with an equilibrium sorting model view. Indeed, if all were fully sorted, the "increasing variance" proposition would not hold.

11.3 Conclusions

The human capital model has provided explanations of the age profiles of earnings and its variance and correlation coefficients. We have shown

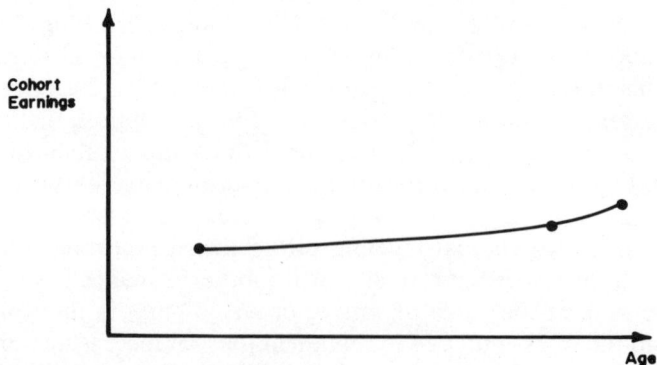

Figure 11.6   Age Earnings Profile

in this paper that a sequential sorting model operating in the presence of uncertainty can also explain all the available empirical evidence. Our explanation is based on the unobserved convexity of the wage function over jobs for workers with expected but uncertain skills. The human capital model explanation is based on unobserved variables with unobserved correlations with measured variables. The two alternative models have different implications for some purposes, and thus it would be useful to devise tests to distinguish them.

Notes

1. Taubman (1977) presents some evidence that the ability correlated with schooling is mostly though not exclusively cognitive. He also presents evidence that noncognitive skills (characteristics) or financing capability that flows from the family explains more of the variance in earnings around age 50 than cognitive skills.

2. We do not include the well-known fact that earnings or wage rates are not normally distributed. This characteristic can be explained by assuming that (unobserved) abilities are not normally distributed.

3. For a recent examination using single cross-section samples, see chapters 3, 4, and 6 in Jencks, et al. (1979). Similar results are found in panel data. See, for example, Fagerlind (1975); Hauser and Daymount (1976); Taubman (1975).

4. As Reder (1969) among others have noted, inability to know in advance a person's marginal product need not invalidate theories which assume that in equilibrium, a person's real wage will equal his marginal product. Reder, for example, suggests that piecework, percentage commissions, and other institutional arrangements can be used to reveal a person's marginal product (MP) before payment is made. Yet there are many occupations and firms where the workers are hired for some relatively lengthy period at a fixed hourly or weekly wage and where a person's MP is not known in advance though perhaps known ex post.

5. Given that the wage structure is open, the worker need not stay with one firm. For some purposes, it is interesting to view each job change as a change in firms. In this sense, the sorting model encompasses external mobility, and it would be a simple matter to append a job-training model that covers internal mobility within the firm. For a discussion of internal labor markets see Williamson, Wachter, and Harris (1975).

Comment   John G. Riley

Ross, Taubman, and Wachter (RTW) have provided us with a useful framework within which to analyze on-the-job sorting. They demonstrate convincingly that the stylized facts linking the variance of earnings and time in the work force can be explained purely as a sorting phenomenon. However, RTW also make it clear that their model can explain almost

John G. Riley is Professor of Economics, University of California, Los Angeles.

any earnings-experience profile, so it is hard to visualize how either cross-section or panel data might be used to distinguish their sorting story from the Mincerian hypothesis of different rates of on-the-job investment.

My own feeling is that it would be interesting to combine sorting with aspects of on-the-job training in an attempt to explain observed differences in earnings growth paths sometimes ascribed to "dual labor markets." To illustrate this point, consider figure C11.1, indicating the productivity of different workers in different jobs. On-the-job training is introduced by making productivity in job 3 (J_3) dependent upon whether or not a worker spends an earlier period in job 2.

Suppose a group with identifiable characteristics α is known to be eighty percent type x and twenty percent type y. In a two-period model it is easy to check that members of this group will be placed first in J_1 and then either held in J_1 or advanced to $J_{3.1}$. Similarly a group with characteristics β which is twenty percent type x and eighty percent type y is optimally placed first in J_2 and then either in J_1 or $J_{3.2}$. So far this is very much the RTW story. However, suppose in addition that the per capita cost of monitoring performance on the job satisfies $.6 < c < 1 \cdot 2$. For such values of c the expected gains to sorting out the twenty percent of type y in group α are outweighed by the monitoring costs. Then monitoring of this group will not take place, and type y will presumably become "discouraged workers" and end up performing at the same rate as type x in J_1. *Opportunities for advancement are then open only to those groups with sufficiently favorable initial characteristics.*

It is natural, therefore, to ask what characteristics firms will use to identify different groups. Educational achievement is an obvious candidate, so RTW are surely incorrect in describing their sorting hypothesis as an alternative to the signaling hypothesis. Instead, the two hypotheses are complementary.

This brings me to the discussion of signaling in labor markets by Spence. The paper, essentially a minisurvey, provides a nice summary of many of the issues. Particularly interesting is the discussion of imperfect signaling and its distributional implications. However there are two issues whose omission is somewhat surprising.

First, various authors (Rothschild and Stiglitz (1976), Wilson (1977), Riley (1979), and indeed Spence himself) have raised doubts about the viability of signaling or "informational" equilibria. To clarify the issues

$$\begin{array}{c} \quad\quad\quad J_1 \quad J_2 \quad J_{3\cdot 1} \quad J_{3\cdot 2} \\ \begin{array}{c} x \\ y \end{array} \left[\begin{array}{cccc} 3 & 1 & -3 & -3 \\ 4 & 2 & 5 & 8 \end{array} \right] \end{array}$$

Figure C11.1

involved, I shall consider a simple version of the model described in section 10.3 of Spence's paper. Let $t_n(y)$ be the time required for an individual of type n to achieve educational level y, and let $M_n(y)$ be the lifetime marginal productivity of type n discounted to the time of exit from the educational system. Higher values of n are associated with higher productivity.

The present value of lifetime productivity is then

$$V_n = e^{-rt_n(y)} M_n(y)$$

Taking logarithms we have

$$v_n = \log V_n = \log M_n(y) - rt_n(y)$$

Under the signaling hypothesis, firms offer workers a discounted lifetime income $W(y)$ which is a function of educational achievement y. An individual of type n then chooses y to maximize

$$\tilde{v}_n = \ln W(y) - rt_n(y)$$

This is depicted in figure C11.2 for types α and β ($\alpha < \beta$). For simplicity, time in school is shown as a linear function of educational achievement. Given the assumption central to signaling that the marginal (time) cost of education is smaller for the more productive workers, there is an earnings function $W(y)$ such that type β chooses a higher level of y and both end up being paid discounted lifetime earnings equal to lifetime productivity. Spence's original work suggested that such an equilibrium was not unique and indeed that there existed a whole family of these earnings functions. It followed that two subsets of the population with identical unobservable characteristics, but differing in an observable characteristic such as race or sex, might be in quite different equilibria. For example, lifetime earnings at every educational level might be strictly higher for one subset. This possibility generated a rich set of policy implications for affirmative action programs, etc.

However, more recent work suggests strongly that the critical equilibrium issue is not whether there are *many* equilibria but whether there are *any*! Consider again figure C11.2. Firms are initially offering lifetime earnings profiles of $W(y)$. Suppose one firm then makes the alternative depicted offer $<\bar{y}, \bar{W}>$. Both type α and type β are just indifferent between their old best offer and the new alternative. Moreover all those types n with $\alpha < n < \beta$ strictly prefer the new offer. Whether or not such an offer is profitable therefore depends upon whether or not the average lifetime productivity of the types in this interval exceeds $\bar{W}$. Recently it has been shown that under relatively weak conditions expected profits will be positive (see Riley 1979). Therefore the signaling profile $W(y)$

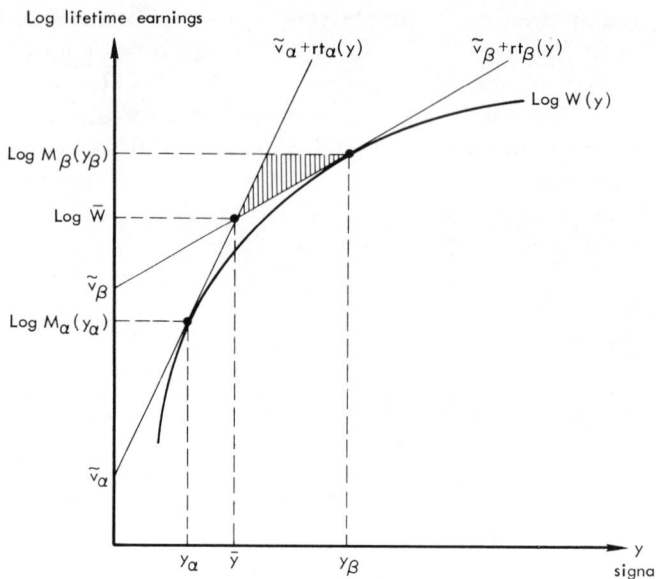

Figure C11.2 Educational Signaling

does not have the stability properties that one would wish of an equilibrium.

However, further reflection suggests that the potential instability described above may not be very damaging. Note that prior to the new offer there is some type $\bar{n}$ for whom

$$M_{\bar{n}}(\bar{y}) = W(\bar{y})$$

Since $\bar{W} > W(\bar{y})$, the new offer loses money on type $\bar{n}$ and hence on all those types n such that $\alpha \leq n \leq \bar{n}$. Therefore the new offer is profitable only on average. It can be shown that there is always a second alternative offer (in the shaded region of figure C11.2) which generates profits to a reacting firm and losses to the firm offering $<\bar{y}, \bar{W}>$. Essentially the reactive offer succeeds in skimming off all the better workers from the pool attracted by $<\bar{y}, \bar{W}>$. Recognition of such an undesirable outcome will then tend to deter firms from making offers above the signaling profile $W(y)$.

While space constraints preclude discussion of the subtleties (see Riley 1979; Wilson 1977), it can be shown that of the family of signaling profiles described by Spence, only one, the Pareto dominating profile is a "reactive equilibrium."

I do not wish to argue that the reactive equilibrium concept provides an entirely satisfactory resolution of the instability problems. However, at the very least it indicates that the signaling hypothesis is not easily rejected on purely theoretical grounds. On the other hand, the elimination of multiple equilibria does eliminate a major difference between the implications of the traditional human capital model and its screening variant.

This brings me finally to the second omission from Spence's paper: the absence of any discussion of the different policy implications associated with the basic signaling model. (As I have already noted, there is an examination of the welfare implications of imperfect signaling.) Accepting the unique reactive signaling equilibrium, I believe that the differences are still very important, especially in the design of programs aimed at improving the education of lower-income groups (see Stiglitz 1975).

The issues are dramatized by considering the simplest case in which there are only two types of workers, type α and type β. With perfect information about productivity, each type chooses a level of education to maximize

$$\ln M_n(y) - rt_n(y)$$

This is depicted in figure C11.3a with type α choosing y_α^* and type β choosing y_β^*. Note that type α would prefer the education-earnings contract of type β. Therefore if, as assumed in the signaling model, productivity is not observable, type β must increase its education level to $\bar{y}_\beta$ in order to be separated out from the less able. The logarithms of the present value of lifetime income of the two types are then v_α^* and $\bar{v}_\beta$ with signaling, rather than v_α^* and v_β^*.

Now suppose funds are allocated for research into the improvement of educational achievement for the less able. The broken lines in figures C11.3a illustrate the effect of an educational innovation which increases value added by the less able. In the traditional human capital model, the gains go to this group alone. However, with signaling, the increase in productivity of type α reduces the amount of signaling needed by type β and hence raises lifetime income of the latter group as well. Adoption of such a policy is therefore enlightened self-interest!

A quite different result follows from the adoption of an innovation which increases the rate of educational advancement of the less able. This is depicted in figure C11.3b. The higher rate of educational advancement implies a reduction in the marginal time costs of education $[t'_\alpha(y)]$ and hence an increase in the education of type α. If productivity is directly observed, workers of type β remain at y_β^* and the gains again go only to type α. However, if there is signaling, the flatter cost curve of type α implies that workers of type β must *increase* their education beyond $\bar{y}_\beta$ in order to be differentiated. This *reduces* their present value of lifetime earnings. To summarize, educational signaling magnifies the potential payoff to increasing value added by the less able and diminishes the payoff to reducing the educational costs of this same group. In both cases the difference is due to first-order spillover effects which alter the income of more able workers.

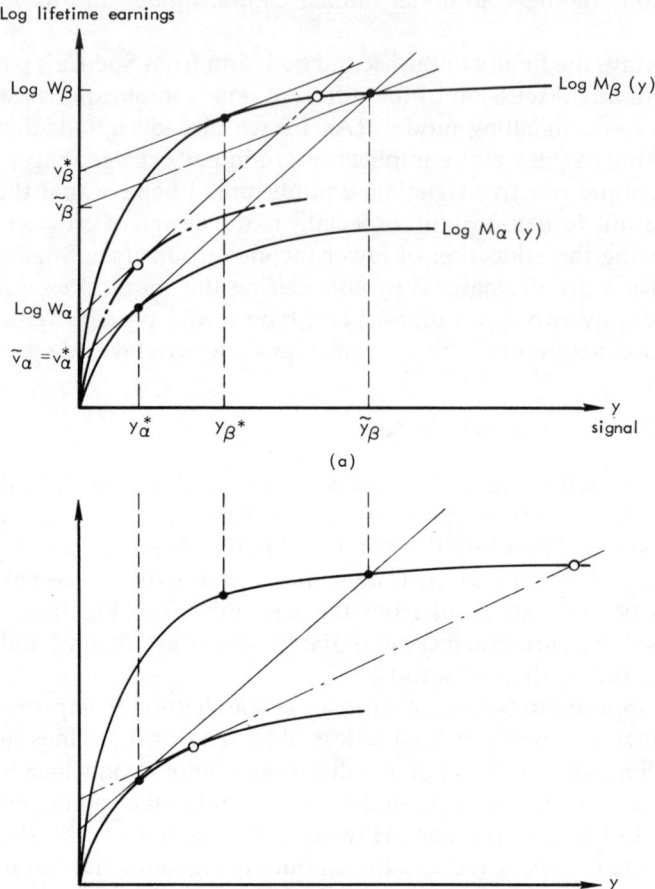

Figure C11.3 Human capital and Signaling Equilibria with Two Types of Workers

Comment   Charles Wilson

Among the several topics treated by Spence in his paper on educational signaling is the role of contingent contracts as an alternative to education for screening workers. I will confine my attention to a closer examination of this issue. My general thesis is that the effect of contingent contracts may be very sensitive to the opportunities of the worker to borrow. In a world with perfect capital markets, contingent contracts are in principle

Charles Wilson is Professor of Economics, University of Wisconsin.

efficient substitutes for educational screening. When workers face an imperfect capital market, however, not only may contingent contracts be inefficient, but the same problems with the existence of an equilibrium associated with any self-selection model also appear.

Contingent Contracts with Adverse Selection

Suppose there are two types of workers both of whom work for two periods. Type 1 workers are least productive and generate a marginal value product of s^1 in each period. Type 2 workers are more productive with a marginal value product of $s^2 > s^1$ in each period. Each worker knows his own productivity at the beginning of the first period. However, firms are unable to determine the productivity of a worker until the beginning of the second period. A contingent contract is a first-period wage w_1 and second-period wage w_2^i for $i = 1, 2$ which depends on the productivity of the worker. Therefore any contingent contract can be represented by a three-dimensional vector (w_1, w_2^1, w_2^2).

Consider first the case where contingent contracts are binding on both firms and workers in the second period. Assuming that firms may borrow and lend at a fixed rate of interest r, they will be indifferent to hiring a worker if the present value of his productivity over the two periods equals the present value of his wage payments. Therefore, a firm just breaks even on a type i worker if $w_1 + (1+r)w_2^i = s^i + (1+r)s^i$. The firm's "break-even" lines for each type worker, labeled $B^i B^i$, are illustrated in figure C11.4. Assume for simplicity that $r = 0$; then both have slopes equal to -1 and pass through their respective marginal productivity points (s^i, s^i).

The workers' preferences across different combinations of first and second-period wage rates depends critically on their access to capital markets. Suppose that workers are able to borrow and lend at the same rate of interest as firms. Then independent of their preferences between first and second-period consumption, they are indifferent between any two income streams with the same present value. In this case, therefore, any indifference curve for each worker has the same slope as the break-even line of the firm.

It should be apparent that under these conditions any contract (w_1, w_2^1, w_2^2) for which (w_1, w_2^1) lies on the $B_1 B_1$ line and (w_1, w_2^2) lies on the $B_2 B_2$ line is consistent with equilibrium in a competitive market. Firms are willing to pay a wage in excess of the marginal value product in the first period if the worker will accept a correspondingly lower wage in the second. Likewise, workers will accept a lower wage in the first period if they are appropriately compensated in the second period.

Some of this indeterminacy disappears if we relax the assumption that workers may borrow at the same fixed rate of interest as firms. Suppose a worker may lend at the fixed rate r but faces a marginal interest rate schedule which increases with the amount he borrows. In this case, his

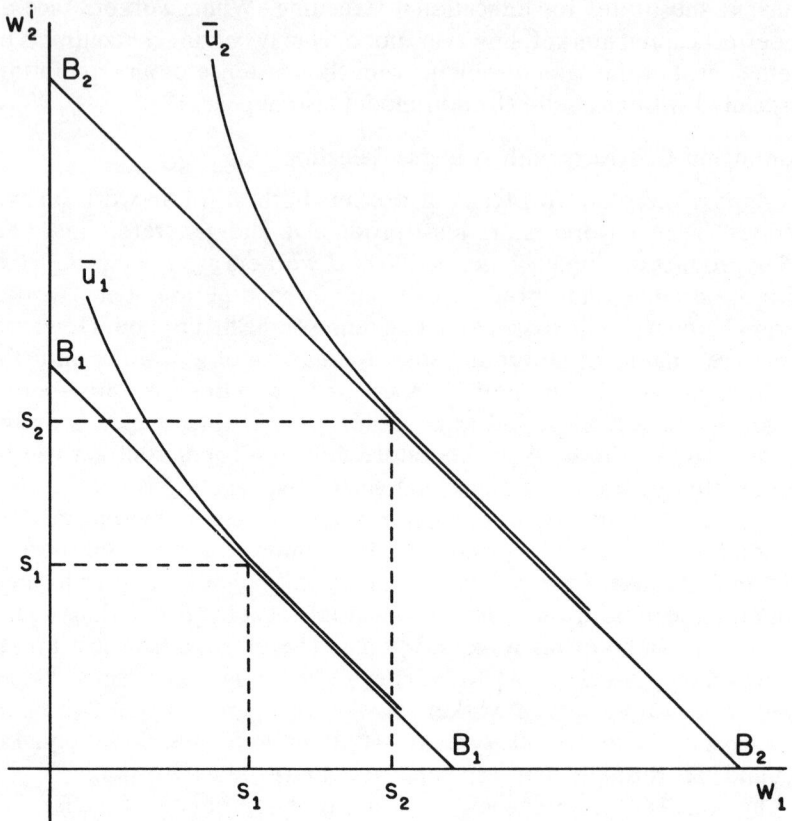

Figure C11.4

feasible bundles of first and second-period consumption depend on more than just the present value of his wages evaluated at interest rate r. Assuming his marginal rate of substitution between first and second-period consumption is strictly decreasing, his marginal rate of substitution between first and second-period *wage rates* will also be strictly decreasing at any combination of wage rates at which he chooses to borrow in the first period. Typical indifference curves are illustrated in figure C11.4. As we increase w_1, the slope becomes increasingly flatter (reflecting a lower marginal interest rate), until a combination of wage rates is reached at which the worker no longer chooses to borrow. Thereafter, the curve becomes a straight line parallel to the firm's break-even line.

Under these conditions, it is no longer true that an equilibrium can be attained given any first-period wage. Because firms may borrow at a lower interest rate than workers, any contract which induces workers to borrow in the first period presents obvious arbitrage opportunities to firms. Competition then forces firms to "lend" to workers at the market rate of interest by increasing the first-period wage to a point at least as large as the workers' desired level of first-period consumption. The equilibrium wage contracts can be illustrated in figure C11.4. For type 1 workers, any contract on their break-even line to the right of s^1 is an equilibrium; for type 2 workers, contracts to the right of s^2 are equilibrium contracts.

In general, it is difficult to enforce the terms of a contingent contract in the second period if the worker can command a higher wage elsewhere. Therefore, let us assume henceforth that the terms of the contract in the second period are binding only on firms. In the second period, workers are free to change employers in order to obtain a higher wage.

Consider first how this affects the worker's preferences among different contracts. As long as the second-period wage is greater than the worker's marginal value product, the worker has no incentive to leave the firm. For these contracts, therefore, the worker's indifference map remains unchanged. However, once the second-period wage falls below the worker's marginal value product, its level becomes irrelevant. The worker can guarantee himself a higher second-period wage by changing (or threatening to change) employers. Therefore, the typical indifference curve for a type i-worker becomes truncated at $w_2^i = s^i$. Once the second-period wage falls below s^i, the worker prefers any contract with a higher first-period wage.

The break-even lines for the firms are also affected. Since the firm must pay a type i worker at least s^i in the second period or lose him to another employer, it can never break even on a type i worker if it pays him more than s^i in the first period. In particular, firms must lose money on type 1 workers if $w_1 > s^1$. Nevertheless, the firm may still break even on average when type 1 workers choose a contract with $w_1 > s^1$, if type 2 workers also accept the contract with a second-period wage low enough to compensate the firm for its loss on the less-productive workers. The only constraint is that the second-period wage for type 2 workers exceed s^2; otherwise, they too will leave the firm in the second period. Let a_i be the proportion of type i workers. Then if the firm is to break even on average when $w_1 > s^1$, w_2^2 must satisfy: (a) $w_2^2 > s^2$; (b) $(a_1 s^1 + a_2 s^2 - w_1) + a_2(s^2 - w_2) = 0$.

This line is labeled $B_a B_a$ in figure C11.5. It starts at $(s^1, 2s^2 - s^1)$ and declines with slope $-1/a_2$ until $w_2^2 = s^2$, at which point the line becomes vertical. The lines labeled $B_1' B_1'$ and $B_2' B_2'$ are the break-even lines for each type individually. Each is identical to the corresponding $B_i B_i$ line up to $w_i = s^i$, at which point it also becomes vertical.

Now consider the equilibrium for this market under the assumption that workers have access to perfect capital markets. In this case, any

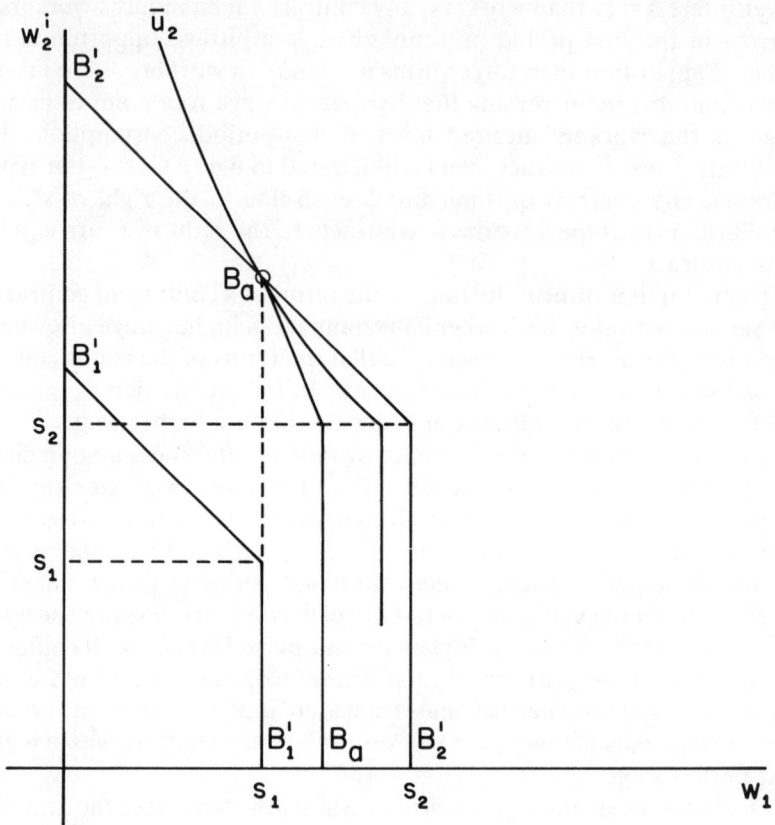

Figure C11.5

first-period wage less than or equal to s^1 is consistent with equilibrium. Both w_2^1 and w_2^2 can be adjusted so that each worker obtains a contract on his break-even line. Furthermore, because the indifference curve of each worker through these points is coincident with his corresponding break-even line, there is no other contract which is profitable for the firm and preferred by this type of worker. Note that because the firm breaks even on both types individually, it is not even necessary for both types to earn the same first-period wage.

The requirement that w_1 be less than s^1 is essential, however. Otherwise, type 1 workers will choose that contract with the highest first-period wage. But in order for such a contract to break even, it must also attract type 2 workers to the corresponding contract on the $B_a B_a$ line. Since any such contract is less preferred than contracts with $w_1 \leq s_1$ on the $B_2' B_2'$ line, no type 2 work will accept it. Therefore $w_1 > s^1$ cannot be an equilibrium.

In short, the restriction on feasible first-period wages resulting from the inability to enforce contingent contracts on workers does not present any serious problems if workers have access to the same capital markets as firms. They are willing to accept any first-period wage if the second-period wage is high enough to generate an income stream with a present value equal to the present value of their marginal product.

This conclusion changes in a fundamental way, however, when we reintroduce the possibility that workers face an upward-sloping marginal interest rate schedule. Suppose that type 2 workers will choose to borrow at any contract on the $B_2'B_2'$ line with $w_1 \leqq s^1$. In this case the indifference curve for the worker will have a slope which is steeper than the $B_1'B_1'$ line at that point. However, in order to obtain a contract with a higher first-period wage, the worker must be willing to subsidize the type 1 workers who will also choose the new contract.

If the slope of the type 2 indifference curve is less in absolute value than $1/a_2$, type 2 workers will prefer to remain at a contract with $w_1 = s^1$, as illustrated in figure C11.5. Consequently, the equilibrium looks no different than when workers could borrow at interest rate r; however, it will be less efficient. There are two distinct problems. First, if there were no type 1 workers, the free rider problem associated with higher first-period wages would disappear and type 2 workers could obtain any contract on the $B_2'B_2'$ line yielding a higher level of satisfaction. Second, if either type workers' preferred consumption point on their B_iB_i line requires a first-period wage greater than s^i, another source of inefficiency results because the firm no longer is able to make loans to its workers in the first period by increasing w_1. Any higher first-period wage becomes essentially a transfer payment when the worker leaves the firm in the following period.

If the slope of the type 2 indifference curve is greater in absolute value than $1/a_2$ where $w_1 = s^1$, then type 2 workers will strictly prefer a contract on the B_aB_a line with $w_1 > s^1$, such as point c in figure C11.6. Firms who offer this contract attract both types of workers. Type 1 workers leave the firm at the end of the first period, but the second-period wage to type 2 workers is sufficiently low so that the firm breaks even on the average worker.

Is this contract then an equilibrium? It is *not* a Nash equilibrium. Suppose some firms are offering contract c and attracting both types of workers. Another firm could offer a contract such as (d) with a lower first-period wage and a type 2 second-period wage sufficiently higher to attract the type 2 workers but still low enough more than to break even on such workers. Note that this contract will not attract type 1 workers because their second-period wage would be no higher than s^1. They would be sacrificing a higher first-period wage without receiving a higher second-period wage in return.

This is precisely the same problem with the existence of equilibrium as was discovered by Rothschild and Stiglitz (1970) and myself (Wilson

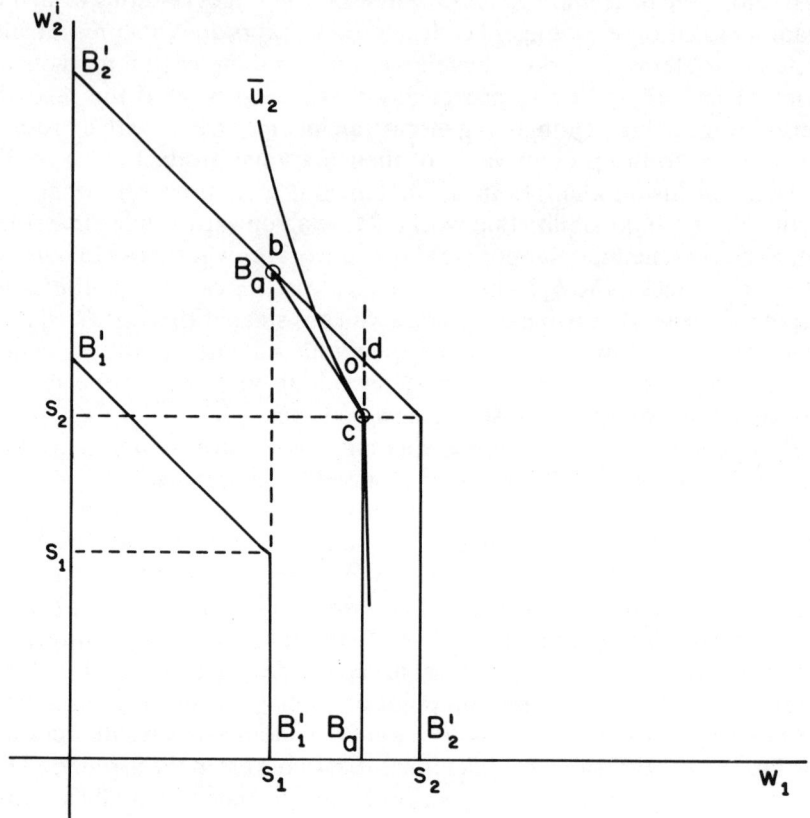

Figure C11.6

1977) in the context of an insurance market. It can appear in any model with signaling or self-selection. If one adopts the equilibrium concept that is employed in Wilson (1977), then point c does become an equilibrium. Firms do not offer a contract like (d) because they anticipate that firms offering (c) will be left with only type 1 workers and consequently will drop the contract. Type 1 workers will then move to (d) and it will lose money as well. On the other hand, if one adopts the reactive equilibrium concept suggested by Riley (1979), then contract b is the equilibrium. Firms will not offer a contract like (c) because they fear retaliation by other firms who may offer contract d.

Little will be gained by discussing in any more detail what is the appropriate equilibrium concept for this market. The issue has already been examined at some length elsewhere. However, a few words about the feasibility of contingent contracts are in order. Recall that the original issue was whether or not contingent contracts can replace signaling as a screen for productive workers. Throughout the analysis the implicit assumption was that such contracts have essentially zero enforcement costs on firms. As a practical matter this may be a difficult assumption to justify.

As I see it, the problem is not so much that firms have an incentive to break the contract. The short-run benefits of breaking a contract will be more than offset by the long-run cost to the firm resulting from its loss of credibility. The problem is in *verifying* that the firm is in fact fulfilling the contract. It is not sufficient that the firm actually pay high-productivity workers a higher wage in the second period; they must be able to convince new workers that they are actually following this policy. An obvious solution to this problem is the use of credentials, either formal or informal. In order to receive a higher wage in the second period, the worker must satisfy certain public criteria. But this "solution" may not be without its own inefficiencies. In fact, we may have essentially reintroduced signaling into the second-period wage decision. Insofar as workers overinvest in credentials which certify their productivity (in the academic market, they may publish too many papers or attend too many professional meetings), the solution may be no more efficient than if education were used as a signal in the first place.

In a more complete model, I suspect that education before the first period would simply supplement other "credentials" the worker must acquire in order to receive a higher wage in the second period. Thus, we have come full circle. In searching for contracts which avoid the inefficiency of educational signaling, firms may require signaling in other forms and in fact may even require educational signaling to enforce the contracts.

The Ross-Taubman-Wachter (RTW) paper presents a convincing and elegant explanation of many of the properties of the typical age-earnings profile. They focus exclusively on the implications for the distribution of earnings when firms optimally assign their employees to jobs based on the workers' performances at earlier jobs. I will confine my comments to two points. The first is that the argument may be strengthened if one takes into account the incentives for intertemporal maximization of a worker's output. The second is that when contingent contracts cannot be introduced efficiently, the problem of adverse selection may tend to generate some inefficiency in the assignment of workers.

RTW argue that depending on the distribution of the worker's productivity and the types of jobs available, incomplete sorting may result. This has the effect of flattening the experience-earnings profile. Although I believe their point is essentially correct, the bias toward incomplete sorting is less severe if firms and workers consider the future benefits of less productive jobs at the beginning of worker careers, followed by a more effective sort later on.

Consider their example with two types of workers and two jobs given by the matrix in figure 11.3. If each worker has a .5 probability of being an X or y worker, the expected payoff from assigning a worker to job 1 is 2; for job 2 the expected payoff is 1.5. Therefore all workers will be assigned to job 1. From this example RTW conclude that complete sorting may not occur even though total output could be increased if type X workers could be identified and assigned to job 2.

This conclusion changes, however, if we consider the implications for intertemporal maximization of a worker's output. Suppose each worker works three periods and the discount rate is zero. If all workers are assigned to job 1 in each period, then total output is 6 per worker. But firms can do better than this. If they assign each worker to job 2 in period 1, the average return is 1.5; however, this permits them to identify each worker's type. In the next two periods, therefore, type X workers can be assigned to job 2 and type y workers assigned to job 1, yielding an average output of 5 which, added to 1.5 in the first period, gives a total of 6.5. Assuming firms pay workers their *expected* marginal product in each period, workers will choose to work for a wage of 1.5 in the first period for a chance to obtain a higher wage in later periods.

Now suppose that workers know their productivity before they take their first job. If contingent contracts can be enforced, then type X workers will immediately choose job 2 and type y workers job 1. In the absence of contingent contracts, however, some inefficiencies appear. In each period, the workers in each job are paid their expected marginal product. Type X workers will immediately go to job 2 in order to establish their productivity. Type y workers will go to the job which pays the highest wage. This will be job 2 unless some type y workers take that job lowering its expected marginal product to 2. Consequently one-third of the type y workers will also take job 2 in period 1. In the following period all workers are perfectly sorted. The firm does not achieve a first best optimum, but does do better than it would if workers had no information at all.

This result need not be obtained in general. Suppose that in job 1, type X workers produced 3 units and type y workers 2, but individual output could not be distinguished. Output would be maximized by leaving all workers in job 1. But, the equilibrium with adverse selection would remain unchanged with one-third of the type y workers assigned to job 2 in period 1.

References

Arrow, K. "Higher Education as a Filter." *Journal of Public Economics*, July 1973.
Diamond, P., et. al. Appendixes in Report to Congressional Research Service by Consultant Panel on Social Security, August 1976.
Fagerlind, I. *Formal Education and Adult Earnings*. Almqvist and Wicksell, 1975.
Fardoust, S. "Risk Taking Behavior, Socioeconomic Background, and Distribution of Income: A Theoretical and Empirical Analysis." Ph.D. Thesis, University of Pennsylvania, 1978.
Hauser, W., and Daymont, T. "Schooling, Ability, and Earnings: Cross Sectional Findings 8 to 14 Years After High School Graduation." Center for Demography and Ecology, University of Wisconsin, 1976.
Jencks, C. "Who Gets Ahead." Basic Books, 1979.
Levhari, D., and Weiss, Y. "The Effect of Risk on the Investment in Human Capital." *American Economic Review*, December 1974, pp. 950–63.
Lilliard, L., and Willis, R. "Dynamic Aspects of Earnings Mobility." *Econometrica*, forthcoming.
Mincer, J. *Schooling, Experience and Earnings*. Columbia University Press, 1974.
Reder, M. "A Partial Survey of the Theory of Income Size Distribution," in L. Soltow, ed., *Six Papers on Size Distribution of Income and Wealth*. Columbia University Press, 1969.
Riley, J. "Testing the Educational Screening Hypothesis." Rand Corporation, mimeo., 1978.
———. "Informational Equilibrium." *Econometrica* 47 (1979): 331–60.
Rothschild, M., and Stiglitz, J. "Equilibrium in Competitive Insurance Markets: The Economics of Imperfect Information." *Quarterly Journal of Economics* 90 (1976): 629–49.
Spence, M. *Market Signalling: Informational Transfer in Hiring and Related Processes*. Harvard University Press, 1974.
———. "Competition in Salaries and Signalling Prerequisites for Jobs." *Quarterly Journal of Economics* 90 (1976): 51–75.
Stiglitz, J. E. "The Theory of Screening, Education and the Distribution of Income." *American Economic Review* 65 (1975): 283–300.
Taubman, P. *Sources of Inequality of Earnings*. North-Holland, 1975.
———. "The Relative Influence of Inheritable and Environmental Factors and the Importance of Intelligence in Earnings Functions." IEA Conference Paper, Nordwijk, 1977.
Taubman, P., and Wales, T. "Higher Education, Mental Ability, and Screening." *Journal of Political Economy*, January/February 1973.

Thaler, R., and Rosen, S. "Estimating the Value of a Life," in Terleckyj, ed., *Household Production and Consumption*. Columbia University Press, 1976.

Weiss, Y. "The Risk Element in Occupational and Educational Choices." *Journal of Political Economy*, November/December 1972, pp. 1203–13.

Williamson, O.; Wachter, M. L.; and Harris, J. "Understanding the Employment Relation: An Analysis of Idiosyncratic Exchange." *Bell Journal of Economics*, Spring 1975, pp. 250–78.

Wilson, C. "A Model of Insurance Markets with Incomplete Information." *Journal of Economic Theory* 16 (1977): 167–207.

Contributors

John M. Abowd
Graduate School of Business
University of Chicago
1101 East 58th Street
Chicago, Illinois 60637

Orley Ashenfelter
Department of Economics
Princeton University
Princeton, New Jersey 08540

Ann P. Bartel
Graduate School of Business
Columbia University
New York, New York 10025

John Bishop
Institute for Research on Poverty
University of Wisconsin
Madison, Wisconsin 53201

George J. Borjas
Department of Economics
University of California
Santa Barbara, California 93106

Frank Brechling
Department of Economics
University of Maryland
College Park, Maryland 20742

Dennis W. Carlton
Law School
University of Chicago
1111 East 60th Street
Chicago, Illinois 60637

Richard B. Freeman
Department of Economics
Harvard University
1737 Cambridge Street
Cambridge, Massachusetts 02138

Gilbert R. Ghez
Walter Heller College of Business Administration
Roosevelt University
430 South Michigan Avenue
Chicago, Illinois 60605

Herschel I. Grossman
Department of Economics
Brown University
Providence, Rhode Island 02912

Daniel S. Hamermesh
Department of Economics
Michigan State University
East Lansing, Michigan 48824

James J. Heckman
Department of Economics
University of Chicago
1126 East 59th Street
Chicago, Illinois 60637

Boyan Jovanovic
Bell Laboratories
600 Mountain Avenue
Murray Hill, New Jersey 07974

Nicholas M. Kiefer
Department of Economics
Cornell University
Ithaca, New York 14853

Jacob Mincer
Department of Economics
Columbia University
New York, New York 10027

Contributors

George R. Neumann
Graduate School of Business
University of Chicago
1101 East 58th Street
Chicago, Illinois 60637

John G. Riley
Department of Economics
University of California
Los Angeles, California 90024

Sherwin Rosen
Department of Economics
University of Chicago
1126 East 59th Street
Chicago, Illinois 60637

Stephen Ross
School of Organization and Management
Yale University
52 Hillhouse Avenue
New Haven, Connecticut 06520

Michael Spence
Department of Economics
Harvard University
Cambridge, Massachusetts 02138

Paul Taubman
Department of Economics
University of Pennsylvania
3718 Locust Walk CR
Philadelphia, Pennsylvania 19104

Warren T. Trepeta
Federal Reserve Board
20th and Constitution Avenue, N.W.
Washington, D.C. 20551

Michael Wachter
Department of Economics
University of Pennsylvania
3718 Locust Walk CR
Philadelphia, Pennsylvania 19104

Charles Wilson
Department of Economics
University of Wisconsin
1180 Observatory Drive
Madison, Wisconsin 53806

Author Index

Abowd, John, 6–8, 168
Akin, J. S., 269
Anderson, R., 61
Arrow, K., 168, 295, 296, 362
Ashenfelter, Orley, 6–8, 168, 169, 282
Astin, A., 249, 254
Astrom, K., 121
Atkinson, R., 96
Azariadis, C., 168, 169, 187, 295

Baily, M., 168, 169, 187, 188, 211, 295
Balcer, Y., 61
Balestra, P., 133
Barlow, R. E., 53
Bartel, Ann, 2–4, 43, 60, 61, 82
Bartholomew, D., 51
Bates, G., 91, 93, 133
Becker, G. S., 22, 44, 54, 83, 87
Becker, J., 206
Ben-Porath, Y., 83, 85, 96
Bergstrom, A. R., 119
Berndt, E. R., 211, 219
Bishop, John, 11–12, 223, 242
Blumen, I. M., 23, 29
Borjas, George, 2–4, 43, 61, 82, 83, 93, 119
Bower, G., 96
Brechling, Frank, 10–11, 188, 190
Brown, A. W., 49
Brudett, K., 47
Burman, G., 282
Burstein, P., 291
Bush, R., 121
Butler, R., 270, 271, 275, 288, 291

Cain, G., 105, 121
Carlton, Dennis W., 15
Christensen, R., 243, 244
Clark, K. B., 218–19, 220
Classen, K., 173, 178, 187, 201, 206
Coleman, J., 96
Coleman, S., 295
Cripps, T., 92
Crothers, E., 96

Da Vanzo, J., 44
Daymont, T., 371
Diamond, D., 61
Diamond, P., 360
Domencich, T., 93
Dreyfus, S., 121
Duncan, B., 290
Duncan, G., 168
Duncan, O., 257, 261, 264, 265, 290

Ehrenberg, R., 173, 178, 187, 201, 206
Epstein, W., 249, 263

Fagerlind, I., 371
Fardoust, S., 361
Fawcett, J., 243
Featherman, D. L., 247, 249, 263, 290
Feldstein, M., 168, 169, 188, 191
Feller, E., 45
Feller, W., 93
Fethke, G. C., 211
Flinn, C., 120

391

Author Index

Freeman, Richard B., 12–14, 61, 218–19, 220, 247, 250, 252, 254, 255, 257, 258, 260, 261, 269, 280, 281, 289, 291

Gallant, A. R., 110
Garfinkle, I., 269
Ghez, Gilbert R., 87, 89
Goldstein, M., 283
Gollop, F. M., 219
Goodman, 93
Gordon, R. J., 187
Greeno, J., 121
Greenwood, M., 22
Griliches, Z., 93
Grossman, Herschel I., 14–16, 295, 300, 301, 314

Hall, R., 247, 249
Halpin, T., 188
Hamermesh, Daniel S., 10, 187, 206, 211, 223
Hanoch, G., 249, 252
Harris, J., 371
Hauser, R. M., 247, 249, 263, 290
Hauser, W., 371
Heckman, James J., 2, 4–6, 23, 61, 66, 83, 91, 92, 93, 94, 96, 99, 100, 101, 102, 103, 104, 105, 110–14, 119, 120, 124, 125, 126–27, 128, 130, 133, 134, 135–36, 151, 169, 173, 176, 270, 271, 275, 282, 283, 288, 291
Hotelling, H., 122

Jaffee, D. M., 315
Jehn, C., 188
Jencks, C., 371
Johnson, N., 121, 133, 176
Jorgenson, D. W., 243, 244
Jovanovic, Boyan, 1–3, 23, 47, 60, 61, 82, 100

Kaldor, Nicholas, 211
Karlin, S., 95
Kasten, R., 247, 249
Katz, A., 187
Keeley, M. C., 169
Kesselman, J. R., 211
Kiefer, Nicholas, 8–10, 173, 174, 175
Kneisser, T., 269
Kogan, M., 23, 29, 62
Koopmans, L. H., 103
Kotz, S., 121, 133, 176

Landes, E., 44
Layton, L., 91
Lazear, E., 82
Leland, H., 343
Lerman, R., 223
Levhari, D., 361
Levin, H. M., 269
Lewis, H. G., 168
Lillard, L., 360
Lucas, R. E., 168

McCall, J., 173
McCarthy, P. J., 23, 29
McFadden, D., 93, 99, 101
McKevitt, J., 216
MaCurdy, T., 126–27, 133, 134, 135–36
Malinvaud, E., 93–168
Marshall, A. W., 53
Masters, S., 249, 276
Michael, R., 44
Mincer, Jacob, 1–3, 27, 46, 60, 61, 82, 89, 96, 360–61
Morgan, J., 134
Mortensen, Dale, 26, 168, 173, 202
Mosteller, F., 121

Nelson, P., 47
Nerlove, M., 93, 133
Neumann, George, 8–10, 173, 174, 175, 178, 179
Neyman, J., 91, 93, 133
Nordhaus, W. D., 214

Oaxaca, R., 173, 178, 187, 201, 206
Oi, W., 22

Padilla, A., 269
Parnes, H. S., 22, 23
Parsons, D., 22
Perloff, J. M., 217
Phelps, E. S., 92, 295
Polachek, S., 89, 269
Pollak, R., 122
Pratt, J., 168
Proschan, F., 53

Rao, C. R., 110, 130
Rapping, L. A., 168
Reder, M., 371
Reiss, A. J., 84
Restle, F., 121

Riley, John G., 16, 359, 372, 373, 374, 382
Rosen, S., 168, 361
Ross, Steven, 18–19
Rothschild, M., 372, 381
Russell, T., 315
Ryder, H., 99, 120

Sahota, G., 82
Samuelson, P., 122
Shakotko, R., 61
Sims, C., 120, 219
Singer, B., 23, 29, 93, 94
Sjastaad, L., 22
Smith, J., 247, 249, 252, 269
Smith, R. S., 283
Smith, V. L., 245
Sorensen, A., 61
Spence, Michael, 16–18, 362, 372
Spilerman, S., 23, 29, 93, 94
Stafford, F., 99, 120, 168
Starrett, D., 296
Stephan, P., 99, 120
Stiglitz, J. E., 295, 372, 375, 381

Tarling, R., 92

Taubman, Paul, 18–19, 359, 360, 371
Taylor, H., 95
Thaler, R., 361
Tobin, James, 211
Trepeta, Warren, 14–16

Viscusi, W. K., 249
Vroman, W., 249, 276

Wachter, Michael L., 18–19, 217, 371
Wales, T., 359
Weiss, L., 247, 250
Weiss, R., 249
Weiss, Y., 361
Welch, F., 247, 249, 250, 252, 257, 269
Williamson, J., 247, 250
Williamson, O., 371
Williamson, S. H., 211
Willis, R., 91, 92, 94, 96, 101, 105, 110–14, 134, 360
Wilson, Charles, 18, 242, 372, 374, 381, 382
Wise, D., 82, 249
Wohlstetter, A., 295
Wolpin, Ken, 169, 283
Wood, D. O., 219

Subject Index

Affirmative action, 247, 281–82
Age-earning profiles, 368–70
Age effect on separations, 53
Antibias activities, 270, 280; effect on demand for black labor, 281

Baily-Feldstein model, 188–206; duration of temporary layoffs amendment, 190–91; experience-rating provision amendment, 191–96
Bayes's theorem, 52
Black labor, demand for, 276, 280–81; relative to white, 269–70
Bureau of National Affairs (BNA) survey, 281

Civil Rights Act of 1964, 269, 270
Contingent contracts, 376–84

Data Resources Data Bank, 244
Discrimination, statistical, 295–96

Earnings, ratio of blacks to whites, 250–52, 254
Economic gains of blacks, measurement of, 248–55
Economic status of blacks, factors contributing to improvement of, 269–83
Education, 359. *See also* Schooling
Employment and Earnings, 197
Equal Employment Opportunities Commission (EEOC), 269
Experience rating, definition of, 188

Family background, effect on labor market position, 263–65; effect on years of schooling, 257–63; measures of, 257–58

Hazard function, definition of, 23–24
Heckman-Willis model, 110–14
Household reading resource, 260–61
Human capital, 21, 22, 42; model, 75, 320–22, 325-32, 338–39, 359, 360–61; theory of, 84

Income. *See* Earnings; Wages

Jobs credit. *See* Wage subsidy
Job search, purpose of, 43
Job search behavior, sample, 178–84; outcomes of, 172–77
Job specific human capital, 25–26
JOBS program, 211

Labor market discrimination, 248
Labor markets, informational aspects of, 319
Labor mobility, analysis of, 22; declines with age, 24; declines with length of tenure, 24; definition of, 23, 67; earlier studies of, 22–23; effects on wages, 43
Labor supply, female, 92
Labor turnover and wage growth, across jobs, 70–73
Labor turnover variable, definition of, 67
Licensure, occupational, 343–48
Local labor market, size of, effect on wage growth, 80

394

Subject Index

Marital status, effect on wage growth, 79–80
Michigan Income Dynamics (MID), 21, 23, 25, 104, 108–9, 127, 132, 142, 151–52
Mobility. *See* Labor mobility
Movers and stayers, comparison of, 53–54, 67–70
"Mover-stayer" model, 22–23, 35, 93
MPSID. *See* Michigan Income Dynamics

National Federation for Independent Businesses, survey, 216–17
National Longitudinal Surveys data (NLS), 21, 23, 24, 30–31, 60, 66, 75, 78–79, 81, 249, 254, 255–68
NBER study, 87
NBER-TH sample, 360
New Jobs Tax Credit, background, 210–13; impact on employment, 213, 240; impact on inflation, 213–15, 240; models, 218–21

Occupation, relative position of blacks and whites, 252–54
Occupational Change in a Generation survey, 249, 263
On-the-job: training, 47; wage growth, 73–77

Panel Study of Income Dynamics. *See* Michigan Income Dynamics
Parental occupation, effect on attainment of blacks and whites, 258–59
Personnel policies, 281
Privacy issue, 348–50

Quality standards, 353–56. *See also* Licensure

Rationing model, 320, 322–23, 337–39
Regional effect on years of schooling, 259
"Residual" discrimination, definition of, 265; background versus, 265–68

Risk-shifting function, 295–314

Schooling, 325–35, 337–39, 350–53
Screening and signaling models, 319–56
Search behavior, 21
Search theory, 22–23
Self-employment, 335–37
Signaling and screening models, 319–56
Signaling model, 320–21, 323–32, 338–39, 340–43, 359, 362, 372–75
Socioeconomic position, measures of, 256
Sorting model, 362–71
Statistical Analysis System, 163–67
Structural state dependence, 120–23

"Tenure effect," 27–30, 53
Tenure turnover profile, 23–24
Time series analysis data, 285
Tobit model, 126
Turnover, 84; job-matching theory of, 47

Unemployment, analysis of, 22; effects of, 172–73; measurements of, 141–42
Unemployment insurance, 145, 147, 148, 161–62, 171, 172, 176, 178, 183–84, 203–6; changes in benefits, 181–82; influence on labor supply, 187; influence on unemployment, 187
Unemployment variable, measurement of, 152–55
Urn models, 94–99, 101–2

Wage growth, 65, 84; and job turnover, 66–81
Wages, determination of, 143–49; tenure effects on, 36–42
Wage structure, 28, 364–68
Wage subsidy program, 172, 182–83
WIN program, 211
Workmen's compensation, 171

LIBRARY OF DAVIDSON COLLEGE